Down by the Riverside

BLACKS IN THE NEW WORLD
August Meier, Series Editor

A list of books in the series appears at the end of this book.

Down by the Riverside

A SOUTH CAROLINA SLAVE COMMUNITY

CHARLES JOYNER

UNIVERSITY OF ILLINOIS PRESS

Urbana and Chicago

LIBRARY OF CONGRESS CATALOGING IN PUBLICATION DATA

Joyner, Charles W.
   Down by the riverside.

   (Blacks in the New World)
   Includes bibliographical references and index.
      1. Slavery—South Carolina—All Saints Parish—History.   2. Afro-
Americans—South Carolina—All Saints Parish—Folklore.   3. Slaves—
South Carolina—All Saints Parish—Folklore.   4. All Saints Parish
(S.C.)—Social life and customs.   5. Folklore—South Carolina—All
Saints Parish.   6. Plantation life—South Carolina—All Saints Parish—
History.   7. Gullah dialect. I. Title. II. Series.
F279.A43J69   1984   975.7'89   83-10369
ISBN 0-252-01058-2 (cloth)
ISBN 0-252-01305-0 (paper)

For Jeannie

Contents

Acknowledgments

I am happy to acknowledge several individuals who have contributed in various ways to this study. First, I am indebted to Genevieve Willcox Chandler, whose work for the Federal Writers' Project in the 1930s justifies my terming her the pioneer collector of folklore, oral history, and sociolinguistics of All Saints Parish. From 1969 until her death in 1980, I cherished her friendship and the rich memories she shared with me out of ninety years of experience. Her daughter, Genevieve Chandler Peterkin, also contributed to this study with suggestions that opened lines of inquiry I might otherwise have missed.

Major portions of the research and writing of this study were undertaken with the financial support of a Social Science Research Council fellowship in Folklore and Folklife at the University of Pennsylvania in 1974–75, a fellowship in Family and Community History at the Newberry Library in the spring of 1977, and a National Endowment for the Humanities seminar at Harvard University in the summer of 1978. Much of the fieldwork and local documentary research was carried out during the course of two generous grants from the South Carolina Committee for the Humanities. In addition, I received support from the institutions where I was teaching—St. Andrews Presbyterian College and the University of South Carolina, Coastal Carolina College. To my long-time friend, George E. Melton of St. Andrews, goes a special note of thanks for his warm encouragement and support over the years.

I have received generous help and courtesy from the splendid library staffs at Harvard University, the University of Pennsylvania, the University of North Carolina at Chapel Hill, Duke University, Clemson University, the College of Charles-

ton, St. Andrews Presbyterian College, the University of South
Carolina, Coastal Carolina College, the Newberry Library, the
Georgetown County Public Library, and the Horry County
Public Library.

I am particularly indebted to Allen Stokes of the South
Caroliniana Library at the University of South Carolina, David
Moltke-Hansen of the South Carolina Historical Society in
Charleston, Wylma Wates of the South Carolina Archives,
James Walker of the National Archives, and Joseph C. Hicker-
son of the Archive of Folk Culture at the Library of Con-
gress, all of whom offered both warm receptions and helpful
suggestions.

For generous assistance in computing various statistical
data, I am grateful to the staffs of the computer centers at St.
Andrews Presbyterian College and the Educational Computing Service in Chapel Hill. Computer tapes of the federal censuses of 1850 and 1860 were made available by the Inter-
university Consortium for Political and Social Research in
Ann Arbor.

Since this study depended so heavily upon fieldwork, I
am especially grateful to a number of persons who smoothed
my path and made the field experience a joy: the Reverends
George Besselieu, Luther Allston, and Porter Singleton, as well
as Abraham Nelson, Prince and Rebecca Washington, Moses
and Anna Washington, Moses Washington, Jr., Mary Small,
Susan "Pigeon" Allston, Sarah Ann Goback, Mamie Goff,
Henry Small, John Beese, Hannah Besselieu, Clint Thompson,
and the Thompson Family Reunion. They became my teachers
and friends. Not only did they share with me memories of
their ancestors, but also their encouragement of my work was
invaluable. Not all of them are still living, but I shall always
cherish the friendships formed during this part of the study.

I owe a special debt of thanks to an able and generous
group of local historians and history-enthusiasts of Georgetown and the Waccamaw region: Charlotte Kaminski Prevost,
Patricia D. Doyle, June Wesley Elliott, Aleen Paul Harper,
Arthur H. Lachicotte, Jr., Thomas P. Davis, Gurdon Tarbox,

Robin Salmon, Sue Mushock, and James Fitch. Their encouragement and counsel are gratefully acknowledged.

Earlier versions of portions of the book were delivered as papers at meetings of the Organization of American Historians, the Southern Historical Association, the American Studies Association, and the Duquesne History Forum, where they were perceptively criticized by Peter H. Wood, Kathryn Morgan, Randall M. Miller, Jacqueline Goggin, Catherine W. Bishir, and Larry R. Morrison. While at the Slave Studies Symposium at the University of Waterloo in the spring of 1979, I had the opportunity to show written material to Winthrop D. Jordan, Michael Craton, Herbert G. Gutman, Philip Morgan, and Paul Escott and to discuss aspects of the study with them. I am grateful for their criticism and encouragement.

I have benefited from the opportunity to draw on the knowledge and insights of many friends and fellow scholars and teachers, who read all or part of various drafts of the manuscript and offered invaluable criticism, encouragement, and advice. While principled criticism is ultimately more valuable than unprincipled praise, encouragement has been indispensable. The penetrating questions raised by several historians helped me to improve earlier drafts. I am especially grateful to Lawrence W. Levine, Peter H. Wood, Theodore Rosengarten, Stanley L. Engerman, George C. Rogers, Jr., John G. Sproat, Walter B. Edgar, George Rawick, Michael P. Johnson, James L. Roark, Richard Jensen, Dan T. Carter, Sydney Nathans, Tom Terrill, Bertram Wyatt-Brown, and John David Smith.

Similarly, several folklorists, anthropologists, linguists, and sociologists provided splendid criticisms and suggestions that continue to influence my thinking. I am indebted to Kenneth S. Goldstein, Barbara Kirshenblatt-Gimblett, John F. Szwed, John W. Adams, Alice Bee Kasakoff, Patricia C. Nichols, William A. Stewart, Henry H. Glassie, John Michael Vlach, Archie Green, Leland Ferguson, Alan Dundes, Dell Hymes, Dan Ben-Amos, Richard M. Dorson, Karl G. Heider, William R. Ferris, Morgan D. Maclachlan, Roger D. Abrahams, and

Orlando Patterson. Many of their criticisms lent support while others challenged certain interpretations I have advanced. Without exception they have served to enrich the discussion and improve the manuscript.

I have profited richly from the close reading and astute suggestions of August Meier, editor of the Blacks in the New World series of the University of Illinois Press, who has made this a better book than it otherwise would have been.

Finally, I owe a very special debt to my family, each of whom uncomplainingly shared, in various ways, in the making of this book. My son Wesley has grown from a baby to a schoolboy, and my daughter Hannah from a child to a young woman, while this work was in progress. They behaved themselves—mostly—while I was working; and they made my life a joy when I was not. But my principal debt is to Jean Dusenbury Joyner, whose contributions have been too diverse and immeasurable to summarize easily. Jeannie believed in this book from the beginning. It was she who first urged me to combine history with folklife and to focus on the local community. She has read and re-read every draft of every page; few pages have not been improved by her questions and suggestions. Neither the dedication nor this brief acknowledgment can adequately express how much her love and emotional support have meant to me over the years. Quite simply, she has helped more than everyone else combined. This book is for her, with love.

However far the stream flows, it never forgets its source.

—Yoruba Proverb

Introduction

His name was Ben Horry, and he was the type of man one would pay attention to. His words were clean and strong and honest and spoke straight to the ironies and contradictions of slavery: the cruelties and kindnesses of the masters, the tragedies and triumphs of the slaves. When Genevieve Willcox Chandler visited him in 1937 to record his memories of slavery for the Federal Writers' Project, he told her, "I the oldest liver left on Waccamaw Neck that belong to Brookgreen, Prospect (now Arcadia), Longwood, Alderly Plantations. I been here! I seen things! I tell you. Thousand of them things happen but I try to forget 'em." When she asked how the slaves had been treated on those plantations before freedom, he answered guardedly but recalled his master's family as good providers of clothing and food. Under the circumstances perhaps one should view Horry's testimony with suspicion. Aged and penniless, struggling to survive during the Great Depression, he may well have looked back too fondly upon a time when it was the master's responsibility to provide for those too old to work. Moreover, the racial etiquette of segregation that prevailed in the 1930s did not encourage him to tell whites, especially local whites, anything that might disturb them. The climate of fear was evident in his wife Stella's response to a question about why they did not have electricity, when the New Deal's rural electrification had run power lines past their door. "White folks run me [off] if I do that!" she replied. And yet Ben and Stella Horry did not hesitate to confide their fear of white opinion to Chandler. Nor did Ben Horry hesitate to describe to her numerous atrocities visited upon the slaves, atrocities he had witnessed with his own eyes.[1]

It has been tempting for scholars using such ex-slave testi-

monies to evaluate them by reference to a priori assumptions
about the character of the institution, a temptation that not all
scholars have resisted. But if evidence is to be analyzed on the
basis of whether or not it supports certain conclusions, by
what criteria are conclusions to be tested? Should not conclusions be evaluated on the basis of evidence, rather than the
other way around? Slavery can be made to appear either be-
nign or barbaric from ex-slave testimonies, depending upon
what evidence is emphasized and what evidence is suppressed.
Reliable conclusions can only emerge from a diligent sifting of
every kind of record available from sources both white and
black, written and oral. All evidence must be taken into account, regardless of where it originated or in which direction it
points. To say that all evidence must be taken into account,
however, is not to say that all evidence is of equal credibility or
of equal value. The testimony of Ben Horry must be evaluated
in comparison not only with the records of the masters and
white visitors, but also with the testimonies of more than a
score of other ex-slaves who had experienced slavery in All
Saints Parish, South Carolina, also known as Waccamaw Neck.
If such sources are individually suspect, once tested against
one another they may speak collectively with authority and
eloquence.[2]

   One purpose of this book is to reconstruct life in one slave
community—All Saints Parish, Georgetown District, in the
South Carolina lowcountry—through just such a sifting of
every kind of available record. All history is local history,
somewhere. And yet how little this obvious fact is reflected in
the scholarship of slavery. Historians describe *the* slave community without having probed in depth any *particular* slave
community. A bit of this from Virginia and a little of that from
Texas, seasoned with a pinch of something else from Mississippi, have been presented as a portrait of the slave South.
The unity of the society and the integration of the culture have
been assumed, when in fact that unity and that integration are
merely hypotheses until they have been demonstrated in specific instances. Too many scholars of slavery, as of other fields,

attempt to describe and analyze abstract wholes without having investigated concrete parts. Too few construct wholes from empirically researched parts. Still, no history, properly understood, is of merely local significance. The location of study is not precisely the same thing as the subject of the study. Obviously different subjects may be studied in different places; but some subjects—such as slave folklife—would seem promising topics to study in particular communities.[3]

A second purpose of this book is an effort to recreate the emotional texture of slave life—the dreams and hopes, the illusions and anxieties, the human values that animated the slaves of All Saints Parish. Endeavoring to penetrate the mind of a people is formidable, certainly presumptuous, and perhaps hopeless. Nevertheless, unless one makes the attempt, one can hope neither to comprehend the collective experience of the slaves nor to be even reasonably fair to the men and women involved. Delineating their folk belief, world view, and habits of mind is even more troublesome than describing patterns of slave behavior. This aspect of slave life is only indirectly revealed in the historian's normal sources, but it is no less important for being imprecise. Conceding the difficulties and acknowledging the uncertainties, one might still suggest a certain value in combining the kinds of sources and methods of analysis used by historians with those used by folklorists, anthropologists, and linguists in the pursuit of such elusive matters. This approach has been deeply influenced by two scholarly traditions that developed in Europe and have in recent years begun to affect American scholarship—the "folklife studies movement" pioneered by European students of *Volkskunde* or regional ethnology and the *Annales* school of French social historians.

While American folklorists were preoccupied with lore, European folklife scholars were more interested in the folk themselves, embracing in their work the customs and material culture of the folk as well as their oral traditions.[4] According to Don Yoder, a leading American folklife scholar, "not only does the researcher study the verbal arts of folksong, folktale, riddle, etc.—which the folklorist has long ago made his province—but also agriculture and agrarian history, settlement patterns, dialectology or folk speech, folk architecture, folk cookery, folk costume, the folk year, arts and crafts." The term "folklife" designates "the total range of folk-cultural phenomena." In practice, however, it must be acknowledged that most American folklife scholars concentrate on material culture and eschew analyzing what Yoder calls "this exciting totality of the verbal, spiritual, and material aspects of a culture."[5]

The *Annales* historians, so-called after the journal founded by Marc Bloch and Lucien Febvre in 1929, pioneered what Febvre called "a new kind of history" concerned with the social and cultural past of human beings previously considered inarticulate. They sought out new kinds of evidence in census reports, court records, deed registries, and church records; and they asked new kinds of questions of their evidence—questions about the *mentalité* of human beings in the past. Rather than wars, treaties, and monarchs, the *Annalistes*, in a monumental series of studies, stressed the intersection of environments, economies, and cultures. Emphasizing the "structures" of social, cultural, and economic life in a given geographic environment over long time periods (the "*longue durée*"), they achieved "a history whose passage is almost imperceptible," according to Fernand Braudel, "a history in which all change is slow."[6]

The novelist Julia Peterkin, whose stories of black folklife were set in All Saints Parish, noted a similar pace of change on the plantations: "The plantation is somewhat removed from the beaten track of civilization; and changes take place here slowly, quietly, almost too quietly to be noticed when they come. Few things appear to happen except what the seasons bring or what the sky sends of cloud and sunshine and wind and rain. But here, the same as in the world outside, change is the only permanent thing." Through an interdisciplinary approach, then, this study attempts to portray not only the outer history of day-to-day life on the rice plantation of All Saints Parish, but also what Braudel calls "that other, submerged, history, almost silent and always discreet, virtually unsuspected either by its observers or its participants, which is little touched by the obstinate erosion of time."[7]

I share the *Annalistes'* concern for the interaction of culture with environments and economies, and I have adopted much of their methodology. I have drawn upon plantation records, visitors' accounts, court records, wills, estate inventories, and vestry records. I have also employed quantitative analysis of demographic and economic data in the manuscript federal censuses and other sources. But slave folklife can never be comprehended using only sources emanating from the masters and their guests, despite the preponderance of such evidence. There are also numerous sources from the slaves themselves— including rich sources in oral tradition—that facilitate the study of slave folklife. In this study I have drawn upon oral traditions from All Saints Parish of three types: (a) testimonies of ex-slaves, embodied in Chandler's interviews of the 1930s; (b) testimonies of children and grandchildren of slaves regarding what information and attitudes their ancestors had deemed important enough to pass on to them, taken from my own interviews; and (c) the testimony of folktales, legends, proverbs, and songs, which, while not explicitly concerned with slavery in most cases, in conjunction with other evidence yields crucial insight into slave folklife. This last testimony is embodied in Chandler's folklore field collections of the 1930s, in John A. Lomax's disc recordings of folksongs for the Library of Congress—made in Chandler's front yard in the summers of 1936, 1937, and 1939—and my own folklore field recordings in the 1960s and 1970s.[8]

A third purpose of this book is to examine the process of culture change in a slave community. To limit this account to a description of slave folklife would seem to shirk an obligation to try to explain the transformation of diverse African cultures into an Afro-American culture, one of the most far-reaching examples of culture change in human history. The very bulk of the literature on slavery tends to conceal that much of the slaves' cultural experience remains unexplained. If the effort simply to describe the transformation has been difficult (and the results uneven), the effort to explain the process promises to be more difficult still. Explanation is notoriously elusive; but, without denying the formidable problems involved, one might nevertheless suggest that slavery constituted a special environment that compelled the slaves to fashion a precarious new folklife in the face of enormous constraints. To acknowledge the influence of environment on culture change is not to embrace environmental causation. Nor is culture itself causal; rather cultural patterns serve as models *for* behavior as well as models *of* behavior that provide humans with guides to appropriate behavior in various situations. Both environment and culture, then, are contexts within which change takes place. Of course, no cultural change is ever so neat that it can be explained as the product of wholly external or wholly internal forces. At some level it must always involve a tension between tradition and environment, between older and newer ways of thought and behavior. The nagging question is not whether there were continuities or discontinuities with African cultural patterns—clearly there were both—but rather, given the nature of the "peculiar institution," how slave folklife developed from the interaction of various African cultural traditions and the new natural, social, and cultural environment. If the African tradition provided models and the environment provided pressures and opportunities, what mediated among them?[9]

Perhaps the transformation can best be illustrated by looking, for the moment, at one aspect of the slaves' culture change: their acquisition of a common language. The earliest African slaves in South Carolina did not constitute a speech community, as the term is used by sociolinguists. The slaves' various African languages were often mutually unintelligible. The common language that they acquired was a pidginized form of English. Pidgins are developed as a means of communication among speakers of diverse languages. A pidgin is by definition an auxilliary language. It has no native speakers. But when the pidgin was passed on to the American-born children of those enslaved Africans, it became the children's native tongue. If a pidgin acquires native speakers, it is no longer considered a pidgin by linguists but is said to be a creole language.

As a native tongue it has to serve all the functions of a language, not merely the restricted functions of a pidgin. Linguists call the process of change in which two or more languages converge to form a new native tongue "creolization." The creole language of the slaves, Gullah, continued to develop—both in inner form and in extended use—in a situation of linguistic contact. There was reciprocal influence of English and African features upon both the creole and the regional standard. The English contribution was principally lexical; the African contribution was principally grammatical.[10]

Language was, of course, only one aspect of the transformation from African to Afro-American culture. As the English labor historian E. P. Thompson notes, both "resistance to change and assent to change arise from the whole culture."[11] But the process of linguistic change provides a model for explaining other aspects of culture change. What might be called the "creolization of culture" involves the unconscious "grammatical" principles of culture—the "deep structure" that generates specific cultural patterns. Such "grammatical" principles survived the middle passage and governed the selective adaptation of elements of both African and European culture. Herded together with others with whom they shared only a common condition of servitude and some degree of cultural overlap, enslaved Africans were compelled to create a new language, a new religion, and a precarious new lifestyle.

The concept of creolization used in this book is influenced by, and is consonant with, the notion of creolization put forward by the Jamaican poet and historian Edward Brathwaite, who defines creolization as "a cultural action—material, psychological and spiritual—based upon the stimulus/response of individuals within the society to their environment and—as white/black, culturally discrete groups—to each other."[12] In adopting the linguistic model of creolization, however, this study attempts to go beyond Brathwaite's usage to isolate the principles that governed that cultural action.

The concept of creolization applied to slave folklife is not an absolute, let alone absolutely proved. Other influences were undoubtedly present and sometimes predominant. The quest for central themes seems to have exercised a perennial fascination for scholars throughout history, but the search has repeatedly run aground on the shoals of human diversity, which has stubbornly resisted synthesis. To make this admission, however, is not to dismiss the importance of creolization. It cannot be denied that the transformation of African culture into Afro-American culture has been one of the major themes of American history, with innumerable implications for every aspect of American life. Granting the imprecise nature of some of my interpretations, I am nevertheless convinced that creolization has a special importance in the effort to comprehend that transformation and that the emphasis on creolization in this book is justified. At the same time I wish to stress that creolization is not the whole story of slavery. In All Saints Parish, as elsewhere, a common historical experience has not necessarily produced a uniformity of culture or a conformity of character.

The path to consensus on explanation may well be even longer and more contentious than the path to consensus on what is to be explained. Much remains to be explored before a convincing explanation can be found for the development of a viable Afro-American culture in slavery, and the explanation is more likely to be complex than simple. Still, if a subject as inherently controversial as slavery can be examined with sufficient detachment and patience, scholars may find in the convergence of the folklife model and creolization theory a promising approach to Afro-American culture change.

Down by the Riverside

Prologue

The old rice fields are deserted now. Once thousands of black slaves labored on the lowcountry plantations, toiling in the intense heat and humidity of these rice fields, raising and lowering their hoes to the rhythm of work songs not unlike those of their African ancestors. They sang not so much because the overseers and drivers made them sing, for each slave had a specific task to accomplish regardless of whether the others kept up or not, nor even because they remembered, in some dark recess of their consciousness, the songs of the Mandingo or Fullah, or Gola or Guinea, or Yoruba or Ibo, or Fante or Ga, but rather because it seemed appropriate to sing and work together. Toiling and singing, the slaves produced immense crops of rice, the fabled Carolina Gold Rice, which the Waccamaw (wȯ-kə-mȯ) River carried away and converted into immense profits that made their masters wealthy. Now the rice fields have been reclaimed by river and swamp; and bobolinks—locally called rice birds—have the banks to themselves. All Saints Parish, lying between the Waccamaw and the Atlantic Ocean, bounded on the south by Winyah Bay and on the north by the state line, was once the site of the richest plantations on the South Carolina rice coast. Lower All Saints Parish was in Georgetown District; it was here that the rice plantations were concentrated. Upper All Saints Parish was in Horry District, by and large an area of yeoman farmers who had more children than slaves, although the Lower All Saints planters also owned a few rice plantations in Upper All Saints Parish. A rice aristocracy of incredible wealth and power developed in Lower All Saints Parish. It supplied much of the leadership that took South Carolina out of the Union in 1860 and precipitated the Civil War.[1] Here, too, there developed a creolized Afro-

American folk culture that drew upon richly diverse African traditions and adapted them creatively and dynamically to a new physical and social environment. The ratio of nine blacks to each white in Lower All Saints Parish was the highest in South Carolina, and more Africans came to South Carolina than anywhere else on the North American mainland.[2]

Today pleasure crafts crowd the Waccamaw as part of the Intracoastal Waterway system. Racers propelled by 200-horsepower engines speed across the upper river in a blur of spray and fiberglass. Skiers move in a wide arc, skimming across the wake of a Thunderbird or a Marquis. Fishermen in bass boats, outfitted with graphite rods and 6,600 c. reels, probe the dark waters for bream and large-mouth bass. Luxurious yachts ply the Waccamaw as well, transporting wealthy refugees from northeastern winters to warmer climes. Most of the people now on the river have come from nearby cities or towns, but some have come from as far away as Canada to enjoy Myrtle Beach and the well-advertised "Grand Strand."[3]

Clad in jeans and our necks encircled with cameras like so many other tourists, we purchase our tickets at Wachesaw Landing for a cruise down the Waccamaw on the *Island Queen*. Before boarding we buy an aerosol of Sportsman, an insect repellant that is supposed to protect us from mosquitos and river flies. I apply the lotion to our daughter Hannah, while my wife Jeannie coats our little Wesley.

> *Good morning, ladies and gentlemen. You are cordially welcome aboard the Island Queen II. Your boat is Coast Guard–approved and travels at ten knots. There are rest rooms aboard on either side of the pilot house, and the snack bar will open presently.*[4]

We board today as tourists, but the river, its wildlife, and its people are no strangers to us. Both Jeannie and I—and many of our ancestors before us—grew up in Upper All Saints Parish in Horry County. Moses Paul, my great-great-grandfather, and Zaccheus Dusenbury, Jeannie's great-grandfather, had been farmers rather than planters and grew corn and sweet potatoes rather than rice. But the river was the highway to the world for farmers as well as for planters and slaves. And the river had been part of our lives, too, for as long as we could remember.

The *Island Queen* forges out into the middle of the river. Across the stern I can see the boat's wake churning a foamy triangle into the shimmering surface of the river, the apex of a larger triangle of long, gently undulating ripples that dissolve far up the shore.

> *You are now cruising down the Waccamaw River and Intra-coastal Waterway. The river was named by the Waccamaw Indians and means "happy water."* . . . *The color of its water resembles overbrewed tea, the result of tannic acid leached from the bark and fallen leaves of the cypress.*[5]

The "tea" looks rather weaker to us than to the *Island Queen* guide. Perhaps tea with cream would be a better color description, with a slightly greenish cast. I remember thinking as a child how dark the water seemed, almost like Pepsi Cola; and I wonder, as we cruise down the Waccamaw, what color it was in 1860.

A skier comes by, literally skipping across the wake of the Thunderbird which pulls him, but falling in the wake of the *Island Queen*. Our guide makes a few general remarks about "the rice industry" and about "the richest of the rice planters"—the Allstons. Her treatment of slavery is succinct:

> *Rice was particularly successful in South Carolina because of the large amount of labor supplied by the system of slavery. The dependability of the labor supply ended with the abolition of slavery.*[6]

The only mention of contemporary blacks on the Waccamaw is patronizing and limited to the residents of Mt. Arena Landing, on Sandy Island.

> *The people on Sandy Island are popularly governed by a self-styled leader from among their community who acts as a sort of mayor.*[7]

We note the absence of any trace of Gullah influence on her speech patterns. Clearly she did not grow up here, among the descendants of those rice planters and those slaves.

Along the eastern shore of the river, interrupted here and there by the old plantation landings, lies a dense forest of oak and pine, cypress and sweet-gum, poplar and hickory. The forest, novelist Julia Peterkin once wrote of the area, "is the oldest thing on the plantation except the earth itself." Her novel *Black April* was set on Sandy Island, and her *Scarlet Sister Mary* was set on "Blue Brook" (Brookgreen) plantation here, beside the Waccamaw.[8]

As we head south from Wachesaw Landing, we note off the port bow, on a bluff overlooking the river, the magnificent residence built by a twentieth-century owner of Wachesaw Plantation.[9] An eery sense of anachronism falls over us. It is a modern structure, shaded by centuries-old oaks whose low spreading limbs could have developed in the clearing of an earlier plantation Big House. The sense of anachronism is deepened as a yellow fiberglass boat floats closer to an ancient, moss-draped live oak, their flickering shadows on the water eerily symbolic to the present and the past.

There are those who believe the Waccamaw is haunted. Ghostly legends abound in oral tradition and popular culture alike.[10] But All Saints Parish is haunted by history as well. A pervasive historical consciousness seems to permeate the atmosphere. I am acutely conscious, here on the Waccamaw, that the river and the forest are the same river and forest that silently witnessed events that took place long ago. It was here, on the Waccamaw, in the shade of some of these very same trees, that Spaniards and Africans are said to have planted in 1526 the first Old World settlement in what is now the United States—Lucas Vasquez de Ayllon's ill-fated San Miguel de Gualdape. It was here on the Gualdape, as the Spanish named the river, that Africans were first brought to this country as slaves, and it was here that the first slave revolt in what is now the United States took place. According to some historians, the rebellious Africans joined with the Indians to drive the Spanish out, and Africans remained here as settlers—144 years before the English founded Charles Town.[11]

The American Revolution is part of the historical consciousness of the Waccamaw. When the French Marquis de Lafayette and the German Baron de Kalb crossed the Atlantic on the *Victor* in 1777 to join the American colonists' struggle for independence, they first came ashore, led by a black slave, in All Saints Parish. Here, as guests of the prominent Waccamaw rice planter Benjamin Huger, the two young Europeans vowed to conquer or die in the cause of American independence.[12] And Francis Marion, the Revolutionary guerrilla leader known as "The Swamp Fox," fought the British in these forests along the Waccamaw and rested his men—former black slaves as well as whites—on the Waccamaw plantations of his in-laws, the Allstons.[13]

The Waccamaw is also haunted by presidential ghosts. George Washington became the first American president to visit All Saints Parish in April 1791, enjoying the hospitality of Brookgreen and Clifton plantations. Standing on Clifton's broad piazza overlooking thousands of acres of rice fields across the Waccamaw, Washington said he felt as if he were in a fairyland.[14] Other presidents have followed Washington to the Waccamaw over the years. James Monroe was a guest at Prospect Hill in April 1819, cruising the Waccamaw on down to Georgetown on "one of the plantation barges, profusely decorated and adorned for the occasion with the United States colors proudly floating at its head. Eight negro oarsmen dressed in livery propelled the barges."[15] Martin van Buren was feted by the Georgetown rice planters in March 1842 and was awarded an honorary membership in their social club— the Planters Club.[16] Grover Cleveland fell overboard during a well-publicized duck-hunting expedition in 1894.[17] In the twentieth century Bernard M. Baruch entertained Franklin Delano Roosevelt and Winston Churchill at his Waccamaw estate, Hobcaw Barony.[18]

The haunted and haunting quality of the Waccamaw had an indirect, but nevertheless important, influence on the devel-

opment of American art. Brookgreen plantation was the birth-
place of Washington Allston, the most important American
painter of the Romantic period. The tales of haunts, hoodoos,
and plat-eyes that young Allston heard from the blacks at
Brookgreen inflamed his youthful imagination and influenced
his leanings toward the supernatural subject matter that characterized his paintings.[19]

It was here, too, on the Waccamaw, that the ambitious
young politician Joseph Alston brought his bride, Theodosia,
the beautiful daughter of Vice-President Aaron Burr.[20] It is said
that her spirit still haunts DuBordieu Island, her summer
retreat.[21]

Off to our right we now come in sight of Sandy Island. As
our guide explains rice culture to the passengers, ten boats
with waving passengers come by in rapid succession between
us and Sandy Island. The water skier this time wisely steers
clear of our wake. Long since abandoned by the mighty rice
princes—the Allstons, the Petigrus, and the Heriots—Sandy
Island has no white residents. The absence of either bridge or
ferry long discouraged most visitors, and the island became
known locally as a black republic.[22] The black islanders travel
to and from mainland jobs by boat. The children are taken to
school by a school boat. Until recent years there was no electricity on the island. The only vehicles were ox carts. Even today two or three pick-up trucks constitute the only motorized
vehicles. But Sandy Islanders are no longer left alone. As we
pass by the old landing for Sandy Knowe plantation, we count
eight boats pulled up on a tiny beach covered with sunbathers
and scampering children.

The old rice fields on this immense river island have long
since been reclaimed by the wilderness. Through the years
the island has been a favorite with local hunters in search of
wild game. Jeannie's grandfather, Paul Herbert Wesley, often
hunted on Sandy Island in pursuit of two special quarries—"a
huge bronze wild turkey gobbler" known as "The Deacon"
and a phantomlike deer known as "Slewfoot, the Island King,"
who "many, many times" had been "jumped and fired upon by
hunters" but who "always eluded them."[23] Wesley described

the wildlife of the Waccamaw in his *Bits of Driftwood*. Of "The Deacon" he wrote: "There was a great dead pine with a long bare limb that extended out from the edge of the swamp, and on this perch the great gobbler would often strut and gobble in pompous dignity. . . . 'The Deacon' made a wonderful picture as he stood there upon the bare limb, his feathers having the appearance of a blaze of burnished bronze as the red rays of the setting sun fell upon them."[24] Elsewhere he described a doe going into a clump of bushes "to rest, after her hard journey from the rice fields where she had passed the night in search of the tender buds that grew along the banks of the many creeks."[25]

Genevieve Willcox Chandler, as a fieldworker for the Federal Writers' Project of the Work Projects Administration, visited the various black settlements on Sandy Island—Pipe Down, Ruinsville, and Brickwell. She talked with Gabe Lance and other "old livers" who had been slaves on the old rice plantations. She recorded their testimonies that the story of those rice plantations could someday be told as they had known it and remembered it.[26] She was impressed with the Sandy Islanders' sense of pride and with their strength of tradition: "The floors I remember well. Wide planks. Scrubbed to an antique gray polish with shucks and lye. We all felt if our biscuit were to fall on these floors it would still be edible. The clear sand did not discolor. The white-haired elderly women in calico and white apron delighted the eye sitting in comfort before six-foot chimney places where embers smoldered. Songs were sung. Stories told. Mothers in the shade of small porches continued to nurse babies unabashed."[27] Fifty years later she was struck by the same anachronistic juxtaposition of past and present that seems so characteristic of the Waccamaw region: "The oaks, the Creek, the Waccamaw are the same. But times have changed. From New Yorks and Baltimores come the ones who went out to seek a fortune. They return in boxes. They sleep under the live oaks near Mont Arena."[28]

As the *Island Queen* passes the southern tip of Sandy Island, I think back on another part of the past—my own visits to Sandy Island during the past decade, hitching a ride on somebody's boat. I have learned much from the Sandy Islanders—from their music, their stories, their oral history, their language, and especially from their dignity, a quiet sense of pride and self-reliance. I remember the good times, and I remember that bitterly cold Sunday boat ride one January to an "anniversary" preaching, when the temperature dipped down to ten degrees, and the guest preacher feared "that lake might freeze." [29]

As the *Island Queen* cruises past areas almost totally reclaimed by nature, it is impossible not to ponder what this area was like when rice culture was at its apex, and other vessels carried other passengers up this same river.

CHAPTER ONE

"Down by the Riverside"

In 1860 a traveler would not have visited the rice plantations of All Saints Parish in the summer—the height of "the sickly season." Most visitors came in the winter or spring by way of Charleston and Georgetown. Typically they boarded the steamship *Nina* in Charleston at night and slept aboard, as the vessel put out to sea quite early in the morning.[1] After leaving Charleston the *Nina* steamed north, hugging the coast for ten or twelve hours. Visitors have left picturesque accounts of the often stormy passage.

> The sea was rough and our boat was small. We staggered in the trough of the sea to our heart's content; and many persons who were visible before we crossed the bar, were seen no more until we re-entered smooth water; having long since passed my own apprenticeship to the rolling of a vessel, I was fortunately exempt from that disagreeable epidemic which so suddenly prevails among landsmen at sea and was able to enjoy as usual the wild careening of waves below and of clouds above. A fellow passenger, however, was so horribly frightened at the harmless commotion that he offered the captain fifty dollars to put him ashore anywhere.

Ultimately the vessel entered Winyah Bay. "As we approached the Georgetown bar a heavy cloud arose, muttering hoarse thunder, and bringing upon us a lively little squall of wind and rain. The landmarks were all concealed, and after trying in vain to make for port, our brave little cockleshell turned its face to the sea and breasted the billows until the offing was sufficiently clear for us to see our way along the channel."[2] As the vessel dropped anchor in Georgetown, visitors from the North were often less prepared for the sight of so many black faces than they had been for the coastal storms. As the *Nina* "rounded up to the long, low, rickety dock, lumbered breast high with cotton, turpentine, and rosin," one northern visitor was struck that "not a white face was to be seen. A few half-clad, shiftless looking negroes, lounging idly about, were the only portion of the population in waiting to witness our landing."[3]

During the stopover of perhaps an hour, visitors had an opportunity to stroll about Georgetown. William Gilmore Simms described Georgetown as a place of 1,500 inhabitants, with "a handsome Court House," bank, jail, market place, public library, two weekly newspapers, and a school for orphans run by the Winyah Indigo Society, founded in 1756. Almira Coffin, a New England visitor, pronounced the town "quite pretty" in 1851, finding its abundance of mills, lumberyards, and trading activities reminiscent of a New England town. She even noted the number of ships from Massachusetts and Maine being loaded at the wharves off Front Street. Another visitor remarked that "two handsome churches and several pleasant residences peep through the trees, and together with green grassy streets, a feature at once of beauty and desertion, relieve the mind of the inspector from the first dreary impression."[4]

Not all visitors were so favorably impressed. "Georgetown *District* is the wealthiest portion of the state," a visitor noted with irony, "but a more miserable collection of decayed wood domiciles and filthy beer shops than are clustered together to make up the *Town*, it would be difficult to find." A northern visitor wrote in a similar vein. "Though situated on a magnificent bay, a little below the confluence of three noble rivers, which drain a country of surpassing richness, and though the centre of the finest rice-growing district in the world, the town is dead. Everything about it wears an air of delapidation." Another wrote that "for the last thirty years it has been going so rapidly to decay that 'Ichabod' is written on every street and mansion." Many visitors remarked on the unhealthiness of the climate. Simms described Georgetown's climate as "so sickly as to impair most of its advantages as a place of trade." Laurence Oliphant, an Englishman who visited the area in 1860, found Georgetown "a dull, unhealthy place," merely a shadow of its earlier importance.[5]

There was some truth to such uncomplimentary observations. "It was never so much of a town in spite of its royal claims," according to J. Motte Alston, a leading Waccamaw rice planter. "After the introduction of rice it became very unhealthy." Georgetown seemed to be recovering somewhat in the 1850s. A visitor was impressed that "two large lumbermills whose tireless 'gangs' of saws are moving day and night, turn out annually about six millions of feet, which are valued at the wharf at about ten dollars per thousand or sixty thousand dollars in the aggregate—a fine turpentine distillery is in process of erection and will soon be ready for the coming crop; a shoe manufacturing company in successful operation producing the most substantial working brogans."[6]

But the town's recovery was only relative. Its importance continued to decline during the rice era as political, social, and cultural power followed economic power to the rice plantations up the Waccamaw Neck, as the land between the Waccamaw River and the Atlantic Ocean was called. The celebrated South Carolina lowcountry stretched from the Waccamaw Neck on the north to the Savannah River on the south, embracing the districts of Horry, Georgetown, Charleston, and Beaufort. The epicenter of the lowcountry, however, was Lower All Saints Parish, on the Waccamaw.[7]

2

From Georgetown the *Nina* steamed north up the Waccamaw River. The Waccamaw is a very winding river, but its overall course is nearly parallel to the Atlantic and less than four miles inland as far as twenty-four miles upstream from its mouth in Winyah Bay. Much of its course was lined with swamps of cypress, magnolia, oak and pine, reeds and rushes, and marsh. Here was the haunt of the alligator and the water moccasin. Great flocks of mallards inhabited the swamps in season, but the wood ducks were here year round, as were the crane and the bittern. The river and its banks teemed with life. Ospreys (fish hawks) and eagles nested in the tops of tall cypress trees, a mother osprey peering around anxiously while her mate swooped around with shrill cries threatening any intruder. Birds of every color and song flew from tree to tree. Little turtles (called "cooters") sunned themselves on logs, either lodged against the shore or floating down the river. They seemed to be trying to see just how many a log would hold, and there were so many it was difficult to count the number seen on one trip. Visitors were told what a delicious soup they make, but they found the sight of snakes dangling from the trees overhanging the river somewhat less pleasant.[8]

Steaming up the Waccamaw, the traveler beheld an ingenious adaptation of technology to environment—miles of serpentine embankment enclosing thousands of acres of rice fields. Here relations among the land, the sea, and the river system were optimal for rice cultivation. The rice fields were "surrounded by dams high enough and strong to resist the highest spring tides," according to prominent rice planter Robert F. W. Allston. "The entire area is divided into 'squares' or fields, containing twelve to twenty acres each, by a series of check-banks."[9] Tides from the sea pushed fresh water up the Waccamaw and into the rice fields, irrigating the fields, feeding the rice plants, and drowning out weeds and undesired sprouts. Opening the gates at high tide flooded the fields; opening them at low tide drained the fields. During the growing season it was often necessary to keep the fields flooded with river water until it became stagnant. When this happened, Allston's daughter later recalled, "the whole atmosphere was polluted by the dreadful smell."[10]

The Big Houses of the rice planters were situated on high land near the river, surrounded by well-tended flower gardens and sheltered by immense live oaks, with lawns reaching down to the water and rice fields extending to the distant woods. Here, in this "deep mould of inexhaustible fertility," was America's premier rice-growing area. In 1860 Georgetown District alone produced nearly one-third of the total national rice crop, and almost as much as all the other South Carolina rice-growing areas combined. In 1850 Georgetown

District had produced nearly one-fourth, and in 1840 almost half of the rice grown in the United States.[11]

Here, too, there developed a slave society that more nearly resembled Caribbean than other mainland societies. In fact, in everything but the strictest geographic sense, the rice coast of South Carolina might be considered the northernmost of the British West Indies. In the colony's first generation, settlers were drawn from all over the Caribbean—the Leeward Islands of St. Kitts, Nevis, Antigua, and Montserrat as well as Jamaica, Barbados, the Bahamas, and as far north as Bermuda. The Bahamian connection was an especially close one, but closer still was the tie with Barbados. Carolina was originally established as an offshoot of Barbados. The Caribbean immigrants brought a certain West Indian milieu with them. Most of the slaves who came into Carolina during the first generation also came from the West Indies, especially from Barbados. Migrants from the major sugar-planting families brought whole gangs of slaves with them, establishing by 1680 a large labor force of African slaves "seasoned" in the West Indies. Thus from earliest settlements immigrants from the West Indies, black as well as white, gave a decidedly Caribbean cast to the struggling Carolina colony.[12]

Africans were in South Carolina from the beginning of settlement and played a major role in establishing rice culture. Indeed the first seed rice was introduced into the colony from Madagascar.[13] The early technological knowledge was supplied by Africans, not Europeans. To support this statement it is not necessary to establish that all, or even most, of the Africans who came to South Carolina were experienced in rice culture. All that is necessary is to point out that none of the Europeans, whether from the British Isles, Western Europe, or the Caribbean, had any experience with rice culture at all. They could not have learned rice culture from the local Indians, who gathered small quantities of wild rice but did not cultivate the crop. Rice, however, was plentiful along the entire West African coast (as well as on the East African island of Madagascar), especially in the Senegal-Gambia region that supplied nearly 20 percent of the slaves imported into South

Carolina. While over the years the Europeans contributed their engineering and management skills to extending and rationalizing the system of rice cultivation developed by the Africans, striking continuities between African and Afro-Carolinian methods of planting, hoeing, winnowing, and pounding (dehusking) the rice persisted through slavery and on into recent years.[14]

The unpleasant truth is that there could hardly have been successful rice culture in South Carolina without the strength and skills of enslaved Africans. This common dependence on their slaves was readily acknowledged by the rice planters. "Only the African race," wrote Elizabeth Allston Pringle, the daughter of Robert F. W. Allston and herself a postslavery rice planter, "could have made it possible or profitable to clear the dense cypress swamps and cultivate them in rice by a system of flooding the fields from the river by canals, ditches, or floodgates, drawing off the water when necessary, and leaving these wonderfully rice lands dry for cultivation." The relationship between the African experience and the development of rice culture in South Carolina is dramatically illustrated in the import-export figures for rice and slaves in the period of greatest expansion in rice production. From 1720 to 1726 an average of about 600 slaves were imported into the colony annually, while an average of over 71,000 hundredweight of rice were exported. From 1731 to 1738 the colony imported an average of more than 2,000 slaves each year, compared to average exports of almost 143,000 hundredweight of rice. By 1740 Africans in South Carolina numbered nearly 40,000, and exports of rice numbered over 308,000 hundredweight.[15]

The colony early began to import slaves directly from Africa. The preferences of Carolina planters among certain African tribes were reflected in the slave markets of Charleston. The most sought-after slaves were from Senegal-Gambia and the Gold Coast, but a high preponderance of Africans from the Congo-Angola region entered the colony during the formative period of the 1730s. Certainly any effort to explain the planters' preference for Senegambian Africans must take into account the prevalence of rice culture in those areas. By

1740 two-thirds of South Carolina's settlers were Africans, nearly 40,000 people. On the Waccamaw the proportions were even more demographically lopsided.[16]

The impact of the racial imbalance on culture change in All Saints Parish was momentous. It is true, as far as it goes, that newly arrived Africans were socialized into the ways the British colonists would have them behave; but it is also true that the preponderance of Africans furthered a constant renewal of African cultural patterns on the rice coast. Furthermore, initiation of European settlers into the ways of the Africans was also inevitable, given the demographic dominance of Africans. Growing up on her father's Georgetown rice plantation, Elizabeth Allston Pringle eagerly absorbed the stories "Daddy Tom" and "Daddy Prince" and "Maum Maria" told her of their own childhoods in Africa. It was, she said, a "very peculiar life, surrounded by hundreds of a different race." A northern visitor to the Waccamaw region noted, in tones of mixed envy and distaste, a degree of intimacy between the races unknown in other parts of the country: "In infancy the same nurse gives food and rest to her own child and to her master's; in childhood the same eye watches and the same hand alternately caresses and corrects them; they mingle their sports in boyhood; and through youth up to manhood there are ties which link them to each other by an affinity that no time or circumstances can destroy."[17]

Here and there along the river the *Nina* would pass boats rowed by stalwart black crews, commanded by black captains. The black oarsmen kept time with their oars to improvised songs sung in the familiar antiphonal (call-and-response) pattern.[18] Welcome Beese, a former slave, recalled one such song many years later:

> Oh, where Mausser William?
> Sing "Glory in my soul!"
> One day gone—another come!
> Sing "Glory in my soul!"
>
> We'll broke bread together!
> Sing "Glory in my soul!"

Pender meddlesome—meddle everybody!
Sing "Glory in my soul!"[19]

The Englishman Oliphant described how "these chants break
with their pleasant melody the calm stillness of the evening, as
we glide down the broad bosom of the Waccamaw, and our
crew with measured stroke keep time to the music of their own
choruses." He wrote down some of the verses:

> Oh, I takes my text in Matthew
> And some in Revelation;
> Oh, I know you by your garment—
> There's a meeting here to-night.[20]

Every now and then the oarsmen would stop their song a
moment to look at a great alligator basking fast asleep in some
sunny cove or on the reeds and marsh. When the sound of the
oars reached it, it plunged into the water with a mighty splash,
sending out great waves that caused the *Nina* to sway gently
back and forth as though on the ocean.[21]

3

The first group of plantations passed by the *Nina* belonged to
absentee landlord William Algernon Alston, Jr.—Michaux,
Calais, Strawberry Hill, Friendfield, and Marietta. Next came
his uncle Charles Alston's Bellefield, then William's Youngville,
followed by two plantations belonging to the estate of Joshua
John Ward—Oryzantia and Alderley. Rose Hill, Forlorn Hope,
and Clifton rounded out the holdings of William Alston, whose
combined plantations—containing more than 16,000 acres
and 567 slaves—dominated the southern tip of All Saints Parish.[22] Tables 1 and 2 summarize the distribution of slaves and
amounts of rice production, by plantation, in All Saints Parish.
Next the *Nina* came in sight of Fairfield, with its rice fields
stretching nearly a thousand acres on both sides of the river.
Moss-draped live oaks lined both sides of the drive leading up
to the Big House, and a wide green lawn extended down to
the river. On the pond behind the terrace garden were both
wild and tame geese and ducks. Here 190 slaves produced

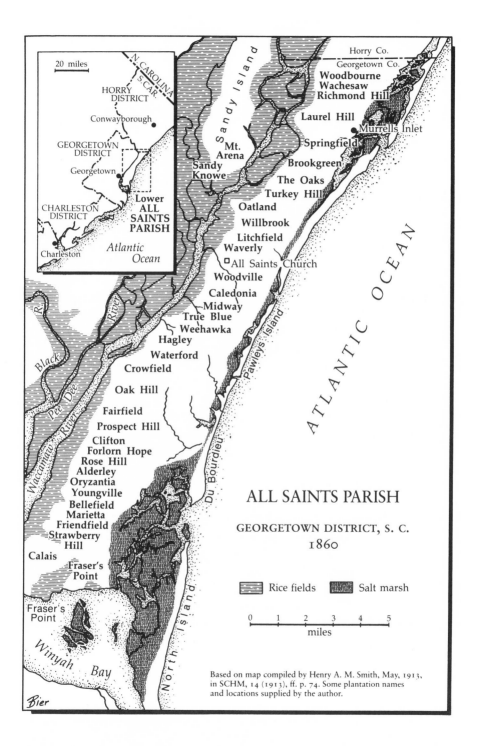

20 miles

N. CAROLINA
S. CAR.

HORRY
DISTRICT

Conwayborough

GEORGETOWN
DISTRICT

Georgetown

CHARLESTON
DISTRICT

Charleston

Lower
ALL
SAINTS
PARISH

Atlantic
Ocean

Horry Co.
Georgetown Co.

Sandy Island

Woodbourne
Wachesaw
Richmond Hill

Laurel Hill

Murrells Inlet

Mt. Arena

Springfield

Sandy Knowe

Brookgreen

The Oaks
Turkey Hill

Oatland

Willbrook

Litchfield

Waverly

All Saints Church

Woodville

Caledonia

Midway

True Blue

Weehawka

Hagley

Waterford

Crowfield

Oak Hill

Fairfield

Prospect Hill

Clifton
Forlorn Hope
Rose Hill
Alderley
Oryzantia
Youngville
Bellefield
Marietta
Friendfield
Strawberry
Hill

Calais

Fraser's
Point

Fraser's
Point

Winyah Bay

Bier

Black R.

Pee Dee R.

Waccamaw River

Du Bourdieu

Pawleys Island

North Island

ATLANTIC OCEAN

ALL SAINTS PARISH

GEORGETOWN DISTRICT, S. C.
1860

Rice fields   Salt marsh

0   1   2   3   4   5
miles

Based on map compiled by Henry A. M. Smith, May, 1913,
in SCHM, 14 (1913), ff. p. 74. Some plantation names
and locations supplied by the author.

nearly a million pounds of rice annually for their master, Charles Cotesworth Pinckney Alston.[23]

The passengers on the *Nina* now passed estates of John LaBruce and John Izard Middleton. At Oak Hill LaBruce's 150 slaves turned out over half a million pounds of rice annually.[24] LaBruce's neighbor was the ardent secessionist Middleton, whose 201 slaves at Crowfield (formerly Bannockburn) produced more rice per slave than those on any other plantation in the parish—one and a half million pounds annually.[25]

Now the plantations of Plowden C. J. Weston—Waterford, Hagley, Weehawka, and True Blue—came into view. The Weston plantations stretched on both sides of the Waccamaw. Disembarking visitors found Hagley House situated on a rise about a five-minute walk from the boat landing, surrounded by a variety of trees, including an orange tree that shaded the kitchen.[26] An Englishwoman who accompanied the Westons upon their return from a holiday visiting Mrs. Weston's family in England reported the mutual reactions of slaves and visitor: "I cannot describe the excitement and joy at the return of the master of the plantation, neither can I express my own feelings at the sight of so many black faces, for they appeared to me to have come up out of the earth, and they were as pleased to see me as if I had long known them. I must say I was not sorry when the shaking of hands was over."[27] For the slaves, the ceremonial ritual surrounding the return of the master must have been a welcome relief from the drudgery of field work.

Among the slaves at Hagley who might have watched the *Nina* steam her way up the Waccamaw were Prince and Melissa, Renty and Josephine, Agrippa and Frank. Prince, the favorite coachman, was twenty-eight years old in 1860. His wife Melissa, a "prime hand" in the rice fields, was twenty-five. They had a little son named Napoleon, and Prince had an assistant groom, twelve-year-old Agrippa. Prince always took a book along while driving the Westons on their various missions. While they visited, he read. His favorite book was said to be *Pilgrim's Progress*. Prince's untidiness in dress was the despair of the Westons, who liked their personal servants dressed in neat livery; but his skill as a driver more than offset his sar-

Table 1.
Distribution of Slaves in All Saints Parish,
by Plantation, 1860

| Plantation(s) | Number of Slaves | | | Slaveowner |
	Male	Female	Total	
Clifton *et al.*	293	274	567	William Algernon Alston, Jr.
Bellefield and Fairfield	136	154	290	Charles Alston, Sr.
Oak Hill	68	82	150	John LaBruce
Crowfield	103	98	201	John Izard Middleton
Hagley *et al.*	196	138	334	Plowden C. J. Weston
Midway	74	61	135	Benjamin F. Dunkin
Caledonia	82	78	160	Estate of Robert Nesbit
Woodville	83	68	151	William Allan Allston
Waverly	84	100	184	Joseph Blyth Allston
Litchfield and Willbrook	167	168	335	Estate of John Hyrne Tucker
Oatland	100	115	215	Martha Allston Pyatt
Turkey Hill	44	46	90	William Heyward Trapier
Brookgreen *et al.*	493	628	1,121	Estate of Joshua John Ward
Laurel Hill	175	86	261	Daniel W. Jordan
Richmond Hill	89	100	189	John D. Magill
TOTAL	2,187	2,196	4,383	
MEAN	145.8	146.4	292.2	
MEDIAN	100	100	201	

SOURCE: Figures derived from 1860 Census, Slave Schedules.

torial shortcomings. He was held in such high esteem on the plantation that he could refuse to carry out certain tasks and get away with it. Once, when asked to drown some unwanted kittens, he replied, "I don't tink I can, for I hear day say tant right kill cats." He was never asked again.[28]

Renty Tucker was a skilled carpenter and builder who also served part-time as a house servant. He was twenty-eight years old in 1860. His wife, Josephine, a seamstress, was twenty-six; and their little Benjamin was six. Renty built the Westons' summer home on Pawleys Island, a sea island just off the Waccamaw Neck. The building was described as "a castle so lofty that we could find a cool place almost in any part of the

Table 2.
Distribution of Rice Production in All Saints Parish,
by Plantation, 1860

| Plantation(s) | Number of Acres | | Annual Production of Rice (in pounds) | Pounds of Rice per Acre | Pounds of Rice per Slave |
	Unim- proved	Cultivated			
Clifton *et al.*	15,000	1,106	1,450,000	1,311	2,561
Bellefield and Fairfield	2,617	907	957,500	1,055.6	3,302
Oak Hill	5,000	600	540,000	900	3,600
Crowfield	1,675	885	1,500,000	1,694.9	7,462
Hagley *et al.*	2,171	900	1,253,000	1,392.2	3,751
Midway	3,000	290	450,000	1,551.7	3,333
Caledonia	2,000	540	700,000	1,296.3	4,375
Woodville	2,000	105	562,950	5,361.4	3,728
Waverly	3,100	370	450,000	1,216.2	2,445
Litchfield and Willbrook	10,000	475	1,012,950	2,132.5	6,173
Oatland	3,000	575	675,000	1,173.9	3,169
Turkey Hill	——	250	225,000	900.0	2,500
Brookgreen *et al.*	10,100	3,500	4,410,000	1,260.0	3,933
Laurel Hill	13,000	900	——	——	——
Richmond Hill	2,265	635	450,000	708.6	2,380
TOTAL	74,928	12,038	14,636,400	21,954.3	52,712
MEAN	5,352	803	1,045,457	1,568.2	3,765
MEDIAN	3,000	600	675,000	1,260	3,333

SOURCE: Figures derived from 1860 Census, Agriculture Schedules.

house." Renty is said to have been trained for fine carpentry in England. For most of 1859 he had been deeply involved in planning and constructing a model of a plantation chapel for the slaves. Weston had secured permission from the vestry at All Saints Church Waccamaw for the erection of such a chapel and had ordered stained glass windows and a chiming clock for the tower from England. The chapel was constructed in the shape of a cross, with a high, deep chancel with a roof beam, three tall lancet windows, and high, deep transepts. The chapel's Gothic architecture, tall steeple, and clock impressed visitors.[29]

At the age of fourteen Frank was already entrusted with the care and cleaning of his master's collection of guns. In 1859 Mrs. Weston had taught him to read and write. When he was baptized into the church, she gave him a Testament. In the summer of 1862 he would escape from slavery to a Union gunboat.[30]

After the Weston plantations, the next estate up the Waccamaw was Midway, the home of Massachusetts-born Benjamin Faneuil Dunkin, chancellor of the Court of Equity of South Carolina. The Big House at Midway was set back several hundred yards from the wharf on high ground. Access was across a wide bank through the rice fields and through a big gate bordered on each side by a Pride of India (Chinaberry) tree, each covered with hundreds of roses. Visitors walked to the house between wild orange hedges four feet tall and six feet thick. The house was a square, two-story building, with wide piazzas extending north and south, each fronting formal gardens of roses, flowering vines, and evergreens. Leading away from the Waccamaw toward the main road was the avenue, a quarter of a mile in length, bordered by 100 live oaks on each side, planted by slaves.[31]

Mariah, a five-year-old slave in 1860, undoubtedly watched the comings and goings of the *Nina* more than once. She would be given soon as a wedding present to Chancellor Dunkin's daughter, Washington, upon her marriage to Charles Alston, a nephew of the owner of Fairfield. Dunkin's 135 slaves brought in a crop of 450,000 pounds of rice at Midway. He also owned another plantation in Prince George Parish of Georgetown District.[32]

The *Nina* steamed into sight of Caledonia, belonging to the estate of the Scottish-born Robert Nesbit (1799–1848). The plantation was managed by his son, Ralph Nesbit. Here 160 slaves produced 700,000 pounds of rice annually.[33] In the summer of 1852 one of his slaves, Jeffrey, successfully escaped from the plantation only to be arrested as a runaway in Horry District, which bordered Georgetown on the north. The advertisement placed by the sheriff of Horry in the *Winyah Observer* described Jeffrey as "about 25 years of age, five feet six inches high, dark complected." The advertisement requested the owner "to come forward, prove property, pay expenses and take him away." [34]

The next plantations, Woodville and Waverly, were owned by the brothers William Allan Allston and Joseph Blythe Allston. Their father had died in 1834 while they were infants. They were raised by their uncle, Robert F. W. Allston, who managed the plantations until the brothers assumed the responsibility in 1857. [35] Among the 335 Allston slaves at Woodville and Waverly were Ben, Bina, Desdimona, Isabel, Lavinia, Molly, Peter, Philander, Prince, Sancho, and Venus. R. F. W. Allston had purchased Venus, Desdimona, and her son Sancho, along with forty-eight other slaves, in March 1851. One of them, London, ran away before he could be delivered to his new master. The following month Venus and Sancho, along with ten other slaves, were mortgaged by their new master. Bina was received by Allston from his niece in exchange for another slave, Lavinia, although no titles were exchanged at the time. The niece had inherited Bina from an aunt. In the meantime, Bina became the mother of a daughter, Isabel, who technically belonged to Allston's niece. The dilemma was resolved in 1854 by an agreement that Allston "should take back the said Lavinia and retain Bina and the child" for the sum of $800. Woodville, with its 105 cultivated acres, was the smallest plantation in All Saints Parish, but it had the highest yield of rice per acre. Its 151 slaves raised over half a million pounds of rice each year. The 184 slaves at Waverly raised 450,000 pounds. [36]

The next two plantations, Litchfield and Willbrook, were owned by the estate of the late John Hyrne Tucker (1780–1859), who left them to his sons—Litchfield to Dr. Henry M. Tucker and Willbrook to Dr. John Hyrne Tucker, Jr. Among the young slaves on the Tucker plantations were Jupiter, Sally, Tom, and Venus, who were being instructed in religion by the Reverend Alexander Glennie, the English-born rector of All

Saints Church. The elder Tucker, whose faith in the Episcopal church was said to be absolute, insured the attendance of his slaves at services in the Litchfield chapel by having his overseer call the roll after service. Any slave missing who was not on the nurse's sick list for the day forfeited a weekly allowance of either bacon, sugar, molasses, or tobacco. The 335 slaves at Litchfield and Willbrook brought in over a million pounds of rice on 475 acres of rice land.[37]

The next plantation up the river was Oatland, owned by Martha Hayes Allston Pyatt, widow of John F. Pyatt (1791–1820). Mrs. Pyatt continued to manage Oatland herself. Welcome Beese, a slave carpenter at Oatland, was twenty-seven years old in 1860. He and his eleven brothers and sisters were all born at Oatland. His father, Sam, and his mother, Dolly, had been bought from Virginia. They both worked in the rice fields, in which 215 slaves produced 675,000 pounds of rice in 1859.[38]

Bordering Oatland was Turkey Hill, owned in 1860 by William Heyward Trapier, who had acquired it by marrying into the Pyatt family. One of his slaves was little Louisa Brown. Her parents had married at Turkey Hill with a wedding feast to celebrate. She described it as "Hot supper. Cake, wine, and all. Kill cow, hog, chicken, and all. That time when you marry, so much to eat." [39]

Now the *Nina* steamed into sight of Brookgreen, the seat of the rice empire owned by the estate of the late Joshua John Ward (1800–1854). In addition to Brookgreen, the Ward empire included Oryzantia, Alderly, and Prospect Hill, which the *Nina* had already passed on its trip up the Waccamaw. Springfield, adjoining Brookgreen, and Longwood and Rose Hill were further up the river in Horry District. The entire estate was managed by his eldest son, Joshua Ward.[40] More than 1,100 slaves cultivated the Ward plantations, making Joshua Ward the largest slaveowner in the nation. Ben Horry, one of his slaves at Brookgreen, called Ward "the head rice Cap'n in dem time." Ben Horry was four years old in 1860. His father, Define Horry, was the "head man," or driver. He was thirty-

nine years old in 1860 and his wife, Bess, was thirty. In addition to Ben they had a daughter, Daphny, who was two. Ben's
uncles, Daniel and Summer, were musicians who played fiddle,
fife, and drum. Ellen Godfrey, one of Ward's Longwood slaves,
was a weaver. She was twenty-two in 1860. The slaves on the
Ward plantations produced almost four and a half million
pounds of rice annually on 3,500 cultivated acres.[41]

Among blacks Ward's reputation as a master is somewhat
mixed. Ex-slaves told Federal Writers' Project interviewer Genevieve Chandler that he was a good master, but they did so
rather guardedly. Centenarian Ellen Godfrey recalled, "Massa
was kind—you know." Ben Horry said, "Well now, fore freedom we were treated by our former owners I will say good—
'cording to situation of time." Horry described numerous
atrocities at the hands of the overseer, but was quick to add,
"If Marse Josh been know 'bout that obersheer, the obersheer
can't do 'em," but "everybody can't go to boss folks." Present-
day descendants of the slaves are more openly critical of Ward
as a slaveholder.[42]

Adjoining Springfield was Laurel Hill, purchased by Colonel Daniel W. Jordan from Plowden C. J. Weston in 1859, but
not occupied until January 1860.[43] Jordan offered to purchase
Weston's Laurel Hill slaves as well; but Weston, through his
agents, "answered most emphatically that no person in the
state could have them, not even his best friend" and that "unless he can find a purchaser to carry them away, he would keep
them himself."[44] In December Weston found a purchaser in the
West for his Laurel Hill slaves, including March, his driver;
Tie, a carpenter and engineer; Dido, the nurse; and Sarah, the
plantation cook. Christmas week for the Laurel Hill slaves was
especially sad as they said good-byes to friends and relatives
from nearby plantations. Emily Weston wrote from Hagley of
the departure of the Laurel Hill slaves: "More than half of
those here went out to see them off; saw the 'Nina' pass up the
river at ½ 8 and down again with the people on board at 1
o'clock. Those left here assembled on the wharf and the vessel
steamed along for a little while very slowly. Tears filled my eyes
as I *looked* and *listened* to the wail from those on shore echoed

by those on board! On onward they went till both the boat and cry were lost in distance."[45]

Unsuccessful in his efforts to buy Weston's Laurel Hill slaves, Jordan attempted to populate Laurel Hill with experienced rice hands from Arundel plantation on the nearby Pee Dee River. Arundel planned to sell a number of slaves "at public or private sale, and either as a gang or in families. We will receive offers at private bid up to the 1st of January next. If not disposed of before that time the negroes will be, probably, offered at auction in Charleston some time during the second week of January."[46] Apparently this attempt was unsuccessful. Nevertheless, by the summer of 1860 Jordan had 261 slaves cultivating 900 acres of rice land. Some, like the house servant Doby, had been with him at Little River. Others were bought here and there, singly or in lots, some of them in Virginia. In January 1860 he purchased an undetermined number of slaves from a man named Wagner. Jordan's 1862 slave list shows several black families with the surname Wagner, which may or may not be an indication of prior ownership.[47] Another group of slaves had been purchased by Jordan in 1859 from Samuel Atkinson in Georgetown—Boston; Andrew, his wife Amy and their children; Adam, his wife Dye and their children; Quash and his daughter Affie; and Fatima and her grandson Christmas.

Boston was an extraordinary man. Atkinson considered him "extremely confidential and intelligent." At the age of thirty, Boston "has been my driver and *overseer* for 9 years." According to Atkinson, "he is capable of turning his hands to anything;—fine size, active, strong, and likely." In a day when the average price for a prime field hand in the Charleston market was $1,200, Atkinson valued Boston at $2,000.[48]

Andrew, "a tall fine looking man," was thirty years old and a trained cooper. "By an act of imprudence in bathing while heated, he took the rheumatism," Atkinson confided to Jordan, "but he is almost entirely restored, and if kept at his trade (which I have not been able to do with him) I have not a doubt he would soon be as perfect as ever." His wife Amy was described as "a prime woman about 29 or 30 years old." Their

children, eight-year-old Robbin and two-year-old May, were
"both handsome boys." [49]

Adam, though described as "slightly *herniaed*," was ex-
tolled by his former master as "active, strong, and ambitious."
Atkinson assured Jordan that Adam "has never laid up a day
during the 9 years I have had him, nor have I ever given him a
dose of medicine—doing whatever the other men do as a full
hand however laborious." His wife Dye was "a very tall and
commanding woman about 30 years of age." Their sons, John
and Paul, were "two remarkably fine looking and promising
boys of 8 and 6 years of age." [50]

Quash, a prime ploughman and field hand, was accompanied by his daughter Affie, "a fine little girl of 3 years of
age." Fatima, "a thrifty old woman midwife and nurse," was
fifty. She was considered "invaluable as a worker about patches
and yards and for the purpose of raising poultry and little
negroes." Her grandson, Christmas, was sixteen or seventeen.
He was described as "active, smart, and faithful." All of this
group were related except for Quash and Affie, whom Atkinson had purchased from another estate. [51]

The next plantation up the Waccamaw was Richmond
Hill, which belonged to Dr. John D. Magill. Magill also owned
Oregon plantation further up the Waccamaw in Horry District. [52] One of the Richmond Hill slaves, Bruce Williams, must
have seen the *Nina* come and go many times in his twenty-
eight years. Dr. Magill taught young Bruce, an obviously intelligent youth, to read and write. After emancipation, at the age
of thirty-three, Williams would go off to attend high school in
Raleigh, North Carolina. In 1874 he would be elected to the
South Carolina House of Representatives; and in 1876, at the
age of forty-four, he would begin the first of his five terms in
the South Carolina Senate. He served until 1902. [53]

The plantation carpenter at Richmond Hill was Hardtimes Sparkman. His family included his twenty-six-year-old
wife, Pleasant, their eight-year-old son, Richmond, and their
four-year-old daughter, Kate. Hardtimes at the age of twenty-
eight was a second-generation carpenter. His father, Hardtimes, Sr., was a carpenter at Dirleton plantation on the Pee

Dee. Dirleton was part of the rice estate left by Edward Thomas Heriot and managed after his death by his son-in-law, Dr. James R. Sparkman.[54]

Titus Small, age thirty-six, was a sheep minder at Richmond Hill. His wife, Silvey, was thirty-four. They were the parents of a daughter, seven-year-old Caroline. Silvey was pregnant with another child, who would be their first son, Toby. Titus Small may be the same Titus who ran away from Richmond Hill in 1858 but was captured before he could get away from Georgetown District and was committed to the Georgetown jail until Magill could come and reclaim him.[55]

Dr. Magill's reputation as a master is uniformly poor, the poorest of any All Saints planter. Ellen Godfrey reported that "Doctor McGill people hab to steal for something to eat."[56] Throughout the 1850s sporadic advertisements for runaway slaves appeared in the Georgetown press. Usually they were placed by the sheriff, who requested the owner "to come forward, prove property, pay expenses, and take him away." (The wording was invariably the same.) Magill was often requested by the sheriff to come and reclaim Titus, or Sampson, or John, or others.[57] Magill also advertised for the return of runaways who had not been apprehended. The *Winyah Observer* ran the following advertisement from June 23 to December 29, 1852: "Runaway from the subscriber on the 24th May last his boy Gabriel. Said negro is a bright mulatto aged about 22 yrs, and is about 5 ft. 7 or 8 in. high; frowns a little when spoken to and has a contraction of 3 fingers on the right hand occasioned by a burn when quite young. He had on when he absconded a brown coat, dark vest, and woolen pants. I will give a liberal reward for his apprehension and safe delivery to me at my plantation on Waccamaw, or at any jail in the state that I may get him." Dr. Magill ran a similar advertisement in the *Wilmington Journal* in North Carolina.[58] Escape from the Waccamaw rice plantations was not easy. There do not appear to have been many All Saints runaways until the Civil War, when the presence of Union gunboats on the Waccamaw vastly improved a fugitive's chances of success. Only one other Waccamaw planter, Robert Nesbit, was mentioned in a sheriff's ad-

vertisement—and he but once. No other Waccamaw planter
advertised for the return of a runaway. When twenty-eight of
Magill's slaves escaped to a Union gunboat in 1862, they described Magill as a cruel master.[59] Perhaps as a result of his
treatment of the slaves at Richmond Hill, rice production per
slave and per acre was the lowest in All Saints Parish.[60]

Dr. Allard Belin Flagg, nephew of Washington Allston
and son-in-law of Joshua John Ward, owned Wachesaw, the
last rice plantation before the *Nina* crossed the line into Horry
District. Flagg was also the master of Oak Lawn on Sandy Island and The Hermitage, a summer retreat on the coast at
Murrells Inlet.[61] Among his slaves at Wachesaw were Margaret
One and her twin brother, Michael. Their father, Michael
One, Sr., was the principal plantation carpenter, and their
mother, Mary One, was a weaver. Their aunt, Ritta One,
nursed the children in the children's house while the mothers
were in the field.[62]

Woodbourne, in Horry District, was the last of the great
rice plantations to be developed. It represented a momentous
achievement by the slaves of J. Motte Alston. Located between the Waccamaw and Bull Creek, on the western shore of
the river, Woodbourne was laboriously cleared from virgin
swampland of "enormous cypress, gum, ash, etc., matted together with huge grape vines, and cane from fifteen to twenty
feet high." It had taken the slaves fourteen years to build the
rice plantation. Its yield was high. According to Alston, "Forty
bushels of rough rice (rice threshed, but not pounded) is the
average number of bushels per acre though I have made sixty-
five bushels per acre on 600 acres of land."[63]

The Big House at Woodbourne, a red, twelve-room structure with a slate roof of seven gables, was constructed and
painted by an especially talented slave, Alston's head carpenter
and engineer, Richmond. Richmond also constructed Alston's
summer home, Sunnyside, on a hundred-acre tract of land on a
salt water creek near Murrells Inlet, wooded with live oaks,
magnolias, and cedars. Alston had purchased the land from
Weston. "Richmond did the whole work," wrote Alston, "of

course with the assistance of some of my men to lift the heavy timbers, etc."[64]

Around 1857, Alston sold Woodbourne to his neighbor Henry Buck for approximately $45,000. In the same year he sold Sunnyside to his brother Charles, taking in payment "so many negroes which my father had given to him." After briefly hiring out his slaves to Buck, Motte Alston sold all but thirty-five to Governor John L. Manning. The thirty-five, who had been in his family all their lives, he hired out to work on a railroad near his new home in Columbia.[65]

Henry Buck, the new master of Woodbourne, was the grandson of the founder of Bucksport, Maine. He had emigrated to the Waccamaw around 1825. Energetic and ambitious, he built a small sawmill and a log hut. Working side by side, Buck and his few slaves carved out of the mighty Waccamaw pine forests one of the world's largest sawmills. Buck's lumber was shipped to every quarter of the globe on his own vessels.[66] A northern visitor wrote of Buck, "It seems to me a marvel that this man, alone and unaided by the usual appliances of commerce, had created a business, rivalling in extent the transactions of many a princely merchant of New York and Boston."[67] The achievement was remarkable, but it was not accomplished alone. Buck owned increasing numbers of slaves. By 1860 there were 311 of them.[68]

The Woodbourne slaves were described by James Roberts Gilmore, a northern traveler who visited the Waccamaw region in December 1860: "A more healthy, and to all appearance, happy set of laboring people, I had never seen. Well fed, comfortably and almost neatly clad, with tidy and well-ordered homes, exempt from labor in childhood and advanced age, and cared for in sickness by a kind and considerate mistress, who is the physician and good Samaritan of the village, they seemed to share as much physical enjoyment as ordinarily falls to the lot of the 'hewer of wood and drawer of water.'"[69] The apparent comfort and happiness of the slaves came as a surprise to Gilmore, who—while no abolitionist—was staunchly antislavery. After seeing conditions at Woodbourne,

Gilmore admitted, "I began to question if Slavery is, in reality, the damnable thing that some untravelled philanthropists have pictured it."[70] According to Gilmore, he was told by a slave that "all de brack folks 'bout har want de Captin [Buck] to buy 'em. He bery nice man—one ob de Lord's own people. . . . Bery good man, massa, but de white folks don't like him, 'cause dey say he treats him darkies so well, all dairn am uncontented."[71] Buck's opposition to the prevailing secessionist sentiment seems also to have earned him some local hostility. Gilmore describes him as "a staunch unionist" and says he was considered "obnoxious to the Secession leaders for his well-known Union sentiments."[72] Despite Buck's unionism, his sons were eager Confederate volunteers after the outbreak of hostilities at Fort Sumter.[73]

Further up the Waccamaw in Horry District were smaller plantations belonging to John M. Tillman and D. W. Oliver. Tillman's 3,000-acre plantation, The Ark, raised 400 bushels of rice on the labor of sixty-three slaves cultivating 250 acres.[74] Tillman's driver was Rodrick Rutledge. Four generations of the Rutledge family lived at The Ark. Rodrick's aged mother, Veenia, enthralled the children with her memories of pirates and the American Revolution. Rodrick's son Tass was twenty-eight in 1860, just beginning his own family. He and his wife Ellen, age twenty, were the parents of a two-year-old, Sabe, and a newborn named Agnes. Their son Sabe would become one of the informants of the Federal Writers' Project.[75]

The 2,000-acre Oliver plantation was cultivated by eighteen slaves producing corn and other foodstuffs instead of rice. Caesar Oliver was the driver. He was thirty years old in 1860 and his wife, Janie, was twenty. Sarah was six, Martha was four, William was two, and little Mary was newborn. William would also pass on the memories of what he had learned of slavery from his parents and from his experience to Chandler, when she was interviewing ex-slaves for the Federal Writers' Project.[76]

But these marked the northernmost penetration of rice culture up the Waccamaw. All the rice plantations passed by the *Nina* south of Woodbourne were on the eastern shore of the river. Moving southward again along the western shore of the Waccamaw, visitors passed Grove Hill and Hasell Hill, the Sandy Island plantations of Mary Ann LaBruce Petigru, the sister-in-law of Governor Robert F. W. Allston. She had sold her other Sandy Island plantation, Pipe Down, to Allston in 1859.[77]

Pipe Down, with its thirty-four slaves in 1859, was but a minor part of the extensive holdings of Robert F. W. Allston, whose other plantations included Chicora Wood, Exchange, Guendalos, and Nightingale Hall, all on the Pee Dee. Altogether Allston owned 630 slaves in 1860.[78] He purchased Pipe Down from his sister-in-law rather reluctantly. A recent widow, she felt herself unable to manage Pipe Down in addition to Grove Hill and Hasell Hill. She promised the Pipe Down slaves that she would obtain a good master for them. The hesitant Allston finally consented when the Pipe Down slaves sent deputations, led by the driver, Philip Washington, to persuade him that he was their choice for future master.[79] If this seems a rather romanticized depiction of slavery, it should be noted that in South Carolina in 1859 the alternative to belonging to a good master was not freedom, but belonging to a bad one. Whether Governor Allston lived up to the Pipe Down slaves' expectations is another question. Careful comparison of the list of thirty-four Pipe Down slaves that he purchased in 1859 with the list of ninety slaves in his estate inventory in 1864 reveals that of the original thirty-four Pipe Down slaves, at least twenty-four had died, run away, been sold, or transferred to other Allston plantations.[80]

Philip Washington, the spokesman for the Pipe Down slaves, was fifty-three in 1860. His daughter, 'Minder, was thirty, and his sons Dunkin and Esau were seventeen and nine, respectively. Washington was described by Allston's daughter as "a splendid specimen" of his race, who "pleaded the cause of his friends with much eloquence." Present-day oral tradition says that "the finest blood of both races" ran through his veins. Quite tall and almost black in complexion, Washington had been highly regarded by his late master, who is reported to have freed him in his will. Since for all practical purposes manumission was prohibited by South Carolina law, Philip Washington was sold to Robert F. W. Allston with the other Pipe Down slaves. After emancipation, however, Philip Washington managed to purchase land on Sandy Island and to establish a settlement of ex-slaves.[81]

There were also newly purchased slaves added to the work force at Pipe Down as well as other Allston plantations. James was a twenty-eight-year-old carpenter. His twenty-four-year-old wife, Hagar, was pregnant and near delivery when purchased in 1859. "James," Allston noted, "has epileptic attacks produced by drink," but added that he "would be valuable if kept from drink." The family of fifty-year-old Levi, his forty-year-old wife Betsey, and their children—Murria, eighteen, and Toby, fourteen—were also new. Allston described Betsey as "delicate" and Murria as "half-witted." This family also included, in Allston's words, "the incumbrance of an old man of eighty years, father of Betsey." Abby and her children—Caleb, Charlotte, Eliza, Sandy, and Lambert—were purchased in 1860 from Allston's niece, so that they could be with their husband and father, Will, who was already an Allston slave.[82]

Mt. Arena, the next plantation down the Waccamaw on Sandy Island, had been part of the extensive estate left by Dr. Edward Thomas Heriot (1793–1854). Managed for several years by Heriot's son-in-law, Dr. James R. Sparkman, it was sold to Heriot's son, Francis Withers Heriot, in 1859. He and his mother made their home at Mt. Arena and summered at Woodland, the Heriot retreat at Murrells Inlet. Under Dr. Sparkman's management, the slaves at Mt. Arena produced 355 barrels of rice in 1855, 384 barrels in 1856, 344 barrels in 1857, 388 barrels in 1858, and 367 barrels in 1859, on 225 acres of rice land.[83]

Gabe Lance was one of the Mt. Arena slaves. His grandfather, Nelson Lance, was the driver at Mt. Arena. Gabe described Frank Heriot as a "good master all right. Give plenty to eat. Reasonable task." He added, however, that if a Mt. Arena slave "didn't done task, put 'em in barn and least cut they give 'em (with lash) been twenty-five to fifty." In addition

to the whipping, the offending slave would have to suffer reduced rations for the following week.[84]

The slaves of Edward Thomas Heriot had to be divided
among his various heirs in 1859. There was an effort made to
keep immediate families together, but it was not always possible to keep grown children on the same plantation with parents. Some favored slaves were singled out for special treatment. Tom and Molly were assigned to lot number one, "in
order to go with their children. . . . They are never to be sold
out of the family—Under the will they are to be provided for
as long as they live." Lot number one went to Mt. Arena and
Francis Heriot, with the understanding that "should it ever become necessary or advisable to transfer them to one of the
other heirs of Dr. E. T. Heriot . . . the money at which they
have been appraised will be paid by such heir to Col. F. W.
Heriot." Tom was appraised at $1,000 and Molly at $600. The
most valued of the Mt. Arena slaves was Jack, who was listed
at $1,200. Other highly valued slaves at Mt. Arena included
Charles, Hammon, Summer, George, John, Frank, Joe, Trim,
Jim, and Peter, each appraised at $1,000.[85]

4

The slaves on the rice plantations of the Waccamaw made
their masters wealthy. Since the vast All Saints rice plantations
were largely self-sufficient, much of the planters' income from
the sale of rice was clear profit. Ward was described as making
"$360 clear to every hand that hoes." Robert F. W. Allston re-
ported the return on "a rice plantation of good size and local-
ity" to be about 8 percent annually. In addition to the cash
return on the staple crop, the fringe benefits of rice planting—
mansion, servants, stable, food crops—were of considerable
value. Furthermore, the planters' capital investment in slaves
appreciated considerably in two ways. First, the market value
of an individual slave doubled between 1850 and 1860 (and
many of the All Saints rice plantation slaves were much more
valuable than the market average for prime field hands). Second, the natural increase in the slave population in a single

generation was sufficient, as a Georgetonian noted, "to educate the children in high-grade seminaries at home or abroad
and to provide marriage portions for the daughters."[86]

The rice plantations of All Saints Parish were certainly not
of average size, wealth, or importance. According to the 1860
census, only eighty-eight slaveholders in the United States
owned more than 300 slaves. Twenty-nine of those slaveholders were rice planters, and seven of them planted on the
Waccamaw. Only fourteen planters owned more than 500
slaves. Nine of them were rice planters, and three of them
planted on the Waccamaw. Only one planter owned more than
1,000 slaves—Joshua Ward, a Waccamaw rice planter.[87]

The slaves of All Saints produced rice of high quality as
well as in large quantities. At the annual fairs of the Winyah
and All Saints Agriculture Society the slaves of Joshua John
Ward and of John Hyrne Tucker consistently earned silver
medals for their masters. The society was founded in 1842 to
improve agriculture and livestock breeding in Georgetown
District. Ward and his slaves were recognized for developing a
new strain of big grain rice. The society also sent exhibits to
such international competitions as the Crystal Palace Exhibition at the 1851 London World's Fair. There Dr. Edward
Thomas Heriot of Sandy Island was awarded a medal for the
prize-winning rice produced by his slaves. Similarly, Robert F.
W. Allston won a silver medal at the Paris Exhibition of 1855
for the rice produced by his slaves on the Waccamaw, on
Sandy Island, and on the Pee Dee.[88]

The rice planters of All Saints Parish were thus at the apex
of the antebellum plantation aristocracy. The rice coast aristocracy was held together by blood as well as by class. The genealogical relationships among them were extensive and complex. By 1860 virtually all the planter families discussed above
were related to one another, with kinship alliances branching
out to include politically and socially prominent families elsewhere in the state as well as in England and Scotland. Such
planters as Joshua Ward and Plowden Weston constituted an
elite who dominated a grudging but increasingly powerless

group of smaller planters and others in 1860. Not only did the elite planters dominate the society, but there was a growing disparity between those who possessed truly fabulous wealth and those who possessed little or nothing by 1860. Between 1850 and 1860 the lower three quartiles of the white population had their share of land ownership reduced from 13 percent to less than 2 percent, while the upper 3 percent of the population increased their share of land from 26 percent to 50 percent.[89] See also Tables 3 and 4.

The fabulous rice economy could not entirely compensate for a hostile environment. Simms found the climate to be "moist, hot, and unhealthy; subject to fevers in summer and agues in autumn." Standing water in thousands of acres of rice fields, stretching beyond the horizons without a stump showing above water, assaulted the nostrils with a horrible stench for much of the growing season. An observer noted that "Europeans have scarcely any idea of the low lands of Carolina. What would they think of travelling through endless and almost impervious woods, where the air is in a state of stagnation, and where, in some seasons, stagnant water lies upon the ground in most parts to the depth of twelve or eighteen inches? Even so early as the month of April, I have . . . observed that in driving along the public road, where it led through a swamp, the white passengers in a carriage were obliged to apply a handkerchief to their noses, so noxious and intolerable was the effluvium." Heriot, writing to a cousin in Scotland, marveled that the slaves seemed impervious to the consequences of sun and swamp, when their effect on whites was so devastating. "This is one of the singular facts connected with our negro population," he said, "that while they thrive and are healthy in the midst of our rice fields, and hot summer sun, a white man particularly foreigners sink under their influence." The interaction of sun and swamp in the flooded rice fields produced "marsh miasma, which engenders fevers of a dangerous nature; fatal, indeed, to white men in most cases; and even negroes, in some seasons, suffer greatly from it." Ship captains refused to take their vessels up the Waccamaw during the

Table 3.
Distribution of Wealth in Land,
All Saints Parish, 1850 and 1860

Total Value of Real Estate (in dollars)	1850		1860	
	Percentage of White Population	Percentage of Real Estate	Percentage of White Population	Percentage of Real Estate
0	33.7	0.0	37.3	0.0
1–1,000	28.2	10.7	28.2	0.7
1,001–10,000	11.3	2.7	14.2	0.5
10,001–50,000	19.1	34.6	12.7	25.8
50,001–100,000	5.2	26.0	3.8	22.9
100,000+	2.5	26.0	3.8	50.1
TOTAL	100.0	100.0	100.0	100.0

SOURCE: This table is computed from 1850 and 1860 Censuses, Agriculture Schedules.

Table 4.
Cumulative Distribution of Wealth in Land,
All Saints Parish, 1850 and 1860

Total Value of Real Estate (in dollars)	1850		1860	
	Cumulative Percentage of White Population	Cumulative Percentage of Real Estate	Cumulative Percentage of White Population	Cumulative Percentage of Real Estate
0	33.7	0.0	37.3	0.0
1–1,000	61.9	10.7	65.5	0.7
1,001–10,000	73.2	13.4	79.7	1.2
10,001–50,000	92.3	48.0	92.4	27.0
50,001–100,000	97.5	74.0	96.2	49.9
100,000+	100.0	100.0	100.0	100.0

SOURCE: This table is computed from 1850 and 1860 Censuses, Agriculture Schedules.

sickly season. The enormous wealth of the Waccamaw was reported by a visitor to be "the product of a sun that dashes his benefits with malaria, pestilence and death." Despite his riches, noted the visitor, "the planter walks forth in the morning unrefreshed, yet he must heed his steps, for the poisonous reptiles lie in his path—the shark watches for him when he laves his burning body in the surf, and the alligator pulls him down in the rivers. For nearly half the year he cannot visit his own plantation. . . . if he comes back before the frost, it is like the return of the banished Foscari, on pain of death. Thus he becomes an absentee." Attributing the deadly malaria to "marsh miasma," the visitor nevertheless complained of abundant mosquitoes. "The insects that, single, are insignificant," he wrote, "have yet, when they come in swarms, powers of intolerable annoyance. The night is no season for rest; they must be kept at bay by nets, that break the freshening breeze which should fan the feverish limbs." Such was the climate of All Saints Parish in the mid-nineteenth century.[90]

Thus the slaves of All Saints Parish lived and shaped the patterns of their folk culture in an environment of distinctive social, economic, and physical characteristics. As a result they shared distinctive demographic characteristics as well (see Table 5). They lived on larger plantations than most slaves elsewhere, and their families had usually been in the district longer, often on the same plantation. They lived in an environment of few whites, and one virtually devoid of free blacks and of mulattoes.[91] The economic and cultural implications of that environment were momentous. Economically, it meant more continuity with African work patterns than one might otherwise have expected. Culturally, it facilitated continuity with various patterns of African folk culture.

As late as 1860 there were still slaves on Waccamaw rice plantations who retained vivid memories of Africa. "Old Pemba," at Hagley plantation, had been brought to South Carolina from Africa as a child toward the end of the eighteenth century. Scipio, at Woodbourne plantation, was another aged

Table 5.
Age and Sex Distribution, Slave Population,
Georgetown District, 1860

Age	Number of Males	Per-centage of Males	Number of Females	Per-centage of Females	Total Number	Percentage of Total
0–4	1,386	7.65	1,291	7.12	2,677	14.78
5–9	974	5.38	1,011	5.58	1,985	10.96
10–14	1,033	5.70	877	4.84	1,910	10.55
15–19	840	4.63	977	5.39	1,817	10.03
20–29	1,705	9.42	1,523	8.41	3,228	17.83
30–39	1,229	6.79	1,353	7.47	2,582	14.26
40–49	1,189	6.57	1,080	5.96	2,269	12.53
50–59	384	2.12	474	2.61	858	4.74
60–69	245	1.35	231	1.28	476	2.63
70–79	96	0.53	70	0.39	166	0.91
80–89	27	0.15	34	0.19	61	0.34
90–99	12	0.07	25	0.14	37	0.20
100+	2	0.01	1	0.01	3	0.02
Unknown	21	0.12	19	0.10	40	0.22
TOTAL	9,143	50.49	8,966	49.51	18,109	100.00

SOURCE: 1860 Census, Slave Schedules.

African who had been taken from his homeland as a young
man. Motte Alston wrote that "Scipio, with many others, was
bought by my grandfather from a New England slave-ship
which came into Charleston to dispose of her cargo. He was
never resold, but like most of his (my grandfather's) large number of negroes, lived and died in the same family. I can't say
that I owned the old man; I simply moved him from my father's place to mine." Even the white children on the rice plantations grew up with stories of Africa. Elizabeth Allston Pringle described

three quite remarkable, tall, fine-looking, and very intelligent Africans who had been bought . . . from the ship which

brought them to this country. Tom, Prince, and Maria . . . had been of a royal family in their own land, and had been taken in battle by an enemy tribe with which they were at war, and sold to a slave ship. No one ever doubted their claim to royal blood, for they were so superior to the ordinary Africans brought out. They were skilled in the arts of their own country and had artistic taste and clever hands. Daddy Tom and Daddy Prince told tales of their wild forests, which the children were never tired of hearing, nor they of telling.

Other African-born slaves on the All Saints plantations were recalled as late as the 1930s by ex-slaves interviewed by Chandler for the Federal Writers' Project.[92]

All Saints slaves were not merely highly aware of their African roots, but also they could and did make minute and invidious distinctions among Africans. For instance, Ancrum, on one of Robert F. W. Allston's plantations, evaluated some of his fellow slaves on the basis of their ethnic origins: "Peter and Sampson and David, dem ben an' outlan' people Afrikan, one ben Gullah and one ben a Guinea—the Gullah ben a cruel people—and de Fullah ben a cruel people, but Guinea ben a tough workin' people, an' Milly ben a Guinea."[93] The continuing presence of African-born slaves, plus the continuing influence of African criteria in slave evaluation of other slaves, indicate rather more cultural continuity with Africa than has been generally credited.

To probe the relationship between the African inheritance and the environment of All Saints Parish requires more speculation than one would wish, but it is unavoidable. What Afro-American culture would have become with different combinations of economy, environment, and heritage it is impossible to say. Certainly it would not have developed as it did. Of course, relatively few African economic and cultural patterns survived unchanged, unaffected by the new physical and social environment. How the slaves responded to the pressures and challenges of work in a rice economy based on African patterns of rice culture, but transformed by Euro-American systems of economic organization, is the subject of the next chapter. The slaves' response to the cultural constraints and cultural opportunities of the new environment—in their material culture, their folk tales, their religious expression, their use of off times, and even their use of language—will be examined in the chapters to follow.

CHAPTER TWO

"All Dem Rice Field"

It was work—work consistently sustained and ruthlessly enforced, work in the rice fields and the rice mills, in the barns
and the barnyards, in the kitchens and the carpentry shops, in
the slaves' cabins and in the masters' mansions—that dominated the waking hours of the slaves of All Saints Parish. From
the slaves' point of view, toil from sunup to sundown was part
of the natural rhythm of the land and was a constant part of
their collective experience. No picture of slave life can be adequate without an attempt to penetrate more deeply into the
work patterns of the rice plantations, the jobs to be done, the
labor system by which the work was arranged and managed,
and the emotional texture of work—the slaves' attitudes toward their jobs. Work patterns on the rice plantations were extremely complex; the adaptation of African labor traditions to
a new environment is not the whole story. Nevertheless, it is an
important part of the story and merits treatment here. Before
exploring their cultural implications, however, it is necessary
to examine the work patterns themselves.

Rice planting, although not exploited commercially until
more than a decade after its introduction into the South Carolina colony, steadily increased in importance after 1695. By
the mid-eighteenth century the labor of rice plantation slaves
in the South Carolina lowcountry afforded their masters the
highest per capita income in the American colonies. They continued to earn huge profits for their masters up to the Civil
War. The slaves of Georgetown District were the leading producers of rice in antebellum America. The Waccamaw plantations were the most productive in Georgetown District.[1]

Africans and their descendants had been cultivating rice
on the Waccamaw since the eighteenth century, clearing the

swamps and marshlands to create the great plantations, digging and ditching, building the banks to hold back the waters
when not desired, digging the sluice gates—called trunks—to
let in the waters when the fields were to be flooded. At low tide
one can still see the innumerable stobs driven into the ground
along the shores of the Waccamaw to hold mud and protect
the banks against erosion, high tides, freshets, and alligators.
Carving useful growing land out of swamp and marsh required
considerable engineering skill. The laborers simply had to
be knowledgeable to have undertaken such an enterprise
successfully.[2]

As late as the mid-nineteenth century black slaves understood and took pride in their own achievement and that of
their ancestors in creating the great rice plantations. Gabe
Lance, who had been a slave at Mt. Arena plantation on Sandy
Island, recalled many years later, "All dem rice field been
nothing but swamp. Slavery people cut kennel (canal) and cut
down woods—and dig ditch through raw woods. All been
clear up for plant rice by slavery people."[3] The slaves' pride in
what they had achieved was perhaps best expressed in 1937 by
Ben Horry, who had been a slave at Brookgreen plantation. He
told Genevieve Chandler, a field worker for the Federal Writers' Project, "Missus, slavery time people *done* something!"[4]
The slaves developed a strong sense of ownership of these
plantations that their ancestors had created and that they continued to make productive. That a slave, considered to be
property, might enjoy a sense of ownership that rivaled his
master's claim seems paradoxical; but a slave was not *merely*
property. A slave was also a human being who had an immense
investment in the plantation both by inheritance and by personal contribution. An ex-slave named Morris, born on one
of William Algernon Alston's plantations on the lower Waccamaw, learned early in the twentieth century that the new
owner's superintendent considered him lazy and wished to put
him off the plantation. Morris went to his new landlord, the
noted financier Bernard M. Baruch. "I was born on dis place
and I ain't agoin' off," he began. "I was born on dis place before Freedom. My Mammy and Daddy worked de rice fields.

Dey's buried here. De fust ting I remember are dose rice banks. I growed up in dem from dat high. . . . De strength of dese arms and dese legs and of dis old back, Mist' Bernie, is in your rice banks. It won't be long before de good Lord take de rest of pore old Morris away too. An' de rest of dis body want to be with de strength of de arms and de legs and de back dat is already buried in your rice banks. No, Mist' Bernie, you ain't agoin' to run old Morris off dis place."[5] Morris stayed. But Morris was not alone in such attitudes, nor were they merely a postslavery phenomenon. J. Motte Alston, the master of Woodbourne, noted that his "head man," Cudjo, shared this same sense of ownership. Alston wrote that Cudjo "looked upon my property as belonging to him."[6]

2

The labor system under which the slaves of All Saints Parish worked and took justifiable pride in their work output was the task system, in general use on rice plantations during the antebellum period. Unlike gang labor on cotton plantations, under the task system the owner or overseer assigned each slave a certain task each morning. When that job was finished, the slave was free to pursue personal interests. Tasks were calculated to last the whole day, but some slaves finished early. For example, if the task was completed by 11 A.M., the slave could quit for the day. If the task was not finished until 5 P.M. or later, the slave had to work until it was completed.[7] J. Motte Alston wrote in his memoirs that tasks were never increased, regardless of the number of slaves who finished early, because the free time served as an incentive to work harder.[8] However, according to present-day black and white oral tradition, if too many people finished too early, the tasks probably *were* increased.[9]

The work day began at sunrise on the rice plantations, partly to avoid the heat as much as possible. As ex-slave William Oliver put it, "When you come right down to the truth, we always got up fore day most of the time." An English visitor described rice planting as "easy work: begin at sunrise, breakfast at nine, dinner at three; by which time the task-work is usually finished." For the slaves, however, the work—the clearing, the plowing, the planting, the harrowing, the hoeing, the harvesting, the threshing—was anything but "easy work." [10]

For every kind of work on the plantation there was a specified task. For instance, the ground-breaking task for an able-bodied hand was to break up 1,200 square feet with a spade after the ground had been plowed. A trench-digger, or trencher, was expected to dig three-quarters of an acre per day with a hoe. A sower was expected to sow half an acre per day. According to Gabe Lance, a "reasonable task" was a quarter-acre to half-acre per day with a hoe. "Ditching man ten compass. Got to slush 'em out. Got to bail that water out till you kin see track." [11]

Tasks were allotted by taking into consideration the age and physical ability of each slave: there were full-task hands, three-quarter-task hands, half-task hands, and quarter-task hands. Plowden C. J. Weston, the master of Hagley plantation, made explicit in his overseers' contract his concept of how much work a task should be: "A task is as much work as the meanest hand can do in nine hours, working industriously." James R. Sparkman, who planted Mt. Arena on Sandy Island until 1859, said that the tasks on his plantation were "easily accomplished, during the winter months in 8 to 9 hours and in summer my people seldom exceed 10 hours labor *per day*." Weston cautioned his overseers that slaves were not to be assigned impossible tasks, nor was more work to be given once a day's task was completed. During severe winter weather tasks were not assigned. Only such work as required least exposure was attempted. In case of heavy rains and thundershowers the slaves were dismissed from work and allowed to return home. [12]

Plowden Weston specified clearly to his overseers that slaves were not to be assigned tasks beyond their capabilities: "No negro is to be put into a task which they cannot finish with tolerable ease. It is a bad plan to punish for not finishing task; it is subversive of discipline to leave tasks unfinished, and contrary to justice to punish for what cannot be done." [13] Weston's practice may not have been the norm on the Waccamaw. No other masters instructed their overseers so specifically as did Weston; furthermore, it is unlikely that Weston's overseers always followed his orders to the letter. Both the slave narratives and present-day oral tradition are replete with instances of slaves having been beaten for not having finished tasks, as well as cases of slaves having been assigned impossible tasks and then having been beaten for failing to complete them. [14]

Both men and women worked in the rice fields during planting, growing, and harvesting; but only men did the ditching, embanking, and other tasks that prepared the fields for rice cultivation. [15] Pregnant women were a special case. Dr. James R. Sparkman of Mt. Arena described his policy regarding pregnant field hands: "Allowance is invariably made for the women as soon as they report themselves *pregnant* they being appointed to light work as will insure a proper consideration for the offspring. No woman is called out to work after her confinement, until the lapse of 30 days, and for the first fortnight thereafter her duties are selected on the upland, or in the cultivation of the provision crops, and she is not sent with the gang on the low damp tide lands." [16] In theory the slaves' tasks were assigned by the owner or overseer, but in practice they had to consult the black drivers, who were in direct charge of the field hands and who, in fact, made numerous major decisions regarding the cultivation of rice. While planters such as Weston, Sparkman, and Joshua Ward tried to run their plantations by minutely predetermined rules, even they found in practice that numerous decisions had to be made on the spot—in the rice fields. [17]

3

The slaves of All Saints Parish planted, cultivated, and harvested their enormous rice crops almost exclusively by hand. The work cycle was dangerous and tiring and involved a full year of strenuous labor in swampy, snake-infested lowlands under the scorching Carolina sun.[18] The slaves began to prepare for a new crop almost immediately after the previous harvest. They plowed under the stubble in the field so that the sod could benefit from the winter frosts. Spring was the time for preparing the fields. Harrowing, plowing, and trenching were the dominant tasks during March. Only the soil preparation made use of animals. Oxen or mules, outfitted with special boots because of the soft boggy earth, pulled the plows. Otherwise, the condition of the soil necessitated hand labor. After the ground was plowed, slaves broke the clods, leveled the surface, and dug trenches roughly twelve to fifteen inches apart to receive the rice seed. All of this they did with their all-purpose eight-inch hoes. Ben Horry of Brookgreen plantation described the tasks: "A quarter (acre) if you mashing ground. Ten compass digging ground, cutting rice one half acre a day. . . . Mashing raw ground half acre some quarter. Mash 'em—take hoe full up them hole, level dem, chop dem big sod! . . . My day I trenching hoe trench dat!"[19] By the end of March the fields would be ready for planting.

April was the planting month. Workers tried to get all the rice planted by the first of May. A planter's wife exulted in her diary April 29, 1859, "Will have planted the whole in two more days."[20] The seed rice was first soaked in mud and dried to prevent its floating to the surface when the field was flooded. "The best hands," according to Robert F. W. Allston, "are chosen to sow rice. In fine April weather it is pleasing to behold the steady, graceful progress of a good sower." Slaves dropped the seeds into the trenches and covered them with the foot.[21] As soon as the fields were planted, the trunks—or sluice gates—were opened at high tide and the fields were flooded. This first flooding, known as the sprout flow, remained on the fields only until the grain sprouted (usually three days to a week) and was then drained. Otherwise the delicate plants would rise to the surface with the least agitation and float away.

During the sprout flow most of the slaves shifted their work to higher ground, where they planted the plantations' provision crops—potatoes, corn, collards, peas, and the like.[22]

Ward's slaves at Brookgreen won their master an award from the Winyah and All Saints Agricultural Society by raising 700 bushels of sweet potatoes on a single acre.[23] Shortly after the rice seed germinated, however, the slaves were back in the rice fields, hoeing in tempo with work songs, moving across the fields in a row.[24]

After this hoeing the fields were again flooded. This flooding, known as the long water, completely submerged the rice fields in order to destroy insects and the young grass that had sprung up among the rice plants. After two or three days the water was drained to half the plants' height and kept there until the plants grew strong enough to stand erect. Some slaves went back to the high ground for more work on the provision crops. Most, however, remained to work the flooded rice fields with hand tools, raking off trash that had risen to the surface from the previous hoeings. About three weeks later the long water was drained and dry cultivation was begun. For the slaves, the three weeks of dry cultivation were excruciating. They worked under intense heat and humidity on muddy ground with short, narrow hoes. They had to complete two or three complete hoeings with the small hoes during this period—the last very lightly and carefully.

Toward mid-July, two or three days after the last hoeing, the final flooding—called the lay-by flow or harvest flow—commenced. The heavy heads of the ripening rice were supported by the water, which was changed often and kept fresh, but never completely drained. This inundation meant nearly two months of lighter work for the slaves, mostly plucking grass and shooing away the yellow and black bobolinks, called rice-birds, as they began their southward migration in August and early September.

The tempo of work picked up early in September as the harvest started. When the rice heads were nearly ripened, the trunks were opened and the fields were drained overnight. At dawn of light the next day the harvest commenced. Standing shoulder-high among the rice plants, the field hands dexterously harvested the grain with sickles known as rice hooks. The rice was dried on the stubble for a day, then tied in sheaves

and stacked on shallow boats, called flats, for transportation
to the threshing yards.

Threshing—separating the heads from their stalks—was
an onerous task. Slaves still did much of the threshing by hand
as late as the mid-nineteenth century. Bundles of grain were
placed on the ground with their heads facing out, while skilled
slaves walked down the rows of bundles beating the heads off
the grain with flailing sticks. The next stage was winnowing,
to separate the grain from the chaff. The threshed grain was
"fanned" in the wind in wide, flat fanner baskets with small,
slanting rims crafted by talented slave basketmakers. Next the
rice was "pounded," a somewhat misleading term for the process by which the outer husks and inner cuticle were removed
from the rice grains. The slaves put a few pecks of unhusked
rice, called rough rice, into wooden mortars made of hollowed-
out logs and, using a grinding motion, worked them with a
pestle made of pine. The outer husks came off easily, but removing the inner cuticle without breaking the rice grains required considerable skill.[25]

The perfection of threshing and pounding mills by the
mid-nineteenth century increased the output of rice. By 1860
there were eleven rice mills in Georgetown District, including
mills at Fairfield, Hagley, Waverly, and Laurel Hill in All Saints
Parish. Most of the planters had their milling done at the mills
on the larger plantations; others sent their rice to the rice mills
in Charleston.[26]

The earliest rice mills were water-powered. The same
fields in which the rice was cultivated from late spring to early
fall served as a power source in the winter for milling the rice.
J. Motte Alston, who planted at Woodbourne, recalled the water mill at his father's Fairfield in his memoirs: "The mill was
erected near the river, and the fields in the rear were flooded at
high water. Then the floodgates were closed, and when the tide
fell in the river, the water held back in the fields was some four
or five feet higher than that in the river. This then was the mo-
tive power which set the machinery of the mill's waterwheel in
motion; the huge stones to rotate and the heavy pestles to
pound."[27]

The sketches and photographs on the following pages illustrate the rice-growing year, from planting through harvesting through threshing. The sketches were made by Alice R. Huger Smith as illustrations for Elizabeth Allston Pringle's memoir, *A Woman Rice Planter* (1914). The photograph of rice loaded on a flat dates from circa 1900, Georgetown, South Carolina. Courtesy, South Caroliniana Library. The other photographs were made by Bayard Wooten for the Federal Writers' Project, All Saints Parish, circa 1937. Courtesy, Brookgreen Gardens. Although both sketches and photographs were done many years after slavery, the processes involved in rice culture had changed relatively little over the decades, and the pictures show graphically the kinds of work slaves in All Saints Parish performed.

Rice plantation barnyard. On the left is a threshing and pounding mill, which vastly increased rice output. There were four such rice mills in All Saints Parish by 1860. On the right is a winnowing house. The use of the hoe as an all-purpose implement continued an African practice.

Preparing the fields for planting. Oxen occasionally wore special boots to keep from sinking in the boggy earth of the rice fields.

Planting rice. Slaves dropped seed rice into trenches and covered them with the foot in the African manner.

Carrying harvested rice to the flats. The rice was loaded onto flatboats, called flats, for transportation to the threshing yard.

Rice loaded on a flat. Flatboats carried the rice—and the slaves—back to the plantation barnyard.

Tying the rice into sheaves. The harvested rice was tied into sheaves for threshing.

Rice sheaves stacked in the plantation barnyard.

Threshing the rice. Slaves beat the heads off the grain with flailing sticks. Threshing was still done by hand on many plantations as late as the mid-nineteenth century.

Pouring "fanned" rice into mortar. Threshed rice was winnowed by being "fanned" in the wind in hand-coiled fanner baskets. Both the baskets and the method of winnowing represent continuity with African tradition.

Above, winnowing and "pounding" the rice. The threshed grain was "fanned" in the wind in wide, flat fanner baskets before being "pounded," a process of removing the outer husks and cuticle from the rice grains with mortar and pestle. "Fanning," "pounding," and coil basketry all represent continuities with African traditions.

"Pounding" rice. Unhusked rice is gently ground in this hollow-log mortar with a wooden pestle in a manner identical to that of West African rice producers.

Most of the water-powered mills had been adapted to steam power by 1840. Robert F. W. Allston, whose extensive holdings in Georgetown District included Waverly, an All Saints rice plantation with a steam mill, vividly depicted the steam mill's operation:

> By steam power, the rough-rice is taken out of the vessel which freights it, up to the attic of the building—thence through the sand-screen to a pair of (five feet wide) heavy stones, which grind off the husk—thence into large wooden mortars, in which it is pounded by large iron-shod pestles (weighing 250 to 350 pounds), for the space of some two hours, more or less.
>
> The rice, now pounded, is once more elevated into the attic, whence it descends through a rolling-screen, to separate whole grains from the broken, and flour from both; and also through wind-fans, to a vertical brushing screen, revolving rapidly, which polishes the flinty grain, and delivers it fully prepared, into the barrel or tierce, which is to convey it to market.[28]

But water mills, steam mills, and hand labor were not mutually exclusive. Almira Coffin, a New Englander who visited Midway, the All Saints rice plantation of Benjamin Fanuiel Dunkin, in 1851, noted that Dunkin had a large water-powered pounding mill by the river, an equally large steam-powered threshing mill, and a smaller winnowing house where the slaves winnowed the grain by hand. "Some planters," she wrote, "have steam mills for these purposes, others have none, but send here and have it hulled at an extensive set of steam mills and pay a certain amount of toll."[29]

The intricate machinery of the rice mills required skilled mechanics, some of whom were slaves especially trained for the purpose.[30] The mills required constant attention to protect the machinery from overheating and fire. It was necessary for the slaves to keep the mill and its environs scrupulously clean. The mills were normally closed in time to allow the slaves to clean the machinery and the mill yard before sunset. Plowden Weston warned his overseers: "The proprietor considers an overseer who leaves any straw or tailing during the night within 300 yards of the mill as unfit to be trusted with the care of valuable property." Thus the rice mills, and the slaves who worked in them, functioned under the direct supervision of the overseers.[31]

Rice that was broken during pounding was kept for consumption on the plantations. The blacks also recycled the various by-products of rice processing for use on the plantations— the husks as fertilizer, the bran as livestock feed, the stubble for livestock bedding. The bedding itself was later used for fertilizer. In the meantime, while the long and tedious process of threshing, winnowing, and pounding were going on, other slaves were harvesting the food crops. By mid-November the provision crops had been gathered and the rice was ready for shipping. Plantation activity slackened. Field hands repaired the dikes and began to prepare the fields for a new beginning of the cycle of rice culture in the spring.[32]

4

The pace and intensity of the slaves' work varied from season to season throughout the growing cycle. It also varied from slave to slave. A common condition of servitude did not necessarily produce a common response or a conformity in work attitudes. Some slaves were energetic; others were slothful. Some gave their labor with apparent willingness; others with obvious resentment. Some refused to work; others found more subtle ways of avoiding toil. For their part the masters wanted more from their slaves than the grudging performance of only enough work to avoid being beaten. To that end the masters tried to motivate the slaves with a flexible system of incentives—rewards for performance, punishments for failure to perform. Their effectiveness in the slave South has been a controversial question, and it is difficult to be certain about even so small an area as All Saints Parish, although the enormous productivity of the Waccamaw plantations would seem to indicate a certain success on the part of the incentives system.[33] To say that the slaves' work performance might have been influenced by the masters' incentives, however, is not to say that the incentives caused the slaves' productivity, nor is it to contend that the slaves could not behave in accordance with their own cultural traditions but could only react to particular modes of the masters' domination. On the contrary, the masters' power to make their slaves work, however omnipotent in theory, was never absolute. The slaves, however abject their legal status, were never completely powerless. If the slaves knew that an absolute refusal to work could bring them swift and certain punishment, they also knew that indolence, malingering, dilatory performance of tasks, and negligent handling of machinery, tools, and animals could bring their masters possible financial loss. But who would suffer most in such an event, the masters or the slaves? Before exploring work patterns on the rice plantations as a matter of cultural continuity and adaptation, then, it is first necessary to examine the positive and negative incentives by which the masters attempted to promote their work.

It was out of enlightened self-interest that Plowden C. J. Weston wrote into his overseers' contract the stipulation that the overseers' performance would be judged first and foremost by "the general well being of the negroes; their cleanly appearance, respectful manners, active and vigorous obedience; their completion of tasks well and early; the small amount of punishment; the excess of births over deaths; the small number of people in hospital, and the health of the children."[34] A plantation where such conditions prevailed, he believed, would be less likely to produce sullen and discontented slaves who procrastinated, malingered, and sabotaged their work. Such a plantation would therefore be more likely to produce up to its capacity. However, only a few masters clearly perceived such implications, and their overseers varied in their effectiveness in carrying out the planters' desires.

The task system itself tended to promote short-range performance. When a slave finished a task, his work day was normally completed. When it was necessary for a slave to work over task, the master paid the slave for it. On some plantations if a slave performed two tasks in one day, the next day was a holiday. As a result the incentive system, in addition to rewarding short-term, immediate performance, was designed to promote longer-term motivation.[35]

The various annual rewards given on the rice plantations also attempted to promote long-term motivation. Slaves who had not lost a single day's work because of illness were rewarded with an extra bushel of rice. Slaves who passed the annual tool inspection and who had not been guilty of any serious offense during the year received a week's extra ration of rice, peas, molasses, meat, and tobacco. The number of slaves claiming such rewards seems to indicate that All Saints slaves did not routinely malinger, feign illness, and deliberately mishandle tools as a means of day-to-day resistance. The rice crop depended on straightly plowed furrows, trenches of an even depth, removal of grass and weeds without damage to the rice or its roots, and careful manipulation of the rice hooks so that the long, golden rice heads were carefully laid to dry on the stubble during harvesting, rather than on the wet ground. Slaves were awarded annual prizes for skill in plowing, hoeing, and hooking.[36]

Another means by which the masters attempted to motivate slaves over an intermediate time period was to purchase hogs, poultry, produce, or cord wood from them. Slave families on some plantations were assigned a portion of land on which to grow rice for themselves; and slaves on most plantations raised pigs, poultry, or cattle. Plowden Weston purchased cows, calves, hogs, poultry, eggs, pumpkins, and rice from his slaves. James Sparkman bought hogs, chickens, and eggs from his slaves; and Ben Sparkman bought hogs and cord wood from his slaves. Robert F. W. Allston gave each slave who was head of a family a hog to raise. Each winter the slave was to produce two yearling hogs, for which he was paid. The slave could keep the rest of the litter for family consumption. It should be noted in this instance, however, that during Allston's lengthy absence from his plantations to serve as governor of South Carolina the slaves had already taken de facto possession of his herd. His gift merely served to legitimize an existing practice on the plantation.[37]

The other side of the incentive coin was punishment for recalcitrant or rebellious slaves. "I like to be kind to my people," Robert F. W. Allston maintained, "but I imperatively require of them honesty, truth, diligence and cheerfulness in their work, wherever and whatever it is."[38] Slaves who did not meet those requirements were punished. Punishment seems to have been administered most commonly for failure to finish tasks; testimony for such punishment is abundant in the Slave Narratives and in my own interviews. Wyndham Malet, an English visitor, reported the most common punishment on plantations to be "shutting up for a certain time."[39] Margaret Bryant, a slave at Wachesaw, was somewhat more explicit regarding being shut up: "Put you in 'Bull pen.' Hab 'um a place can't see you hand before you. Can't turn round good in there. Left you in there till morning. Give you fifty lash and send you to work."[40] Whipping seems to have been in more general use. Ex-slave Albert Carolina recalled many years later: "Mausser gin (give) the woman a task. Didn't done it. Next day didn't done it. Saturday come, task time out! Driver! I tell th' truth, you could hear those people, 'Murder! Murder!'"[41] Hagar Brown of The Oaks described bloody beatings for failure to finish a task: "Don't done you task, driver wave that whip, put you over the barrel, beat you so blood run down."[42] Gabe Lance, from Sparkman's Mt. Arena, remembered the punishment for unfinished tasks on Sandy Island: "Put 'em in barn and least cut them give 'em (with lash) been twenty-five to fifty."[43] One of Robert F. W. Allston's overseers administered twelve lashes each to eight women for "hoeing corn bad."[44] Whippings were also administered for offenses such as theft, illicit slave meetings, being off the plantation without a ticket or pass, and attempting to run away.[45] The testimony of the ex-slaves and the oral traditions of their descendants do not bear out the notion that whippings were rare or that positive incentives outweighed negative ones in the masters' efforts to promote slave performance.[46]

It would be untrue to history, and unfair to the planters, to leave the impression that no masters in All Saints Parish attempted to restrain the use of the lash. Robert F. W. Allston reduced the authority of overseers who applied the whip too readily.[47] Weston instructed his overseers that confinement was preferable to whipping and that the imposition of a whole task rather than a half task on Saturday would be sufficient punishment for most offenses. When whippings were deemed necessary, they were not to exceed fifteen lashes and were not to be administered in the heat of the moment. Twenty-four hours were to elapse between discovery of the transgression and its punishment. In particular, Weston warned the overseers that they must take special precaution "to prevent any *indecency* in punishing women." In Weston's opinion proper management of the plantation required "a system of *strict justice*." That meant, he said, that "no person should ever be allowed to break a law without being punished, nor any person punished who has not broken a well-known law." It was important that persons being punished should understand why they were being punished. Nor should they be punished in anger or capriciously. The overseer was cautioned to avoid abusive language and "violence of demeanor," because such displays "are hardly ever forgotten by those to whom they are addressed."[48] Present-day black oral tradition suggests that there were still other masters who used the lash rarely if at all, but it is doubtful that their numbers were large. The system that Weston articulated represented the ideal toward which some planters strived rather than the reality most planters achieved.[49]

In many cases, in fact, offenses carried even more severe punishments. Robert F. W. Allston once withheld all Christmas celebrations among his slaves until they found out which of the slaves had stolen hogs from Allston's pen. When two suspects were discovered, they were forced to run the gauntlet.[50] On another occasion, Allston gave instructions regarding Brass, a slave who repeatedly failed to fulfill his tasks: "Now if any one about you is going to Charleston, give Brass a new shirt and send him to Robertston Blacklock and Co. to be turn'd into money, forthwith."[51] After some of his slaves had failed in a runaway attempt in 1862, Plowden C. J. Weston sold each of the would-be runaways to different people, deliberately separating them from their wives.[52]

And there were at least rumors of quite grisly punishments, although direct testimony in such cases is unavailable. Hagar Brown told Genevieve Chandler many years after emancipation that she had heard stories of slaves having been buried alive for punishment: "Dey put 'em in the grave live! And you holler under the dirt till you weary and hafter dead. Old timey people talk. My ma does talk before she dead."[53] Ben Horry of Brookgreen also reported hearing of such cruel and unusual punishments. When Chandler asked him about reports of slaves having been buried alive, he answered: "Bury live? I did hear some talk o' that. I didn't know whether they bury 'em to scay 'em (scare 'em) or what. I DID hear tell bout it. I most know that man name. Some these white people that day something. They either manage you or kill you."[54]

The harshest punishments were reserved for those who attempted to run away. Public hanging was the punishment for six slaves—three men and their wives—apprehended in 1862 while trying to escape the plantation of Dr. John D. Magill. "I hear about them slave try to run away," Mariah Heywood of Chancellor Dunkin's Midway recalled. She described how another group of slaves belonging to Magill had tried to escape; but the baby cried and alerted the patrol, who fired toward the sound, shooting out the eye of one slave woman. "Mr. McCuskey told us Nemo Ralston was one," she said. "Say they put four horses to him—one to every limb. Stretch 'em. And cut horses and each horse carry a piece! Mr. McCuskey was one help lynch Nemo."[55]

Just as the general leniency of Weston probably does not represent the norm in All Saints Parish, such atrocities as burying slaves alive or pulling slaves limb from limb with horses are surely exceptional, if true at all. One must be very cautious with hearsay evidence. Neither Hagar Brown nor Ben Horry, both credible witnesses, professed personal knowledge of slaves having been buried alive, only that they had heard rumors. Mariah Heywood, on the other hand, did profess to have heard about the lynching directly from one of the participants. In any event, it is no longer possible, if it ever was, to determine with precision what the norm was in negative incentives. What is possible, and ultimately more meaningful, is to specify the *range* of variation in punishments on the rice plantations of the Waccamaw.[56]

The overt use of coercion may have been a sign of a master's weakness rather than his strength; for punishments, whether mild and sporadic or cruel and persistent, represent the dark underside of plantation paternalism. The kindly, patriarchal role in which the masters liked to cast themselves required that they play their parts with benevolence, indulgence, and understanding, in an attempt to provide a standard of accommodation and benevolent despotism to mediate between conflicting relationships and interests.[57] "I manage them as my children," wrote Edward Thomas Heriot, the proprietor of Mt. Arena plantation on Sandy Island until his death in 1854. The planters proclaimed their belief that they had achieved such a paternalistic community, free from tension and violence, in which master and slave lived together in a spirit of accommodation and understanding. Heriot expressed to his Scottish cousin his belief that, compared to his slaves, "there is no class of people, as far as I have seen in this country, or Europe, of the same grade, where there is so much real happiness, where the wants of nature are so abundantly supplied, where the requirements of labour are as little, and where the guaranty against poverty and distress from all the conditions of existence is so great."[58] If the rice planters sometimes fell short of their aspirations and their pretensions (and some of them *often* fell short), it should be noted that paternalism did provide standards of kindness and benevolence to aspire—or pretend—to.

But every slaveholder and every overseer had to contend with troublesome slaves at some point. Their attempts to impose discipline on sullen and rebellious bondsmen made a grim, ugly contrast to the public face of paternalism. The rituals of punishment on the rice plantations were as much a part of the paternalistic system as the rewards for faithful service, the Christmas largesse, or the slave wedding feasts. When a master supervised—or administered—punishment, no less than when he dispensed gifts and favors, he did so in rituals that contrasted the dependent position of the slave with his own status of dominance. The ritual of slave punishment dramatized the fundamental concern of a slave society—status. Thus formalized public punishment dramatized in a particularly acute way, free of etiquette, euphemism, and illusion, the enforcement of rules of deference and social behavior.[59]

5

Granting that the rice planters attempted to regulate closely the labor of their bondsmen, and conceding that they were able to impose their economic and management techniques to a considerable degree, it is nevertheless unduly myopic to fail to see a vital continuity with various African traditions in several features of the rice cycle. Work patterns might not seem, at first, to be the most fruitful area in which to seek evidence of cultural creolization. One would hardly expect the subsistence work activities of West African villages to have any continuing relevance on the large, highly organized, commercially prosperous rice plantations of All Saints Parish. Setting aside for the moment the question of creolizaton, it may at least be said that enslaved Africans responded to the labor demands of their masters and of their new physical and economic environment in their own ways—their African ways. Doubtless many of their African ways no longer made sense in the new environment. Meaningless customs and practices, like such traditions in all cultures, were discarded and remembered—if at all— only as reminders of a lost world. But those traditions that remained meaningful continued and were passed on to succeeding generations. Along the way some traditions took on new forms as they were adapted to the needs of the new environment. Many persisted along the Waccamaw—both as survivals and as adaptations—into the mid-nineteenth century.

Many of the Africans who came to the South Carolina lowcountry, although certainly not all, came from rice-producing areas of Africa. I have already discussed their contribution in the establishment of rice cultivation in chapter one. As late as the Civil War, Africans and their descendants in All Saints Parish continued to use African methods of planting, hoeing, winnowing, and threshing the rice. They planted by pressing a hole in the trenches with the heel, dropping in the seeds, and covering them with the foot in the West African manner. Their use of the hoe as an all-purpose implement also represents continuity with African practice. Winnowing the rice in fanner baskets marks a continuation of two important African traditions—that of winnowing rice and that of coil basketry. Moreover, while the mortar and pestle are universal, they are not universally used in the same way. The lowcountry slaves' manner of pounding the rice was identical to the West African practice. It would seem unlikely that All Saints bondsmen adopted African methods of seeding, hoeing, and winnowing rice, but somehow forgot the African mortar and pestle tradition, only to learn of such implements from others.[60]

These features of rice culture are examples of African retentions—practices that continued more or less unchanged in the New World. So long as African-born slaves continued to live on the rice plantations of the Waccamaw (and they did so as long as slavery lasted), at least some elements of African culture would be expected to persist. It should occasion no surprise, either, that certain African work patterns in rice culture survived with little change among second and third generations of Afro-Americans under favorable circumstances. As in all cultures, however, the utility of various cultural features was dependent on environmental factors. If the introduction of rice mills after 1830 brought a relative decline in African methods of winnowing and threshing rice, the inability of animals or machinery to adapt readily to the soft, boggy ground of the rice fields helped to ensure the continuing vitality of African traditions of seeding and hoeing.[61]

More significant than such static retentions was the successful imposition by All Saints slaves of a cooperative work ethos upon the highly individualistic task system through which their masters attempted to regulate their labor. This syncretic achievement exemplified cultural continuity with Africa at a deeper and more fundamental level than did simple African retentions. Here the slaves adapted a basic African work orientation to a vastly different labor system and, in the process, adapted the masters' labor system to their own sense of appropriateness. Moving across the fields in a row hoeing side-by-side to the rhythm of work songs, the slaves imposed a group consciousness on their field work. The task system treated them as individuals with individual work assignments; nevertheless, they continued to work in groups, corresponding to cooperative work patterns widespread in West Africa. Stronger and faster slaves helped weaker and slower ones to keep up with the group. Hagar Brown recalled long after emancipation how her mother had helped Hagar's weakly Aunt Henritta with her tasks so that Henritta would not be beaten. Even their masters were forced to accept the slaves' preferred work-styles. James Sparkman acknowledged in 1858 that "it is customary (*and never objected to*) for the more active and industrious hands to assist those who are slower and more tardy in finishing their daily tasks." Thus did the slaves on Waccamaw rice plantations develop an accommodation to the necessities of the task system that allowed them to continue to develop a cooperative slave community through mutual self-help.[62]

6

Cooperative work patterns were employed most fully by the field hands, of course; but not all slaves were field hands. The testimonies of ex-slaves, no less than plantation records and travelers' accounts, testify to numerous slaves employed in managerial or professional capacities, or as skilled craftsmen or semiskilled workers. The difficulty in determining proportions is less a matter of quantification than of classification. If managerial slaves may be taken to comprise drivers and black overseers, and plantation professionals to include such diverse men and women as boatmen, butlers, carpenters, cooks, coopers, nurses, tailors, tanners, and weavers, how are house servants, mill hands, and stock minders to be classified? And are such specialized field workers as ditchmen and plowmen to be considered field hands or skilled workers? Indeed, one could plausibly argue that virtually all the field hands on a rice plantation should be classified as skilled laborers, in view of the level of competence required in rice culture.

It is difficult to consider such thorny questions as what jobs belong in what classifications without having some knowledge of how many slaves were involved in which jobs. The most detailed source of information on the distribution of slave occupations on the Waccamaw rice plantations is Plowden C. J. Weston's meticulous inventory of the estate of his father, Francis Marion Weston, in 1855. The list of slaves gives names, ages, and occupations for each slave on the elder Weston's plantations. Even if the designation skilled is limited to such artisans as blacksmiths, carpenters, carters, coopers, bricklayers, nurses, midwives, and seamstresses, excluding stock minders, ditchmen, and plowmen, it can be said that one out of every four or five male slaves in the work force was employed in a managerial or skilled occupation.[63] Tables 6 and 7 indicate the number and proportations of various occupations among slaves on Weston's Laurel Hill and Hagley plantations.

In addition, the occupations of adult slaves who died the year prior to June 1 of the census year are listed in the mortality schedules of the manuscript federal census. The mortality schedules for Georgetown District for 1850 and 1860 show slaves working as butchers, boat hands, hostlers, and millers, in addition to the occupations listed in the Weston inventory. Any examination of slave occupations based on the mortality schedules of the census must be interpreted with care. Statistics from such data are automatically skewed upward in median age by the number of elderly persons who died during the year. Nonetheless, to control for slaves over sixty years of age—that is, to eliminate slaves over sixty from the sample—would obscure the extent to which elderly slaves continued to work. In some occupations listed in the mortality schedules—butchers, carpenters, coopers, drivers, hostlers, millers, nurses, seamstresses, trunk minders, and watchmen—half or more of the slaves employed were over sixty.[64] Table 8 indicates the distribution of elderly slaves in occupation groups.

Normally slaves on the Waccamaw rice plantations continued to work at physically lighter jobs throughout their six-

Table 6.
Distribution of Occupations among Slaves
on Laurel Hill Plantation, 1854

Occupation	Number of Males	Percentage of Males	Number of Females	Percentage of Females	Total Number	Percentage of Total
Prime Hands	——	——	13	15.1	13	7.6
Full Hands	——	——	42	48.8	42	24.6
Half Hands	3	3.5	15	17.7	18	10.5
Highland Hands *	2	2.4	5	5.9	7	4.1
Ditchmen *	28.5	33.5	——	——	28.5	16.7
Plowmen *	6.5	7.7	——	——	6.5	3.8
Drivers	3	3.5	——	——	3	1.8
Blacksmiths	1	1.2	——	——	1	0.6
Carpenters *	10	11.8	——	——	10	5.9
Carters	1	1.2	——	——	1	0.6
Coopers *	4	4.7	——	——	4	2.3
Bricklayers *	0.5	0.6	——	——	0.5	0.3
Engineers *	2.5	2.9	——	——	2.5	1.5
Mill Hands *	6	7.1	——	——	6	3.5
Mill Watchmen	1	1.2	——	——	1	0.6
House Servants *	2	2.4	3.5	4.1	5.5	3.2
House Cooks *	——	——	1.5	1.7	1.5	0.9
Plantation Cooks	——	——	2	2.3	2	1.2
Overseer's Cooks	——	——	1	1.2	1	0.6
Miller's Cooks	——	——	1	1.2	1	0.6
Overseer's Girls	——	——	1	1.2	1	0.6
Cattle Minders	2	2.4	——	——	2	1.2
Hog Minders	2	2.4	——	——	2	1.2
Mule Minders	1	1.2	——	——	1	0.6
Poultry Minders	1	1.2	——	——	1	0.6
Sheep Minders	2	2.4	——	——	2	1.2
Yard Minders	1	1.2	——	——	1	0.6
Trunk Minders	1	1.2	——	——	1	0.6
Cow Feeders	1	1.2	——	——	1	0.6
Gardeners	1	1.2	1	1.2	2	1.2
Stablemen	1	1.2	——	——	1	0.6
Watchmen	1	1.2	——	——	1	0.6
TOTAL WORK FORCE	85		86		171	

SOURCE: Inventory of the estate of Francis Marion Weston, 1855, Office of Probate Judge, Georgetown County Court House.
* Includes part-time workers.

Table 7.
Distribution of Occupations among Slaves
on Hagley Plantation, 1854

Occupation	Number of Males	Percentage of Males	Number of Females	Percentage of Females	Total Number	Percentage of Total
Prime Hands	——	——	21	44.7	21	24.1
Full Hands	——	——	2	4.3	2	2.3
Half Hands	4	10.0	11	23.4	15	17.2
Quarter Hands	——	——	1	2.1	1	1.2
Ditchmen*	17.5	43.8	——	——	17.5	20.1
Plowmen	4	10.0	——	——	4	4.6
Drivers	1	2.5	——	——	1	1.2
Carpenters*	2.5	1.6	——	——	2.5	2.9
Carters	1	2.5	——	——	1	1.2
Coopers*	0.5	1.3	——	——	0.5	0.6
Gardeners*	0.5	1.3	——	——	0.5	0.6
Coachmen	2	5.0	——	——	2	2.3
Nurses	——	——	2	4.3	2	2.3
Midwives	——	——	1	2.1	1	1.2
Seamstresses	——	——	1	2.1	1	1.2
House Cooks	——	——	3	6.4	3	3.5
Children's Cooks	——	——	1	2.1	1	1.2
Overseer's Cooks	——	——	1	2.1	1	1.2
House Servants	2	5.0	2	4.3	4	4.6
House Boys	3	7.5	——	——	3	3.5
Overseer's Boys	1	2.5	——	——	1	1.2
Overseer's Girls	——	——	1	2.1	1	1.2
Trunk Minders	1	2.5	——	——	1	1.2
TOTAL WORK FORCE	40		47		87	

SOURCE: Inventory of the estate of Francis Marion Weston, 1855, Office of Probate Judge, Georgetown County Court House.
* Includes part-time workers.

Table 8.
Distribution of Slaves over Sixty Years of Age
in Occupational Groups

1850		1860	
Occupation	*Percentage over 60*	*Occupation*	*Percentage over 60*
Cooper	100.0	Hostler	100.0
Butcher	100.0	Watchman	100.0
Trunk Minder	100.0	Seamstress	100.0
Nurse	66.6	Field Hand	20.0
Driver	50.0	Invalid	100.0
Miller	50.0		
Carpenter	50.0		
Laborer	25.0		
None	100.0		
Unknown	100.0	Unknown	100.0

SOURCE: Censuses for 1850 and 1860, Mortality Schedules, Georgetown District, S.C.

ties and became retired around the age of seventy. The Weston inventories listed only one retired slave younger than seventy. The oldest slave still employed was a seventy-year-old driver. The wide variety of occupations necessary on a large rice plantation meant that there were several plantation jobs particularly suited to the enhanced knowledge and diminished physical capacity of elderly slaves. For example, elderly men were assigned to such crucial jobs as trunk minder, which required considerable experience and mature judgment, even though the physical demands were slight. Others became stock minders or gardeners. Elderly women were often assigned to the day nursery or "chillun house." But elderly slaves were not always assigned to new occupations. The task system made it possible to alter even field work to fit an aging slave's abilities. The Weston inventories reveal several elderly slaves continuing to work in the fields as three-quarter hands, half hands, or quarter hands. Apparently retired drivers and carpenters stayed involved with the plantation work force. Unlike other retired slaves, they are identified in the inventories both as drivers and carpenters and as superannuated.[65]

Visitors were struck by what they called these "curious fossil specimens of negro humanity," some of whom could "recall reminiscences of three or four generations back of the family to which they have belonged for nearly a century."[66] Elderly slaves in All Saints Parish were treated with respect and deference by blacks and whites alike, in conformity with classical African attitudes. "Anybody older than you," Hagar Brown taught her children, "you must honor them." In many West African societies considerable prestige and authority are accorded the elders, for the spirits of the ancestors exercise power over the efforts of the living. The elderly are regarded as partially liminal, symbolically poised between this world and eternity. Soon they will become spirits themselves and will exercise the power of spirits. To respect the elderly in this world is to earn a blessing from the spirits; to abuse the elderly is to anger the spirits. Mariah Heywood, born in slavery on a Waccamaw rice plantation, inherited and transmitted these African traditions, syncretized somewhat with the Ten Commandments. A black woman in the 1930s recalled of Mariah Heywood:

> Aunt Mariah tell me 'bout how she totin' water, when she a little missy girl—totin' way from the spring to the Big House— and she'd meet one them old women, and they say: "Dater (daughter), give the old woman a drink!" And Aunt Mariah say the old person'd say: "Tank you, dater! You'll have long life!" She say she never couldn't refuse when the old people ask for a drink, not even when the sand deep, and the sun hot, and she know if they take the drink it mean she have to walk clean back down the hill, and up the hill, for another bucket. But some [of] the girl wouldn't let the old people drink out their bucket, and Aunt Mariah say they'd tell em: "Go long! You nasty no manners thing! You'll never live out you days!" And you know Aunt Mariah say all them girls GONE, and she [only] one [left]!

On the Waccamaw plantations, as well as throughout the Caribbean, the elders were addressed as Uncle and Aunty or Mauma and Daddy by all the younger slaves as well as by the children of the Big House, not because of kinship ties, but as a mark of respect.[67]

7

The respect accorded managerial slaves on the rice plantation was a measure of their importance, as both oral and written sources agree. Not merely drivers and black overseers, but also boat captains and master craftsmen exercised positions of authority over other slaves. An English visitor described how Captain Charlie called his crew together by blowing a loud blast on a conch, how the crew rowed merrily in tempo with work songs, and how Captain Charlie took his wife along with him on the boat trips. Renty Tucker, the extraordinarily talented carpenter of Hagley plantation, seemed virtually free. He was sent, unsupervised, with a crew of carpenters under his direction to various locales around All Saints Parish. Similarly, Thomas Bonneau, head carpenter for Robert F. W. Allston, trained four or five apprentices a year to be skilled carpenters.[68]

The highest-ranked slaves were the drivers, who necessarily worked in close cooperation with the overseers. Overseers were dependent upon the black drivers to make the major decisions regarding everything from the supervision of the labor force to the regulation of the water flow in the fields. The drivers were in a difficult position. As slaves they were aware that no achievement they might accomplish could change their condition. But they were favored slaves, nevertheless. To maintain their status and privileges they had to assert their authority and demand a high level of discipline and performance from the laborers under their supervision.[69]

Several of the ex-slaves who were Chandler's informants for the WPA Slave Narrative project in the 1930s were children or grandchildren of drivers. Gabe Lance said, "My grandfather [was] the Driver—slave Driver. Name Nelson."[70] Sabe Rutledge recalled, "My grandfather, Rodrick Rutledge, driver from a boy. Time he big nuff to handle it till Freedom." Rutledge had been a slave on The Ark plantation in upper All Saints Parish in Horry District, where "Old man John Tilgh-

man at the Ark plantation have no overseer—have 'Driver.'
Most folks on Waccamaw have overseer and 'Driver.'"[71] William Oliver described his father as "head man" on the plantation. Ben Horry said that his father was the "boss man" on the plantation and carried the keys to the rice barn.[72]

The drivers' responsibilities were spelled out in detail by Plowden C. J. Weston: "Drivers are, under the Overseer, to maintain discipline and order on the place. They are to be responsible for the quiet of the negro-houses, for the proper performance of tasks, for bringing out the people early in the morning, and generally for the immediate inspection of such things as the Overseer only generally superintends." Each morning the drivers were charged with having the field hands, except for the sick and for nursing mothers, on the flats (or barges) and ready to go to the rice fields by sunrise. "One driver is to go down to the flat early, the other to remain behind and bring on all the people with him. He will be responsible for all coming down." Once in the field the driver pointed out to each slave the task for the day, which had been determined in consultation with the overseer. It was also the driver's responsibility to inspect the completed task and approve the performance before a slave was allowed to go home.[73]

Since drivers were expected to maintain a high level of performance and discipline in the work force, they were charged with meting out punishment to slaves who fell short of the expected standards. Some drivers abused their positions and used punishments not merely to enforce discipline, but as a means of bending other slaves to their will. For instance, a slave woman who rejected the sexual advances of a driver might be assigned an impossible task and then whipped for not finishing it. "If one them driver want you," according to Ben Horry, "they give you task you CAN'T DO. You getting this beating not for you task—for you flesh!"[74] Such abuses are doubtless the reason such planters as Plowden C. J. Weston strictly regulated the administration of punishment on the plantations. "No driver," Weston specified, "is to be allowed to punish any person in any way, except by order of the Overseer, and in his presence."[75] But such stipulations were easier made than enforced. At least two drivers, both of them named Cudjo, were murdered by fellow slaves for abuse of power.[76]

If their merits and defects be fairly balanced, it must be acknowledged that the slave drivers were neither saints nor demons. Unwilling to turn their backs upon their own people, they also wished to avoid violating the expectations of their masters. If some were savagely cruel, few were so barren in nobler qualities as not also to exhibit signs of virtue and compassion. Often the drivers were the most outstanding male slaves on the plantations. Many of them were elderly and may have derived some of their authority from their role as patriarch of a large kin network. There are instances of sons taking up their fathers' roles as drivers, but it would appear that the positions were filled on merit rather than by heredity.[77]

Drivers were invested with their powers publicly by the masters. In some cases they were confirmed in their authority by the clergy. For example, Daniel, Benjamin Allston's driver, was confirmed by a bishop. This is a natural process of ritual; people not only move from one status to another, but also they mark such moves with appropriate symbolic actions. In such prescribed formal rituals, the act of delegating authority symbolically enhanced both the dominance of the driver over other slaves and the dominance of the master over the driver. While such sanctions did not insure that drivers would never abuse their power, the rituals did promote an almost mystical aura of high seriousness in the delegation of command.[78] It would appear that most of the drivers attempted to mediate between the other slaves on the one hand and the masters on the other. The attempt required not merely the ability to balance competing interests and competing pressures, but also a considerable amount of guile as well, as was exemplified by James Sparkman's Orinoco, whom Robert F. W. Allston described as "a smart intelligent driver but tricky." In their effort to meet their responsibilities to each group as humanely as possible the drivers of All Saints met with considerable success. Because of the efforts of such drivers as Define Horry at Brookgreen, Nelson Lance at Mt. Arena, Caesar Oliver at the "Old Oliver Place," Rodrick Rutledge at The Ark, and Philip Washington at Pipe

Down, the institution of slavery was perhaps a bit more humane than it otherwise would or could have been.[79]

8

On most plantations the drivers were closely supervised in their day-to-day activities by the overseers. Occasionally these overseers were black, but typically they were young white men from the poorer classes of Georgetown District who became overseers as a means of gaining experience and getting a start in life. Among eighty-three overseers in the district in 1860, all were literate, 88 percent were under forty years of age, 58 percent were married, 30 percent possessed real estate of their own, 18 percent possessed considerable personal property, and 22 percent were themselves slaveholders.[80] These statistics support the prevailing belief in present-day oral tradition that the overseers were "adequately taken care of" and "pretty well paid."[81] If overseeing gave young white men a start toward the ownership of land and slaves, however, there is no example of an overseer ever climbing up the economic ladder into the planter class in All Saints Parish. Black overseers, of course, could hardly aspire to become planters in any event.[82]

In at least one instance early in the nineteenth century the overseer was a free black, a mulatto who had some connection with the family of his master, Joseph Alston.[83] There were cases of overseers who were themselves slaves. Boston, a thirty-year-old slave, was purchased by Daniel W. Jordan in 1859 to be his overseer at Laurel Hill. Boston's former owner described him as "my driver and *overseer* for nine years—extremely confidential and intelligent he has carried my plantation keys during all that time, making harvesting, preparing for market and shipping my crops yearly." Ben Horry testified to Chandler many years later that there had been an African-born black overseer at Brookgreen.[84] On smaller plantations head drivers or other slaves might serve as de facto overseers. Rodrick Rutledge, driver at The Ark, a smaller unit on the upper Waccamaw in Horry District, was such an overseer. The

Ark did not have an overseer; thus the driver functioned at a managerial level immediately under the master.[85]

Whether white or black, official or de facto, the overseer bore a heavy burden of responsibility. Plowden C. J. Weston specified his expectations in the overseer's contract: not only would the overseer's performance be judged by the condition and productivity of the slaves but also by the physical condition of the plantation—its buildings, grounds, livestock, implements, rice fields, banks, and trunks—and, not least in importance, by the amount and quality of rice produced.[86] Other Waccamaw planters were less explicit in stating their expectations. Although it is unlikely that they expected less from their overseers, they may well have ordered their priorities differently.

Some overseers attempted to imitate their employer's paternalism by using persuasion and positive incentives, but the general performance of overseers seems to have been as spotty in All Saints Parish as elsewhere in the South. A few overseers were downright sadistic. The Slave Narratives, while generally picturing the All Saints masters favorably, fairly seethe with hostility toward the overseers. There are numerous stories of brutal and inhumane treatment by the overseers. Hagar Brown said her overseer would whip a man or woman for failure to finish a task. The usual punishment was fifty lashes. Masters and slaves, furthermore, did not always share the same evaluation of an overseer. For example, Robert F. W. Allston always considered the Hemingways, Thomas and J. A., to be good overseers. In Ben Horry's opinion, "Mr. Hemingway been severe." White overseers, according to the Slave Narratives, tended to be even harsher and stricter than black overseers. Ben Horry explained that "white obersheer want to hold his job. Nigger obersheer don't care too much. He know he going stay on plantation anyhow." The single most vicious overseer that Ben Horry encountered, however, was not white but black. "The worst thin I members was the colored obersheer . . . he have it in for my mother and lay task on 'em she ain't able for do. Then for punishment my mother is take to the barn and strapped down on thing called the Pony. Hands spread like this and strapped to the floor and all two both she feet been tie like this. And she been given twenty-five to fifty lashes till the blood flow. . . . I stay there look wid DESE HERE (eyes)! Want you to know one thing—MY OWN DADDY DERE couldn't move. Couldn't venture dat ober-sheer!" Horry said that such things could not have happened had his master, Joshua Ward, known about it, but "just the house servant get Marse Josh' and Miss Bess' ear." The planters' source of information regarding their overseers was often a trusted servant. When his father was later made overseer, Ben recalled, "them things different."[87]

Perhaps the judgments of the Slave Narratives are overly harsh, but there is little evidence to the contrary. Robert F. W. Allston's high regard for his overseers, especially Jesse Belflowers, may have been well merited. "Of course there were brutal overseers," admitted Waccamaw planter J. Motte Alston, "but they were the exceptions." Whether such overseers as are described in the Slave Narratives are the exception or the norm, for six to seven months of each year they had virtually complete dominion over the rice plantations of All Saints Parish as the masters and their families fled the malarial swamps of the Waccamaw for the seashore, for Charleston, for Flat Rock in the mountains, or for Europe.[88]

9

Overseers and drivers normally performed their supervisory duties in the rice fields among the field hands. Another group of slaves—skilled artisans—were employed in non-field pursuits. The number of skilled occupations necessary to run a rice plantation is astounding. The following list, compiled from probate inventories and plantation records, gives an idea of the range of skills: animal raisers, baby keepers, barbers, blacksmiths, boatmen, bricklayers, butchers, butlers, carpenters, coachmen, cobblers, cooks, coopers, engineers, gardeners, gunkeepers, laundresses, lumbermen, maids, nurses, pantry minders, saltworkers, seamstresses, shoemakers, stock minders, tailors, tanners, tinsmiths, trunk minders, valets, waiters, and weavers. Many of the skilled slaves followed two or more of these occupations, receiving careful training for their particular jobs.[89] The skilled slaves of All Saints Parish gave the lie to George Fitzhugh's obtuse advice to planters regarding blacks: "But don't attempt to make carpenters, or manufacturers, or house-servants, or hostlers, or gardeners of the men, nor seamstresses, nor washerwomen, nor cooks, nor chambermaids of the women. They are too slow, too faithless, too unskillful to succeed in such pursuits."[90]

West Africa was a land of consummate craftsmen, and enslaved Africans had brought with them to South Carolina highly developed technologies in metalwork, woodwork, leatherwork, ivorywork, pottery, and weaving. The natural environment of South Carolina was sufficiently like that of West Africa to render many of the skills learned in the Old World indispensable in the New World. Africans excelled not merely in heavy labor such as clearing land, but were so successful as bricklayers, butchers, carpenters, coachmen, farmers, fishers, and herdsmen that they were imported in larger and larger numbers. Not least of the ironies of the slave trade was that the skills of the Africans helped to strengthen the rationale behind their enslavement. The contribution of skilled slave craftsmen and mechanics to the economic development of the plantations has yet to be adequately credited.[91]

Not only were these skills retained and syncretized in the New World, but blacks responded eagerly to incentives to acquire new skills. As a general rule, young slaves aiming for plantation professions were apprenticed to senior craftsmen or craftswomen to be taught and trained. In some cases slaves were sent to Charleston or even to England to be taught particular skills such as cabinetry. The achievement of the slaves in building the plantation Big Houses, with their elaborate hand-fashioned iron grill work, magnificent cabinetry, and other decorative embellishments, is adequate testimony that the African inheritance of southern aesthetics included skills in wood and ironworking that went far beyond mere physical labor. The slaves took a possessive pride in the Big Houses that they built, despite the humbler circumstances of their own cabins.[92]

Perhaps the elite of the slave craftsmen were the carpenters. Not only did the carpenters build the Big Houses and the rice mills, the slave cabins and the barns, using such hand tools as the saw, plane, axe, hatchet, auger, adze, chisel, and drawing knife, but also the trunks, or floodgates, that flooded and drained the rice fields, and the plantation fleet of flats, rowboats, and dugout canoes.[93]

One of the most talented carpenters in All Saints Parish was Renty Tucker of Hagley plantation. Said to have been trained for fine carpentry in England, Tucker built the famous chapel of St. Mary's, Weehawka, on Plowden C. J. Weston's plantation, working closely with the Westons on the design for the structure. He built a scale model of the chapel in January 1859 and started work on the foundation a few weeks later. By early May he had covered the nave and chancel. When the Westons returned from England at the end of November 1859, he had erected the church tower. By spring the stained-glass lancet windows and the clock and chimes for the tower had arrived from England, and St. Mary's, Weehawka, was formally opened. It featured carved oak stalls and double walls for coolness.[94]

Renty Tucker also built the summer home of the Westons on Pawleys Island, which Elizabeth Collins, their English housekeeper, described as "a castle so lofty that we could find a cool place almost in any part of the house." He made the building of cypress boards, probably hewn in the carpentry shop at Hagley and transported to Pawleys Island. Roman numerals were chiseled into the boards so that the building could be properly constructed on the island. Both wooden pegs and hand-cut nails were used to hold the framework together. The Weston home was considerably more elegant than the cottages of other planters on Pawleys Island.[95]

Richmond, of J. Motte Alston's Woodbourne plantation, was another extraordinarily talented slave carpenter. Purchased by Alston from his father, Thomas Pinckney Alston,

Richmond built the Big House at Woodbourne, assisted only when he had to handle timber too heavy for him. He also built the Alston summer cottage on the creek at Murrells Inlet–Sunnyside. Richmond built the frame at Woodbourne, moved it across the Waccamaw on flats, and hauled it to the shore by teams of oxen. Alston was so impressed that he made provisions in his will to free Richmond and his wife.[96]

Carpenters were trained by master craftsmen in large carpenter shops on the plantations. Four or five apprentices studied annually under Thomas Bonneau, a slave who was chief carpenter for Robert F. W. Allston. Bonneau took pride that he did not turn out "jack-legs," his term for mediocre craftsmen, but men of skill. Bonneau built a plantation chapel for Allston, although not so elaborate as that built by Renty Tucker at Hagley.[97] Among the prized slave carpenters of the Waccamaw were Hardtimes Sparkman of Mt. Arena, Welcome Beese of Oatland, and the large battery of carpenters at Brookgreen plantation—Lazrus, David, Joe, Cato, Sam, Tom, Jacob, Jim, Philip, Cain, Moses, and Aaron.[98]

Good carpenters were in demand and were able to hire out their labor off the plantation, paying their masters a portion of their income. James Sparkman, whose extensive holdings included Mt. Arena on Sandy Island for a period, hired a carpenter from Benjamin Dunkin in 1846 to help build a house. In 1854 he paid $120 for the hire of a carpenter, a sum nearly twice the cost of a horse and four times the cost of a boat. Four years earlier he had *sold* a slave named Bella for less. Robert F. W. Allston also hired carpenters frequently.[99]

The tools carpenters had to work with were crude. When Anthony started working for Sparkman in January 1853 (probably hired), he had the following available to him: 1 jack plane; 1 fore plane; 1 hand saw (all old); 1 axe (broad); 1 adze; 1 square; and 2 chisels (good). The carpentry crew at Brookgreen had a slightly larger repertory of tools to choose from: band saw; 1-inch chisel; ½-inch chisel; 2-inch augur; 1 ½-inch augur; 7.8-inch augur; adze; hatchet; broad axe; square; compass; plane; and saw. Thus the achievement of the skilled carpenters on the Waccamaw rice plantations is all the

more remarkable for having been accomplished with such limited tools.[100]

Among the skilled occupations on the rice plantations,
blacksmiths were necessary to shoe the horses, make horse-
shoes and nails, and keep the axles, wheels, and other metalwork used on the plantation in repair. The blacksmith shop on
the Robert F. W. Allston estate was described as completely
equipped and up-to-date, with apprentices being trained under
the careful eye of the master blacksmith, a slave named Guy
Walker. Among the tools the young apprentices would learn to
use were the bellows, anvil, vice, hammer, tongs, dog, coal
chisel, and nailmakers.[101]

Other young slaves, men and women, who showed prom-
ise of development were trained as coopers, slatworkers, or as
mechanics to work in such rice mills as Robert F. W. Allston's
pounding mill, reputedly the largest in the state. Salt boiling
was carried on by slaves without supervision, according to Allston's daughter. "My father had the faculty for organization,"
she wrote, "and his negro men were remarkably well-trained,
intelligent, and self-reliant."[102]

Slave women were employed in the tasks of spinning, dyeing, weaving, and sewing to provide clothing for the plantation. Much of the dyeing was done with black walnut and indigo. Some of the weavers managed to weave beyond their
task-limit without the overseers noticing. They sold the extra
cloth to poor whites in the parish. Occasionally they sold more
than they had woven beyond their quota and had to work up
into the night so as not to get caught, as in the case of Margaret Bryant's mother. "Po-buckra come there and buy cloth
from Mom," Margaret Bryant recalled to Chandler. "Buy
three and four yards. Ma sell that have to weave day and night
to please obersheer."[103] The looms were manually operated.
William Oliver recalled, "My mother was a weaver, old timey
loom. Cotton and wool, sheckel (shuttle)." Margaret Bryant
said that while her mother wove, there were also two women
carding and two women spinning. "Ma wop 'em off. Send duh
sheckel (shuttle) through there."[104]

After the yarn was spun, dyed, and woven into cloth,

seamstresses sewed it into clothing and other household furnishings. Margaret, the head seamstress at Hagley plantation, worked with other seamstresses to make new drawing-room curtains and covers. Most of the plantation sewing, however, involved making clothes. For example, Margaret worked closely with Emily Weston during April and early May 1859 in cutting out and sewing clothes for the children on Weston's plantations. While many of the seamstresses worked closely with "Ole Miss," as Margaret did, a well-trained seamstress did not require close supervision. When Emily Weston left for an extended visit to England early in May 1859, she left minute instructions with her seamstress Dolly as to the type and quantity of garments to be produced. In December, upon her return, she inspected the work done by the plantation seamstresses. Given the clothing necessities of the large plantation work force, most plantations had a crew of seamstresses who worked more or less full time on sewing.[105]

One of the most important of the crafts practiced by skilled slave artisans on the Waccamaw was the making of an earthenware that has come to be called Colono-ware. Colono-ware shards have been excavated at plantation sites in All Saints Parish as well as throughout the South Carolina lowcountry. This unglazed, low-fired ceramic, once thought to have been produced by free Indians for trade with the colonists (because it was found on plantation sites rather than in Indian settlements), is now recognized as the product of slave potters. It is most commonly found on slave sites in the South Carolina lowcountry. A similar unglazed earthenware was produced by slaves on plantations in Barbados and, in fact, may have been brought to South Carolina by the large number of slaves imported from there. South Carolina Colono-ware constitutes an especially interesting example of cultural syncretism in that it incorporates elements of both African and Indian pottery traditions. Production of Colono-ware appears to have ended in the early nineteenth century with the increased accessibility of ceramics and ironware and with the end of the slave trade.[106]

Talented slave basketmakers were responsible for producing the fanner baskets used for winnowing rice. These and other baskets made by the slaves were examples of coil basketry, which is indubitably of African origin. Coil baskets, unlike the woven baskets of American Indians, were made by wrapping dried palmetto fronds around bundles of sweetgrass roughly eighteen to twenty inches long and one-third to one-half inch in diameter. Pine needles were sometimes mixed with the sweetgrass for decorative effect. Maria, an African-born slave of Robert F. W. Allston, was one such basketmaker. "Maum Maria," recalled Allston's daughter, "made wonderful baskets and wove beautiful rugs from the rushes that grew along Long Cane Creek." [107]

Africans such as Maria and their descendants responded to incentives to learn new skills on the Waccamaw plantations; but they blended the new, acquired modes of expression with ancestral, remembered modes of expression in a process of artistic creolization. The acquisition of preferred positions on the plantations by virtue of inherited and acquired skills may be seen as part of the process by which the slaves of All Saints Parish helped to create a more orderly and predictable world for themselves, one in which the old virtues of beauty and skill and craftsmanship still counted for something. The practice of these skills—and the status that accrued to skilled workers— gave talented slaves both a sense of self-esteem and a certain measure of freedom from supervision, which enabled them to make their work patterns more tolerable, and even occasionally glorious, parts of a meaningful culture, however artificially constricted it may have been. [108]

10

Not all the skilled workers on a rice plantation were involved in rice cultivation or craft production. Each plantation had certain slaves designated and trained to serve its transportation needs. Boatmen, for example, took charge of the fleet of flats, rowboats, and dugout canoes. Boats were valuable property, and the boat crews were charged with their use and care. All the boats were kept sheltered from the sun, except when being used, and were locked up at night. Captain Charlie, chief boatman for the plantations of Plowden C. J. Weston, was assisted by a crew of eight men, described by an English visitor as "fine, strong, good-natured fellows." Even vessels as large as schooners were occasionally manned entirely by slaves. One of Robert F. W. Allston's overseers wrote of the *Waccamaw*, which picked up rice at the Allston rice mill, that "there is no white men in her when she comes to the mill."[109]

Although the Waccamaw River served as the principal avenue of transportation in All Saints Parish, land transportation had to be used as well. The head coachman on a rice plantation was an elite figure and one of the most privileged slaves. The chief coachman for Plowden and Emily Weston was Prince, a man of enormous talent and dignity. He never resorted to the whip with his horses, but commanded them with his voice alone. Aleck Parker, Governor Robert F. W. Allston's head coachman, commanded even greater deference among the Allston family. Once, when young Elizabeth Allston and her friends began to sing in the carriage as it rode through the streets of Charleston, he addressed her sternly, "Miss Betsy, if unna [second person plural] kyant behave unna self, I'll tek yu straight home! Dis ain't no conduk fu de Gubner karridge!"[110]

The term nurse was used to designate two plantation occupations—those who cared for the sick and those who cared for the children. The medical nurses (men and women) were responsible for helping the physicians who were employed by the plantations, usually on a contractual basis. The physicians extracted teeth, lanced carbuncles, dressed wounds, performed obstetrical services and minor surgery, and prescribed medicines, liniment, and porter.[111] The nurses' principal duties involved keeping the floors, bedding, blankets, and utensils of the plantation hospitals clean and caring for the immediate needs of the sick. They did not normally administer medicine to patients except upon orders of the physician. Typical medicines given to ailing slaves included magnesia, calomel, tartar emetic, paregoric, laudanum, quinine, cream of tartar, castor oil, and opium.[112] Typically there was one person designated plantation nurse, who might be male or female. Many women received some nursing training, because seriously ill patients often required nursing full time. Slaves who needed surgery or specialized medical care were sent to Charleston for treatment.[113]

The job of children's nurse was typically assigned to slave women who were either too old or too young to work in the fields. This followed a common West African practice of utilizing the skills of the elderly. These nurses would keep the little slave children in a special "chillun house," or day nursery, while their parents worked in the rice fields or other jobs. Margaret Bryant recalled many years later, "My Pa sister, Ritta One, had that job. Nuss (nurse) the chillen. . . . All size chillun." Some nurses became exclusive nurses for white children, as in the case of the mother of Ben Horry: "My mother nuss (nurse). Get up so high—natural nuss for white people."[114]

The cooks were an important part of the skilled work force on a rice plantation. Food for the sick was prepared by the nurses; otherwise the cooks were responsible for cooking food for everyone on the plantation. Plowden C. J. Weston had one cook who specialized in cooking for the rice-field workers and another who cooked for carpenters, millers, and high-ground workers. By having two cooks working closer to the scene of the work, it was possible to serve meals while they were still hot without requiring time-consuming boat rides to and from the rice fields. James Sparkman assigned a cook especially for the field hands. Most of the plantations had a separate cook for the children. The midday meals were served communally, either in or near the fields, or at some central location on the plantation. Morning and evening meals were usually eaten at home. The renown that the slave cooks earned for their cooking was equalled by the admiration they attracted for their imaginative use of spices. The taste for highly spiced cooking, at least partially inherited from Africa, was transmitted to the whites through the Big House kitchens. The various dishes developed by slave cooks, which would later become famous as soul food, were by no means restricted to blacks, nor even to the poorer segment of the white plantation.[115]

Other slaves served as gardeners for the Big House flower

gardens. Emily Weston wrote in her diary of her efforts to have
the road to Hagley House smoothed and made into an integral
part of the landscaping: "Fine and warmer, but again in the
road and finished cutting. Then walked to see the Rosa's and
Mr. R took me to see the garden really getting into order and
showing seeds coming up." And again, "Fine and warm, but in
the road again but did not quite finish there being so many
stumps to dig out." Weston also commented in her diary on
the progress of one of the slaves in learning the skill of gardening: "Agrippa just now beginning to hoe weeds in the garden,
going there every day, and I hope may turn out a trifle (at any
rate) of a gardener."[116]

The stable hands were responsible for all the horses,
mules, oxen, and other livestock on the plantation. One slave
was in charge of all the oxen, and he was responsible for half a
task of plowing as well. The overseer was to provide the stable
hands with straw, tailing, and coarse flour for the oxen. Plowing and carting depended upon the appearance of the oxen.
Mules were also under the year-round care of a single person.
The mules were fed on flour and cut-up tailing. During periods
of hard work the mules' diets were supplemented with corn
and cut-up crab grass mixed with straw and flour. During the
summer, when not in use, they were turned out on the marsh
to feed. Plowden C. J. Weston probably spoke for many planters when he wrote, "It is easy to keep an animal once fat in
good condition, but extremely difficult to get one into condition who is worked down." Therefore, the slaves charged with
taking care of the livestock had significant responsibilities. Not
only must the livestock be kept in good condition, but the livestock implements—harness, chains, yokes, and plows, along
with the carts and wagons—as well. Stables and ox-houses
were to be cleaned out weekly, and the oxen and mules were
cleaned down each evening.[117]

The yard watchman was responsible for the crops in the
yard and for the barns. Rice was stored in the barns and
threshing took place in the barnyards. Weston instructed his
overseers to keep a close watch on the barnyard: "As soon as

the people come in in the morning the barnyard doors should be locked and not be opened again until work is over, except to admit the suckling children."[118]

The rice plantations also had poultry yards where fowl were raised and pastures for sheep and dairy cattle. Almira Coffin wrote a friend in New England that "the cows are the meanest looking animals you ever saw" but thought "the sheep are very decent." Simmon was in charge of the sheep and dairy cows on the estate of Plowden C. J. Weston, while Tamar had charge of the poultry yard. Occasionally slaves who were otherwise employed also raised poultry. Gabriel, for instance, tried to raise ducks. One of the Weston hogs caused him to lose two ducks. He reported to Emily Weston, "Your hog, ma'am, done eat two my ducks." "How so, Gabriel?" she replied. "You should keep them in." "See, ma'am, young duck bery lobe run bout, and your pen broke. . . . I like sell my duck when dem big enough." She promised to have Simmon mend the hog pen.[119]

The skilled workers, especially the carpenters and mechanics, enjoyed a measure of status, deference, and independence in their work patterns on the plantations. The children of field hands were taught respect for these skilled workers because of their talents. Their status did not, however, seem to create a gulf between them and the field hands. The inventories reveal numerous examples of skilled craftsmen married to prime field hands, or ditchmen married to house servants. On the rice plantations of the Waccamaw, mechanics, craftsmen, and other skilled workers generally made common cause with house servants and field slaves. Together they created and maintained, against frightful odds, a slave community.[120]

11

A wide variety of occupations is subsumed under the general label house servants—butlers, cooks, valets, maids, waiters and waitresses, laundresses, and children's nurses, among others. When Adele Petigru Allston was a young bride, she became quite upset when she discovered what a large household staff she was expected to manage. She went to her husband on the verge of tears:

> There are too many servants; I do not know what to do with them. There is Mary, the cook; Milly, the laundress; Caroline, the housemaid; Cinda, the seamstress; Peter, the butler; Andrew, the second dining-room man; Aleck, the coachman; and Moses, the gardner. And George, the scullion, and the boy in the yard besides! I cannot find work for them! After breakfast, when they line up and ask, "Miss, wha' yu' want me fu' do to-day?" I feel like running away. Please send some of them away, for Lavinia is capable of doing the work of two of them. Please send them away, half of them, at least.

Her husband, Robert, told her that he could not. They were house servants, trained for house work and not for field work. It would be cruel, he said, to send them into the fields. "As soon as you get accustomed to the life here you will know there is plenty for them to do. The house is large and to keep it perfectly clean takes constant work. Then there is the constant need of having clothes cut and made for the babies and little children on the place; the nourishment, soup, etc. to be made and sent to the sick. You will find that there is really more work than there are hands for, in a little while." She found her husband's prediction to be accurate, their daughter wrote, "but it took all her own precious time to direct and plan and carry out the work."[121]

The duties of the house servants included cooking, cleaning, washing, nursing, looking after the children, and generally waiting on the master and mistress and their family. There seems to have been a considerable degree of specialization in household tasks, but regardless of specialty a house servant might find duties quite varied, as the following sequence in the diary of Emily Weston indicates:

> Tuesday, March 15. Hector and Caesar went to Laurel Hill to pack up all those things Plowden has determined to bring out of the house, and also the wine.
> Wednesday, March 16. Plowden off early to Laurel Hill to see after the things there to be sent down in flats. These arrived at 4 o'clock and very busy we were having them brought up—not

finished until ½ past 8. Such a collection of articles I scarcely knew where to stow them.

Thursday, March 17. Busy putting things a little in order, un-packing china, glass, etc., and about 4 another flat came with the portion of wine already packed. Had it put into baskets and deposited in the new-made cellar under the portico.

Friday was rainy, and Saturday and Sunday were holidays, but on Monday the house servants returned to packing.

Monday, March 21. Off early to superintend the packing up the remainder of the Laurel Hill wine, Hector and Jack going with me. All was in the flat by 4 o'clock, and quite a business it was!... Hector staid to mind the wine and flat started for Hag-ley in the evening.

Tuesday, March 22. The flat with wine arrived and began to unload about 10. I and Margaret, with one of the boys, put up the wine as it was brought in baskets and tired enough I was when the business was over.[122]

When a planter acquired a new plantation, it was often house servants who were entrusted with seeing to housing for the slaves, as when Plowden C. J. Weston moved some of his Laurel Hill slaves to his newly acquired True Blue plantation. In addition, when the master's family moved to a new resi-dence (as many of them did during 1862 when Union gun-boats cruised the Waccamaw, raiding the plantations), the task of preparing the new residence for occupancy normally fell to a house servant. When Emily Weston moved to Snow Hill plantation near Conwayborough in Horry District while her husband was in the army, Gabriel was sent ahead to get the house ready.[123]

Some house servants, such as Jemmy, the Westons' butler, and Nelson, the Allstons' butler, also acquired managerial re-sponsibilities, being left in charge of other house servants when the master's family was away. When Emily Weston moved to Snow Hill, Dolly, a house maid, was left in charge of a skeleton staff at Hagley.[124]

In many cases there was a white woman who served as something of an overseer to the house servants. Almira Coffin spoke of the daughter of Benjamin F. Dunkin having "a first rate white woman for housekeeper who has the care of everything." Elizabeth Collins, a young English woman, served essentially the same function for Emily Weston. Collins kept the household women at Hagley occupied during part of the day with sewing: "The women's house work was generally done about eleven o'clock, and the rest of the day spent in making garments for the field hands. Of course, the cutting out, &c, came to my lot, which was no play game, the number of negroes being between three and four hundred." [125]

Male domestics were sometimes especially trained to serve at the Hot and Hot Fish Club, an elite social club of the Waccamaw planters, where liveried servants served elaborate meals and drinks, and planters bowled and played billiards in the comfortable club house each Friday from June to mid-October. Other male domestics were trained to be valets, or "body-servants." Julia Peterkin, who lived on the Waccamaw in the early twentieth century after her father became a co-owner of Brookgreen plantation, described some of the duties of a valet: "A gentleman . . . is not considered extravagant if a 'body-servant' brings his coffee before he gets out of bed in the morning, presses his clothes, shines his boots, saddles his horse and attends to his hounds and bulldogs. The body-servant's duties may also include making his employer's mint julep in the summer, hot toddies in the winter, and keeping his spirits cheered whenever he gets down at heart."

The duties of male domestics could be quite varied. On one occasion Adele Allston went to look at a rice field ready to be harvested, traveling in a small boat steered by her husband and rowed by Nelson the butler and another slave. Robert F. W. Allston asked Nelson to put out his oar to steady the boat as Adele began to depart. Just as she was stepping on the bank, Nelson removed his oar from the water. The boat spun around and Adele plunged into the water up to her waist, greatly agitated. [126]

Planters regarded house servants to be of a higher status than that of field hands because of their training and the higher price they commanded in the marketplace. Slaves generally seem to have shared a sense of status stratification ranging from house servants at the top through drivers and artisans on down to field hands. The Allston house servants were said to have felt themselves "vastly superior to the ordinary run of negroes, the aristocracy of the race." Ben Horry regarded his mother as "up so high" because she was a nurse to the white children. Ex-slave Mariah Heywood, according to Chandler, felt herself to be of a higher status because she was a house servant who identified closely with her master's family. "The fact that she was raised by aristocrats," Chandler wrote, "shows plainly in her dealings with both races." Elizabeth Allston Pringle, on the other hand, contended that "Negroes are by nature aristocrats, and have the keenest appreciation and perception of what constitutes a gentleman."[127]

House servants generally had lighter work than field hands on the rice plantations of All Saints Parish. Their closer contact with the master and mistress, however, had both advantages and disadvantages. They typically obtained better and more clothing and food, often from the master's own table. The Reverend James L. Belin specified in his will his desire that the inheritors of his house servants furnish them daily with "a plentiful supply of such food as they eat themselves; for my servants have been accustomed to such as my table afforded." Similarly, their housing, located between the street of the field hands and the Big House, was often superior to that furnished other slaves. Their relationships with the whites were more amiable, and house servants as well as skilled slaves were taken along on trips with the master or mistress. The closer relationship with the master and his family, or, as Ben Horry put it, the fact that "just the house servant get Marse Josh' and Miss Bess' ear" enabled some house servants to move to more favored positions on the staff than field hands could.[128]

Despite the advantages that accrued to house servants because of their closer association with the master's family, however, these servants were more constrained to behave as their masters wished them to behave, in contrast with field hands who managed to make even work activities occasions for socializing and had more occasions to socialize away from the watchful eyes of the masters and overseers. Field hands could work for themselves or relax on weekends, evenings after tasks were completed, and holidays. House servants, by contrast, were on constant call and had to take turns working on holidays. An extreme example was the situation of women house servants, who were sometimes overpowered and raped by a master or the master's son while the mistress was not at home. Ben Horry described one case: "Susan was a house women," he told Chandler. "To my knowledge she had three white chillun. Not WANT 'em HAB 'em. Women overpowered." Although their tasks were more arduous and their tangible rewards more meager, field hands nevertheless had some advantages denied house servants.[129]

No great gulf separated house slaves from field hands or other slaves, although it is true that a strong undercurrent of hostility toward house servants by other slaves is evident in black oral tradition. House servants were sometimes regarded as traitors by other slaves because of their more amiable relationships with the whites. In fact, however, house servants seem to have been runaways to a larger degree than field hands, perhaps largely because of greater opportunities. For instance, Plowden Weston's young gunkeeper, Frank, escaped in 1862, when Union gunboats were cruising the Waccamaw. And Adele Allston entertained suspicions of her "highly favored servant" Mary in 1864. Not only had Mary's sons Thomas and Scotland run off, but also her daughter and her family and her brother Tom the carpenter and all his family. Mrs. Allston considered that "too many instances in her family for me to suppose she is ignorant of their plans and designs." She felt that Mary should not be allowed to remain in her position "in charge of the house with the keys, etc. unless she can prove her innocence."[130]

The expectation of group loyalty and solidarity seems to be part of the culture of institutions in which the group is essentially isolated from the broader society and has to live and work within a more-or-less controlled daily round. Those who appear to defy or disregard that expected solidarity may become the objects of extreme hostility on the part of the others.

Real group loyalty is rarely more than tenuous in such situations, however, as each individual pursues personal strategies of adaptation. On the Waccamaw rice plantations it would seem more appropriate to think in terms of degrees of solidarity as one attempts to understand the many ways in which slaves deftly blended accommodation and resistance as a means of putting up with what they had to put up with and of getting out of what they could get out of. Nowhere were these twin forms of the adaptive process more subtly tested than in the Big House, with its interracial interdependence, attachments, and hostilities, its ironic affections and hatreds. The highly ambiguous situation of the house servants made it possible for them to occupy a special position between the street and the Big House and to play an intermediary role in the creolization of each. House servants took elements of black culture into the culinary, religious, and folkloristic patterns of the Big House and brought elements of white culture to the street. It was through the house servants that black southerners derived much of their European heritage, and white southerners derived much of their African heritage.[131]

12

Not all slaves worked on their masters' plantations. Some slaves, especially those with exceptional skills, hired out to work on other plantations, on the docks, or in hotels or stables in nearby Georgetown. Masters normally arranged for the hiring of field hands and domestics, but skilled carpenters, craftsmen, and others often made arrangements for themselves. While slaves who hired out had to hand over to their masters a certain portion of their earnings—often the major portion—they otherwise lived more or less outside a masters' jurisdiction for the duration of the job.[132]

Scipio, a slave who hired his time as a teamster, carriage driver, and porter in Georgetown, captured the imagination of a New York visitor. James Roberts Gilmore made Scipio a central figure in his pseudonymously published *Among the Pines*:

He was a genuine native African, and a most original and genuine specimen of his race. His thin, close-cut lips, straight nose
and European features contrasted strangely with a skin of
ebony blackness, and the quiet, simple dignity of his manner be-
tokened superior intelligence. When a boy, he was with his
mother, kidnapped by a hostile tribe, and sold to the traders at
Cape Lopez, on the western coast of Africa. There, in the slave-
pen, the mother died, and he, a child of seven years, was sent in
the slave ship to Cuba. At Havana, when sixteen, he attracted
the notice of a gentleman residing in Charleston, who bought
him and took him to "the states." He lived as house-servant in
the family of this gentleman till 1855, when his master died,
leaving him a legacy to a daughter. This lady, a kind, indulgent
mistress, had since allowed him to "hire his time," and he then
carried on an "independent business," as porter, and doer of all
work around the wharves and streets of Georgetown. He thus
gained a comfortable living, besides paying to his mistress one
hundred and fifty dollars yearly for the privilege of earning his
own support.[133]

Slave carpenters were especially in demand. James Sparkman hired a carpenter from Benjamin Dunkin on a nearly regular basis. Henry, a carpenter on Ralph Nesbit's Caledonia
plantation, was hired by All Saints Church, Waccamaw, for
carpentry work on the church. William Oliver's father, Caesar
Oliver, hired out at some point in his career. "Hire they self out
as stevedore—anything they could—and pay massa so much
for the time," William Oliver recalled. "Smart slave do that.
Oh, yes, my father do that." Robert F. W. Allston sometimes
hired as many as twenty carpenters to work on the rice mill at
Waverly plantation.[134]

The South Carolina General Assembly in 1845 made it
unlawful for a master to let slaves hire out, but the law was
never enforced and was widely flouted. Newspapers openly advertised slave hirings, as for example the following from the
Winyah Intelligencer in Georgetown:

Field negroes to hire. The subscriber will hire, before the Market House, at auction, on Monday the third of January next, if

fair, and if not, the first fair day after, between twenty and thirty
field hands, with their families.

Persons who hire will be required to give notes with approved
personal security, and to furnish each negro with a suit of summer and winter clothes, and each of the laboring negroes a pair
of shoes.[135]

During the Civil War the Confederate government hired
slaves, by conscription, from Robert F. W. Allston, his son
Benjamin, Charles Alston, John Magill, Ralph Nesbit, Martha
Pyatt, Joshua John Ward's sons Maham and Benjamin, and
Plowden C. J. Weston, among other Waccamaw planters. One
of the slaves hired from Mrs. Pyatt was her carpenter Welcome
Beese, who was sent to work on fortifications and to help build
artillery batteries at Little River on the northern end of the
Waccamaw Neck, at Florence about seventy miles inland, and
at Charleston.[136]

13

Thus the slaves of All Saints Parish worked—as field hands or
yard workers, as drivers or occasionally overseers, as skilled
artisans, boatmen, coachmen, nurses, cooks, or house servants—and took pride in their achievements. On one level, at
least, they certainly responded favorably to their masters' incentives. They claimed the rewards for highly developed skills
and for perfect work attendance, and they produced enormous
crops of rice. They responded more favorably to positive incentives than to punishments, as evidenced by their lower productivity at Richmond Hill, the seat of the most notoriously
cruel of All Saints masters. To say, however, that the slaves
were generally productive and proud, and to say that they did
not routinely malinger or deliberately mishandle tools and
livestock, is not to say that they had internalized the values of
their masters. When opportunities for escape were few and
chances for success were slim, the slaves of All Saints Parish
were cooperative and productive. When the pressure of Union
gunboats on the Waccamaw after 1862 vastly increased the
possibilities of a successful escape, they deserted in droves.

Slave work patterns on the Waccamaw illustrate a particularly interesting example of cultural creolization. There was certainly strong continuity with African work patterns in both field work and in skilled crafts; however, slaves responded positively to incentives to learn new skills from the whites and even from the Indians. Furthermore, the imposition of African communal work behavior on the masters' individualistic task system illustrates an even more striking adaptation of elements of African culture to a very different environment. The status distinctions made by the masters, which set managerial slaves, skilled craftsmen, and house servants apart from field hands were observed by many slaves as well. Nevertheless, there was a strong sense of solidarity among the slave community, in which ditchman married weaver and butler married field hand. Rice plantation slaves were neither Sambos nor Horatio Algers. If they were efficient workers *within* the system of paternalism, they were also effective workers *of* the system, and they knew how to work it for their own ends. How efficiently the slaves worked within the system to produce rice is illustrated by examining the total number of slaves on the various plantations from Table 1 and the output they produced (both in terms of acres cultivated and the pounds of rice obtained) from Table 2. How effectively the slaves worked the system to require the masters to provide them more time for their own purposes—and what they did with that time—will be examined in the following chapters.

CHAPTER THREE

"Sit at the Welcome Table"

A walk through the slave village in the late afternoon, when the dark pines cast lengthening shadows on the weathered cabins, with their cypress-shingled roofs and broad front porches, was one of the remarkable experiences of the rice plantations. There, after the slaves' field tasks were done, a visitor could observe not only the sights and sounds of the street—the women in their bright gingham dresses and white headkerchiefs, the men in their indigo-dyed homespun shirts and red jackets combining work with socializing as they went about their various chores—but also smell wood smoke from the cabin chimneys and the aromas of cornbread, peas and rice, pork or fish cooking over open fires in skilletlike ovens and iron cooking pots, stirred from time to time with cedar paddles. An understanding of the material environment of slavery—the food, clothing, and shelter of the slaves—would seem to be an indispensable prelude to comprehending other aspects of their culture. The material environment not only reflected the cognitions and perceptions of the slaves; it was itself a major influence on their behavior. One who would seek to understand cultural persistence and adaptation can ignore the material environment only at the cost of accuracy. Granting that attempts to probe such cognitions and perceptions are at best presumptive, and conceding that such matters are easier to assert than to demonstrate, one might still profit by an effort to go beyond the consideration of artifacts alone to the consideration of the slaves' material culture—that is, the knowledge that enabled them to produce and appreciate material things—as a means of untangling the complex strands of slave folklife.[1]

2

In the social relations of slavery in All Saints Parish, food served several functions. The relations between any folk group and its foodways are complex and reciprocal: concepts of appetite and hunger are partly shaped by the culture of the group, but culture itself is partly shaped by the basic human need for food. On the Waccamaw rice plantations slaves ate the grains, fruits, vegetables, and meats of the New World environment; but to those foodstuffs slave cooks applied an African culinary grammar—methods of cooking and spicing, remembered recipes, ancestral tastes. They added the soul ingredients. Not only did food provide the nourishment necessary to sustain life among the slave community, but it was also one of the few sources of pleasure they enjoyed. Thus food—creolized as soul food—became one of the symbols of group identity in the slave community.[2]

The slaves' rations were usually distributed on Saturday afternoons and had to last until the following Saturday, supplemented by food from the slaves' gardens and animals they raised. If the allowance ran out before the end of the week, as it did on some plantations, the slaves had to steal or do without.[3] James R. Sparkman reported his own weekly allocations to be "of Meal 10 quarts, of Rice or Peas 8 quarts, and of Sweet Potatoes one Bushel. This is the full allowance of every adult, and the younger negroes the same, no matter what their age, as soon as they are put to task work. Molasses is given throughout the year at proper intervals, Salt Fish only in winter, Pork or Bacon and Beef during summer. The allowance of Molasses is 1 pint (for one week), of Salted Fish (Mullet or Mackerel) 2 or 3 according to size, of Pork or Bacon 2 lbs." Sparkman also said he distributed two quarts (8 cups) of beef-and-rice soup daily to each slave from the first of June to the first of November.[4] On John D. Magill's plantations, however, according to Titus Small's daughter, "a week's food for a slave family was a peck of sweet potatoes, a dozen salted fish; if there was a baby in the family you got one peck of grits and one piece of fat back. In the summertime you got one peck of meal and one quart of syrup."[5] Plantations had to contract for the purchase of beef, tongue, and molasses. It was sometimes necessary to substitute mutton from the plantation's sheep when excessive heat made it impossible to preserve the beef.[6]

Some slaves prepared and ate all their meals in their cabins, but more typical on the Waccamaw were the big kitchen and central eating place where all the slaves ate together. Kitchens were separate buildings from the Big Houses, usually situated strategically between the smokehouse and the Big House. Often the morning and evening meals were eaten at home in the slave cabins, while the midday meal was eaten at the central eating shed, or, in some cases, in the field. J. Motte Alston described cooking rice in the field at Woodbourne plantation: "Uncover, as you walk along the banks of the fields, one of their little three-legged iron pots with its wooden cover, and try, if only from curiosity, the rice which they have prepared for their midday meal." On the plantations of Plowden C. J. Weston breakfast was eaten in the fields at nine and lunch at three, after most task work had been completed.[7]

House servants often ate the same food as the master's family, and they usually ate in the kitchen either before or after the master's family was served. Breakfast, served anytime between 7 and 9 A.M., was a light meal for the planter's family and the house servants. Wyndham Malet wrote of breakfasting on stewed peaches, bread, and clabber. Dinner, the midday meal, constituted "the great business of the day." Dining around 2 P.M., the lowcountry gentry—and their servants— might enjoy a variety of meats (ham, mutton, venison, turkey, oysters, and turtle in combination were not uncommon) topped off by desserts (assorted puddings and pies), wines, and cordials. The Weston family continued the English tradition of high tea, but most All Saints planter families ate a lighter meal—supper—in the evening.[8]

Slave cooks were skilled workers who established enviable reputations among the plantation community, black and white. Most plantations had both plantation cooks and children's cooks who were responsible for the midday meal. Some idea of the magnitude of the cooks' task can be gained from the "schedule of allowances" drawn up for the cooks at Hagley plantation. The plantation cook was responsible for cooking for approximately 200 adult slaves, while the children's cook had to prepare food for approximately 130 children. The following rations were given out daily except Sundays:

DURING POTATO TIME
> To each person doing any work, 4 qts.
> To each child at the negro-houses, 2 qts.

DURING GRITS-TIME
> To the cook for public-pot, for every person doing any work, 1 qt.
> To the child's cook, for each child at negro-houses, 1 pt.
> Salt to cook for public pot, 1 pt.
> Salt to child's cook, ½ pt.

Other rations were distributed biweekly or weekly.

ON EVERY TUESDAY AND FRIDAY THROUGHOUT THE YEAR
> To cook for public pot, for whole gang of workers, tradesmen, drivers, &c., Meat 30 lbs.
> To child's cook for all the children, Meat 15 lbs.

ON EVERY TUESDAY AND FRIDAY FROM APRIL 1ST TO OCTOBER 1ST
> To the plantation cook for each person doing any work, instead of the pint of grits, Small Rice 1 pt.
> To the child's cook, for each child instead of the ½ pt. of grits, Small rice ½ pt.
> To plantation cook for the whole gang of workers, tradesmen, drivers, &c., Peas; quantity depending on produce.

EVERY THURSDAY THROUGHOUT THE YEAR
> To the child's cook, for all the children, Molasses, 2 qts.

Other food was apportioned directly to individual slaves to be cooked and eaten in their own houses:

WEEKLY ALLOWANCE THROUGHOUT THE YEAR—TO BE GIVEN OUT EVERY SATURDAY AFTERNOON
> To each person doing any work, Flour, 3 qts.
> To each child at negro-houses, Flour, 3 pts.

To each person who has behaved well, and has not been sick during the week, 2 Fish or 1 pt. Molasses.

To each nurse, 4 Fish or 1¼ pt. Molasses.

To head carpenter; to head-miller; to head-cooper; to head-ploughman; to watchman; to trunk-minders; to drivers; to mule-minders; to hog-minder; to cattle-minder; and to every superannuated person, 5 Fish, or 1½ pt. Molasses each.

MONTHLY ALLOWANCE—ON THE 1ST OF EVERY MONTH

To each person doing any work, and each superannuated person, Salt, 1 qt.

To each person doing any work, and each superannuated person, Tobacco, 1 hand.

CHRISTMAS ALLOWANCE

To each person doing any work, and each superannuated person, fresh Meat, 3 lbs.; Salt Meat, 3 lbs.; Molasses, 1 qt.; Small Rice, 4 qts.; Salt, ½ bushel.

To each child at negro-houses, Fresh Meat, 1½ lbs.; Salt Meat, 1½ lbs.; Molasses, 1 pt.; Small Rice, 2 qts.

ADDITIONAL ALLOWANCE

Every day when rice is sown or harvested, to the cook, for the whole gang of workers in the field, Meat 40 lbs.; Peas, as above.

No allowances or presents, besides the above, are on any consideration to be made—except for sick people, as specified further on.[9]

There are few descriptions of the cooking implements. Ellen Godfrey, a slave at Longwood plantation, recalled long after emancipation a great iron skilletlike oven with three legs and a snug lid, on which coals were piled for baking.[10] Slave cooks had at their disposal a rather elaborate inventory of cooking utensils on James R. Sparkman's plantations. These implements, however, were more likely used for preparing the Sparkman family's meals than those of the slaves. An inventory of 1845 listed the following implements:

2 pr shovel & tongs	2 enameled Digestind
2 wrought iron kitchen dogs	1 sauce pan (covered)
1 wrought spit dog	1 tin kettle (large)

3 trammels	1 iron mortar
3 trivets	2 frying pans
1 cook, ladle, fork & skimmer	3 ovens (baking)
2 toasters	1 roaster
2 gridirons	2 iron tea kettles
1 griddle	1 coffee mill
1 steak pan	8 pots (various sizes)
2 thin wafer iron	

The following appeared in a list dated May 1847: 2 large pots—6 gal.; 2 pots—6 qts.; 2 pots—4 qts.; 4 pots—3 qts.; 2 pots—2 qts.; and 2 new spiders. An 1848 kitchen inventory listed 1 copper chelten kettle; 3 enameled saucepans; 1 trimont tea kettle; 1 meat cleaver; 1 cook knife w/saw; and 1 cullender.[11]

If cooking for the Big House required a wide array of implements, cooking in the public pots was often a crude affair. Sabe Rutledge recalled that his grandmother, a plantation cook, "had two pots going. Boil all day and all night. Biling. Biling till he ticken (thicken). Cedar paddle stir with." Utensils for eating were as crude as implements for cooking, if they existed at all. Sometimes wooden spoons, clam shells, or pieces of broken pottery served as eating utensils. On some plantations the slaves ate with their hands.[12] Most of the plantations had special cooks for the children, who ate together and were served half-portions. Joshua Ward employed four full-time cooks for the more than 400 slave children on his plantations.[13]

The basic ingredients in the slaves' diet were vegetables. Although some plantations had a large communal garden for the whole plantation, a more typical pattern was for the slaves to have small plots for their personal use. These gardens were worked by the slaves after their tasks for the day were finished and on weekends and other off times. Whether the plantation had one big garden or each slave had a small one, it was the work and sweat of the slaves that went into the soil to grow corn, sweet potatos, Irish potatos, tomatos, collards, turnips, peanuts, okra, eggplant, beans, and peas. "There is no vegetable of which negroes are more fond than of the common field

pea," wrote a planter in 1851. "They are very nutritious, and if
cooked perfectly done, and well seasoned with red pepper, are
quite healthy." Other slaves mixed peas with rice and salt meat
to make the popular "Hoppin' John." Since few of these vegetables were mentioned in the tables of allowances or rations, it
would appear that most of these vegetables were grown by individual slaves.[14]

Such fruit as the slaves were able to obtain came from the
plantations' grapevines, orange, lemon, and fig trees, and
melon patches, or was purchased from the Caribbean by the
masters. J. Motte Alston wrote in his memoirs of vessels from
the West Indies steaming up the Waccamaw to pick up lumber
from Henry Buck's large sawmills. "These vessels would pass
in front of my house," he recalled, "and I would frequently lay
in all the fruit I wanted at a trifling cost." On most plantations
fruits were preserved in some way—dried, canned, or bran-
died—for enjoyment during the winter. Slaves perhaps ate the
wild berries that grew in abundance along the Waccamaw as
well.[15]

Rice was a staple food as well as the cash crop on the
Waccamaw.[16] Goliah, a slave of Robert F. W. Allston, told Allston's daughter how rice should be cooked: "Fust t'ing yo' roll
up yo' sleeve es high as yo' kin, en yo tak soap en yo' wash yo'
hand clean. Den you wash yo' pot clean, fill um wid col' wata
en put on de fia. Now w'ile yo' wata de bile, yo' put yo' rice
een a piggin en yo' wash um well, den when yo' dun put salt
een yo' pot, en 'e bile high, yo' put yo' rice een, en le' um bile
till 'e swell, den yo' pour off de wata, en put yo' pot back o' de
stove, for steam."[17] "Rice," according to J. Motte Alston,
"when properly cooked is the best cereal for man; by far the
most wholesome and nutritious." Rice was only cooked properly, in his opinion, when it was "boiled till *done*, the water
'dreened' (drained) off, and set on the ashes to 'soak.' Around
the pot there is a brown rice-cake, in the center of which are
the snow-white grains, each thoroughly done and each separate. Unless one has eaten rice cooked in this way, he knows
nothing about it. The stuff called rice—soft and gluey—may
do to paper a wall, but not to feed civilized man."[18] Rice, espe-

cially cracked rice which was the slaves' usual ration, was also prepared as pilau—boiled with salt pork, fish, or game and vegetables. Sparkman claimed an allowance of eight quarts of rice or peas weekly to his slaves at Mt. Arena—the equivalent of ten cups of cooked rice daily.[19]

On some plantations rice was distributed every working day throughout the year. On others, slaves resorted to theft to augment their diet. At John D. Magill's Richmond Hill and Oregon plantations "they would steal rice and hide it in the straw. . . . They would have to tote rice straw to put in the corn field to use as manure, they would put a basket in the straw; steal rice and hide it in the basket in the straw; carry it out on their heads to the corn field; when they got the chance they hid the rice in the swamp marking the spot. . . . They would beat the rice out in the swamp. They burned out a stump and made a round hole; then they took a piece of pole and sharpened the edge and beat the rice out. This was a homemade kind of morta[r] and pestle; was used to beat the rice." When slaves on Brookgreen plantation broke into the rice barn and stole more rice, the wife of Joshua Ward told the overseers that the slaves should be given more rice rather than being punished for trying to steal it. As Ben Horry, one of Ward's slaves, later recalled, "Anybody steal rice and they beat them, Miss Bessie cry and say, 'Let 'em have rice! My rice—my nigger!'"[20]

Running close behind rice as a staple in All Saints Parish were grits and hominy, both derived from corn. The term hominy designates corn with the hull and germ removed; grits refers to the ground grains of corn. Elizabeth Collins, the English housekeeper at Hagley plantation, apparently learned her recipe for grits from the slave cooks:

The corn having been ground, and the grits well sifted through a wire seive, which then divides the flour from the coarse grits, the former is reserved for making bread, and the latter transferred to a pot of cold water and let boil until the water is nearly gone; then the little water, which is only left to keep it from burning, is poured off, and the hominy is ready for the table. It is generally eaten for breakfast, when, if people choose to be stingy enough, the overplus can be deposited in a vessel with the flour, and mixed with a quantity of water or clabber, put to rise until the evening, when a couple of eggs or a sweet potato must be well stirred in, and of course, a little salt. Bake it at once, and then the economical housewife will have a good and light loaf for supper.[21]

Some of the slave children expressed a dislike for yellow corn. Sabe Rutledge recalled, "I cry many a day bout that yellow corn! 'Pa, this here yellow corn make hominy look like he got egg cook in 'em; red corn look like hominy cook in red molasses!' But yellow corn stronger feed! Stronger feed! And pa know 'em."[22]

Cornbread was by far the most common bread in the slaves' diet, although it occasionally included rice bread, rye bread, and wheat bread (called sweet bread). Buttermilk biscuits, baked in one of the great iron skilletlike three-legged ovens with live-oak coals heaped on top, were especially prized. Cakes and other baked delicacies, such as gingerbread, were reserved for special occasions such as Christmas and weddings.[23]

The slaves' provisions included allowances for sugar, honey, and molasses, often eaten with cornbread. The consumption of large quantities of molasses led Wyndham Malet to credit slaves with a sweet tooth, but such an interpretation both ignores the importance of molasses as a source of iron and calcium (in a diet low in meat and dairy products) and glosses over the role of condiments and seasonings in slave food. Furthermore, one way of making ill-tasting—or tasteless—food palatable was to pour molasses on it. Molasses spiced with vinegar and diluted with water made a common beverage for All Saints slaves. It tasted somewhat like treacle, or so it seemed to Emily Weston's English housekeeper, who marveled that such a refreshment "is what the negro is very fond of."[24]

Among dairy products clabber was the most common and apparently the most enjoyed. Milk, especially buttermilk, was common enough during the winter, but quickly soured in the intense heat of a Carolina summer. Cheese was a rare delicacy.

Elizabeth Collins contended that cheese could not be made in Carolina, "for on account of the intense heat, the milk quickly turns sour; in fact, if it is let to stand for about two hours, it becomes a thick curd which is called clabber." She acknowledged that clabber was considered by many to be "a dainty dish," but she was happy that she had "never been obliged to eat it." An English relative of the Westons, however, considered clabber to be "quite a godsend in the absence of tea. It is simply 'curds and whey,'" he noted. "A bowl of milk is put by in the evening, and by atmospheric operation becomes *claber* in the morning." Another dairy product in use among the slaves was butter, usually churned on the flood tide so that the butter would come "wid de tide."[25]

Meat, whether supplied daily or irregularly, was especially prized. Mt. Arena slaves ate beef soup thickened with rice daily from June to November, with occasional substitutions of mutton. Goat, cheese, and chicken were also well liked, but pork was easily the favorite. Hog-butchering time meant spare ribs, bacon, and chitterlings for the slaves, the other parts being reserved for the master. Salt was scarce in All Saints Parish. The slaves of Robert F. W. Allston boiled it from sea water on the salt creeks between the Waccamaw Neck and Pawleys Island. While some plantations had saltworks, meat was usually preserved by smoking. Near the plantation kitchens stood smokehouses, where hams, sausages, side meat, and other meats were cured and stored.[26]

Seafood ran a close second in popularity to pork among Waccamaw slaves. Oysters, clams, crabs, shrimp, fresh fish in the summer, and smoked or brined fish in the winter were all part of the standard diet for inhabitants of this coastal area. The waters teemed with salt and fresh water fish: shad, trout, pike, perch, and sturgeon. The slaves added to their allowances of food by using their off times for fishing, crabbing, oystering, and clamming. They caught autumn mullet at night in cast nets and hauled quantities of them home in sacks. Mullet was described by Motte Alston as "a fine fish and the roes especially so." Sabe Rutledge recalled that he and his family ate mullet and rice for the three fall months. Fish were plentiful not only in the salt creeks and ocean but also in the fresh-water lakes, which swarmed with pike and other varieties.[27]

A very special and rare seafood delicacy was turtle eggs. An English visitor found 115 turtle eggs on the beach at Pawleys Island in the summer of 1862. He had to learn how to prepare them from an elderly slave who was in charge of the Pawleys Island summer home of Plowden and Emily Weston. The slave informed him "they were 'first rate eating,' which, on having some for breakfast, I found to be the case. They have a delicate flavour, and must be very nutritious; their coating is tough instead of brittle."[28]

Among other seafood sometimes eaten by slaves were eel and alligator. Hagar Brown described how to prepare eel for eating. "Dress 'em. Strip 'em down the back. Stuff 'em and bake 'em." In addition to its nutritional value, eel skin was reputed to be good for rheumatism: "wrap 'em 'round leg," she advised, "keep 'em till pain gone." Regarding the alligator, she said that one could "eat every part but don't eat the head and feet. Eat body part and tail. Makes chillun fat."[29]

Game meats were also popular among the slaves. The woods bordering the Waccamaw abounded in deer, foxes, rabbits, racoons, opossums, black bears, geese, ducks, turkeys, woodcocks, snipes, rice birds, pigeons, partridges, and plovers. William Oliver recalled the abundance of game. "Possum and squirrel all we could get," he said. "Wild turkey, possum. Don't bother with no coon much." According to Hagar Brown, however, racoon was a greater delicacy than opossum. "Coon better than possum; heap cleaner than possum. Coon won't eat everything a possum does." She also supplemented her diet with fox, crow, and hawk. "Fox? I eat 'em," she recalled, but added, "fox hard to lay hand on. Them thing kin out run a ghost. Possum good! Easy to catch possum."[30]

There are indications that slaves may have owned firearms. In any event they used them for hunting. Elizabeth Allston Pringle recalled in her memoirs that her father's slaves shot rice birds on the plantations. A northern visitor to the Waccamaw in 1831 reported, "The blacks are never better pleased than when they are hunting in the woods; and it is seldom that they have not in the larder the flesh of a raccoon or opossum." J. Motte Alston noted that, despite his requirements that slaves attend evening church services every other week, "there were some who preferred to hunt [or] fish."[31]

Hunting and fishing served at least two functions for All Saints slaves. On the one hand, they supplemented the sometimes meager or monotonous diet portioned out by the master. On the other hand, they were sports—two of the slaves' few recreations. While some slaveholders allowed little or no time for slaves to enjoy such pleasures, it appears from most accounts that the majority of the All Saints rice planters not only encouraged their slaves to hunt and fish but also often hunted and fished with them.[32]

Occasions for elaborate feasts included weddings, Christmas, and other holidays. On the Waccamaw, slave weddings were occasions of great celebration, marked by festive banquets. On the plantations of Plowden and Emily Weston wedding cards were sent out, and the couple were feted with cake, turkeys, hams, molasses, and the like. Louisa Brown recalled that slave weddings were often accompanied by a feast; the marriage of her parents at Turkey Hill plantation had included such a repast. The planter and his family joined with the rest of the plantation community in wishing the bride and groom health and happiness, and the marriage was celebrated with wedding cakes baked in the kitchen of the Big House.[33]

Christmas exemplified the importance of food in the plantation holidays. The daughter of Robert F. W. Allston recalled many years later that "there was much feasting at Christmas, for a beef and several hogs were always killed and extra rations of sugar, coffee, molasses, and flour were given out, and great quantities of sweet potatoes. Altogether it was a joyful time." Christmas called for three days of holiday on many lowcountry rice plantations. Three days before the beginnings of the celebration, Emily Weston, mistress of Hagley, Weehawka, True Blue, and Waterford plantations, visited the slave houses and gave out sugar to the children. On Christmas Eve, she and her husband distributed meat, salt, rice, and molasses to the adult slaves. Typically Christmas was a time of extra rations—

and of special rations, which the slaves had but rarely at other times, especially plum pudding and gingerbread, apples, oranges, currants, and other fruits, and heaping plates of ham, turkey, and goose.[34]

Christmas was also one of the few times slaves were permitted to drink intoxicating liquors. On Christmas morning 1856 the slaves of Robert F. W. Allston gathered to toast—repeatedly—his election to the governorship of South Carolina. Adele Petigru Allston wrote their son, "The next morning there was a great demonstration, the negroes coming as usual to wish Merry Christmas and the compliments of the Season, but more than usual to greet their master the Gov. They made a great noise and drank the Governor's health in many a stout glass of whiskey." Weddings were also occasions at which spirits—wine more often than whiskey—might be served.[35]

Not all slaves, of course, limited their imbibing to occasions permitted by their masters. Define Horry, a trusted driver at Brookgreen plantation, stole rice from the rice barn and pounded it with a makeshift mortar and pestle in the woods in order to have money to buy liquor. His son, Ben Horry, later recalled

> My father love he liquor. That take money. He ain't have any money but he have the barn key and *rice* been money! . . . *That* rice he been take to town sat'dy when the Colonel and Father go to get provision like sugar, coffee, pepper, and salt. With the money he get when he sell that rice, he buy liquor. He been hide that sack o' rice fore day clean in the prow of the boat and cover with a thing like an old coat. I members one day when he come back from town he make a miss when he unloading and fell and broke he jug! The Big Boss see; he smell; and he see WHY my father make that miss step; he already sample that liquor! But the Boss ain't say too much. Sat'dy time come to ration off. Every head on the plantation to Brookgreen line up at smokehouse to draw he share of meat and rice and grits and meal. . . . Well, headman reach down in the corner and pull out a piece of that broke whiskey jug and put on top my father rations where all could see! Colonel Ward cause that to be done to broke him off from that whiskey jug. My father was a steady liquor man till then and the Boss broke him off.[36]

The Waccamaw planters were keenly sensitive to the potential of alcohol to disrupt what they regarded as normal role boundaries in a slave society. The crossing of boundaries, they feared, might promote contradictions and tensions within the social relations of the plantation. Even the slightest transgressions were sufficient to send forth ripples of alarm. Dr. Andrew Hasell sent a stern note chastising Colonel Daniel W. Jordan for giving whiskey to Hasell's slave Isaac: "I heard from Mayham Ward yesterday that my man Isaac was intoxicated at Club—I regret it—Some temptation must have been made—either in the dregs—left by members—or by some other dose. He has never been intemperate here for 14 years—& has never been seen intoxicated—or suspected of having taken liquor during that long period—You will confer a favor upon me in not offering liquor to any servant of mine." Jordan responded by downplaying the significance of the event but insisted that he was "not in the habit of offering liquor to your servant, or to the servants of other people." According to Jordan, "Your servant put me in the way of obtaining a cooking utensil which I expected to have found in the Club House. When he returned from showing my boy the fork of the road—I happened, as is sometimes to the case, to be taking a drink he offered me ice water and for his politeness I gave him about 2 table spoons full of whiskey. This is my agency in the matter. The boy was a little lively but I do not think he was by any means drunk." Jordan added, significantly, "It is not difficult for negroes to get whiskey if they want it." [37] Despite Jordan's efforts to minimize the occasion, the use of alcohol by slaves was a threat to the slave system. Perhaps its disruptive potential was most memorably epitomized in a slave aphorism from Hagar Brown: "Likker'll make you not know you mama." [38]

How well fed were the slaves on the rice plantations of All Saints Parish? Certainly there were incentives, both economic and humanitarian, for the planters to provide their slaves with sufficient food for good health. Masters had invested in their slaves not merely their money but also their chances of success. Self-interest, if not human kindness, should rule out food deprivation as an issue. Incentives and logic, however, are not the same as evidence; and there remain substantial doubts regarding the nutritional value of the slaves' diet. A commonly voiced criticism by historians has been that the slave diet lacked ingredients necessary to good health. The charge that a niacin deficiency caused widespread pellagra symptoms does not stand up, however, to an intensive examination of the evidence from All Saints Parish—the Slave Narratives, plantation records, census mortality schedules, or the records of physicians in the area.[39]

The slaveholders' self-portrait was predictably flattering. J. Motte Alston wrote in his memoirs that rice plantation slaves on the Waccamaw were "bountifully" fed. Plowden C. J. Weston, in his overseers' contract, specified that "great care should be taken that the negroes should never have less than their regular allowance: in all cases of doubt, it should be given in favour of the largest quantity. The measures should not be *struck*, but rather heaped up over."[40]

Most of the All Saints ex-slaves interviewed by Genevieve Willcox Chandler for the Federal Writers' Project recalled their masters as good providers of ham and chicken, collards and peas, cornbread and molasses, rice and grits. Ellen Godfrey reported, "Colonel [Joshua] Ward keep a nice place. Gie 'em rice, peas, four cook for chillun." Gabe Lance said his master, Francis Heriot, was a "Good master, all right. Give plenty to eat." None of the Waccamaw ex-slaves reported having been poorly fed. However, several did point out that while they had personally been well fed, other slaves on the Waccamaw had not fared as well. In particular the slaves at Magill's Richmond Hill and Oregon plantations were singled out as having been poorly fed. Ellen Godfrey reported that "Doctor Magill people hab to steal for something to eat." Interviews that I conducted in 1972 and 1975 among the children and grandchildren of All Saints slaves present a similarly mixed picture. John Beese—whose father, Welcome Beese, was a carpenter at Oatland plantation—had heard that there was always plenty to eat, that no one went hungry at Oatland. On the other hand, Mary Small—the daughter of Hagar Brown—

reported that her mother told her many a meal consisted of nothing more than corn meal mush and molasses in a pan.[41]

The cultivation of rice on the Waccamaw was quite lucrative for the planters. Cotton planters were sometimes faced with the necessity of cutting costs in order to maintain their incomes, a necessity some met by cutting the food allowance of their slaves. All Saints rice planters faced no such alternative. The demographic pattern of a steady natural increase in the slave population of the parish supports the notion of a generally adequate slave diet on the rice plantations, although the proportion of the population over sixty was quite small. In fact, the relatively short life span of rice plantation slaves may be related to nutrition. In any event, it is highly unlikely that many All Saints slaves ate just what their masters ate, although the slaves of the Reverend Belin may have been exceptional in that regard. Belin owned only a few house servants, not a large army of field laborers, while most of the All Saints slaves lived on large plantations with numerous other slaves, most of them field hands. It was logistically impossible for most slaves to have been fed as Belin may have fed his house servants. For the most part, slaves appear to have had enough to eat on the Waccamaw (despite the conspicuous exceptions on Magill's plantations); but their starch-heavy, high-energy diets may have concealed dangerous nutritional deficiencies. Certainly All Saints slaves were better fed than the Irish peasants who were found by a royal commission investigating conditions among the poor in the 1830s to be subsisting on a diet of "dry potatoes, and with these they are . . . obliged to stint themselves to one spare meal on the day. . . . They sometimes get a herring, or a little milk, but they never get meat except at Christmas, Easter, and Shrovetide."[42]

But such comparisons may mislead as much as they illuminate. The amount of food stolen on the rice plantations would seem to indicate a certain amount of dissatisfaction. Slaves in All Saints Parish regularly stole food through a variety of means and for a variety of reasons. A northern visitor noted in 1831 that "slavery seldom fortifies honesty; and, besides, the slave may fancy that it is just to make reprisals on his master's property for violence done to his own person; it often happens, then, that there is more flesh in the house of a negro than he would willingly exhibit to the overseer." While food theft might have been motivated by aggression and revenge, or even by a desire to make money with which to buy liquor, at least some of the theft must be attributed to dissatisfaction with the rations. In any event slaves who stole food did not always think of it as stealing. They just moved Maussa's hog from inside Maussa's smokehouse to inside Maussa's slave. How could one species of property, after all, steal another? As "Miss Bess" said, "My rice—my nigger!"[43]

Food played a role in slave culture beyond mere sustenance. It had immense cultural and ideological significance: the choice of particular foods and particular means of preparation involved issues of crucial importance to the slaves' sense of identity. Slave cooks not only maintained cultural continuity with West African cuisine but also adapted the African tradition creatively to the necessities and opportunities of a new culinary environment. The importance of food to the slaves of All Saints Parish is perhaps best revealed in two of their proverbs: "A full belly makes strong arms an' a willin' heart," but "hunger tame wild beast."[44]

3

Costume is one of the basic symbols of any community, expressing not only distinctions of age, sex, marital status, religious affiliation, wealth, and social status within the community, but also distinctions among various social contexts, from everyday to occupational to erotic to ceremonial contexts. The clothing worn by All Saints slaves was not, strictly speaking, folk costume, at least not in the sense that folk costume is an outward symbol both of group identity and of the individual's place within the group. Just as in a folk community individuals are not completely free to express their individuality in dress, on the rice plantations slaves were not completely free to express group consciousness and solidarity in their dress. Slave costume cannot be taken as a direct symbol of their own sense of identity as a community. Nor is slave costume a direct symbol of the stereotypes held by the masters, who found the physical appearance of the slaves—their very blackness— quite sufficient to set them apart. There was no pressing need for clothing to serve that function as well. To be sure, there was an attempt in eighteenth-century South Carolina to control slave costume by statute, to require slaves to wear coarse clothing only; it proved unenforceable, as the slaveholders themselves felt no pressing incentive to compel compliance. The extent to which the law was ignored is illustrated by the letters to the editor of the *South Carolina Gazette* complaining of slaves openly dressing beyond their station less than five years after the law was passed.[45]

To maintain that the slaves' clothing did not directly express their sense of identity as a folk community is not to say that there is no relationship at all. It merely acknowledges that folk costume needs to be studied in relation to community life as a whole, that *how* clothing is worn may be as significant as *what* clothing is worn. The significant point to be noticed is clothing behavior rather than clothing. If slaves were subject to more external constraints upon their dress than were free persons, they were nevertheless not quite devoid of choice both in how clothing was worn and to some extent in how it was cut.[46]

Antebellum reports of slave clothing on the Waccamaw differ little from one another. J. Motte Alston, proprietor of Woodbourne plantation, maintained that the slaves were "bountifully clothed." Visitors to the Waccamaw region who observed slaves working in the field or about the plantation often called attention to the quality of the slaves' clothing, frequently enough, in fact, to lend considerable credence to their observations. New Yorker James Roberts Gilmore, for example, described an elderly slave woman "arrayed in a mass of cast-off finery, whose gay colors were in striking contrast with her jet-black skin and bent, decrepit form. Her gown, which was very short, was of flaming red and yellow worsted stuff, and the enormous turban that graced her head and hid all but a few tufts of her frizzled, 'pepper-and-salt' locks, was evidently a contribution from the family stock of worn-out pillow cases." Almira Coffin noted slaves dressed in clean suits on Sunday, while Elizabeth Collins took notice of the "very thick woolen" of the slaves' winter clothes. She also emphasized that the women's dress was "very gay," but she lamented that "they have no taste whatever to cut or trim a garment. I have seen many very pretty prints sewn together upside down." The Englishman Wyndham Malet described the slaves as "well clothed." Informants for the Slave Narratives as well as the children and grandchildren of slaves whom I interviewed usually recalled at least adequate clothing on the All Saints plantations. Ellen Godfrey said that her master "sent slam to England gie me good clothes and shoe."[47]

Some planters purchased clothing for their slaves ready-made, but most ordered woolen cloth from England and had the clothing made on the plantation. Cloth was also woven on the large, generally self-sufficient rice plantations of All Saints Parish where a number of slave women were assigned full-time work as weavers and seamstresses. The plantation mistress supervised the work of making clothes, a demanding year-round task.[48] She was often directly involved in cutting out and sewing the clothes, as the following extracts from the diary of Emily Weston make clear:

> *Monday, May 2.* . . . I busy with Margaret cutting out children's clothes, and after school gave them all out, both to True Blue & Hagley.
>
> *Saturday, May 7.* Settled the sewing with Dolly. . . .
> 184 men's red flannels, R. & P.
> 235 women's robins, D.
> 16 boy's red flannels, M.
> 13 Baby bundles, D. & S.
> 27 house-servant's shirts, S. & G.
> and 3 pieces of trousering &
> 1 piece of shirting, to cut from, if necessary about 100 yds of the first & 40 of the other.

Saturday, December 3. Looking over work done by servants.
19 Fine shirts
7 Coarser do [shirts]
63 Pr Pants
6 Shirts (blue.)
13 Baby bundles
236 Robins
184 Red jackets
16 boys' do [red jackets]

In addition to the full-time seamstresses, women house servants often devoted a part of their time to making clothes.[49]

The materials used consisted principally of woolens and cottons, neither of which was produced on the rice plantations. J. Motte Alston maintained that cotton was used only for summer wear; winter clothing was all wool, with no "admixture of cotton." The material was often bought already woven into drilling, broadcloth, flannel, plush, "mixed cloth," and both coarse and fine shirting. Shirtings, however, were more often woven on the plantations.[50] The quality of the material varied from plantation to plantation. At John D. Magill's Oregon, "cloth was called homespun; it looked like crocker sack or burlap." On the other hand, Robert F. W. Allston had some of his own clothes tailored from the same material used for that of the slaves. He gave instructions regarding a particular tweed to be used for slave garments: "If there is enough of it left I would like a coat of it for myself."[51]

The most common colors were blue, red, and gray. William Oliver emphasized "lots of gray" in his recollections in the 1930s. J. Motte Alston's liveried house servants were dressed in green. Red, however, seems to be the color mentioned most commonly in the various sources. Maple and indigo dyes were used on the plantations to color the woven materials. Plaids seem to have been even more popular than solid colors—brown and white or blue and white Welsh plaids, cotton plaids for the summer dresses of the house servants, plaid winter shirts for the men, gingham dresses for the women.[52]

On many of the Waccamaw rice plantations, the semi-annual distribution of clothing and blankets was treated as something of a paternalistic ritual that reflected the social significance of clothing. The distribution process itself had multiple meanings. First, by dramatizing mutual obligations between master and slave, it helped promote a sense of community. Second, in transforming a necessary task of organization into a ceremony of personal largesse, the All Saints rice planters underscored their own dominant status in contrast with the slaves' position. Thus, the giving itself served to emphasize the masters' benevolence and to evoke the slaves' gratitude while simultaneously enhancing the masters' status and power.[53] The daughter of Robert F. W. Allston recalled the process on her father's plantations:

> It was an interesting thing to watch: a name was read out by mamma, papa, or my sister from the book, and up the step came the little girl, dropped a courtesy [*sic*] to each of us and then to Maum Mary, and stood before her to be measured. Maum Mary was sometimes inclined to be very impatient and cross, but she dared not give way to the inclinations openly, with us all watching her. She would just jerk the timid ones around a little; but if papa was there he would say quite sternly: "Gently, Mary, gently." The little girl, as she went out loaded with her things and the things of her little brothers and sisters, would drop another courtesy of thanks.[54]

Clothing was generally distributed in May and November, although Emily Weston's diary shows periodic distribution between early April and mid-May and from early to late December. On the plantations of Robert F. W. Allston, clothes were given out the day after New Year's Day.

> Maum Mary began early in the morning after New Year's Day to bring out and pile in log-cabin fashion in the piazza roles of red flannel, rolls of white homespun (unbleached muslin) and of thick homespun, and of calico for the women. Then for the men, rolls of jeans, dark colored, and rolls of white for the shirts, and then rolls of the most beautiful white stuff like the material of which blankets are made. This was called *plains*, and with the jeans was imported from England, as being stronger and warmer than any to be got in this country. There were buttons and threads and needles in each roll of stuff, suit-

able for that thickness of material. All these little piles made of rolls filled up the very big piazza, and it took nearly all day for the long lists to be read out and each individual to come up and get their stuffs. Each woman had a red flannel roll, two white homespun rolls, two colored homespun, and two calico. The men had one red flannel, two white homespun, two jeans, and one white plains.[55]

Children were allocated yardage according to their size. On Allston's plantations children's clothing was distributed on the day following the distribution of clothing for adults. "Each child came up to Maum Mary where she sat surrounded by whole bales and stuff, and stood in front of her. She took the end of the homespun, held it on top of the child's head and brought the material down to the floor and then up again to the head. This would make one full garment for the child, and was the way to assure there being enough, with no waste. The red flannel was handled the same way, and the coloured homespun for every-day frocks, and the calico for Sunday frocks."[56]

James Sparkman gave each man and woman six yards of "widest cotton Osnaburgs" and six yards of unbleached cotton shirting. For winter, the men's ration was "one Kersey or Pilot Cloth Sack, ready made, and one pr. Kersey Pants, or if they cant be had, 6 yds best white welsh plains, also 6 yds Cotton Shirting." The women were alloted six yards each of "best Welsh Plains and Cotton Shirting." Both the quality and the quantity of clothing varied from one plantation to another.[57]

On some plantations buttons, needles, and thread were supplied, for some slaves were expected to make their garments. On other plantations specialized tailors and seamstresses made garments for everyone. J. Motte Alston noted that, after the material was distributed, "the cloth and all necessary 'trimmings' can be taken, if so desired, to the tailor and seamstresses at Fairfield to be cut and made according to the wish of its owner."[58]

The fabrics were heavy and durable, and with proper maintenance the clothes were expected to last for years, even though new clothes were distributed annually. Some plantations held regular inspections to insure that the clothes fit and that they were kept clean and mended. Even the most generous masters, however, seldom provided their slaves with an opportunity to wash and change their clothing more than once a week. On Plowden C. J. Weston's plantations a slave woman named Rachel was detailed to wash for the men servants. One week she washed white clothes, the next week dark clothes. These were called "white week" and "black week," respectively. One day in May, after the rice had been planted, was set aside for washing all woolen clothing and blankets before they were put aside until cold weather. On the large plantations clothes were mended regularly. At Hagley mending day was the day before washing. Prince, Hagley's head coachman, was generally regarded as the least tidy of all; his clothes were mended first. Elizabeth Collins, the English housekeeper at Hagley, wrote that "on being asked one week to bring in his clothes to be mended, he walked to the house with two pairs of trousers hung on his arm. I looked at them and told him that I thought them past mending, for there was not a piece bigger than a quarter of yard square without holes, not worn from any length of time, but torn by the bushes. . . . After a good deal of planning, the two were made into one pair, and the owner wore them for some time, and seemed more pleased than if they were new." [59]

One of the social functions of clothing is the visible marking of differentiations among the members of the community according to age, sex, and status. Status within the slave community involved a number of different relationships, but the one most clearly marked by costume was that between house servants and other slaves. Butlers, maids, valets, and coachmen were expected to reflect the status of their master and mistress. Individual planters clothed their servants according to their individual fancies. Sparkman said that he supplied his own "without limit to insure a genteel and comfortable appearance." J. Motte Alston's house servants were dressed in coats of dark green broadcloth, trousers of green plush, and vests faced with red and trimmed in silver braid. [60]

Head coverings for men included caps and hats. The slaves at Woodbourne wore Scottish caps, which J. Motte Alston had imported from Britain. "Macknaw caps" were distributed at Christmas to Sparkman's slaves. Plowden Weston's English brother-in-law reported that many of Weston's slaves wore in their caps a small palmetto tree—the South Carolina emblem—made of palmetto leaves. But many slaves wore hats instead of caps. Sabe Rutledge recalled that the first time he was old enough to remember seeing his grandfather—driver Rodrick Rutledge—the old man was wearing an "old beaver hat on he head. Top of crown wear out and I member he have paste-board cover over with cloth and sew in he hat crown." At Hagley and the other Weston plantations, hats were distributed to the slaves for the summer.[61]

For women the ubiquitous head covering was the headkerchief or bandanna. Elizabeth Collins noted that slave women tied their bandannas tightly about their heads, with a thick piece of paper stuffed at the back part to look like a comb. These headkerchiefs were almost invariably white and marked the status of the "mammies" in the South Carolina lowcountry. It is ironic that such headkerchiefs have become a symbol of subservience, for the custom of wearing headkerchiefs in the slave community reflected continuity with African tradition and expressed a high degree of personal pride. The custom was widely practiced in those parts of the New World with the highest concentrations of African descendants and where other African cultural traits were retained in the highest degree.[62] A similar continuity with distinctive African ways of hair dressing was practiced by slave women on the Waccamaw: Margaret Bryant continued her grandmother's practice of wrapping each little strand of hair securely with white twine. "Grandma old timey," she said, "she wrap her hair."[63]

The suit seems to have been the most prized of the male articles of clothing. Ben Horry recalled with relish the time when he became old enough for a suit of his own: "They brought a great deal of this cloth they call blue drilling to make a suit for every boy big enough to wear a suit of clothes and a pair of shoes for every one. I thought *that* the happiest 'set up' I had in boyhood. Blue drilling pants and coat and shoe."[64] Coats and jackets were also valued. Plowden C. J. Weston annually gave each of his male slaves a coat and a red jacket. Female slaves often wore shawls instead of coats. Overcoats were a more expensive item and were probably not furnished to every slave. Dr. James R. Sparkman purchased an overcoat for a slave named Jacob for $8, a substantial price on the eve of the Civil War.[65]

Shirts ranged from the fine and coarse shirts described by Emily Weston to the "weave shirt—die with blue indigo boil with myrtle seed"—that was worn by Rodrick Rutledge. Blue drilling and tweed were more common for trousers of most slaves than the green plush worn by J. Motte Alston's house servants. Sometimes the men, except for liveried house servants, wore overalls rather than trousers. Rodrick Rutledge was described by his grandson as having worn "something built kinder like overall and have a apron. Apron button up here where my overall buckle and can be let down. All been dye with indigo."[66]

Red flannel underwear was distributed to men, women, and children for the winter. Women's lingerie was probably plain, for the most part; however, Elizabeth Collins emphasized that the house servants liked to show off their lingerie: "some of the women being very gay, and they would now and then give a swing, so as to display their taste."[67]

No article of slave dress was mentioned so often, nor evoked so wide a range of opinion, as shoes. Ellen Godfrey recalled that her master sent to England to get slaves on his plantation good shoes. William Oliver said that the big plantations purchased shoes ready-made. No doubt the quality varied from plantation to plantation. Rodrick Rutledge was described as having "old brogan shoe on he foot." Children and grandchildren of slaves told me of their having heard of some slaves going barefoot in summer and having to improvise shoes of wooden soles and feet wrapped in tow bags. Julia Small, daughter of a slave on Magill's Oregon plantation, recalled that "Grandmother knew men to ditch and crack the ice with their bare feet."[68]

Apparently most rice planters attempted to provide the

slaves on their plantations with comfortable shoes. They measured the feet of their slaves and ordered accordingly. Elizabeth Allston Pringle described how the process worked on her father's plantations.

> Every man, woman, and child on the place . . . was called on to give their measure—a nice, light strip of wood about an inch wide the length of their foot. Each was supposed to put the weight of the foot down on the piece of wood and have some one mark and cut it off the right length; then take it himself, so that there would be no mistake, to Mr. Belflowers [the overseer], who wrote the full name upon it. These measures Mr. Belflowers brought to papa, all clearly and distinctly marked in pencil; and they were sent to the factor in Charleston, who took them to a reliable shoe dealer, and each measure was fitted into a pair of shoes.

The lack of measure of width accounts for the poor fit of some of the shoes, but the poor fit was usually attributed to vanity by the masters: "darkies have a very great dislike of big feet, so many of them were tempted to send too short a measure; and then what a disappointment and what suppressed groans and lamentations when the new shoes were tried on! 'Somebody change my meshur.' And often I was called on to examine the stick and read out the name on it. No mistake there. But these victims of vanity were few, and were always much ridiculed by the others who had wisely given the full length of the foot."[69] The time when shoes were distributed varied from plantation to plantation. James R. Sparkman distributed shoes in November after the rice was harvested. Plowden C. J. Weston distributed shoes in April. Robert F. W. Allston distributed shoes in early January on the third day after New Year.[70]

Carrying the shoes rather than wearing them was not an unusual practice among the Waccamaw slaves, owing partially, no doubt, to poor fit. As late as the 1930s Ben Horry, then in his eighties, would "take my foot in my hand" and walk the thirty-mile round trip from his home to Conway, S.C., about once a week. Another reason for carrying rather than wearing shoes was given by a lowcountry slave who ex-

plained, "Oonah see dese duh me shoosh; me feet dem blonx
tuh Maussah!" (You see, these are *my* shoes, but my feet belong to the master!)[71]

Blankets, often imported from England, were distributed
annually. "In distributing to my people generally," Sparkman
wrote, "my habit has been for years to give in rotation, viz to
the men, 1 year, to the women the 2d year, and to each child
the 3d year no matter what its age or how many in the family.
This insures one new blanket 2 years out of three to each family and to those with several children the supply is abundant
every 3d year to make the average large." There was also a certain amount of sporadic distribution as necessary, as indicated
by a note Adele Allston wrote to herself on the back of an en-
velope: "I must give to Dido a large blanket for Lucy & Abraham & take back the small one—give to Lavinia a large blanket for Iris & Charles—give to April a large blanket for Hariet
[*sic*] & Lotta—take back the small one—send to Hannah a
large blanket for Murfy and Terina from H. P. Hale—give a
large blanket to Becky for Jane and Stella—take back the small
one—give a small one to Violet's Alice—give a small blanket
to Hager—give to Mary a small blanket for Albert."[72]

One significant function of costume in any folk community is that of differentiating between the workaday world and
the festive world. The same rhythmic alternation between
work and festivals that is evident in the temporal life of the
community is symbolized in the costume. For the slaves on All
Saints rice plantations that alternation distinguished between
the workaday world of the weekdays and the festive air the
slaves gave to the weekends—the distinction between the time
owed to the master and the time available for their own purposes. Slaves on the rice plantations of the Waccamaw would
clean themselves up after a strenuous week's work in the
scorching Carolina sun and put on clean clothes for Saturday
night visiting or partying (or both) and for church on Sunday.
They might even put on shoes that fit so badly they had been
barefoot all week. To be sure, some masters required their
slaves to be clean and neatly dressed for church on Sundays,
but the slaves made Sunday the occasion for displaying

not merely cleanliness but finery that they had purchased with hard-earned cash from extra work or sales from their gardens.[73]

The clothing of the slaves exemplified not merely the ways slaves wished to present themselves; but it also identified the way the masters liked to present themselves—as kindly, paternalistic, and generous. Many masters believed that encouraging their slaves to take pride in their appearance and permitting them to possess a few frills was good management and conducive to health and morale. For the slaves, the profound significance of costume is most apparent when one considers the occasions for dressing up. During weekdays they belonged to the masters, but on Sundays they emerged as self-respecting men and women. Through their self-respect they demonstrated their mutual respect for one another as members of a community.[74]

4

Behind the Big House, beyond the kitchens, barns, stables, carriage houses, and other plantation outbuildings, were the cabins of the slaves. These slave quarters were known on the rice plantations of the Waccamaw as the street. They were built in settlements, often on named streets, and reminded an English visitor of a country village. There were three such settlements on Robert F. W. Allston's plantation, with houses about fifty yards apart on both sides of the street. Each village contained about twelve houses along each side of the street. In these villages the slaves lived more or less to themselves, although on some plantations the white overseer's house was at the end of the street, "so that watchful eyes and ears could know how the slaves behaved when not at work."[75]

People are influenced by the space around them. They may be crowded, or awe-struck, or comfortable. Their work may be made easier or harder; their personalities may be stimulated or relaxed by the space they inhabit. A proper orientation in space is essential to sanity and survival. Architecture, by giving form to space, brings space under human control.

Vernacular architecture—that is, folk building, done without benefit of formal plans—is the immediate product of its users, forming a sensitive indicator of their inner feelings, their ideas of what is and is not appropriate. Through the analysis of vernacular architecture one can begin to penetrate the minds of people in past time and to recognize that, just as changes in people's cognition, perception, and values may bring about changes in their architecture, changes in their housing may shape changes in their world view as well.[76] Unfortunately, the archaeological evidence for All Saints Parish is thin. A few surviving slave houses at Friendfield Village on Hobcaw Barony and some turn-of-the-century photographs are all that remain.[77]

The houses were built by the slaves, although the rice planters organized the process and usually provided the specifications. It is for that reason that most of the slave houses exemplify British house-types. All of the surviving cabins in Friendfield Village are single-story structures, as are all of the slave houses visible in the turn-of-the-century photographs of slave streets at Brookgreen and elsewhere. Early accounts, however, describe two-story slave dwellings as well as one-story cabins. At Hagley, for example, each slave house was said to have an upstairs and separate bedrooms for male and female children. This may have been an example of the southern I house, a very common two-story dwelling two rooms wide and one room deep.[78]

Most of the slave houses in the old photographs appear to be of the British hall-and-parlor type. This rectangular, one-story, gable-roofed house is patterned closely after originals in England and northern Ireland. James R. Sparkman maintained that the slave cabins on his plantation contained "a hall and 2 sleeping compartments"—an apt description of the hall-and-parlor house. Appearances may be deceptive, however. The surviving slave houses at Friendfield Village exemplify the facade, but not the floor plan, of the hall-and-parlor house. The floor plan, on the other hand, is identical to that of the Yoruba two-room houses of Nigeria.[79]

Another common folk house-type in the South was the

double pen, in which a one-room cabin (or single pen) had another room added. Several double-pen cabins are visible in the
old photographs of Waccamaw slave streets, all of them examples of the saddlebag-type, with the additional room added to
the chimney end, resulting in a double-pen cabin with a central
chimney. Double-pen cabins may have sheltered two slave families, in which case their single-room spatial units were the
same as the single-pen houses in spatial orientations. Some visitors, however, clearly described the double-pen house as a
single-family dwelling. Whether or not the double-pens
housed single families, however, the British single-pen house-
type is conceptually equivalent to *half* of a common two-room
Yoruba house. Thus, the floor plan of the double-pen house is
similar to an African proxemic environment. Here, too, one
finds a convergence of African floor plan and British facade.[80]
Nearly all the surviving slave cabins at Friendfield reflect the
convergence of elements of African and of European culture.
Outwardly the cabins were marked by European notions of
symmetry and control, but inwardly they concealed interiors
marked by African spatial orientations. The two-room house
was crucial to the Yoruba architectural tradition, and its continuity in Waccamaw slave cabins was not accidental. That continuity is eloquent testimony that West African architecture
was not forgotten in the crucible of slavery.[81]

James R. Sparkman's claim that the slaves on his plantations lived in houses measuring eighteen by twenty-two feet
hardly seems credible to contemporary scholars of slavery. But
the lively debate over the adequacy of slave housing—based on
unspoken Euro-American assumptions regarding optimum
spatial dimensions—has obscured as much as it has revealed.
By Euro-American standards the amount of living space available to the slaves would seem to compare favorably with that
of the Pilgrims. The average dimensions of extant seventeenth-
century houses in Plymouth, Massachusetts, measured sixteen
by twenty-one feet. On the other hand, by Afro-American
standards, the slave cabins may have been too large, not too
small. Optimal dimensions in African architecture are small—
nine by nine in Benin, eight by eight in Angola, ten by ten gen-

erally. Buildings throughout West Africa feature rooms small enough to facilitate intimacy in social relations. Slaves who came to All Saints Parish from Senegal and Gambia in the north all the way to Angola and the Congo in the south shared a cultural preference for such arrangements. Thus, the relatively small dimensions of slave housing may be taken less as evidence of the physical deprivation of the slaves than as evidence of cultural continuity with Africa. Despite the imposition by the planters of European symmetrical facades and construction techniques, slaves on the rice plantations of the Waccamaw built their houses in compliance with an undisrupted African sensitivity toward optimal dimension.[82]

Seen from a distance, the slave cabins, with their exterior walls darkened by the weather, seemed to create a grim, brooding effect on visitors. New Yorker James Roberts Gilmore wrote of an All Saints slave street as a "little collection of negro huts, which straggled about through the woods for the distance of a third of a mile." While the general drabness of the outside might be partially offset by colorful flowers in the yard, the interiors often seemed as forbidding as the exterior.[83]

The old photographs indicate that the slave houses were covered with shingle roofs. Cypress roofs were the most common. The inside walls were constructed of "hewn or sawed frames, milled weatherboarding, cover'd with best cypress shingles." Slaves of less affluent planters, such as those on Henry Buck's Horry turpentine plantation, lived in log cabins. The spaces between the logs were chinked with clay, which had the disadvantage of letting in too little air in the summer and too much in the winter. Flooring was "raised two feet from the ground" and was "closely jointed." Sometimes "a worn but neat and well-kept carpet partly covered the floor."[84]

The broad front porches of the slave cabins helped to modify the steamy Waccamaw summers by providing both shade for the house and a shady place where one might catch the faintest stirrings of a late afternoon breeze. The absence of such porches in Europe suggests that the African slaves and their descendants may have taught their masters more about tropical architecture than has been generally credited.[85]

The twentieth-century mastery of light and darkness was not part of the life of the slaves. Slave houses on the plantations of such planters as Plowden C. J. Weston and James R. Sparkman had glass-paned windows. Others, however, had fewer windows, shuttered but not glazed. Gilmore, visiting the estate of Henry Buck, commented that "the one window, though destitute of glass, and ornamented with the inevitable board-shutter, had a green moreen curtain, which kept out the wind and the rain." The curtain and shutter could not, of course, keep out the hordes of mosquitoes and other insects in the summer. They could only offer the slaves a choice between heat or fresh air in the winter. Such cabins must have remained relatively dark even in the day, and nightfall only intensified the darkness. Slaves made their own candles, but they were often in short supply. Without the ability to control the darkness to any marked degree, the slaves lived their lives in more or less separate compartments of day and night, light and dark, work and the inability to see.[86]

"We had here reached the negro cabin," wrote a northern visitor to the Waccamaw in 1860. "In all respects it was like the other huts on the plantation. A bright fire lit up its interior." The fireplace provided heat as well as light. One of the major considerations in slave housing was the problem of heating. Despite the semitropical temperatures of coastal Carolina summers, artificial heat was necessary for several months of the year. Slaves on the rice plantations depended on their open fireplaces for keeping warm. "A huge log stayed in the back of the chimney summer and winter," said Julia Small, daughter of one of the slaves at Magill's Oregon. "People would carry fire to and from each other's house." The slaves rarely had matches. A tinder horn "was beat against a rock until it sparked and a piece of rag was lit." It was considered bad luck to let a fire die out in a house. In Julia Peterkin's novel of Afro-American folklife on Sandy Island, *Black April*, the fire in Maum Hannah's cabin had never died out completely since it was first started by her great-grandfather who had been brought from Africa to be a slave. All the fires in the village had come from that same first fire. The fireplace was thus a central structural consideration. The usual building material for fireplaces and chimneys in All Saints Parish was brick or clay; but a composition of clay, sand, and tar was also common. Sparkman said such a composition was "quite equal" to brick "if properly done."[87]

The slaves of wealthy rice planters such as Plowden C. J. Weston and James R. Sparkman may have enjoyed rather better housing than was common in the cotton South. Even on the rice plantations of the Waccamaw, however, the problems of intense heat and humidity in the summer and the few months of severe cold in the winter were only partially ameliorated by the slave cabins. Moreover, the winter chill was often intensified by bitter winds whipping in off the Atlantic a few miles away.[88]

All of the rooms in a slave house might serve as sleeping quarters. Slave carpenters built sturdy bedsteads on some rice plantations. On others boards were simply nailed against the wall to form crude bunks. Slave women made mattresses and stuffed them with rice straw. Blankets were normally distributed every third year in rotation. Slave women often got together at night, after a day's work in the rice fields, to make warm and often beautiful quilts to supplement the supply of blankets. They made quilting an occasion of social interaction as well as an occasion of work, thus helping to ease the burden of bondage. The most common quilt made by the slaves was the patchwork, in which a design was created like a mosaic from numerous patches of cloth. Slave women made both pieced and appliqued quilts. Africans who came to the Waccamaw as slaves brought with them a rich heritage of textile art, including some quilting, but slave women learned many quilting techniques from Euro-American quilting traditions. It does not necessarily follow, however, that all—or even most—of their quilt patterns were derived from the Euro-American tradition. On the contrary, many of their patterns—especially the ubiquitous strip or string quilt—exemplified clear continuities with a widespread West African textile tradition in which the strip was the basic structural and design unit.[89]

A slave's home was the site of all sorts of activities—

cooking, eating, quilting, sewing, prayer meetings, storytelling, dancing, music-making, and sleeping. Each activity had its own physical equipment. Slaves collected crockery and glasses and obtained wood and tinware utensils, sofas, rocking chairs, and carving knives. Talented slave carpenters—such as Renty Tucker, Welcome Beese, Hardtimes Sparkman, Thomas Bonneau, and Richmond, the head carpenter at Woodbourne plantation—made furniture for the houses of the street. Slaves did not accumulate much in the way of personal property, of course, but there does appear to have been a trend toward more diversity in household furnishings during the closing years of slavery.[90]

The main room had to serve as both kitchen and dining room. In most slave cabins a table and some chairs stood in the middle of the main room. Gilmore noted "an old fashioned table, covered with a faded woolen cloth" as the centerpiece of one slave cabin. Other tables ranged from small pine tables to planks set across trestles. On Magill's Oregon plantation the slaves did not have chairs but sat on crude benches made from a single piece of wood with four spokes serving as legs. Basic cooking utensils were concentrated near the fireplace. A New England visitor noted that the slaves of Joshua Ward had utensils of wood and tinware. Utensils for cooking and eating were stored in chests or sideboards, such as the one described by Gilmore: "In the corner near the fire was a curiously contrived sideboard, made from narrow strips of yellow pine, tongued and grooved together, and oiled so as to bring out the beautiful grain of the wood. On it were several broken and cracked glasses, and an array of irregular crockery." Some slave houses were furnished with the cast-off finery of the Big House. "Against the side of the room opposite the door stood an antique, brass-handled bureau," wrote Gilmore. "The rocking chair, in which the old negress passed most of her time, was of mahogany, wadded and covered with chintz, and the armseat I occupied, though old and patched in many places, had evidently moved in good society." By "good society" Gilmore clearly meant "the master's society."[91]

Each of the slave cabins in Friendfield Village featured a

steep roof with a loft entered through a ladder and a hole in the ceiling. The lofts were used for sleeping by the children as well as providing storage space. The lofts not only gave additional space but also facilitated a certain minimum of privacy.[92]

With an enhanced appreciation of the relationship between cleanliness and health, due to considerable attention to that subject in the agricultural journals, planters increasingly required regular cleaning and inspection of the slave houses. James R. Sparkman set aside three days annually at Mt. Arena for a thorough cleaning of the houses on the street—in May, in October or November, and just after Christmas. Joshua Ward required all of the houses on the Brookgreen street to be scoured each Saturday, with houses and cooking and eating utensils inspected for cleanliness.[93]

The rice planters of the Waccamaw, while making efforts to improve the quality of housing on their plantations, boasted that their slaves, unlike most of the world's peoples, lived under decent conditions. Heriot wrote to his Scottish cousin his belief that "there is no class of people, as far as I have seen in this country, or Europe, of the same grade, where there is so much real happiness, where the wants of nature are so abundantly supplied, where the requirements of labour are as little, and where the guaranty against poverty and distress from all the conditions of existence is so great. . . . [T]he greatest evil that I could inflict upon them would, if in my power, be to put them just in the condition that I saw the labourers upon the Castle Mains farm [in Scotland] under Mr. Todd—not very distant from you."[94] Judged by modern standards slave housing exemplified something less than decent conditions. But other, more contemporaneous perspectives may be illuminating. The slave streets of All Saints Parish were clearly superior to the grim and ugly slave barracks of Cuba or to the thatched huts of sticks and cane trash in which slaves were housed in Barbados and Jamaica. And the housing of rice plantation slaves compared favorably not only with that of other slaves but also with that of poor whites in the South and free workers in the North. Furthermore, houses on the slave streets of the

Waccamaw were often better than the "wretched hovels" in which whole families "slept upon straw or upon the bare ground" in Ireland. Heriot's moral narcissism, as he boasted of the "happiness" of his slaves compared to the "poverty and distress" of most of the world's workers and peasants, may seem particularly hypocritical by modern standards. The opulence of the Big House only accentuates the shabbiness of the slave quarters. But judged by the standards of his day, not ours, Heriot was neither liar nor hypocrite, nor was he inhumane. His slaves did enjoy better material conditions than most of the world's working class.[95] See Table 9 for the distribution of slave housing on the plantations in All Saints Parish.

If the slave houses served the masters as a symbol of their own kindness and of the vaunted superiority of their labor sys-

Table 9.
Distribution of Slave Housing in All Saints Parish,
by Slaveowner, 1860

Slaveowner	Number of Slaves	Number of Slave Houses	Average Number of Slaves per House
William Algernon Alston, Jr.	567	90	6.3
Charles Alston, Jr.	290	90	3.2
John LaBruce	150	35	4.3
John Izard Middleton	201	21	9.6
Plowden C. J. Weston	334	80	4.2
Benjamin F. Dunkin	135	30	4.5
Estate of Robert Nesbit	160	31	5.2
William Allan Allston	151	30	5.0
Joseph Blyth Allston	184	28	6.6
Estate of John Hyrne Tucker	188	20	9.4
Martha Allston Pyatt	215	40	5.4
William Heyward Trapier	90	——	——
Estate of Joshua J. Ward	1,121	194	5.8
Daniel W. Jordan	261	69	3.8
John D. Magill	189	——	——

SOURCE: 1860 Census, Slave Population Schedules.

tem, it must be noted that the houses provided the slaves with something more than merely a place to eat and sleep. In several significant ways they helped to support and sustain the slaves' sense of family. Analysis of the slave population schedules of the 1860 census indicates that on the average a single family occupied a plantation slave dwelling. According to plantation records, travelers' accounts, and oral tradition among the descendants of the slaves, the typical pattern on the Waccamaw was for the slaves to live in family units, each family having a house of its own.[96]

The foregoing details of household arrangement are perhaps insignificant in themselves, but they possess profound implications not only for the comprehension of the slave family but also for some of the more intangible aspects of slave culture. The slave cabins did not lend themselves to much privacy, but out of the context of a small-scale spatial environment not unlike that of the African homes of their ancestors the slaves developed patterns of behavior that included various gestures of touching—the hand on the shoulder, the slapping of the thigh, the ritualized handshake—all of which denoted identity as members of a cultural community.[97]

Perhaps even more significant was that when the slave family was together in its home, gathered around the fireplace, the master and his power were shut out for the moment. Around that fireplace the young slave learned a language, heard stories of how Buh Rabbit outsmarted Buh Bear and of how the slave John outsmarted Ole Maussa, watched the grownups cook and quilt and dance to the music of fiddle and banjo, observed the spirited weekly prayer meetings, and prayed quietly in the family bosom. In short, it was largely around that fireside that the young slave acquired a rich creolized culture. The cabin may have been dark and stuffy, prone to drafts in the winter and insects in the summer, but its importance is nevertheless underscored by Hagar Brown's invocation: "God bless the house and keep the soul."[98]

Ben Horry, born in slavery on Brookgreen plantation, was a principal informant of Genevieve Willcox Chandler's ex-slave interviews. Photograph by Bayard Wooten, courtesy of Brookgreen Gardens.

Hagar Brown spent her childhood as a slave on The Oaks plantation. She was a major informant for Genevieve Chandler's ex-slave interviews. Photograph by Bayard Wooten, courtesy of Brookgreen Gardens.

Born a slave of All Saints planter Benjamin F. Dunkin, Mariah Heywood was given as a wedding present upon the marriage of his daughter, Washington Dunkin, to Charles Alston. Her memories of slavery times were an important addition to Genevieve Chandler's ex-slave interviews. Photograph by Bayard Wooten, courtesy of South Caroliniana Library.

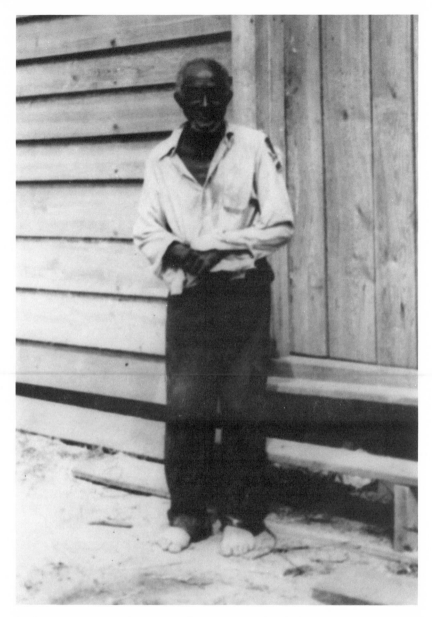

Welcome Beese was born into slavery on Oatland plantation. At 104, he was the oldest living ex-slave in All Saints Parish at the time of Genevieve Chandler's interviews. Photograph by Bayard Wooten, courtesy of South Caroliniana Library.

Stella Horry sits on the porch of her cabin, where she and her husband, Ben, were interviewed by Genevieve Chandler.

The summer home of Plowden C. J. Weston, a prominent All Saints rice planter, was built by the talented slave carpenter Renty Tucker. It is still in use in the 1980s as the Pelican Inn. Photograph by Bill Edmonds.

The slave street at Friendfield plantation. From a lantern slide, circa 1905; courtesy, Belle W. Baruch Foundation.

The slave street at Brookgreen plantation. Drawing by the author from a photograph, circa 1900, in the William D. Morgan Photograph Collection, Georgetown County Public Library.

CHAPTER FOUR

"Off Times"

It was not the days of drudgery in the rice fields but the hours of off time that most shaped the contours of slave culture. This natural process of cultural formation is the heart and soul of slave folklife: for people not only work, but they also pray and frolic, hunt and fish, cook and clean, court and marry, bear and raise children, love and hope and dream. Surrounded by such needs and seizing every opportunity for negotiation, the slaves resolved to claim as much time for themselves as possible. So powerful was the force of tradition that planters granted privileges with caution for fear of their becoming customary expectations; but increasingly the slaves asserted claims to off times and holidays, in which the masters reluctantly acquiesced. Plowden C. J. Weston, for example, guaranteed the time due slaves to use for their own purposes by specifying in his overseer's contract:

> No work of any sort or kind is to be permitted to be done by negroes on Good Friday, or Christmas day, or on any Sunday, except going for a Doctor, or nursing sick persons; any work of this kind done on any of these days is to be reported to the Proprietor, who will pay for it. The two days following Christmas day; the first Saturdays after finishing threshing, planting, hoeing, and harvest, are also to be holidays, on which the people may work for themselves. Only half task is to be done on every Saturday, except during planting and harvest, and [except by] those who have misbehaved or been lying up during the week.[1]

These off times and the cultural developments they fostered may be examined in the daily, weekly, annual, and life cycles of the slaves and in the spatial arenas in which they took place: in the slave quarters, in the Big House area, in the plantation chapels, carpentry shops, barnyards and provision grounds, in the fields and forests, and on the rivers and seashore. That off times were set apart from workday activities gave them special meaning and alerted special expectations.[2]

The time provided by such guarantees as Weston's was not *leisure* time, in the usual sense, but part of the moral economy of the plantation: time, as Weston noted, when "the people may work for themselves." The slaves used the time, in part, for the transmission of cultural patterns from generation to generation; but off times fostered creativity as well as continuity. Not only did the slaves retain and share features of their diverse African cultures, but they also used their off times to forge new folkways out of varying traditions and uncertain circumstances. How they did so provides insight into many other aspects of slave folklife, for all aspects were linked in such a way that understanding one helps comprehend others.[3]

Even while toiling in the rice fields, slaves found that they could lighten the burden of labor through their social relations. An Englishman who visited the Waccamaw in 1856 was only partly misled by his walk through the plantation, where he observed "all the papas and mamas of these little urchins at work, the former taking it uncommonly easy, and the latter perpetually giggling over jokes known to themselves, and very ready to shake hands upon all occasions, and afterwards to titter and blush unseen." The boat crews on the Waccamaw socialized by singing as they worked. Once they rowed guests home from a plantation wedding as far as twenty miles up the Waccamaw, keeping time to their rowing as they improvised songs in honor of the bride and groom. And Sabe Rutledge recalled in the 1930s how he and his brothers and sisters had worked until ten o'clock at night in their cabin during the winters by the light of the fireplace. "How come I know all these Buh Rabbit story, Mudder spin you know," he said. "Mudder and Father tell you story to keep you eye open."[4]

2

Daily off time began when the individually assigned daily tasks were completed, for within the task system there was no uniform quitting time: when slaves finished their tasks, they were through for the day. Weston calculated tasks at nine hours for "the meanest full hand." On his plantations it may be assumed that most slaves finished their tasks more quickly, but probably not much more quickly. Weston's brother-in-law reported that the task work began at sunrise and was usually finished by three. On other plantations the tasks may have been longer. In view of Weston's reputation in oral tradition as a very generous master, it is unlikely that they were shorter, although a New England woman who visited Midway plantation in 1851 described the slaves' tasks as "only half day ones if they are ambitious."[5]

The slaves' daily off time promoted a protopeasant internal economy on the rice plantations of the Waccamaw. After tasks were completed, All Saints slaves cultivated their own provision grounds and raised livestock for themselves and for sale. Such economic activity was a striking example of the moral economy of the rice plantations. Weston "gave a piece of land to each person for cultivation of rice; 1 acre among five. The people all followed us and each received *his or her own*, so there should be no mistakes." If the slaves did not literally own their land, but held it at their masters' pleasure, they did own livestock in actuality and sold it to their masters and others. Wyndham Malet, Weston's brother-in-law, reported that all of Weston's slaves had pigs, poultry, and cows. James R. Sparkman purchased eggs, chickens, hogs, and the like from his slaves at Mt. Arena. Sparkman contended that with "reasonable industry and ordinary providence," his slaves could "add materially to their comforts and indulgencies." Robert F. W. Allston purchased hogs from his slaves. Other masters purchased hogs, chickens, cows and calves, eggs, cord wood, rice, and pumpkins from their slaves. Purchase of rice or other supplies from slaves was contrary to South Carolina law—as the All Saints planters surely knew, since they included in their ranks a governor, two lieutenant-governors, numerous legislators, and the chancellor of the South Carolina Court of Equity—but the planters perceived such social relations to be positive incentives to the slaves. The law obviously was not enforced, and the ownership and sale of livestock remained part of the body of rights asserted successfully by the slaves, even in the face of specific legislation to the contrary.[6]

Daily off time lent itself equally well to crime or to worship. Some slaves used their evenings for illegal economic activities. For instance, Define Horry, trusted driver on Joshua Ward's estate, slipped into the swamp at night to thresh stolen rice on a hand-made mortar and pestle in order to earn extra money in a kind of underground economy. But other slaves spent their evenings in the service of the Lord. Many slaves held family devotions or went to one another's houses for worship. Numerous slaves gathered at such praise meetings to sing spirituals, to pray, and to shout.[7] (So central was the role of religion in slave folklife that it will be treated in some detail in chapter five.)

Slaves on the Waccamaw rice plantations who could perform two tasks in a single day were entitled to a full day off the following day. Masters encouraged the earning of holidays because they had learned that such conspicuously positive incentives were more successful in motivating their slaves to work than negative incentives. Slaves who earned the two-task holiday often used the time for fishing and clamming. J. Motte Alston reported that "the said hand would usually go to the seashore and lay in a supply of fish and clams. Large numbers of mullet were caught at night in cast nets, and sacks full brought home." The slaves also gathered oysters in the creek.[8]

3

Saturday afternoons and Sundays were part of the weekly cycle of off times. Half-tasks were given on Saturdays to allow slaves time for themselves, and they used the time for washing and cleaning, for working in their own gardens and tending their own livestock, for visiting friends on neighboring plantations, and for hunting and fishing.[9]

Saturday nights were sometimes given over to dances and social get-togethers. Talented slaves such as Prince, the head coachman at Hagley, would entertain the slave community with banjo and fiddle music while the slaves danced away at least some of their cares. Malet described Prince as "a capital fiddler" who often played his fiddle to the accompaniment of a banjo or tambourine. Daniel and Summer Horry of Brookgreen plantation were also highly regarded musicians who played for the master's entertainment as well as for dances in the slave community. "You can put it down that they were Colonel [Joshua] Ward's musicianer," their nephew, Ben Horry, told interviewer Genevieve Chandler. "Play a fiddle, beat drum, blow fife. . . . Great fiddlers, drummers." The universality of the fiddle among the slaves was attested by Malet: "Never a company of negroes, but someone plays a fiddle."[10]

A northern visitor condescendingly described one such musical gathering on an All Saints plantation:

> Marc Antony was rattling away at the bones, Nero fiddling as if Rome were burning, and Hannibal clawing at a banjo as if the fate of Carthage hung on its strings. Napoleon . . . was moving his legs even faster than in the Russian retreat; and Wesley was using his heels in a way that showed *they* didn't belong to the Methodist church. . . . about twenty "gentleman and lady" darkies joined, two at a time, in a half "walk-round" half breakdown. . . . Such uproarious jollity, such full and perfect enjoyment, I had never seen in humanity, black or white.

Here is a case in which an observer from outside the culture, and an obtuse and racist one at that, nevertheless provides rare, firsthand evidence of an important function served by slave music and dance—temporary release from the soul-crushing burdens of bondage. He also describes the socialization process by which the young were initiated into the cultural patterns of the slave community: "The little nigs, only four or five years old, would rush into the ring and shuffle away at the breakdowns till I feared their short legs would come off; while all the darkies joined in the songs, till the branches of the old pines above shook as if they too had caught the spirit of the music."[11]

The All Saints slaves also sang—their secular songs as well as their spirituals remaining quite close to West African singing style, their words making incisive comments on the world of the rice plantations. The African-born slave Scipio was quite popular among other All Saints slaves for his singing of such songs as

> Come listen, all you darkies, come listen to my song,
> It am about ole Massa, who use me bery wrong:
> In de cole, frosty mornin', it ain't so bery nice,
> Wid de water to de middle to hoe among de rice.[12]

Not all of the slave songs were intended for the ears of the masters.

On weekends slaves who were able to obtain passes, or tickets, could visit friends or relatives or go courting on other plantations in the parish. Tickets were given as rewards for good behavior, although practice in this matter varied from plantation to plantation. Weston instructed his overseers that "no one is to be absent from the place without a ticket, which is always to be given to such as ask it, and have behaved well." Slaves visiting other plantations were to bring their tickets back signed by the overseer; slaves visiting Weston's plantation were required to show their tickets to the overseer, who signed them. Some slaves visited other plantations without benefit of a ticket; but they ran the risk of being caught by the overseer, when he checked the cabins from time to time at night, or by the slave patrols. Ben Horry recollected, "Got to have paper. Got to carry you paper. Dem patroller put you cross a log! Beat you to death." One of the principal enjoyments of visiting, with or without tickets, was courting. Ben Horry remembered, "Very FUSS girl—FUSS one I go with name was Teena. . . . Go there every Sunday after school. Oatland plantation—belong to Marse Benjamin Allston. Stay till sunset."[13]

Such visiting patterns created a network of associations—a slave community—larger than any given plantation community. This slave community was bound by numerous ties of kin, friendships, culture, and sometimes associations kept secret from the masters. Scipio, who had hired out as a coachman to James Roberts Gilmore, a northern visitor to All Saints Parish, eavesdropped on a conversation regarding South Carolina's impending secession among Gilmore, Henry Buck, and Robert F. W. Allston. He told the northerner after they had left Woodbourne, Buck's rice plantation, that he had stayed up all night "wid some ob de cullud folks" discussing secession and the likelihood "dat if day gwo to war de brack man will be FREE!" Gilmore feared the other slaves would tell on Scipio and get him in trouble. "Tell!" Scipio exclaimed. "Lord bless you, massa, *de bracks am all free-masons*; dat are old man and woman wud die 'fore dey'd tell." [14]

Sunday was a special day on the plantations, the only full day of off time in the weekly cycle. Some masters, such as Plowden C. J. Weston, allowed no work at all to be done on Sunday, so Sunday food had to be cooked on Saturday. Other Waccamaw plantation owners also designated Sunday as a day of rest. On most of them each family cooked for itself. Most slaves attended church, typically in the afternoon or evening. Most masters expected, and some masters compelled, their slaves to attend services. But other slaves used Sunday to hunt and fish. William Oliver recalled nearly three-quarters of a century later, "Game was all over the woods. Everybody could hunt everybody land those days. Hunting was free." Fishing, too, was good—fresh water as well as salt water. "Could get pike out the lakes. Go fishing Sabbath. That was day off." [15]

On some plantations Sunday was the day when rations and provisions were distributed. Whether or not Sunday was provisioning day, however, on many plantations the slaves gathered at the Big House on Sunday morning. Ben Horry recalled that at Brookgreen and Springfield each Sunday "every gal and the young one must dress up and go to the yard and Miss Bessie give 'em candy. . . . Glad to see young women dance." Another reason they gathered at the Big House was "For Marse Josh to see how the clothes fit. And him and Miss Bess make us run races to see who run the fastest. That the happiest time I members when I wuz a boy to Brookgreen." On the plantations of Robert F. W. Allston, Sunday afternoons meant a ritual of catechism and cake for some slaves. [16]

4

In the annual cycle of off times no holiday was more important than Christmas, when three days were allotted for celebration. On many plantations the slaves gathered early on Christmas morning at the Big House to receive portions of rum or whiskey and tobacco, extra rations, and small gifts. John Pierpont, a northerner serving as a tutor at Clifton plantation, described his first Christmas in All Saints Parish: "On my first waking, the sound of serenading violins & drums saluted my ears, and for some time continued. . . . During almost the whole of the second and third afternoons, the portico was crowded with these dancers . . . fiddlers & drumming. . . . Some of them who were native Africans did not join the dance with the others, but, by themselves gave us a specimen of the sports & amusement with which the benighted and uncivilized children of nature divert themselves." [17]

Among the plantation Christmas customs was that of caroling on Christmas morning. A nothern visitor to Georgetown District described being awakened on Christmas morning by the "chanting of a Christmas hymn" below his window.

> I arose, and looking cautiously from the corner of the lattice, that I might not be discovered, found that a group of little negro girls, dressed in their favorite colors of green and white, were rendering their morning salutations to the various members of the family. The words of the hymn ran nearly thus:
>
>> Brightly does the morning break
>> In the eastern sky; awake!
>> Cradled on his bed of hay
>> Jesus Christ was born today.
>> Let a merry Christmas be,
>> Massa, both to me and thee!
>
> This was sung, with a slight variation, two or three times; and then whispering together for a moment, the blithe party scampered off to another chamber to repeat the same ceremony. I learned afterward . . . that this was an old custom on the plantation.[18]

Christmas, which lasted three days (December 25–27) on the Weston plantations, is described in some detail in the diary of Emily Weston and in the memoirs of her English housekeeper, Elizabeth Collins. On December 22 Mrs. Weston visited the cabins, giving out sugar to the children. On December 23 she noted in her diary that her husband was getting things ready. On Saturday, December 24, she entered in her diary the following: "Dined early and P[lowden] then gave out Xmas to the whole of men, women, and children, which took 2½ hours. Hector looked over the meat, Prince the salt, Caesar the rice, Jimmy and Jack the molasses, and Frank the tobacco." Christmas day many of the Weston slaves, including some of the house servants, had tickets to visit other plantations and to stay overnight. On December 26 Mrs. Weston visited the street and gave out gingerbread to the children. A number of other slaves had tickets to visit friends. On December 27 there were four weddings. Wednesday, December 28, was the last day of Christmas, since Christmas day was on a Sunday, which was a holiday anyway. She sent over apples and gingerbread to the carpenters' shop, where "a great deal of dancing" was going on. Again she visited the street and gave out gingerbread to the children. The Westons' English housekeeper described the slaves as having "a jolly time" at Christmas, enjoying themselves "with singing and dancing, both of which the negro can do well." House servants received the same holidays as the field hands, but had to "take turns, so as not to interfere with the comforts of the family." Among the culinary delicacies enjoyed by the slaves during Christmas were "a ham, turkey, goose, plum pudding, gingerbread, apples, oranges, etc."[19]

On the lowcountry plantations house servants made a game of saying "Merry Christmas!" or "Christmas gift!" before a member of the master's family did, followed by "I ketch yu!" if successful. Upon being caught the member of the master's family was expected to produce a gift, whereupon the slave would reciprocate with two, three, six, or a dozen eggs wrapped in a handkerchief. On the plantations of Robert F. W. Allston dancing commenced on the piazza before the Allston family finished breakfast, with fiddles, triangles, and bones beating the rhythms until ten in the evening, with the pattern repeated for three days. On Christmas night the master and one of his slaves set off elaborate fireworks for the entertainment of black and white alike.[20]

Some Christmases were more elaborate than others. On Christmas morning of 1856, the year Robert F. W. Allston was elected governor of South Carolina, there was a particularly joyous celebration on his plantations (as previously discussed). Allston himself did not arrive home until the evening before Christmas, and the festivities did not begin until Christmas day. Adult slaves were issued a ration of whiskey and drank toasts to the new governor.[21] If Christmas 1856 was more elaborate than usual for the Allston slaves, Christmases during the Civil War, when the patterns of plantation life were interrupted in a thousand ways, were marked by fewer material resources for everyone. Collins noted in 1861, "Christmas passed without any enjoyment for the negroes, but fortunately a few figs and currants were saved for their Christmas pudding, and with the exception of apples and gingerbread, their suppers passed off with great satisfaction."[22]

On the plantations of James R. Sparkman, including Mt. Arena on Sandy Island, Christmas day was marked by the inspection of all plantation tools. Sparkman noted in 1858 that tool inspection had taken place each Christmas day since 1844. An extra ration of rice, peas, molasses, and meat, equivalent to a week's ration, was given to "all who are not defaulters in showing their working utensils and who have not been guilty of any *greivous* offense during the year." Each woman received a handkerchief with her ration; each man a woolen cap. One of the three days of Christmas holidays on the Sparkman estates was to be given over to cleaning the cabins.[23]

5

Christmas was a popular time for slave weddings, one of the most important rites of passage in the life cycle. The purpose of the rituals accompanying birth, marriage, and death was to cushion the disturbing transition from one status to another, which could not be accomplished without social and individual adjustment. Such rites of passage were occasions for off times on the rice plantations of the Waccamaw. At Hagley, for instance, the bride and groom were allowed a holiday of three days. There were four weddings on the Weston estate during Christmas 1859 and seven weddings on the R. F. W. Allston estate during Christmas 1858. Christmas was also a popular time for young slave couples to become engaged, with weddings being postponed until spring.[24]

Despite the fact that slave marriages were not recognized by South Carolina law, the All Saints planters usually had them solemnized by clergy. The planters were eager to promote viable slave families for a variety of reasons. First, as Christians they believed wedlock sanctioned by Scripture and considered cohabitation outside wedlock to be living in sin. Second, as practical administrators of large plantations with hundreds of slaves they regarded the family relationship as the key to a stable social order. In promoting for each slave a stake in the social order through marriage, they discouraged runaways far more effectively than the threat—and example—of dire punishment could. By encouraging stable slave families, moreover, they also encouraged the natural increase of the slave population. Thus, for reasons both sincerely altruistic and at the same time self-serving, the rice planters of the Waccamaw actively promoted slave marriage.[25]

The strength of the slave family rested upon a firmer foundation, however, than the masters' promotion. The slaves' creative response to the masters' notions of family was mediated by the cultural grammar of African familial traditions. If the slave family served the master as a mechanism for imposing social control, it served the slaves as a mode of structuring sexual and kinship relations and the rearing of children, and as a focus for psychological loyalty and devotion. It was in the bosom of the family that the young slave acquired much of his cultural heritage, and it was through the medium of the family that the individual slave was related to the larger slave community.[26]

Slave weddings, whether celebrated at Christmas or at some other time of the year, represented a focused gathering in which both blacks and whites on the rice plantations were engrossed in a common flow of activity. The weddings of slaves were occasions of great celebration. At Hagley they were said to be "kept with good cheer; wedding cards were sent out to all their friends; the master gives them cake, turkeys, hams, molasses, coffee, &c." Louisa Brown remembered hearing her parents describe their wedding feast: "Hot supper, cake, wine, and all. Kill cow, hog, chicken, and all. That time when you marry, so much to eat." The white owners joined the other celebrants in wishing health and happiness to the bride and groom. Ceremonies were performed in the yard of the Big House, and the wedding cakes were often baked in the master's kitchen.[27]

Slave funerals were as elaborate a part of the slave life cycle in All Saints Parish as weddings. Such African continuities as leaving pieces of crockery on the grave were strongly evident in such rituals; and, in accordance with old African custom, they were marked by considerable pageantry and display. For blacks on the Waccamaw—as in Africa and elsewhere in the New World—funerals were the real climax of life, the time when one was reunited with one's ancestors. The slaves emphasized the necessity of an appropriate funeral to prevent the spirits of the ancestors from returning—possibly in malevolent form. As one ex-slave recalled, "Us doan want 'e sperrit lebe behin." This emphasis represented a direct link of continuity with West African funereal tradition. When "Old Charles"—the superannuated driver on the plantations of Francis Marion Weston—died, the planter's daughter-in-law wrote a brief account of the funeral in her diary: "A rainy morning, but cleared somewhat about 10. Mr. Quimby came to lead the burial service, Mr. Lance & Mr. Rosa also came & we were a large party at the grave, all the Guendalos folk here and at Laurel-Hill being present, and most of the Hagley people. Mr. Quimby asked me to raise the hymn." Quimby and Lance were white ministers, and Rosa was ordained as a lay minister. It is difficult to determine whether the presence of white ministers was typical. Generally the slaves seemed to have preferred their own preachers, but certainly the presence of white ministers at slave funerals was not uncommon in All Saints Parish.[28]

Hagar Brown recalled that when her mother was dying she had said, "'I gone leave. I gone leave here now! . . . When I gone I ax the Master when he take me, to send drop o' rain to let true believer know I gone to Glory!'" And when they lifted the body to take it to the church, "Rain, 'Tit! 'Tit! 'Tit! on the house! At the gate, moon shine out!" The processions to and from the burial ground as well as the graveside services were marked by music, mournful dirges on the way to the burying ground, happier music on the return. Many funerals were held at night, as much because of the slaves' preference as the masters'. "Especially emotional their funeral gatherings," noted one master who had witnessed them, "and when conducted by torchlight the whole ceremony seems to be a mimicry of the savage war dance."[29]

6

The off times of Waccamaw slaves can also be studied in the spatial arenas in which they took place. One such arena was the home, in which such activities as family devotions, various home tasks, storytelling, praise meetings, and singings (which met weekly in various homes) occurred. The slave quarters— generally referred to as the street—constituted another arena. Here were held the parties and frolics, with dancing, singing, and instrumental music. Singing-dancing parties were also held on Christmas in the carpenters' shop at Weston's plantations and on the piazza of Allston's Big House.

These were but two examples of the kinds of activities associated with off times, especially in the Big House area. Weddings usually took place in the yard of the Big House, as did Sunday morning gatherings and races. Elsewhere, on the immense tracts of woodland that were part of every All Saints plantation, hunting and fishing were pursued. In addition, fishing and crabbing were activities of the river and the seashore.

Funerals were usually held in the plantation chapel, with burial at a designated burial ground on the plantation. Off-
plantation activities involved visiting and courting, among
others, all governed by a ticket system.

Several genres of expressive culture can be discerned
within these off-time activities. Music and song seem to have
been involved with virtually every temporal and spatial context, while dance, necessarily involving more social interaction, seems to have been more pronounced on weekends and
holidays. Storytelling was rather heavily oriented toward home
and family, although not exclusively so. Games and pastimes
could be solitary or social. Hunting and fishing were often solitary, but were sometimes social. Foot races and the like were of
necessity social.[30]

Through these genres of expressive behavior, and their
performance of these genres in the temporal, spatial, and social contexts considered appropriate within their shared cultural grammar, the slaves responded to the demands—and the
few opportunities—of the environment of slavery in such a
way as to protect themselves and their children from the worst
ravages of life in bondage. At least two of the genres of the
slaves' expressive behavior, their religion and their folktales,
are so significant to the study of slave folklife that they are
treated in separate chapters.

CHAPTER FIVE

"Come by Here, Lord"

Visitors to the Waccamaw rice plantations were struck by the religious fervor of the slave community—the slaves' active participation in church services, their ecstatic prayers and energetic shouts, and especially their spirituals. Of the origins and beliefs of that religion, as well as its meaning to the slaves, most of the visitors knew nothing. They never reflected that they were witnessing a remarkable cultural transformation: from a diversity of African beliefs and a multiplicity of African rites and practices to a distinctive Afro-Christianity that voiced the slaves' deepest ancestral values as they responded to a new and constricting environment. The All Saints slaves, uprooted from a culture in which religion applied to all aspects of life, were objects of intensive proselytizing efforts on the part of their masters. They did not so much adapt to Christianity (at least not to the selective Christianity evangelized to them by their masters) as adapt Christianity to themselves. Just as the masters converted Christianity to their own culture, so the slaves converted Christianity to theirs. It was not God the judge of behavior—God the master or overseer—who was the object of worship in Afro-Christianity, but a God more like African deities: God the transcendant spirit. They worshipped this new Christian deity in traditional African ways, and they made European religious forms serve African religious functions. Christianity did, as the masters hoped, promote both a certain amount of slave forbearance and a faith that those who suffered most on earth would be rewarded in heaven. But Afro-Christianity also demonstrated that the slaves were as concerned with freedom in this world as with salvation in the next.[1]

Slave religion on the Waccamaw may be examined as a

process of cultural interaction between acquired Christianity and inherited African religious traditions. It is important to draw a distinction between the religious instruction of the slaves and the religious behavior of the slaves, although the two are by no means unrelated. The masters' attempts to indoctrinate the slaves with the tenets of Protestant Christianity, especially those which would promote their contentment with present conditions, met with considerable success. But African religious beliefs and practices continued to flourish in All Saints Parish in three distinct streams. One stream, which included such practices as ecstatic trances and spirit possession as a part of religious services, merged with Christianity, giving the slaves' religion a distinctive cast. Another stream, which included belief in hags and witches as well as certain malign spirits, continued to exist among slave Christians as a sort of parallel consciousness, neither part of their Christianity nor completely outside it. Yet another stream, which included conjuration and sorcery, flourished as an underground alternative religious system in ways that ran quite counter to the doctrines of Christianity. What had been a unified religious outlook in Africa, in which virtually all experience was religious, had become fragmented and diversified in the new environment.[2]

That unified religious outlook had served important needs in Africa, and those needs continued to exist on the plantations of the New World. Belief in occult phenomena and efforts to manipulate them were not merely irrational and eccentric but also were a natural manifestation of a human world view in pre-industrial societies. In a world at the mercy of harvest and weather, of disaster and disease, lacking technology and education, acceptance of magic and conjuration as a means of attempting to control natural forces was understandable. Such an outlook among Africans and their descendants in the New World was considered primitive and superstitious; but it was part of the mentality of Europe as well, where not that long before belief in ghosts and fairies was more common than belief in Christianity and where witches and astrologers were more influential than priests. If Africans brought with them to All Saints Parish beliefs that the spirits of the ancestors regulated life in this world, Europeans brought with them beliefs in omens and witchcraft; both learned and common folk attempted to regulate their lives with signs, charms, and exorcisms.[3]

Enslaved Africans in the South Carolina lowcountry continued what an observer called "a strong attachment to their native country, and to those friends and relations with whom they spent the early years of life." Afro-American slaves maintained African ethnic distinctions on All Saints rice plantations well into the mid-nineteenth century; and they may have stolen away in the evenings to join with slaves of the same ethnic group from neighboring plantations to celebrate their African religions away from the masters' prying and unbelieving eyes. It would be absurd to minimize the African component in slave religion; however, one must not forget that enslaved Africans in the South Carolina lowcountry came from widely separated areas of Africa. To stress their cultural similarities too much is inevitably to oversimplify. West African religions comprised a deeply complex reality, with diverse religious expression. But a theological affinity among African ethnic groups transcended differences in rites and practices and reflected a common bond, an overall spirit, which stressed the African's mystical relationship to God and the supernatural, as well as the role of the shaman—magician, sorcerer, or conjuror—in the social order. Moreover, the very diversity of African religious practices promoted an acceptance of cultural differences and an openness to cultural interaction. Even large and widespread ethnic groups, such as the Bantu, showed a tendency toward cultural fusion as a basic cultural characteristic. Such tendencies gave African cultural grammars an integral dynamism, an expectation of culture change as a fundamental trait. It is not surprising, then, that Afro-American continuities with African religion are found not so much in static and archaic retentions, but in distinctive modes of expression that were the product of the slaves' creative response to a new environment in which they had to adapt to both Christianity and slavery.[4]

2

The decline and breakup of a unified African religion into separate fragments were especially marked among the slaves of All
Saints Parish. While other streams of African religion either
converged or co-existed with Christianity, belief in magical
shamanism—called voodoo or hoodoo in the New World—
continued an underground existence outside of and hostile to
the Christian tradition. Conjuration was, of course, practiced
in secret, and documentation is inevitably scanty. Discussion of
this aspect of slave religion is, therefore, necessarily more tentative and more speculative than one would wish. The role of
slave conjuration in All Saints Parish remains both largely unknown and at least partly unknowable. Nevertheless, there is
sufficient evidence to assert with confidence the continuity of
an underground stream of magical shamanism throughout the
slavery period and beyond. James R. Sparkman, the master of
Mt. Arena, was astounded to learn that "on one plantation,
where more than ordinary attention had been given to their religious training, there was an open relapse into Feticism or
Voodooism" following emancipation. Appalled by having
"been brought into personal contact with the devil" and having found themselves "powerless," the planters had to invoke
"military interference," according to Sparkman, "before the
outbreak could be contained."[5]

Voodoo—or hoodoo—involved rituals whereby sorcerers
called up the spirits of the dead to offer advice or to perform
cures. The process of dying, according to West African belief,
was not complete for up to five years. The spirits of the ancestors, the living dead, were the closest links between the world
of the living and the world of the spirits, because they were
beings who straddled both worlds. Since illness was regarded
as supernatural in origin, it was necessary—through sorcery—
to call up the spirits for protection. Magical shamanism could
be used for either protective or malevolent purposes: it could
cure an illness, kill an enemy, or secure someone's love. All
misfortune was regarded as the result of sorcery—including,

presumably, slavery. One's only protection was stronger magic. Such were the similarities in Afro-American occultism; with considerable variation it existed throughout the slave societies of the New World.[6]

The perpetuation of hoodoo seems to have been most pronounced in areas where slaves were concentrated in large numbers. It arose with the arrival of slaves from the Caribbean or directly from Africa who adapted African snake cults to a new environment. The African connection in hoodoo was unmistakable. High in the pantheon of African deities, the snake god of so many African cultures—the Ewe, Fon, Bantu, Dahomey, Whydah, and Yoruba—symbolized the cosmic energy of nature, the arbiter of fortune and misfortune. His protective power could be invoked only by his sorcerers. Initiation rites featured snakeskins, and snake-charming was sometimes used in hoodoo. All sorts of supernatural powers were attributed to serpents in the snakelore of All Saints Parish, from little green snakes that made spring water cool and sweet to garter snakes that could break themselves into joints and put themselves back together again to coach-whips that could catch their tails in their mouths and roll like a hoop in pursuit of their victims. A coach-whip killed by wrapping its body around a victim, tying him to a tree, and whipping him to death with its tail. Snakes on the Waccamaw were said to eat eggs out of hen nests and to suck cows dry. If one attempted to kill snakes, they did not die until the sun went down. And they could multiply themselves virtually at will: an ex-slave recalled that someone had come upon "a whoppin' big rattler quiled [coiled] by a old dead, live-oak harricane. When that snake found somebody messin' 'round, she made a kind of strange noise and opened her mouth and that man counted eighteen little ten inch rattlers that run right in that Mammy snake's mouth." The only cure for snakebite was a black chicken, "fer tie on ter dreen out de pizen ef dem rattler pop yuh on yuh laig" (to tie on to drain out the poison if those rattlers pop you on your leg). At no time did voodoo—or hoodoo—on the Waccamaw rice plantations approach the level or internal organization of Haitian

Vodun, but it does appear to have achieved a distinctive character that raised it to a level beyond simple, unorganized conjuring.[7]

All Saints slaves did not always go to their masters when they were troubled by physical or personal problems. Many of them took such complaints to local conjurers, the plantation priests or medicine men of the old religion. Such conjurers often enjoyed considerable influence and power among the slave community, even among some of the Christians. They gained and exercised their powers over the slaves in diverse ways and by various methods, but always by fear and awe. They were relied upon by their patrons both for protection or relief from spells and for laying spells upon their enemies. The conjurers were often marked not merely by an unusual mentality but also by some physical peculiarity that set them apart from other slaves, a peculiarity that typically suggested a relationship with the world of the spirits. One such All Saints conjurer, Obie Hines, was said to "look lak a witch—funny shapted [shaped]."[8]

The position of conjurer was sometimes inherited, but more often was the result of peculiar circumstances of birth, such as being born feet-foremost or with a caul over the face. Such children were considered to have special powers. Babies born with a caul were believed to be gifted—or cursed—with second sight. They would always be able to see spirits and other supernatural phenomena: "Ain't I fer tell yuh Julie ain fer born wid caul but George gal, Zena is? Dat gal bin born wid caul. She kin see w'at de ornary, common run cain't see." Children thought to have been born with second sight were often taught the special lore of the conjurers. Some slave midwives, however, used a countercharm to lift the "curse" of second sight. Hagar Brown said of the caul: "Take that off. Make tea outer um. Feed baby till he all gone. Take the spell off. Can't see 'um. Can't see hant. When born take 'um from he face. Make tea. Feed 'um till he all gone. Drink 'em all. Spell take off. Can't see 'um." Lillie Knox explained to Genevieve Chandler that "Aunt Hagar does that so they won't grow up scared.

When anyone like that they all the time seeing things and it'll scare them."[9]

Other conjurers in All Saints Parish were said to have received their powers by selling themselves to the devil in exchange for the ability to conjure and cast spells. After meeting with the devil at a crossroads for nine consecutive nights, a novice conjurer would procure a lucky black cat bone, which would thereafter be used in conjuration and what was called "rich craft." Minnie Knox recalled to Chandler, "They does say black cat has een 'um uh lucky bone. Doan kill th' cat. Get yuh uh cat ain got on 'um no white hair. Doan kill 'um. Jess drap 'em een uh pot uh biling wautuh (water) en bil 'um till hit all bile tuh pieces. Wan leetle bone will stay on top." There were also reports of marriage between humans and the devil. Ellen Carolina told of one case in which the hapless groom did not know he was riding with the devil until it was too late: "Eber mile pos' day git to, gal countenance change. Ebery mile pos' gettin uglier and uglier. Git to las' mile pos' she tun to Debil wid long tail on em! No gal now."[10]

The conjurers were assisted in their efforts by various combinations of common and uncommon substances that were held to be magical. "Peoples conjers wid grabe yard dirt," one ex-slave told Chandler. "Yuh can tek dat dirt en all kind ob ting en mek conjur bag. Dey bin some kind ob debilmint yuh mix wid dat stuff." An uninitiated person looked into a conjure bag at risk of life. Hagar Brown said, "I know I ain't goin' be the one peep in there. 'Cause I ain't make my peace yet. Know it will make you fall dead. Wouldn't have time to crook." A woman on Sandy Island told Chandler, "I hear tell bout a man ober de ribbah what jus looked on a conjure man bag, an he died." She did describe, however, what a woman she knew found when she looked into a conjure bag. "What dat debbilment look like?" she exclaimed. "It wuz de terriblest lookin sight she eber has saw! She say it wuz all mixin up. De ting fuzz up like a baby head an wukkin up and mixin. Hab eye. Hab nose. Hab mout'. Red eye. Fuzz on em. An de mind come tuh Lutella. 'Stroy dat devil wuk!' And she done what de spirit say." Armed with such charms conjurers made powerful impressions on other slaves. They were said to possess all manner of malign powers.[11]

Not all of the conjurers' spells had sinister intent. If they were considered the perpetrators of most misfortunes, they were also highly regarded as healers. The positive role played by the conjurers (or conjure-doctors as they were often called by the slaves) in the treatment of slave illnesses exemplified the role of religion in every aspect of slave life. The precise role of the medical profession in the treatment of slaves remains controversial, but white physicians did not enjoy a high reputation among All Saints slaves, and the white man's medicine was regarded with suspicion. Depending upon the complaint, conjure doctors might take a pharmaceutical approach to treatment. Africans had brought their highly esteemed pharmacopoeia with them to South Carolina as part of their oral traditions. They found the semitropical lowcountry environment similar enough to that of West Africa that such knowledge was easily adapted to somewhat new flora and fauna. To cure a child of worms, for instance, Margaret Bryant said they would "git the gipsy (gypsum) weed. Beat 'em up for worm. Give 'em when the moon change." Rheumatism was treated by massaging the affected area with eelskin or having the patient ingest a decoction of oakbark or pokeberry tea, which did in fact possess medical properties. Other ailments might call for a sort of psychotherapy, as expressed in divination. The persistent headaches of Lillie Knox's grandmother, Kit, were diagnosed by conjurer Obie Hines as having been caused by a lizard in her head (a common diagnosis among conjurers): "En ole man Obie ax fuh uh hankercher. En he shake it en say, 'Kit! Blow yuh nostril!' 'Can't, man!' 'Blow, Kit, blow!' En she blow! En if she wuz here live ter-day, she'd tell you. She blow en blow out uh lizard out her nose—small, slick black lizard! She kept it en show it tuh us young'uns." If illness were caused by sorcery, it could only be removed by countersorcery: "I had a half-brother like to been run crazy. Pain in the head. Fix! They took some kinder rattlesnake dust and fix him. Nobody didn't know how. Didn't know whether somebody lay something cross that man path or put poison in his cap or what been done." But countersorcery could remove the evil spell: "Mother just give Rich that root woman treatment and turn that spell in time." Conjurers on the Waccamaw sometimes turned spells back upon their perpetrators. Zackie Knox told Chandler of a conjure doctor who was accused of giving a woman the "wandering sickness" by turning a spell back on her when she failed to pay him for putting a charm on her husband. Occasionally conjurers even attempted to "lay a trick" on the master or overseer. Ex-slave Ella Small recalled that at Wachesaw plantation a "conjur been throw at the obersheer (overseer) and hit my Brudder Frank."[12]

Not all slaves believed in conjure, of course. "Conjur?" asked ex-slave Sabe Rutledge. "Wouldn't burn a hucks [crust of] bread for 'em." Lillie Knox recalled that her slave grandmother "didn't b'lieve in nuthin lak goopherin ner conjurin ner nuthin." Some of the ex-slaves were even more emphatic in their expressions of disbelief. "Now, me, I don't b'lieve in no conjur ball ner ritch-craft," said a former slave on Sandy Island. "I don't b'lieve in no coo-coo nor hoo-doo ner nuthin." While the Waccamaw conjurers were never able to command universal adherence, and while they never approached the political power of the Caribbean priests of Obeah, Myalism, or Vodun, it is clear that they exercised influence over the lives of the slaves out of proportion to any power in their charms and spells. It is equally clear that they could neither have gained nor held such influence over other slaves had they not served a real function on the rice plantations. Even if the conjurers are acknowledged to have been frauds and extortionists, one must recognize that they also served the slave community as healers in time of sickness and as comforters in time of suffering, as interpreters of those unobservable spirits whose activities directed everyday life, and as awesome beings whose supernatural powers could be enlisted in the redress of grievances. For the Waccamaw slaves, their conjurers—the underground priests of voodoo—bridged the precarious servitude of the all-too-real world and the mysterious uncertainties of the spirit world. In so doing, they created for even the most credulous slaves a buffer against mental and emotional submission to the slave system. Many, perhaps most, of the All Saints slaves abandoned their adherence to this aspect of their African heritage. Those who did not, by helping to preserve and extend an autonomous African heritage, were making a contribution to community and survival.[13]

3

Voodoo had a continuing appeal to some slaves; most slave Christians, when they did not totally reject that stream of African cosmology, considered the conjurers' powers to be evil and inimical to Christianity. Another stream, the venerable African distinction between hags and haunts, proved to be more compatible with the slaves' new religious outlook. Haunts were the spirits of the dead, returned to trouble the living: a lowcountry version of the Congo zumbi or the Haitian zambi, although carrying a somewhat different connotation on the Waccamaw. Hags, on the other hand, were not spirits of the dead, but rather the disembodied spirits of witches who would shed their skins at night and "ride" people—that is, give them nightmares. "Hag a REAL PERSON," the old-timers emphasized. "They jus' learn dat trade." Slave Christians neither abandoned such beliefs nor incorporated them into Afro-Christianity. Hags, haunts, and plat-eyes—malevolent, shape-changing spirits—persisted in a parallel stream of belief.[14]

Hags were particularly troublesome creatures who could fly through the air and who were given to vampirism: "Dey say hag sperit can go troo de keyhole of de do' en ef dey lak you dey goes in en sucks your blood troo yer nose. Nobody scusin a hag lak dat kin' o' diet, but dey eats dat fer de syrup on dey bread. When hag rides you, you mek noise same lak er little shiverin owl. You can't wake up en you won't wake up twell somebody tech you. You calls dat de hag ridin you."[15] The very young and the very old were particularly susceptible to being victimized by hags. Ex-slave Liza Small believed that a hag was responsible for the death of her grandson: "My daughter have the two boy. Lose one. I low [allow] hag musser lock he jaw.

Couldn't suck." [16] Another aged slave personally struggled with hags until "she ole bones bin gib out." "Maum Nellie she try 'em. She fight hag seben year. Jes she wan. She wressel wid 'em. . . . But atter seben year dey run she. She say she too ole fer de hag fer ride. She say she too tired. She wuk so hard. She hoe. She plant. She harbest. En night come en she crabe fer res'." [17] There were precautions that the slaves might take to keep hags from riding them. Maum Nellie employed traditional preventive measures: "She bed down she fire, en she fall in she bunk. But she ain't fer out she light. She light burn low fer keep hag out. En de sifter bin hang ober de key-hole. Dat, too, fer keep out hag. W'en hag come tru de keyhole en git en dat sifter, he hab de culiosity. En he stay right dere twell he count de hole in dat sifter. En he lose count. En he start ergin [again]. En he git mix. En daylight kotch 'em. En he hab for go." [18] The only certain means of preventing a hag from riding one was to catch the hag, which could best be done by the traditional African method of salting and peppering her skin while she was out of it. "Ef you is marry wid a hag, she gits up en slips out'n she skin an' hide it under de stairsteps or back doorsteps, en when she come back she gits back in en lays back down. Now, when you wife go, you git up en look under de staircase. Ef ye fin' she skin, you salt en pepper it good same lak you salt en pepper fish what you goin fry. Ef she gone haggin, she sho lef' it, en if you salts it, she kain't git back in." [19] Once the hag was caught she must be destroyed: "Put 'em in a barrel o' tar an' B'UN EM UP." As Lillie Knox told Chandler, "Ain' nuttin else ter do." [20]

Whether haunts were more fearsome creatures than hags was a matter of dispute among the slaves. According to one ex-slave the hags were worse: "Dey say de ded can't fer hurt yuh. Hit de libe ones do dat." But another judged haunts to be more sinister: "De hag cain't trouble she. Hag jes human. But she ain't fer manage dem hant." Those who reported having seen haunts described them in inhuman terms. "Dey all two bofe hab on long white robe en er hair hang down, en he face been red same lak de brick en de chimbley," one reported. He added that the haunts possessed inhuman mobility. "Dey walks right

in tru de do', en hit barred!" Haunts were more likely to appear at certain times, such as a full moon, than at others: "De
hant woorser at de full o' de moon. Maum Nellie fer testify it
start way cross de fiel'. It bark lak fox. It howl lak dawg. It
hoot lak squinch owl. It soun lak all de beas' ob de woods. En
fuss news it hit de house. It circle. It prowl same lak stray
dawg. En while she hol' she bref [breath], de door what she
done bolt mube [move] open. De pot lid lif. De rockin chair
rock." Since the spirits of the dead exercised such a disquieting
effect on the living, efforts were made to contain them. Slave
funerals, for example, tried to propitiate the spirits of the ancestors. If the deceased were considered likely to remain as a
malign spirit, the living sought to prevent it. "Ef hit er wicked
wan us bin fer bury us doan want 'e sperrit lebe behin. Us keep
tight circle roun de grabe 'twell 'e well cober."[21]

Perhaps the most hideous and most malevolent of the occult creatures of this stream of African cosmology was the
plat-eye, a malign spirit that took various shapes in order to
lure its victims into danger and rob them of their wits. "Maum
Addie," an aged ex-slave in All Saints Parish, recalled, "De ole
folks is talk bout Plat-eye. Dey say dey takes shape ob all kind
de critter—dawg, cat, hawg, mule, varmint, an I is hear tell ob
plat-eye takin form ob gator. I ain' see dem scusin wan leetle
time [except for one little time]." Hagar Brown described how
the plat-eye "turn bull and turn all kinder sumpting nudder.
Right there that muster shed. Dat been Plat-eye!" Matthew
Grant declared that plat-eyes could "turn to dog, turn to horse,
turn back to people. Turn to lil' bird! The old head tell me if
you try to run from dem they trip you up! Throw you down.
See 'um better on a old moon and a new moon. Stay round
graveyard and all them cross road. 'Specially a road where
they carry dead body cross. When Plat-eye show he self to you,
you got to see dem!"

"Maum Addie," a former slave, told Chandler of her encounter with a plat-eye: "En mah short handle leetle clam rake
been in mah hand en I sing, 'Gawd will take care ob me.' . . .
En den de mine come ter me, 'De Lawd heps dem what heps

deysef.' W'en I raise up mah rake en I come right cross dat critter haid. Ef dat had bin a real cat, I'd er pin him ter dat lawg. My rake bin bury deep en de lawg hol' em. En I clare ter Gawd, Miss Jin, dat he up en prances right onder mah feets, dem eyes burning holes in me en he tail swish, swish lak ole Sooky tail when de flies bad." "Maum Addie" knew of but one means of keeping plat-eyes at bay: "Gunpowder en sulphur. Dey is say Plat-eye can' stan' dem smell mix." Since adopting that preventive measure, "dey ain fer trubble me sense dat wan time." She learned the remedy from a conjurer; but her description of him aptly illustrates the complexities of cultural creolization in the New World: "Uncle Murphy he witch doctor en he bin tell me how fer fend 'em off. Dat man full ob knowledge. He mus hab Gawd mind in 'em." Her defense against plat-eyes was a fascinating blend of tradition and creativity, of conjuration, Christianity, and common sense: "So I totes mah powder en sulphur en I carries mah stick in mah han en puts mah truss in Gawd."[22]

As one might expect of a once-unified religious cosmology shattered into diverse and sometimes mutually exclusive streams, belief in the various components was by no means uniform. Some abandoned belief in all forms of non-Christian supernaturalism. An ex-slave named Hackless recalled a slave preacher who spurned hags, haunts, and plat-eyes with equal disdain. "Dat wan brabe man. 'E all de time fer say Plat-eye ner hag ner hant ner ghos ain fer harm 'em. 'E ain fear de dark no*how*. . . . 'E truss Gawd." But many slaves selectively adhered to some beliefs and abandoned others, as, for example, Liza Small's skepticism regarding the efficacy of the widespread belief that painting the door and window facings blue would ward off hags. Chandler asked her why she had all her doors and windows painted blue. She answered simply, "Board tak' em." When Chandler asked why she used the color blue, she said, "Old man buy 'em." Finally, when Chandler said she had always heard blue would keep the hags out, she exclaimed, "That ain't so! That ain't so! I prove that. Sometimes they ride me till I can't keep up next day!"[23]

4

A third stream of inherited cosmology—which included African ideas regarding polytheism, rebirth, and spirit possession in religious ritual—combined with elements of Christianity to form an influential, and distinctly black, religion on the rice plantations of the Waccamaw. Since this new slave religion was the result of a convergence of African and European religious orientations, it may be helpful for a moment to examine the Christianity evangelized to the slaves in order to gain some perspective on the creolization process by which the slaves blended elements of African religions with elements of Christianity and adapted them to the conditions of rice plantation life. The originality of slave religion on the plantation streets and in the plantation chapels resides neither in its specifically African features nor in its specifically Christian features, but in its unique and creative synthesis in response to the reality of slavery.

While early South Carolina slaveholders had only reluctantly tolerated efforts to Christianize their slaves, the rice planters of antebellum All Saints Parish eagerly supported and participated in missionary efforts on their plantations. James L. Belin, a Methodist pastor at Murrells Inlet, began a forty-year mission to the slaves in 1819. Most of the rice planters were Episcopalians and members of All Saints Church, Waccamaw. They began their own mission to the slaves in 1832 under the leadership of their newly ordained rector, a twenty-eight-year-old Englishman named Alexander Glennie. Glennie preached to slaves on one plantation each Sunday afternoon and another on Sunday evening, and he held services three or four evenings a week as well. He was thus able to visit each plantation in the parish once or twice a month. When he began his mission, he had ten black communicants; by 1862 there were 529. Ex-slave Sabe Rutledge recalled, "Before freedom Parson Glennie—he was piscopal—he would come give us a service once a month on the plantation—so mother said." J. Motte Alston described Glennie's visits to Woodbourne in his memoirs:

The Reverend Alexander Glennie and his wife would come to us once every fortnight. He always came to dinner, after which he would teach the negro children their catechism and preach to all of my negroes at night. They always had a half holiday on these occasions, so as to let them brush up and make a respectable appearance. It was a law that all should attend.

I had a Church built conveniently, and my family, myself, and guests always attended. It was quite wonderful what retentive memories they had, for few could read. The minister would always read the evening services of the Episcopal Book of Common Prayer and always, too, the same Psalter so as to enable the congregation to respond, which they did most accurately and devoutly.

But I do well remember one evening when the Bishop (Davis) accompanied Mr. Glennie and was to preach that evening, and all were rigged out in their Sunday's best, when in the midst of the service, while all were standing, one of the men, full six feet in height, went fast asleep and fell over the benches, and all came down with a crash to the floor, to the amusement of the congregation and to the mortification of the performer, whose specific gravity so greatly outweighed his spiritual zeal.

Perhaps such lapses in spiritual zeal were at least partly explained by the recollections of another ex-slave, Mariah Heywood, who remembered that "Parson Glennie come once a month to Sunnyside. Parson Glennie read, sing, pray. Tell us obey Miss Minna."[24]

Between Glennie's visits the planters held morning devotionals for the house servants. A northern visitor described one such morning at Henry Buck's Woodbourne plantation: "a signal from the mistress caused the sounding of a bell in the hall, and some ten or twelve men and women house-servants, of remarkably neat and tidy appearance . . . entered the apartment. They took a stand at the remote end of the room and our host, opening a large, well-worn family *Bible*, read the fifty-fourth chapter of Isaiah. Then, all kneeling, he made a short extemporaneous petition, closing with the Lord's Prayer; all present, black as well as white, joining in it. Then Heber's beautiful hymn, 'From Greenland's Icy Mountains,' was sung; the negroes, to my ear, making much better music than the whites."[25]

The rice planters supported such attempts at religious instruction of the slaves in part out of genuine concern for the
slaves' spiritual welfare. The religion they taught to the slaves,
however, was a highly selective form of Christianity, which
stressed obedience in the here and now as much as salvation in
the hereafter. When Buck held family devotions for his house
servants, when John Hyrne Tucker and J. Motte Alston compelled their slaves to attend chapel services, when Plowden C.
J. and Emily Weston catechized their slaves and taught them to
read the Bible, they did so out of a sincere Christian concern
for the slaves' salvation. But they were also aware that religion
was a more subtle, more humane, and more effective means of
control than the whip.[26]

Glennie eloquently emphasized this aspect of Christianity
in his sermons to the slaves:

> "Servants, be obedient to them that are your masters according
> to the flesh, with fear and trembling, in singleness of your heart,
> as unto Christ; not with eye service as men pleasers; but as the
> servants of Christ, doing the will of God from the heart: with
> good will doing service, as to the Lord and not to men; knowing
> that whatsoever good thing any man doeth, the same shall he
> receive of the Lord, whether he be bond or free." This passage
> from the Bible shews to you, what God requires from you as
> servants; and there are many other passages which teach the
> same things. You should try and remember these parts of the
> Bible, that you may be able "to do your duty in that state of life,
> unto which it has pleased God to call you." For although a bad
> servant may not wish to know what God requires of him, yet a
> Christian servant will desire to know this, and to do his will in
> every thing.

"Here," Glennie told the slaves, "is a very plain command:
'servants be obedient': be obedient to your masters." Bad servants would neglect this command, "but you, who call yourselves children of God, will do his will" and "every day give
proof that you wish to serve God, by your ready, your cheerful
obedience." He cautioned them against "giving offence by any
conduct that looks like disobedience; for, by disobedience, you
not only offend your earthly master, but you sin against God"

and "bring reproach on Him whose name you bear." Servants should look upon their daily tasks as "the will of God." "Do not attend to your work only while your earthly master's eye is upon you; but remember that the eye of your heavenly Master is always upon you." A bad servant would only work "so long as his master's eye is upon him," but "you, who call yourselves the servants of Christ," will "'do service' cheerfully, 'as to the Lord, and not to men.'" And, in the day of judgment, "it matters not whether we be bond-servants or free men: it matters not whether we be among the high and the rich, or among the low and the poor: we shall in that day receive according as we now live. If we now live as obedient followers of our Lord and Savior Jesus Christ, we shall, through him who loved us, inherit everlasting life."[27]

It would be unfair to Glennie, and untrue to history, to suggest that he cynically reduced Christianity to patience, humility, and the fear of sin, or that he was more concerned with the slaves' discipline than with their salvation. Nevertheless, slaveholders believed his preaching had a significant effect on discipline in All Saints Parish. James R. Sparkman reflected on the success of the slaves' religious instruction in 1858: "The moral and social condition of the Slave population in this district has vastly improved within 20 years. The control, management, and entire discipline has materially changed, crime and rebellion are much less frequent. They have learned in many instances to govern themselves and to govern each other and through this section, '*Runaways*' are fewer and '*less lawless.*'" Colonel Thomas Pinckney Alston, a leading Waccamaw rice planter until his retirement in 1858, tacitly conceded that some planters were less interested in the slaves' understanding of the Christian gospels than with the effect of religious indoctrination on keeping order on the plantations.[28]

The dilemma that Glennie and other ministers had to face was that the Christianity they preached was potentially subversive to the institution of slavery. He and the planters both realized this. During the 1834 legislative debate, which prohibited teaching slaves to read and write, a planter had noted that anyone who wanted slaves to read the *entire* Bible be-

longed in "a room in the Lunatic Asylum."[29] Glennie was no
mere sycophant of cynical rice planters. He did not select
merely the texts that promoted order and discipline among the
slaves. But he did realize that the same religion that so effectively promoted order on Waccamaw rice plantations contained the seeds of disorder. He did not preach to his congregations that Pharoah had enslaved the children of Israel and
held them in bondage in Egypt. He did not tell them that the
Lord visited plagues on the slaveholders or that Moses led
them in a mass escape from slavery to the promised land.[30]

But Glennie did preach the equality of all in the sight of
God. He spoke of "our first parents, Adam and Eve," and told
slave and master alike that "all mankind are descended from
them." He preached the equality of sinfulness. "All are born in
sin," he said, "and if it were not for the love and mercy and
goodness of God, all would live in sin, and would suffer the
pains of hell forever." But "we sinners" are saved because
"Christ Jesus came into the world." Glennie identified Jesus
with the slaves. "And he did not appear as a great and rich
man, but he took the form of a servant." Christianity imposed
obedience not merely upon the slaves, but upon their earthly
masters as well. Glennie preached that "in the day of judgment, the inquiry will be: What have we done in this world;
how did we live in this world? It matters not," he told his congregations, "in what condition we have been here," whether
slave or free, high or low, rich or poor. All would be held to the
same account before God's judgment. "If we are disobedient to
his word, we can inherit only everlasting misery." As servants
were taught in the Bible how they must obey their masters, so
masters were taught in the Bible how they must rule their servants, and the rich were taught how they must do good with
their riches. Masters and slaves alike Glennie admonished to
"remember the account which we shall all have to give before
his judgment seat."[31]

Here was the dilemma for the rice planters. As Christians,
they were committed to the religious instruction of their
slaves. But the religion to be taught to the slaves also called the
masters to account. That the masters were as subject as the

slaves to the requirements of Christianity created a problem of role boundaries on the rice plantations and emphasized internal tensions and anomalies that could not be ignored. Many, perhaps most, of the Waccamaw masters took Glennie's admonitions quite seriously. Plowden C. J. Weston prayed in the chapel at Hagley that God would "give to all masters grace to keep order and discipline in their families, and to treat their servants with mercy, kindness, gentleness, and discretion; knowing that thou has made of one flesh all the nations of the earth. Give to all servants grace to obey their masters, and please them well in all things; knowing that in thus doing they shall please thee who art the Master over all." Robert F. W. Allston believed that the "best inducement" to win the slaves to Christianity was "example on our own part; next a just, consistent, systematic administration of domestic government." [32]

5

The missionary efforts of Glennie and others were an important source of Afro-Christianity among the slaves of All Saints Parish. But the slaves did not simply adopt Glennie's God and his faith. In their efforts to establish a spiritual life for themselves, they interpreted the elements of Christianity taught by Glennie in terms of deep-rooted African cognitive orientations. In stressing the significance of the African contribution to slave Christianity, it would be a mistake to leave the impression that Africa was culturally homogeneous or that it bequeathed to its exiles in the New World a legacy of static survivals. On the contrary, African religious expression was so diverse that borrowings were common among various ethnic groups. But rising above the plethora of rites and practices was a common bond—the concept of a sacred cosmos in which nearly all experience was religious, from the naming of children to beliefs regarding when to plant and how to hunt and fish. And underlying the various African cultures were shared cognitive or "grammatical" orientations—mental rules governing appropriate behavior—which affected the slaves' adoption, adaptation, and application of Christianity. Since slaves could no longer find on Waccamaw rice plantations anything approximating the African context of their sacred cosmos, they worshiped their new Christian God with the kind of expressive behavior their African heritage taught them was appropriate for an important deity.[33]

The persistence of African expressive behavior in slave religion was manifested in a high degree of emotional involvement in worship, including the use of dances and chants to rhythmic accompaniment, culminating in trances and spirit possession. Unlike hoodoo and conjuration, spirit possession was incorporated into Afro-Christianity and reinterpreted in Christian terms. According to one of the Waccamaw rice planters, "Their whole religious worship is proverbially emotional, frequently running into boisterous shoutings, with noisy demonstrations of hands and feet, and extravagant, wild, hysterical gyrations of the body, which are contagious and Exhaustive, sometimes ending in a swoon or semicataleptic condition." At night many slave families went to one another's houses to hold prayer meetings and to sing and "shout." The shout was a series of body motions (usually described as a dance by outsiders) that the slaves performed to the accompaniment of spirituals. It exemplified the creative Afro-Carolinian adaptation of a West African ring dance performed to complex drum rhythms. In the New World the drums, upon which Africans had relied to articulate their spiritual life, were lost; but a substitute was improvised with polyrhythmic hand-clapping and foot-stamping. The slaves called the adaptation "shouting," after the African *saut*, meaning to walk or run around. Similar expressive behavior was widespread among blacks in the Caribbean and elsewhere in the South Carolina lowcountry. While many slave Christians frowned upon dancing itself, they participated in the shouts with great enthusiasm. "Fire take the church! Heart commence to turn over!" recalled Hagar Brown, describing her response as the spirit filled the church. "Great Lord! The whole thing been jump!" As she shouted up and down the aisles, she felt that "anything I want, I hold out my hand and say, 'Jehovah, I pend on you!'" In such prolonged religious fervor many became so stiff from trances that they "cannot buckle." [34]

The phenomenon of spirit possession was the central fact of expressive behavior in the spiritual life of All Saints slaves. The necessity of experiencing spirit possession for conversion marked the continuation in Afro-Christianity of one of the most persistent features of African religion (especially pronounced among the Bantu, the Yoruba, and the Fante-Ashanti) in the New World. Conversion was characterized by a spiritual journey, or retreat, called "seeking." The seeker's prolonged praying and meditating during this period induced an ecstatic trance without which conversion was not considered authentic: "Fore he convert—like any other else man. Had to be borned again." Eventually the seeker "came through" and "found peace." Hagar Brown recalled her own conversion to Chandler: "I 'member and I 'member well when I wuz on my prayin' ground! 'Member when I get my thing!" she said. "I come through. Right there to old Laurel Hill been my prayin' ground." "Coming through" was in itself an ecstatic experience, as Hagar Brown described it: "How happy are the child of God when he know he sin forgiven! Somebody kept tryin' to tech me. I walkin'! Walkin'! And a big man with he hands folded jest so say, 'Let her 'lone! Leave her 'lone. Been that-a-way myself! He layin' down! 'Layin' down hands cross he breast! No common head o' man! Spirit of God! Then I feel somebody tech me. My jaw been lock Thursday night twelve o'clock. Saturday I come through! Couldn't eat; couldn't eat! Them old timey people, couldn't fool em." Only after such an experience was one accepted as a member of the church. Others were considered sinners. [35]

When slave Christians gathered at one another's houses for praise meetings, their expressive behavior provided a release for pent-up emotions in the soaring rhetoric of the prayers, the antiphonal singing, and the ecstatic shouts, unlike the sedate, unemotional Episcopal services that Glennie conducted for the planters at All Saints Church, Waccamaw. A white visitor, observing one such South Carolina praise meeting, remarked that "none can move a negro but a negro." This was not altogether true, but white preachers had to realize that sermons were no more passive experiences for blacks than was singing. A religious service was not a relationship between a performer and an audience, but a mutual performance. Just as songs were characterized by the strong call-and-response antiphony of West African music, so prayers and sermons were punctuated by congregational responses. Glennie "lined out" hymns for his black congregations, who responded antiphonally. A northern visitor described the scene: "We all went to a negro church. . . . The congregation responded and sang the Te Deum with Mr. G[lennie]. Some had books and could read, but as all could not, he would read two lines of a hymn & then they would all sing them & so on!!" [36] Glennie tailored the catechismal style of his Anglican sermons to suit the stylistic expectations of the slaves. "Now do you, all of you, my brethren, receive this saying, that Christ Jesus came into the world to save sinners!" he would ask, and the congregation would respond. "Do you receive this, and live according to it, in the hope of going to heaven?" Again the congregation would respond—and so on through the series of questions and congregational answers that built to a powerful climax: "Do you look upon yourselves as among the sinners that Jesus came to save; and in consequence, are you so repenting of your sins as to forsake them? Do you kneel down upon your knees everyday before the holy God, and confess to him that you are miserable sinners, deserving his anger; and at the same time look to Jesus who was crucified for you, and pray that for his sake your sins may all be forgiven, that they may all be blotted out in his most precious blood? Is it your care too to pray, that the Holy Spirit may abide in your hearts, making you faithful followers of Jesus Christ, willing servants of God, obedient to him in all things?" This long series of questions, answered by the congregation whenever the preacher paused, was followed by three repetitive sentences. "That is what you ought to be doing, if you would have your souls to be saved," Glennie would say, and the congregation would respond. "That is what you ought to be doing, if you would have Jesus Christ to save you from living in sin in this world, and from suffering the punishment which your sins deserve in the next," he would say, and the congregation would respond. "Seriously think of these things, I pray you," Glennie concluded, "and may God bless you, and make you true followers of Jesus Christ, who came into this world to save sinners."[37]

So powerful was the expressive behavior of the African religious heritage that white ministers ignored it at their peril if they wished to preach successfully to plantation slaves on the Waccamaw.

6

It was not merely in expressive behavior, however, that the religion of the slaves was distinctive. Afro-Christianity embodied a broader theology than just the selected portions taught them by Glennie and other white preachers. The slaves did not reject the Christian call to renounce sin and follow Jesus. Many of the slave songs from All Saints Parish reflected the emphasis of Glennie's sermons. There were songs that glorified Jesus:

> The Roman soldier 'round Him
> A thousand army wide
> If He had not been die for us
> We all might not have been save
>
> Now I just want to told you
> How He went down in the grave
> With the burden of nation
> And sinner for to save[38]

And there were songs that urged the renunciation of sin:

> God sent Jonah to Ninevy [Ninevah] land.
> Jonah disobey my God command
> Paid his fare and he got on board.
> Children, don't you do that!
>
> Don't you do that!
> Don't you do that!

God got His eye on you!
Don't you do that!
Don't you do that!
Don't you idle your time away![39]

But the slaves also found in Christianity analogies to their own situation in the enslavement and persecution of the Israelites. And they found in Christianity the heroes and the hopes that could make life in bondage bearable.

If Glennie's sermons concentrated exclusively on the gospels and the epistles of the New Testament, the Afro-American spirituals from All Saints Parish were filled with Old Testament imagery—Daniel in the lion's den; Gabriel's blowing his horn; Ezekiel in the wilderness, chewing on dry bones; the shepherd boy David's felling of the mighty Goliath; God's rescuing Jonah from the whale; God's calling Moses to lead the Israelites out of slavery; God's sending a flood to destroy the wicked world. Such themes had immediate appeal to a people held in bondage and exile. And New Testament references in the All Saints spirituals ran heavily to revelation and to that final judgment day when God would redeem the righteous and punish the wicked for their misdeeds on earth.[40]

There is a haunting quality about the spirituals that partly echoes African continuities in their music and performance style and partly reflects the trials and suffering, the sorrows and tribulations of life in bondage. Despite their inevitable sadness, however, the spirituals were also songs of hope and of affirmation. They reflected an awareness that slavery was an unnatural—and temporary—condition:

God call Moses! (Ay Lord!)
God call Moses! (Ay Lord!)
God call Moses! (Ay Lord!)
Time is a-rollin on!

Moses free the people! (Ay Lord!)
Moses free the people! (Ay Lord!)
Moses free the people! (Ay Lord!)
Time is a-rollin on![41]

They reflected an awareness that God wreaks vengeance on the wicked who have oppressed his people:

> I'm looking for the stone
> That rolling through Babylon!
> I'm looking for the stone
> That rolling through Babylon!
> I'm looking for the stone
> That rolling through Babylon!
> Down from the kingdom of the world![42]

They reflected an awareness that God can work miracles to bring about immediate change, as when the Syrian commander Naaman was cleansed of leprosy by washing in the Jordan River and became a follower of Jehovah:

> God told Naaman to go to Jordan!
> Halleloo!
> God told Naaman to go to Jordan!
> Halleloo!
> Halleloo! Halleloo![43]

They reflected, too, belief that persistence would be rewarded:

> Joshua was the son of Nun
> He never stop till the work was done![44]

and

> Lord, I've started for the kingdom!
> Lord, I've started for the kingdom!
> Lord, I've started for the kingdom!
> I ain't gon' turn back! I ain't goin' turn back![45]

They called upon the Lord for strength to face the burdens of the present:

> Come by here, Lord! Come by here!
> Come by here! my Lord! Come by here!
> Come by here, Lord! Come by here!
> Oh Lord, come by here!
>
> Need your power, Lord, Come by here!
> Need your power, Lord, Come by here!

Need your power, Lord, Come by here!
Oh, Lordy, Come by here!

Sinners moanin' Lord! Come by here!
Sinners moanin' Lord! Come by here!
Sinners moanin' Lord, Come by here!
Oh, Lordy, Come by here. [46]

But they expressed full confidence that heaven awaits them in the life beyond death. No one can enter heaven on the labor of others:

I got to stand
Before the judgment bar!
Oh, there's nobody here
To stand there for me!
Oh, I got to stand there
For myself! [47]

But just as God delivered Daniel from the lion's den and the fiery furnace, He could also deliver His followers from the House of Bondage:

I'm goin' home!
I'm goin' home!
I will overcome some day!
I'm goin' home!
I'm goin' home!
I will overcome some day!

I do believe!
I do believe!
I will overcome some day!
I do believe!
I do believe!
I will overcome some day. [48]

If the specific deities of Africa were left behind, the Christian doctrine of the Trinity was readily comprehensible to slave converts; and legions of saints and angels kept alive the spirit of African polytheism:

I believe I'll count the angel!
I do believe I'll count the angel!

> I do believe I'll count the angel!
> How many angels in the band? [49]

Since the African cognitive grammar underlying the slaves' religion did not make a sharp distinction between the sacred and secular worlds, the perceptions and beliefs expressed in these songs were applied directly to the world of the rice plantations. As they labored in the rice fields under the broiling Carolina sun, they lightened their burdens with songs such as "Don't Get Weary, We're Almost Done." When slaves were sold away from the plantation, those remaining behind would face their grief with the help of such songs as

> Oh my sister done move!
> My sister done move!
> My sister done move her campin' ground!
> Ah Lord! Lord have mercy!
> My sister done move her campin' ground!

and

> Gwine meet my Mother over there!
> Gwine meet my Mother over there!
> We gwine have a good time!
> Way by-and-by! [50]

Other songs, such as this one taken down by an English visitor in 1856, could have served as a kind of code to inform the slaves of a secret religious gathering or a clandestine frolic:

> Oh, I takes my text in Matthew,
> And some in Revelation,
> Oh, I know you by your garment—
> There's a meeting here to-night. [51]

And when the slaves sang of "Going over Jordan," or "I Done Started for the Kingdom," or celebrated the glory of "Canaan's Happy Shore," it is likely that the specific geography in their minds was not always biblical. Such songs as "If You See John the Writer" seem even more explicitly concerned with escape from the House of Bondage:

> If you see John the writer, tell him you saw me!
> Tell him you saw me!

If you see John the writer, tell him you saw me
When you saw me I was on my way!

I'm travelin' up the King Highway!
I'm travelin' up the King Highway!
I'm travelin' up the King Highway!
When you saw me I was on my way!

I was on my way to a heavenly land when you saw me!
When you saw me!
I was on my way to a Heavenly land
When you saw me I was on my way![52]

The old King's Highway, which George Washington had followed on his presidential visit in 1790, runs north and south through All Saints Parish. The slaves knew that route led to the free states.

At the outbreak of the Civil War several slaves were imprisoned in Georgetown for singing

We'll soon be free
We'll soon be free
We'll soon be free
When de Lord will call us home

My brudder how long
My brudder how long
My brudder how long
'Fore we done sufferin' here

We'll fight for liberty
We'll fight for liberty
We'll fight for liberty
When de Lord will call us home

Thomas Wentworth Higginson, who learned this song from Georgetown soldiers in the black regiment that he commanded, the First South Carolina Volunteers, speculated that "'De Lord will call us home' was evidently thought to be a symbolic verse; for, as a little drummer boy explained to me, showing all his white teeth as he sat in the moonlight by the door of my tent, 'Dey tink *de Lord* mean for say de Yankees.'" Higginson's friend William Francis Allen remarked that "in

this case the suspicion was unfounded." Presumably he regarded the suspicion as unfounded because the song was an
old one, but the assumption that slaves only began to dream of
freedom at the outbreak of the Civil War is spurious. Accept-
ing for the moment the dubious proposition that the song ini-
tially meant freedom from sin rather than freedom from slavery, it is difficult to believe it did not take on the latter meaning
during the Civil War. The slaves of All Saints Parish understood perfectly well what was at stake in the fighting. Welcome
Beese told Chandler, "Yankee fight for free WE. . . . THEY
FIGHT TO FREE NIGGER!" In the altered context of the Civil
War—as later during the civil rights movement—old spirituals
could take on more specific meanings.[53]

7

The shouts, spirituals, and religious fervor of the slaves excited
and alarmed their masters. They were encouraged that the
slaves held family prayers and gathered at house meetings to
sing and shout and to be moved by such slave preachers as
Jemmy, a house servant at Hagley.[54] Wyndham Malet, an English visitor to Hagley (and himself an Anglican priest), vividly
rendered the cadence and imagery of one of Jemmy's prayers:

> O Lord,
> in whose palm of his hand be the waters of the ocean—
> who can remove mountains—
> who weights the earth in a balance—
> who can still the waves of the storm—
> who can break the pines of the forest—
> who gives us a land of rivers of waters—
> O Jesus!
> who died on the cross for us—
> O forgive us our sins;
> help us in this time of trial and need.
> Protect our massa far away;
> protect our brothers "Hector" and "Caesar" with him;
> defend us now we are away from home;
> defend our friends and relatives at home, &c.

Jemmy was a man of status within the slave community, held in high regard as a man of words. The continuing social importance of the man of words marked the adaptation of African tradition to Afro-Christianity. Jemmy, who straddled the sacred and secular worlds, was regarded as having the ability to employ the powers of the sacred world within the secular domain.[55]

Such "gifted" men—as Malet termed them—often acted as mediators between Christian belief and the everyday world of the plantation. One example of the African sense of the total involvement of religion in everyday life was the role of the slave preachers as arbiters in settling disputes among the slaves. As a Sandy Island slaveholder put it, the "mandates and decrees" of Afro-Christianity were regarded by the slaves to be "more authoritative & binding than the laws of the commonwealth or, as they express it, the laws of the white man." If the decision was not accepted, the offender might be ostracized by slave Christians as a "sinner," but repentant sinners were easily accepted back into the group, often enjoying extra attention in the process. "Here's the wandering sheep come back in the fold," the preacher said when Ben Horry repented. His return is illustrative: "Poor old Uncle Ben! In church after services he stay in. Tears just pour out his eyes. Th' pitifulest thing in this world. Pitiful! Pitiful! He make you cry. Realize he doing wrong and turn back. And they read the scripture bout the prodigal son have returned." Through such mediation, the slave preachers not only promoted social order on the plantations but also helped to solidify a sense of slave community and served as role models with strong cultural identities not dependent upon their positions as slaves.[56]

Furthermore, while Glennie and other white ministers preached Christianity at least partly to promote contentment, the slave preachers often sowed the seeds of discontent in the community. Much of the slaves' spiritual life was hidden from the masters' eyes. According to Sparkman, the black church was "regarded by many of its members as a *social but secret* society." The slaves of All Saints Parish often held religious services independently of the whites, and sometimes without their knowledge. Mariah Heywood recalled that they held secret prayer meetings throughout the Civil War in which they prayed for freedom from slavery. Such slave revolts as those of Gabriel Prosser, Nat Turner, and—closer to home—Denmark Vesey had been planned under cover of religious associations (although the conjurer Gullah Jack figured prominently in the Vesey plot). Slave preachers may also have played a role in slave revolts in Georgetown District in 1802 and 1829. Certainly charismatic slave preachers seem to have been involved in virtually every known slave revolt. In any event such spirituals as "We'll Soon Be Free" gave evidence not only that enslavement could not crush the love of freedom from the hearts and minds of the slaves but also that Afro-Christianity provided an appropriate vehicle for expressing that love of freedom.[57]

Of course, Christianity did not take with every slave. For one thing, at least a few African-born slaves in the South Carolina lowcountry retained their belief in Islam as late as the mid-nineteenth century. Some lowcountry planters substituted a ration of beef instead of pork for Moslem slaves. Other slaves simply regarded Christianity as a nuisance. One African-born slave in the eighteenth century was reported to have said to another: "I am no such bad man as you think. . . . True I love dance and frolic;—sure Sambo, it's no harm, for make merry now and then. . . . Is nobody good but them praying sort a people? . . . I don't love this praying and going to meeting. What have we black people for do with that? The minister he never say any thing to us."[58] But for others Afro-Christianity played an important role in their day-to-day lives on the rice plantations of the Waccamaw. Through their active participation in praise meetings, in their preservation of African traditions of spirit possession and expressive behavior in ecstatic prayers and energetic shouts, and especially in their transcendant spirituals, the slaves of All Saints Parish voiced their deepest values and proclaimed—and partly shaped—their sense of community.

CHAPTER SIX

"All De Bes' Story"

From Africa, with its long tradition of narrative and its great bestiary of tricksters, came a rich legacy of folktales that delighted both blacks and whites on the rice plantations of the Waccamaw. One of the persistent delusions of the slaveholders, of visitors to the plantations, and of several generations of others was that the trickster tales told by plantation slaves were mere entertainment. What the novel is to twentieth-century readers, the trickster tale was to the slaves of All Saints Parish. Its performance style was their synthesis of inherited and acquired artistry. Its theme was a satirical depiction of their own world and its social relations. Its function was to inspire and educate. Its telling and hearing helped to create the solidarity of the slave community. To attempt to describe the emergence of an adaptive slave culture, to speculate on the response of the slaves to their enslavement, or to delineate the patterns of slave folklife without taking into consideration the evidence of their folktales is to ignore the medium through which the slaves spoke to posterity from their souls. Questions such as the inner world of the slaves' minds will remain egregious speculation until the stories slaves told one another have been carefully analyzed. With no disposition to insist that the narratives—even those told as personal experiences—necessarily took place as told, one might at least observe that narrating such experiences had cultural meaning for the slaves who told them and the slaves who heard them. The cultural meaning may be probed by an examination of the slaves' stories and their storytelling, their continuity with Africa and their creativity in America, their themes and their functions. The animal and human trickster tales of the slaves exemplify language used as symbolic action. By manipulating the words that defined it, the slaves could verbally rearrange their world and turn it symbolically inside out.[1]

In their folktales as in other aspects of their folklife the slaves of All Saints Parish drew upon their African heritage as one of the resources from which they fashioned a response to the slave environment. There were African-born slaves on the Waccamaw as late as the mid-nineteenth century whose memories of Africa were still vivid.[2] The presence of such slaves plus the influence of African criteria in slaves' evaluation of other slaves indicate rather more cultural continuity with Africa than has generally been credited. This is not to say that all the folktales of the slave community were necessarily African. Certainly the repertory of slave tales included many types that were widely diffused throughout Europe and elsewhere. Comparison of tale types tends to indicate that many Afro-American folktales originated in Europe or Asia. This may, however, be simply an impression resulting from uneven collection, both in space and time.[3]

The controversy over origins has unfortunately obscured the question of creativity in Afro-American storytelling. Regardless of the ultimate outcome of that controversy, the cultural continuity of All Saints slaves with their African heritage is not dependent upon proof that their folktales originated in Africa. Nor is the worth of their culture dependent upon the ethnic purity of their continuity with African culture. In fact, the folk narrative tradition of All Saints slaves—like that of their African ancestors—was eclectic and creative. They took their sources where they found them and, like folk groups everywhere, remembered what they found memorable, used what they found usable, and forgot the forgetable. Both inherited aesthetic grammars and the realities of the immediate situation played mediating roles in that process.

2

The best known and most widely collected folktales among both Africans and Afro-Americans are the animal tales, and the best known and most widely collected animal tales are trickster tales. In All Saints Parish, too, animal trickster tales constitute the most common type of folk narrative. The most obvious feature of the All Saints animal tales is their emphasis on small but sly creatures, weak but wily animals who continually get the better of their bigger and more powerful adversaries through superior cunning. Despite physical puniness, the tiny trickster's personality is marked by audacity, egotism, and rebellion. Through the symbolic identification of nature with society the animal trickster tales defined the trickster and his actions as both necessary and good. Such symbolic identification served as a means of transforming the unavoidable into the desirable and of giving a certain freedom of individual action despite group restraints.[4]

Uprooted Africans and their descendants did not simply retain their ancestral trickster tales unchanged, either in All Saints Parish or anywhere else. On the contrary, the African narrative tradition itself was creative and innovative both in Africa and in the New World, where it encountered a strikingly different natural and social environment. Afro-American trickster tales exemplify the slaves' response to that new environment and their efforts to manipulate it verbally and symbolically. It would appear, for instance, that wish fulfillment and role inversion played a somewhat more prominent role in slave trickster tales than in African trickster tales. Nor are trickster tales unique to African and African-derived cultures; on the contrary, trickster tales are universal. But they are not universally alike. What they have in common is the hero who lives by his wits. His behavior is at odds with the cultural values—often deeply held—that restrain him. But what those values are and how the trickster gets around them varies from culture to culture. For example, while the Afro-American slave trickster figure and the Native American trickster figure are both rabbits (and are historically related), they exhibit important differences. The slave trickster, while he may fail or even be repaid in kind for his swindles, is neither a clown nor a self-devourer, as is the Native American trickster.[5]

The intricate combination of realism and fantasy in the animal trickster tales made it possible for them to carry more complex and subtle meanings than simple, unambiguous plots—a trickster tries to deceive another animal and either succeeds or is himself tricked. These tales of thoroughly humanized animals exemplified the process of symboling. The animals think like humans, they behave like humans, they experience human emotions, and they live in a realistic world that is clearly like that of their narrators. But they also remain recognizably animals. The big animals are usually strong and powerful but not very bright; they are constantly being duped by the less powerful trickster figures. This combination of realism and fantasy made it possible for storytellers and audiences in Africa and America alike to identify with the animal characteristics without the identification becoming rigid or allegorical.[6] To miss that identification is to miss perhaps the central meaning of the trickster tales to the slaves; but to magnify that identification out of proportion—to take the trickster tales *merely* as vicarious protest tales—is to miss other levels of their meaning completely. That the animal trickster tales provided slaves with a satirical depiction of the society in which they lived has been somewhat obscured by an overemphasis on similarities between the trickster and the slave. A people's perception of their social and economic system grows out of an identification of the people with nature and their perception of nature in terms of social relations. Thus the struggle between Buh Rabbit (the slave) and Buh Bear (the "maussa") could be perceived as founded in nature and thus inevitable.[7]

The animal trickster appears in many guises in black folktales in Africa and in the New World. On the rice plantations of the Waccamaw he is usually Buh Rabbit (or Buddah Rabbit), although he also appears as Buh Cootah (Cooter, a small turtle), Buh Squel (Squirrel), and Buh Pa'tridge (Partridge). Buh Rabbit is not always the trickster; in his encounters with Buh Pa'tridge he is himself tricked. This shifting of roles in the tales is important, for it underlines the educative function of folktale narration in the slave community. From such role switching, slaves learned not merely how to emulate the trickster but also how to avoid being tricked.[8]

3

The central theme of the animal trickster tales is the struggle for mastery between the trickster and his adversary, as expressed in possession of the two most basic signs of status—food and sex. An ironic inversion of the cultural notion of food-sharing as a hallmark of community runs through a number of the tales. For example, in "Duh Rabbit, Fox, an' Goose," Buh Rabbit has been stealing food from a garden owned by an absentee owner. The owner leaves word with his "lil gal" to watch out for the next time Buh Rabbit breaks into the garden and not let him out. She does so while the man tells Buh Fox to go eat Buh Rabbit. But Rabbit tells Fox he will show him some tasty geese if he won't eat him. Fox goes off after the geese, Rabbit tells him a bear is chasing him, Fox runs away, and Rabbit is free. He has taken his fill from the garden without suffering the consequences. In the universe of the trickster tales there is no food-sharing, merely a continuing struggle among the animals over control of the food supply. In such an environment, as this story and others like it make clear, the slaves were aware of the positive advantages of role playing.[9]

Not the least of the lessons for the slaves embedded in their folktales was that values which are appropriate in some situations may not be useful in others. Friendship and altruism were held up as positive values within the slave community, but such traits were not exhibited by the tricksters in their social relations with the powerful. In the story "Buddah Bear's Fish," Buddah Bear is walking through the woods with some freshly caught fish when he sees what appears to be a dead rabbit in the path. It is Buddah Rabbit playing dead. Scampering ahead after Buddah Bear passes by, Buddah Rabbit repeats this trick three more times. Finally, Buddah Bear sets down his fish and goes back to retrieve the four "dead rabbits." When he returns, he finds Buddah Rabbit already cooking up a fish stew. Bear reclaims the fish, but Rabbit escapes unpunished. In this tale the trickster is unsuccessful, but in many others he succeeds. The lesson is clear—when dealing with the powerful, one has everything to gain and little if anything to lose by adopting the value system of the trickster.[10]

While the possession of food is a common symbol of status and power, significantly the trickster found his greatest satisfaction not in the mere possession of food, but in *taking* it from the more powerful animals. In "De Buttah Tree," Buh Woof and Buh Rabbit are joint owners of a butter tree. While Wolf and Rabbit are hoeing rice one day, Rabbit keeps slipping off and eating some of the butter until he has eaten it all. Not only does he deny having eaten the butter, but also he rubs butter on Wolf's mouth while he is sleeping and accuses him of eating the butter. Were mere survival perceived by the narrators to be the theme of the stories, it is unlikely that the final episode would have remained part of the emotional core of the story. Clearly this story is not about food as a symbol of survival, but food as a symbol of power.[11]

And so it goes in one tale after another. In "Bruh Rabbit en de Cow," Rabbit and Wolf are joint owners of a cow. Wolf tires of the partnership, perceiving that it has no advantages for him and demands that they split the cow in half. He will take the hind part. Rabbit "magnanimously" lets him have the whole cow but continues to steal all the milk. That the slaves understood the positive advantages of food theft—and that at least some slaves took the educative function of such tales as this quite literally—is clear from the amount of food theft on the rice plantations on All Saints Parish.[12]

The trickster in the folktales from the Waccamaw is not necessarily admirable. In tale after tale, despite his sly effectiveness, he is a scoundrel who is always ready to cheat or deceive. His outstanding characteristic is his amorality, his complete disdain for either social or moral values. In the story "Buddah Frog, Buddah Squel, and Buddah Rabbit," Squirrel has eaten some of Rabbit's corn. Rabbit leaves Bull Frog to watch the tree in which Squirrel is hiding while Rabbit goes home for his gun. Squirrel chews on some peas to get Frog's attention. Frog wants some peas, also, and asks Squirrel to throw him some. Squirrel (the trickster figure in this tale) tells him to open his eyes, hands, and mouth, whereupon Squirrel throws down a big handful of salt mixed with red and black pepper, which he always carries around for blinding purposes. While Frog is in agony with his burning eyes, Squirrel escapes. Rabbit returns and angrily clobbers Frog with his gun for letting Squirrel escape. This tale is an object lesson in the danger of the trickster's becoming as vicious and cruel as his oppressor. The essence of such tales as this was not moral judgment, but of vicarious victory over oppression. Nevertheless, to see such tales *only* as vicarious triumphs is to miss an important lesson in the limits of amorality.[13]

In yet another tale of the competition for food the tables are turned on the trickster. Buh Rabbit rarely meets his match; when he does, it is at the hands of even smaller, weaker creatures. "Buh Rabbit and Buh Guinea" involves the theft of a cow by Rabbit and Guinea. Rabbit sends Guinea to look for the sun in order to get fire with which to cook the cow. While he is gone, Rabbit gives away beef to all his friends. When Guinea returns, Rabbit tells him the cow has sunk into the ground. Only his tail is showing. They pull the tail up and Guinea eats it, then pretends to be poisoned. Rabbit desperately scurries off to get the meat back from his friends before they are poisoned, too.[14]

The other basic status symbol in the animal trickster tales of the Waccamaw is sexual prowess. In tale after tale the trickster (Buh Rabbit usually) is engaged in deadly competition with the more powerful animals for the favors of "de gals." In "Buddah Rabbit and Buddah Gatah," for instance, Rabbit is jealous because "all de gals stuck on Buddah Gatah." Rabbit goes to a dance where Gator is fiddling and calling. As he calls instructions to the dancers, Gator repeats the refrain, "Eb'ry day good! Eb'ry day good!" Rabbit persuades Gator to let him call and fiddle while Gator rests. As Rabbit calls instructions, he repeats as a refrain, "Some day good! Some day bad! Some day good! Some day bad!" Gator does not like that refrain, because he says he has never seen any trouble. One day Rabbit finds Gator resting on some dried-up old swamp grass and encircles him with fire while Rabbit hollers at him, "Some day good! Some day bad!" Gator is forced to acknowledge that there is indeed trouble in the world. Here again the essential amorality of the trickster is depicted. Such duplicity and violence, in some cases (such as this) depicted for their own sake, are portrayed as everyday actions for the trickster.[15]

In "Buh Partridge Pay Buh Rabbit Back," Rabbit is the victim, and a frailer creature, Buh Partridge, is the deadly trickster. Rabbit and Partridge are competing for the favors of a particular woman ("Dey lakin de same gal"). Rabbit finds Partridge sitting on a stump with his head tucked under his wing. Partridge pretends that his head has been cut off and grandly extolls the virtues of headlessness. He is even going to the dance without his head. Rabbit wants his head cut off, too, but neither his wife, his mother, nor his daughter will oblige him. Eventually Partridge agrees to behead him. He chops off Rabbit's head, then takes his own head out from under his wing and goes to the dance, where he will have the woman all to himself. Rabbit's cunning is offset by his stupidity, his vanity, and his inability to see when he himself is the butt of a trick. Rabbit's role-switching from trickster to tricked in different stories made it possible for slaves to empathize not merely with the trickster, but with the tricked as well.[16]

The tales made clear to the slaves how important it was for the weak to understand the ways of the strong, for it was through understanding the foibles of the powerful that the weak were able to triumph. In the story "Buddah Deer and Buddah Cootah Run a Race," the sleek Deer and the lumbering Cooter are competing for the hand of the king's daughter. They decide to run a race to see who will marry her. Deer is arrogantly convinced he can outrun any creature in the forest. But at each milepost on the ten-mile race course, he sees Buddah Cootah waiting for him. Actually Cooter has other cooters posted at each marker, to make Deer think he is losing. When Deer arrives at the finish line and sees Cooter already there with the king's daughter by his side, he drops dead. Once again the wit of the lowly trickster, with a little help from his friends, frustrates the power of the speedy Deer. That Cooter and Deer were competing for the favors of the daughter of the most powerful creature in the forest demonstrates unmistaka-

bly that theirs is a contest for *status* as much as for sexual
mastery.[17]

In the All Saints version of another tale, Rabbit is competing with Wolf for the favors of a "pretty girl." Rabbit decides
to demonstrate to her that Wolf is nothing more than his sad-
dle horse. "Start to party. Budder Rabbit ax Budder Wolfe to
be he riding horse. Budder Rabbit so tricky. Got near where
the dancing house Budder Rabbit spur 'em. All the pretty girl
is see Budder Rabbit fine riding horse. All laughed at Budder
Wolfe." Here the trickster does more than simply defeat his
rival; he thoroughly humiliates him, takes his woman, and re-
duces him to servility. This symbolic inversion of roles per-
forms a function similar to symbolic inversions in ritual. Symbolic inversion provides psychic relief from the emotional
constraints of slavery, symbolic attacks on oppressive masters
and overseers, and, most important of all, a continuing reminder that existing power relationships are not necessarily
natural power relationships. Here is evidence of the important
role played by such folktales in shaping the world view of the
slaves.[18]

4

But there is a strong countertheme running through the tales
of competition for both food and sex—the theme of the trickster out-tricked. In tale after tale the victim, realizing he has
been tricked by the trickster, sets about trying to trick the
trickster in revenge, but without success. Nevertheless, Buh
Rabbit, so often the trickster, does meet his match in some of
the tales. When he does, he is not defeated by the powerful
through sheer strength, but by frailer creatures who are trick-
ier than he. As already noted, Buh Rabbit is tricked by Buh
Guinea into thinking the cow he has stolen is poisoned, and by
Buh Pa'tridge into having his head cut off, and his henchman
Buh Frog is duped into letting Buh Squel escape.[19]

Other All Saints trickster stories show Buh Rabbit being
tricked by the king, by Buh Bear, again by Buh Pa'tridge, and

once by the other animals working together. Buh Rabbit's fate as a victim varies from mere embarrassment to violent death. In the tale "Buddah Rabbit and the King," the king calls all the animals together for a board meeting at the church. All are required to be present and on time, on penalty of a five-dollar fine. While the other animals are at the meeting, Buh Rabbit robs their gardens. Then he manages to slip into the meeting late without being observed by the king or anyone else. When he sees the king's hound dog behind the door, however, Buh Rabbit gets so nervous he jumps up, attracting attention to himself and getting caught.[20]

"Buddah Bear Plays Dead" portrays Buddah Bear attempting to be a trickster, but being out-tricked by Buddah Rabbit. Rabbit hears the news that Bear is dead and joins the other animals in viewing the alleged corpse. He tells the gathered animals that he has heard that a dead bear turns over and groans three times. The "corpse" turns over and groans three times, thus giving himself away as alive. Rabbit flees with Bear in hot pursuit but unable to catch him. Here is an example of the educative function of these tales. It is as important for slaves to learn how to avoid being tricked as to learn how to be a trickster.[21]

A notable theme of the trickster tales is the punishment of those who refuse to live up to the obligations of friendship or to come to the aid of their fellow creatures in time of need. The All Saints versions of the classic "Tar Baby" folktale exemplify the rhetorical device that shows things getting worse as the result of the neglect of sacred duties. The other animals seek revenge on Buh Rabbit for his not sharing water from his secret well during a drought. He tells them he gets up early in the morning to drink the dew. One night Billy Goat watches Buh Rabbit and discovers the secret well. Billy Goat hastens back to tell the other animals. They decide to teach Buh Rabbit a lesson and set a trap—the tar baby—for him near his well. When Buh Rabbit comes for a drink, he says, "Hey, oh deah, Putty Gal!" but the tar baby does not answer. Buh Rabbit becomes angry. "You bettah talk wid me! Oh, ef I slaps you one time wid my right han', I broke you jaw!" The tar baby does not answer, and Buh Rabbit hits her. His hand sticks. "Ef I slaps you wid my lef' han' one time, I slaps you face one-sided!" The same result. "Ef I kicks you wid dis foot, I bus you belly open!" The same result again. "Oh, I wouldn' wantuh kick you wid muh lef' foot—Oh, Gal, ah ain' know whut 'e done fo you!" Both hands and both feet are soon stuck. "Well, I knows one ting! Uh got uh belly hyuh. I butt you wid my belly, buss you open!" Eventually even his head and teeth are stuck to the tar baby. Then the goat and other animals come and scold him for lying about the dew before releasing him. Buh Rabbit's selfishness is the reason *why* the other animals revenge themselves upon him; his vanity, boastfulness, and stupidity are the keys to *how* they are able to accomplish that revenge—a valuable lesson to slaves.[22]

Throughout the animal trickster tales runs the reminder that overweening pride, literally hubris, often leads to a tragic fall. It is true of the powerful animals whom Buh Rabbit outwits, but it is also true of Buh Rabbit when he forgets who he is and tries to rise above his fellow creatures. This is well expressed in "Buh Rabbit and Buh Partridge," which, like "Buh Partridge Pay Buh Rabbit Back," depicts a murderous trick played on Rabbit by the tricky little Partridge. Partridge steals Rabbit's new whip, made of an alligator's hide, while it is drying on a persimmon tree. When Rabbit approaches, Partridge hides his head under his wing so as to appear headless. He tells Rabbit his head came off when he ate a piece of the alligator's tail, but "Ah lakes it wid muh haid off. Now wen it cole lak it be or rainin' ah kin leab muh haid tuh de house out de weddah wen ah goes off!" Rabbit can hardly wait to secure the advantages of headlessness for himself as well. He rushes home to his wife, who at first refuses but eventually reluctantly agrees to cut his head off. "So she lif' up de shawt han'le axe en come down 'BLAM.' Ah Buh Rabbit haid roll off tuh one side en Buh Rabbit fluttah and gib 'e las' hop."[23]

Clearly such tales as these provided the slaves with a vicarious satisfaction in the weak overcoming the powerful through cunning. And just as clearly such tales provided didactic lessons regarding behavior. As Sabe Rutledge, a slave at The Ark plantation, later recalled, "Buh Partridge was the onliest one I ever hear bout could get best of Buh Rabbit." Equally clearly, however, neither literalistic interpretations nor clearcut moralizing exhausts the meanings of the animal trickster tales. These folktales represent, perhaps preeminently, the artistic expression of the slaves—the means through which their creative artists present to posterity not merely the social, but also the artistic impulse of their community. In the animal tales they found the perfect vehicle to express those impulses, those often painful cultural truths, in an indirect, and thus less painful, way. Such indirection goes to the heart of African concepts of eloquence.[24]

5

There was another cycle of trickster tales narrated by the All Saints slaves. In this cycle the trickster role is not played by a surrogate slave—Buh Rabbit—but by a real slave—John. John and Ole Maussa continually match wits: John seeks to gain the advantage through trickery and guile while Maussa tries to avoid being tricked by John's mischief. The slaves who told and the slaves who listened to these tales used them to redefine the harsh realities of life in bondage into a realm more attractive, making a virtue of necessity, thereby giving a voluntary color to an involuntary plight. By identifying unpleasant necessities with accepted values and beliefs, slave storytellers sought to find intellectual coherence and emotional unity in diverse experiences and to impose meaning on those experiences that would influence future attitudes and patterns of behavior. John, who shares Buh Rabbit's cheerfully cynical and ironic view of social relations and of life in general, delights in the tug-of-war with Ole Maussa, Ole Miss, and even the devil himself.[25]

As in the case of the animal trickster tales, one of the important themes running through the John cycle is the trick-

ster's theft of food and the victim's attempts to punish the trickster for stealing. In "Another One Mom Phillipa Tales," John
has been breaking into the corn patch and stealing Maussa's
corn. Maussa sets a steel trap and, to his surprise, catches
John, who promises never to steal again if Maussa will just for-
give him this time. Maussa says, "John, you too good a nigger
to take a gun and SHOOT. I'll tell you what I'll do. I'll put you
in a sack and tie a mill stone to the sack and throw you in the
river." Maussa ties John up in a sack and goes to find a mill
stone. After awhile a poor old hungry woman comes by and
hears John inside the sack praying. She asks who is in the sack
and John replies that his master is trying to make him eat, but
he is too full. And Maussa has gone to get more rice, ham,
beans, pork, chicken, and pie. The old lady says she is hungry.
John says, "You loose this sack and get in here and when
Maussa come he'll give you all that good sumptin' to eat."
When Maussa finds the old lady, he lets her go but decides to
take John out to the desert where there are wild animals who
will eat him up. He takes John out and ties him to a tree, but
by and by some hunters arrive. John tells them Maussa has
stationed him there to keep hunters off the property. They release him and tell him to get out. Maussa next tries to drown
John in the mill pond with a big rock tied around his neck, but
John gets the rock loose and swims out on the other side. John
says, "Maussa, I trust the Lord. Lord take care o' John." To
insure that this moral lesson is not lost, the storyteller adds,
"And John's faith turned them all to Christian. They all got to
believin' Christian like John." This tale is one of the clearest
examples of the relationship between the John tales and the
animal trickster tales. Most Afro-American versions of this
tale feature animal tricksters rather than John.[26]

There is a similar story from the Waccamaw about the
master's numerous efforts to kill John in revenge for his many
knaveries. Maussa tells his wife, "You know I'm goin' kill
John! That nigger too wise. He learn too much. He might kill
me!" Here is perhaps as clear a statement as one might find of
the slaves' rationale behind wearing a mask of ignorance and
servility before whites. Maussa takes John to the river and ties

him in a sack, but decides to eat his dinner before killing him.
John, tied up in the sack, begins to sing:

> Anyhow! Anyhow, my Lord! Anyhow!
> At the Holy Ghost we may bide!
> Lord, I goin' up to Heaven anyhow!

An old lady passing by says, "Ain'ts that John?" John tells her
he is going up to heaven today. She says she would like to go
up to heaven. John says, "I can go up any old day. I'll let you
go in my place." She lets him out and replaces him in the sack.
Maussa comes back and unwittingly throws her into the river.
After two or three days, John comes strolling back to the plantation driving a herd of Maussa's cows that he has taken from
the pasture. John says, "Mornin' Maussa!" "John, I thought I
kill you!" "Yes, Cap'n, you kill me! I been all to Heaven and
come 'round by Hell. The Devil have these cow. Say he ain't
want 'em. You want 'em?" "Drive 'em in the stable, John.
John, you know where my money?" "I know where your
money 'fore I leave." "Well you go get that money and spend it
for anything you want." And thus, the narrator emphasizes,
"John come to be a rich colored man." In this tale slave storytellers demonstrated both the advantages and the limits of the
trickster's role. John comes to be like Maussa in more ways
than one. Not only does he become rich and powerful, but in
order to do so he also becomes more selfish and cruel, turning
his trickster's wiles on a poor, helpless old woman. There is a
complexity of vision in this depiction of the price of achieving
power that the simple equation of the trickster with the slave is
insufficient to account for.[27]

In their trickster-creation—John—the slaves personified
the advantages, disadvantages, and dangers of the trickster role.
The hazards of failure were great (although in the surviving All
Saints tales John never fails), but the rewards—money, freedom, status, and power—were greater. One of the most famous tales in the John cycle, widely diffused into a number of
cultures, relates to John's prowess as a seer and prophet. John,
who eavesdrops on the conversations of Maussa and Old Miss,
always knows Maussa's plans for him in advance. Maussa, very

impressed, makes a bet with a neighboring planter. "Well, I'm goin' huntin' tonight with my dogs. I bet you my whole plantation and $700.00 your John can't come here in the mornin' and tell me what I caught!" John's master accepts the bet, and the two planters arrange the test for the following morning:

> Next mornin' here Maussa call John. He have John get on a horse and Maussa get on a horse and here they gone to the Cap'n plantation.
>
> The Cap'n, Cap'n Jule, have the animil he catch under a bit tub on the back porch. When John and his Maussa come ridin' up Cap'n Jule say, "That your fortune teller? All right John! What's under that tub?"
>
> And John were a scared nigger. John study. He study. He roll he fist. He scratch he head. He look up to the sky. He study the cloud but that didn't help him none. John just plumb give up. "Well, Maussa, I tells you the truth, well Maussa, you caught the old coon at last!"
>
> They raise up the tub and there a big, old tiger coon! John was so happy he jump up and knock his heels together six times and say, "Lord! Lord! Maussa, I can tell you the day you goin' die! Cap'n Jule, I can tell you anything you want to know!"
>
> And Maussa give John him freedom and a place, a house and land and all, and made John a rich man.

This tale, climaxed by a lucky pun relating the trapped animal and the all-too-common epithet for black people, provided the slaves not only with vicarious satisfaction at John's gaining wealth and freedom, but also with explicit instructions on how to eavesdrop to learn the masters' plans in advance. Such tales as this also point up the extremely complex set of relationships involved in plantation paternalism. The slaves and the masters were involved, on at least one level, in cooperative endeavors, in which success was vital to both. If the master's financial fortunes fell, the slaves felt the pain acutely. If the master's profits were higher, the slaves were apt to share, however unequally, in the benefits. It is this aspect of cooperation that is reflected in such tales as this and others in which Maussa and John engage in joint endeavors, however uneasy the partnership. Other tales indicate all too clearly the sharp conflict between slave and master, and the necessity for the slaves to use all their ingenuity to improve their lot.[28]

The human trickster also appears in other slavery-time stories under the names "Jack" or "Go-lias." In the story "Strong Man Jack," the hero (John in most versions collected elsewhere) wins a swimming race without getting his feet wet.

> Once upon a time they was Jack was a very wise nigger. Cap'n brag on Jack. Cap'n say, Jack can beat all swimmin'! The he come tell Jack, "Jack, tomorrow a man coming here to swim with you. Want you to swim two three miles. Want you to beat him. I bet money on you. You must beat him so's we can get all that money."
>
> Now Jack can't swim nary lick. He go get him a stove, grits, meal, meat, and lard and ALL and put 'em on his back. Man come to swim with Jack he say, "What you got them bundle for and goin swimmin?"
>
> Jack tell him, "You think I goin' swim three four miles 'thout any sumptin t'eat. You must think I a big fool!"
>
> And the man what come think if Jack goin' swim so far he have to stop and cook rations long the way he better down. Jack Cap'n got all THAT money.[29]

But the slave trickster is not satisfied with outwitting Old Maussa, gaining his freedom, and acquiring wealth and power. The quest is for status. In the following tale the slave trickster (here called Go-lias) tricks the devil himself:

> Devil tell Go-lias he was strongest. Go-lias tell Devil HE was strongest. Devil tell Go-lias "Strongest man can FLING the furrest! And I bet you so many thousand dollar I can FLING the furrest!" Go-lias bet the devil he couldn't. And the Devil he up and shrowed (throwed) 'bout two, three mile. Go-lias told him he'd BEAT him! (Lot o' money up!)
>
> Now the Devil done the first chunkin'. Go-lias said, "Well, my time to chunk, eh?"
>
> Devil tell him, "Yes, your time to chunk."
>
> Go-lias got him a flag and gone to wavin'. Wavin' and lookin' up. Wavin'. Wavin'.
>
> Devil say, "Go-lias, what you donnin'?"
>
> "I wavin' the angel to STOW WAY! STOW WAY!"

Big old sledge! Big old piece o' iron! Wavin the angels to move way! Stow way!

Devil sing out, "Uh! Uh! NO! NO! You done win. You done win. Devil didn't gruss (trust) Go-lias after dat. Go-lias look like sech a strong fellow anyhow and after he find Go-lias was goin' chunk up in Heaven and wavin' the angel out the way he GIVE UP! He done chunk TWO, THREE miles. Know he win. Wavin' the engel (angels) to move back out the way!"[30]

In spite of the subservience and role-playing forced upon John—and by extension upon themselves—the slaves found the trickster tales appealing. The reasons are not hard to understand. The trickster is always one up at the end. One of the tales, for instance, describes the efforts of John and Old Maussa to capture a lion who has been breaking into the master's corn. First the master tells John to go down to the cornfield and capture "what-some-ever 'tis." John finds the lion breaking corn, but when the lion sees John he chases him around and around an oak tree. John reaches around the oak tree and grabs both the lion's paws. Afraid to turn the lion loose, he holds him there all night. When Maussa comes in the morning, he orders John to put the lion in a cage. John says, "Maussa hold right here till I come." So John leaves Maussa holding the lion while he goes home to eat, rest up, and ponder. When he returns, he tells Maussa to turn the lion loose as he runs across the field and under the barn. The lion, thinking John has gone *into* the barn, goes through the barn door, which John promptly locks and bars. Maussa comes and tells John to put him in a cage. "I'll put the cage in the barn and I wants you to put this lion in the cage!" John is frightened but tells Maussa, "All right, suh. All right, suh, Maussa!" Maussa puts the cage in the barn. The lion begins to roar and chase John around and around the cage. John fools the lion into thinking he is IN the cage. The lion jumps in and John locks him up. "Maussa can't 'blive his eyes when he sees John one put the lion in the cage. John TOO smart!" Not only is John a step ahead of the master but also of a creature even bigger and more powerful than the master. The occurrence of the lion in this tale, when there are no lions in All Saints Parish, exemplifies not only an African continuity but also the measure of fantasy that is incorporated into the realistic human trickster tales. It is the counterpart of the realistic element in the animal trickster tales. Only animals that are found on the Waccamaw are portrayed in the animal tales from the Waccamaw. What is important is the combination of elements of realism and fantasy. The realism allows for the identification of the story with the slaves' everyday lives; the fantasy allows the imagination to soar and to perceive differences as well as similarities.[31]

It is not merely in their combination of elements of realism and of fantasy that the animal trickster tales and the human trickster tales are similar. Both exemplify the African tradition of indirection, both emphasize the positive values (and the limits) of trickery, and both portray the triumph of the weak over the powerful through the use of their wits. Both present a combined opposition to the status quo coupled with a distortion of conventional social values. And both promote the idea of personal freedom from the pressures of restrictions from the larger society.[32]

Similarities must not be emphasized out of proportion, however. One major distinction differentiates the slave trickster from the animal trickster. The slaves *knew* John, knew him personally; John was one of them. He helped the other slaves, by his example, to endure and to prevail even when the burden was heaviest. Unlike Buh Rabbit, John was neither allegorical nor symbolic. He expressed the values and attitudes of his fellow slaves directly. In his inevitable victories over the more powerful master (and thus over the slave system), John provided the slave community with perspective by incongruity. Buh Rabbit tales might be narrated to the master's family as well as to one's fellow slaves, but John tales were for telling only among the slaves. John expressed in symbolic action their plight and their hope, their collective experience, and thus their very identity.[33]

6

Storytelling sessions in the slave community functioned as
sources for inspiration and education and transformed pure
rhetoric into quasireligious ritual. The verbal action of the narratives, as Sabe Rutledge recalled, evoked a behavioral response in the hearers. The storytellers' stylistic techniques of
acceleration and retard, their subtle use of verbal dynamics
and vocal imitations of the animals, and the audience's laugh-
ter and interjected comments on the action—matching what
they heard in the story with what they already knew and felt—
all exemplified the social relations that generated the audience's emotional response to the narrative and the narrative's
dependence on the spontaneous cooperation between the storyteller and the slave community in the narration. In the mutually revealing relationships between a society and its folktales,
the interplay of personality and social relations was one of the
prime movers of such symbolic action as storytelling. But the
social situations of storytelling had distinctive structures of
their own, which were not necessarily like those of social
structures of the society at large. It is perhaps less accurate to
think of storytelling in the slave community as a narrator's performance before an audience than to regard it as a mutual performance. Granting that, as stories were told time and again,
they were reshaped with each telling, and conceding that with
changes in context came subtle changes in meaning, one is
nevertheless struck, after all, more with the major continuities
than with the minor variations.[34]

Slave storytelling, then, may be regarded in some sense as
a ritual—an everyday symbolic enactment—that provides
both a condensed representation of cultural ideals and social
necessities, and a frame for experience. In the All Saints animal
trickster tales, the most common introductory frame by far is
some variation on "Once upon a time . . ." ("One time . . . ,"
"One day . . . ," "Once . . . ," "Once 'pon a time . . ."). Other
common introductory framing devices are variations on "Have
you heard the one about . . . ?" ("Did I gib you de tale 'bout
. . . ?"), "This is a story about . . ." ("Dis be 'bout . . ."), and

"It all began . . ." ("What staht duh ting . . ."). The most common concluding frame is inherent in the story itself; the story ends with the concluding event in the plot. Nearly a third of the stories, however, end with some form of moral comment on the meaning of the story by the narrator, indicating the function of the tales in the slaves' moral education. But such framing devices, by shutting in desired themes and shutting out extraneous ones, could make any story a part of that education.[35]

Speculation on the extent to which slave storytellers and their listeners considered their stories to be educational is presumptuous, probably impossible, and perhaps useless. Clearly folktales have functions, but precisely what their function may be is easier to assume than to demonstrate. One of the uses—as distinguished from functions—of trickster tales on the Waccamaw was sheer entertainment, no insignificant contribution in the House of Bondage. Many of the animal tales were seen as light-hearted narratives of the amusing antics of various animals in a wide range of situations. A tally of the cast of characters—alligators, bears, buzzards, cooters, cows, crows, deer, dogs, fish, foxes, frogs, geese, goats, guineas, hawks, hogs, opossums, owls, partridges, rabbits, raccoons, squirrels, turkeys, wolves, and an occasional human being—reveals that the animals depicted were common in All Saints Parish and were well known to the audience. In this regard slave storytellers followed the practice of their African ancestors, as they did when they added to the fun with such paralinguistic features as imitations of the appearance, voices, and demeanor of the animals.[36]

No matter how entertaining, some tales end with a kind of moral, sometimes in the form of a proverb's informing the listeners that they can learn a lesson from the experiences of the characters in the narrative. Some tales depicted the fate of those who failed to acknowledge their dependence on God. In the story "Buzzard and Hawk," a hawk and a buzzard meet and discuss their methods of procuring food. It is clear from the tone of their discussion that Buh Hawk plans on showing off. In the process he impales himself on a sharp fence post.

The tale ends with the buzzard's making a statement that spec-
ifies the moral of the tale: "Hit good to wait on de Lawd."
Many slave folktales, on the Waccamaw and elsewhere in the
slave South, were implicitly or explicitly didactic. Such tales
were widely used in Africa as part of the education of children.
Their descendants on the slave plantations of the New World
continued the tradition of education through folktales.[37]

The educative function of folktales in All Saints Parish
was primarily oriented toward a model that stressed how to
act and how to survive, rather than one that explained how
things came to be. There are no examples of the kinds of cosmological myths found in some cultures that purport to explain all kinds of natural and supernatural phenomena. The
nearest thing on the Waccamaw to such myths were the etiological tales, which ostensibly explained to the slaves the origin of some observable characteristic of some member of the
animal kingdom. This they usually did humorously. Etiological themes in the African prototypes of such tales were not
confined to animal tales (as they were on the Waccamaw); but
the tradition of explaining, in amusing stories, striking animal
characteristics already known to the audience was especially
strong in African animal tales. One such etiological tale from
All Saints is "Buddah Woof Fool Buddah Rabbit." Rabbit
meets Wolf one day after Wolf has caught many fish. Rabbit
asks how he caught so many. Wolf says he caught them with
his tail. Rabbit goes to the creek and dips his tail in the ice-cold
water, in which it freezes fast. Buh Owl, responding to Rabbit's cries for help, grabs him by the ears and tries to pull his
tail out of the creek. Not only does he stretch Rabbit's ears and
eyes in the process, he also breaks off Rabbit's frozen tail.
Thus, because of Wolf's trickery, Rabbit winds up with no fish;
but he has big eyes, long ears, and no tail.[38]

The slaves' folktales also served the important psychological function of projecting personal hopes and fears, frailties
and weaknesses onto a surrogate (usually a weaker animal),
which is then made to defeat his stronger and larger adversaries (usually big but not very smart animals such as Buh Bear
and Buh Wolf). This trickster-surrogate steals his adversaries'

food and women, cheats them in races, shifts the blame for his own misdeeds onto them, and even tricks them into fratricide and homicide. It is signficiant that Buh Rabbit and John do not merely defeat their adversaries; they do so while flaunting a jaunty sassiness and cool imperturbability that slaves were under pressure to conceal from their masters. The trickster shares with the slaves the cynical view of a social order as it is observed from the bottom up. Life in the universe of the trickster tales, as in the House of Bondage, is a constant struggle. These tales make it clear that the struggle is not merely for food and sex for their own sake, but as symbols of mastery over the powerful. The trickster's victories represent projections of the slaves' most acutely frustrated desire—status in a highly status-conscious time and place. These symbolic attacks upon power itself clearly reveal the slaves' irreverence toward the power arrangements of the slavery system, and the trickster's victories over the powerful served to enhance the slaves' self-image.[39]

It is important that one look beyond the surface themes of the trickster tales. The enhancement of self-image, of identity, was an important function of the All Saints trickster tales, however elusive it may be to examine. Like Buh Rabbit, slaves too had to make do with their natural resources and learn to maneuver with what they had. Encompassed within the definition of a situation was a strategy for dealing with its reality. The importance of self-reliance, as indicated in the trickster tales, was underscored in the proverb of one of the All Saints slaves, Hagar Brown, who noted, "Every tub stand on its own bottom." Survival in the slave system depended upon the slaves' ability always to remember who and where they were and upon their ability to "put yuh bess foot fo moss" (put your best foot foremost) in any crisis.[40]

The trickster was an inspiration as well as a projection of frustrations, and he occasionally served as a role model as well. But it is important to note that the trickster was portrayed by slave storytellers in ambivalent terms. In his single-minded pursuit of mastery he becomes as merciless as the master. The slave folktales were full of aggressive humor, perhaps the most useful of humanity's numerous aggressive implements. The trickster's aggressive brutality and destructive cruelty served less as role models for slaves to emulate than as outlets for repressed antisocial hostilities engendered by the slave system. Trickster tales to some extent served as object lessons in the tactics of day-to-day resistance to slavery. A tally of the tactics actually used by slaves in All Saints Parish and in other slave societies reads like a motif-index of slave trickster tales— lying, cheating, theft, "accidental" destruction of property, feigned sickness, and the like. It is clear that such tactics as these ran counter to the values of their African heritage and of their creolized form of Christianity. If the slaves suffered any pangs of conscience over the adoption of patterns of behavior at variance with their deepest values, these trickster tales served as a release valve. These stories provided a rationale for adopting such behavior patterns in particular situations without necessarily regarding them as normal or socially approved behavior patterns. By such situational ethics, theft from a fellow slave was wrong; but theft from the master was not really theft, as the masters were already thieves because they were masters. That slaves perceived the relationship between master and slave to be one of "thief" and "stolen property" is indicated in the Gullah proverb, "Ef bukra [white man] neber tief, how come neggar yer?"[41]

Thus the trickster tales served as an inspiration for and justification of some forms of antisocial behavior and simultaneously served as a release valve for even more aggressive and antisocial repressed desires. In so doing they both promoted day-to-day resistance to slavery and at the same time lessened the likelihood that a large-scale slave rebellion might overthrow the system. Not the least important part of the slaves' deft blend of accommodation and resistance, the trickster tales were in fact a crucial element in the development of an adaptive Afro-American culture. That culture was the most significant form of resistance against the spiritual and psychological, if not the physical, effects of slavery.[42]

The slaves developed a cohesive new culture out of their various African heritages and the necessities of the New World environment, promoting a sense of group solidarity even in the face of the most dehumanizing aspects of the slave system. Conceding that slavery must be recognized as a total institution, one need not conclude that such total institutions necessarily led to the total dehumanization of their denizens. The creolized culture created by the slaves served as a buttress to courage, confidence, and self-esteem and as a buffer to infantilism and dependency. Not only was the masters' stereotype of the slaves as ignorant, carefree, and childlike rejected by the slaves as a self-concept; but, in being perceived by the slaves as denigration, the stereotype actually promoted their sense of solidarity. A common, although unintended, result of denigration is to promote a sense of homogeneity and cohesion even in a turbulent situation. Such examples of traditional expressive behavior as storytelling were among the most striking means by which the slaves proclaimed and reinforced their sense of identity.[43]

CHAPTER SEVEN

Gullah: A Creole Language

Perhaps the most striking aspect of slave folklife to visitors on the rice plantations of the Waccamaw was the strangeness of the slaves' speech. One reason for that strangeness lay in the fact that numerous Africans inhabited All Saints Parish as late as the mid-nineteenth century—including the regal "Daddy Tom," "Maum Maria," and Prince; the "outlan'" Africans Peter, Sampson, and David; Millie the Guinea; young Scipio the coachman; Old Scipio of Woodbourne; and Old Pemba of Hagley. Many of them continued to count and pray in their native African languages and to call objects by their African names. These aging Africans were the last of the thousands who had personally experienced the shock of enslavement and the outrage of the middle passage, the last who still viewed the world through an African lens, and the last who could still speak their unadulterated African tongues. But the speech of American-born slaves was also alien to northern and European ears. Whether they described it as gibberish or jabbering, whether they were able to "overhear some of the words" or required translation from plantation whites, travelers repeatedly confessed their inability to understand the speech of the slaves. "The lowland negro of South Carolina has a barbaric dialect," contended Edward King. "The English words seem to tumble all at once from his mouth, and to get sadly mixed whenever he endeavors to speak." King and other visitors to the lowcountry found the slaves' tones so thick, their enunciations so indolent, and their phrasing so odd as to remain unintelligible.[1]

When one speaks of language among a people so imperfectly understood by visitors, one speaks with inevitable imprecision; but one might at least say that the slaves of All Saints Parish belonged to a distinctive speech community. One who would attempt to understand their folklife must attempt to understand Gullah—the common language that the slaves forged out of diverse traditions and uncertain circumstances—for it was through Gullah that Africans from various backgrounds not only communicated with and entertained one another but also linked themselves into a community, gave shape to a common culture, and handed down that culture to their posterity. And it was through Gullah that the symbolic group identity that the slaves created for themselves was impressed most powerfully upon the generations to come. Thus the study of Gullah is the study of the central element in slave culture. As a moving force in the creation of Afro-American culture in the crucible of slavery, the development of Gullah was comparable to the development of English, German, or French in the creation of these respective national cultures.[2]

2

It is now impossible to say with any certainty what Gullah sounded like as spoken by the slaves. The Gullah speech of present-day All Saints Parish is probably no more than a pale reflection of antebellum slave speech. Such sources as Genevieve Willcox Chandler's interviews with ex-slaves who had learned to speak the language in the mid-nineteenth century offer tantalizing glimpses of its vocabulary and its pronunciation and an opportunity to discover its grammatical rules.

As a language Gullah did not behave like English; it formed plurals and indicated possession and negation differently; it used a somewhat simpler system of pronouns and a somewhat more complex system of verbs than did English. Certain of the most distinctive features of the language merit brief consideration here. To concentrate on Gullah as spoken by the last generation of slaves in All Saints Parish, in the context of slave folklife, is not to imply that their speech was unrelated to black speech elsewhere and at other times—any more than studies of contemporary black speech in comparative linguistics imply that speech exists in isolation from other aspects of culture.

Gullah pronouns in All Saints Parish made no distinction between men and women. In this behavior Gullah retained a structure common to a number of African languages, such as Ibo, Ga, and Yoruba. The initial all-purpose Gullah pronoun was *e*, as in "After de war *'e* come back and took into big drinking and was' 'em till *'e* fall tru" (After the war he came back and took into big drinking and wasted it [his money] until it fell through [i.e., he lost it]). *E* served as the masculine, feminine, and neuter pronoun. Later, under the influence of English, *he* became the all-purpose Gullah pronoun, although *e* was not completely replaced during slavery, when the last generation of slaves was learning to speak the language. The Gullah pronoun *he* was not the same, however, as the English pronoun *he*, but served for masculine, feminine, and neuter gender. Interchangeable with *e*, *he* could serve as a subject or to indicate possession, as in "*He* broke *he* whiskey jug" (He broke his whiskey jug), or "Sam *he* husband name" (Sam was her husband's name).[3] The Gullah pronoun for objects in All Saints Parish was *em*, which served for masculine, feminine, and neuter gender, whether singular or plural, as in "See *'em* the one time" ([I] saw him once); "Grandfather took old Miss Sally on he back to hid *'em* in the wood where Maussa" (Grandfather took old Miss Sally on his back to hide her in the woods where the master [was hiding]); "He couldn't believe *'em*" (He couldn't believe it); and "Flat *'em* all up to Marlboro" ([They] took them all on flatboats up to Marlboro [District]).[4]

Gullah pronouns of the slavery period were more complex than English pronouns in one respect, however: Gullah included a form for second person plural, which English lacks. Standard English pronouns cannot distinguish between singular and plural in second person. Writers variously represent the Gullah pronoun for second person plural as *yinnah* or *unna*. Like other Gullah pronouns, the same form was used as a subject or to indicate possession, as in "*Yinnah* talk big storm hang people up on tree?" (Are you [all] talking about the big storm that hung people up in the trees?) or "if *unna* kyant behave *unna* self, I'll tek yu straight home!" (If you can't behave yourselves, I'll take you straight home).[5]

Two other features of the Gullah nominal system that distinguished it from English should be mentioned. One was that Gullah speakers marked possession by juxtaposition rather than by word forms, as in "*He* people wuz always free" (His people were always free) or "Joshuaway been *Cindy* pa" (Joshua was Cindy's father). The other distinctive feature of the Gullah nominal system was the practice of non-redundant plurals. If pluralization were otherwise indicated in a Gullah sentence, it was not also indicated by the noun, as in "Dan'l and Summer two both my *uncle*" (Both Daniel and Summer were my uncles).[6] This practice was in sharp contrast to English, which required agreement in number between determiners and the nouns they modify.

The prepositions of slave speech in All Saints Parish, unlike English prepositions, did not use different forms to indicate whether one was approaching some location or one was already there. The same form was used for approach prepositions—"Old people used to go *to* Richmond Hill, Laurel Hill, and Wachesaw and have those prayer-meeting"—or for static-locative prepositions—"One stop *to* Sandy Island, Montarena landing" (One [Yankee gun boat] stopped at Sandy Island, Mt. Arena landing).[7]

The verbal system of Gullah was considerably more complex than that of English. First, equating verbs occurred in past tense, as in "When my mother *been* young woman, work in rice" (When my mother was a young woman, she worked in rice); but they were usually omitted in present tense, as in "Dem Yankee wicked kind a people, drive me from me home" (Those Yankees are a wicked kind of people to drive me from my home). The omission of an equating verb is called zero copula.[8] Gullah sentences used zero copula for verbal adjectives, as in "I *glad* for freedom till I *fool*" (I was so glad for freedom that I appeared foolish). In this regard, Gullah retains the verbal adjective construction of several West African languages, including Ewe, Fante, Kikongo, and Yoruba, but contrasts strongly with English.[9]

Another All Saints Gullah construction that retained West African linguistic forms was the combination of verbs both to take an object and to serve as a connective. The most common verbs used in this construction were *say* and *go* (usually in the form *gone*). The following are examples: "One gentman at de gate *tell me say* he Messus broder, is Messus dare in?" (A gentleman at the gate told me he is the Mistress's brother; is the Mistress therein?) and "They didn't do a God thing but *gone and put* a beating on you, darling" (They didn't do a God's thing but put a beating on you, darling). In this usage the slaves retained both the form and the function of the same construction in Ibo and Twi.[10]

Perhaps the most unique feature of the Gullah verbal system was its distinction between continuing and momentary actions (aspect) rather than specifying the relative time of the action (tense). In their emphasis on aspect over time, Gullah speakers in All Saints Parish retained the grammatical rules of such West African languages as Ewe, Kimbundu, Mandinka, and Yoruba.[11] Unlike English, Gullah rarely distinguished between present and past tenses in the verbal system. When the slaves did mark past tense in Gullah, they used the verb form *been*: "When the Yankee come I *been* on the loom" (When the Yankees came I was on the loom). In the preceding sentence, ex-slave Ellen Godfrey used both marked and unmarked verb forms for simple past tense (*been* and *come*, respectively). If the slaves only occasionally marked past tense, they often marked aspect, whether ongoing, completed, or habitual. They indicated continuing actions by using the old creole form *duh* preceding the verb or the newer form *-ing* following the verb: "Yuh can't rest, bubber, w'en hag *duh* ride yuh" (You can't rest, brother, when a hag is riding you [i.e., when you have nightmares]), or "You *getting* this beating not for you task—for you flesh!" (You are getting this beating not for [failing to finish] your task—[but] for your flesh!). *Duh* and *-ing* were interchangeable but were not used together. Waccamaw slaves marked continuing actions in the past with *been* plus the action verb, as in "Aunt Ellen *been looking* for you all day" (Aunt Ellen has been looking for you all day). The slaves indicated habitual actions, past or present, by using *be* plus the action verb, as for example, "You orter *be* carry money with you" (You should [habitually] carry money with you).[12]

Similarly, Gullah speakers on the Waccamaw rice plantations distinguished between ongoing and momentary negation in their speech. Momentary negation was indicated by *ain't*, as in "I *ain't* want him" (I did not want him). The slaves marked ongoing negation by *didn't*—as in "Maussa *didn't* low you to marry till you twenty-two" (The master did not allow you to marry until you were twenty-two)—for past ongoing negation, and by *don't*—as in "They *don't* eat much"—for present ongoing negation. It is perhaps more appropriate to regard *didn't* and *don't* as full negators in their own right, rather than as contractions of *do* or *did* plus a negator. Multiple negation was often used in Gullah for additional emphasis, as in "She say she *never couldn't* refuse when the old people ask for a drink" (She said she could never refuse when the old people asked for a drink).[13]

Furthermore, when Hagar Brown exclaimed, "I *too* glad my chillun ain't born then!" (I am very glad my children had not been born then!), or when one of the slaves at Hagley told Emily Weston, "See, ma'am, young duck *bery* lobe run bout, and your pen broke!" (See, ma'am, young ducks very much love to run about, and your pen broke [and your hog ate two of my ducks]), they exemplified a continuity with African ways of modifying adjectives and adverbs.[14]

Three final distinctive features of slave speech should be discussed. One is that certain verbs that normally take complements in English did not necessarily take complements in Gullah. Margaret Bryant's lament, "Missus, I *ain't wuth*. I *ain't wuth*!" (I am not worth [anything, i.e., I am not feeling very good]), requires a complement in English, but not in Gullah. Second, Gullah speakers expressed passive voice in a construction that would indicate active voice in English, as, for example, "How come you *wanter bury* Watsaw?" (Why do you want to be buried at Wachesaw?) or "A crow *kin eat*" (A crow can be eaten [i.e., is edible]). A similar construction is prominent in Afro-American speech in Jamaica. Third, the slaves transformed declarations into yes/no questions by adding the word *enty* at the end of statements, as in "Chillun, ain't find duh plum, enty?" (Children, you didn't find the plums [did you]?) *Enty* has been variously translated as *n'est ce pas* and *ain't it.*[15]

The last generation of slaves in All Saints Parish thus spoke a language that differed from English in several fundamental features. The slaves did not distinguish between location and approach in their prepositions, nor among genders in their pronouns. They indicated pluralization only once in a sentence, but they used distinctive forms of the second person pronoun to distinguish between singular and plural. They designated possession by juxtaposition. In their verbal system the use of equating verbs was varied, but other verbs were combined in distinctive ways. Both verbs and negators distinguished between ongoing and momentary actions rather than when those actions might have taken place. Negation could be intensified by using multiple negators. Verbal complements could be omitted. The same form was used for active or passive voice; declarative sentences could be made into questions by the use of the interrogative tag *enty*. While house servants may have spoken nearly standard English, many Gullah speakers in the Waccamaw rice fields were quite consistent in their use of these features. Whatever else might be said of the relationships between black and white speech in America, Gullah—as spoken by the last generation of slaves—followed a different set of grammatical rules than did English. Those white commentators who considered Gullah an imperfect result of "a savage and primitive people's endeavor to acquire for themselves the highly organized language of a very highly civilized race" were not only racist, but linguistically ignorant.[16] However much Gullah and English may have shared the same vocabulary, Gullah and English were not the same language.

3

Gullah did not, of course, spring forth full-grown in the mid-nineteenth century. Its roots, however, remain wrapped in linguistic controversy. Linguistic pronouncements are notoriously hazardous, and historians have generally been reluctant to make them. An acceptable explanation is likely to be complex, for the making of a language is not a simple process. If historical and linguistic evidence are put together, however, some of the answers seem neither elusive nor ambiguous. In retrospect it seems clear that the speech of the slaves on Waccamaw rice plantations resulted from the convergence of a number of African languages with English. The resulting speech, Gullah, exemplified a creole language, which in turn developed from an earlier pidgin. The terms *pidgin* and *creole*, although frequently misunderstood, are technical linguistic terms and imply no value judgments, derogatory or otherwise. A pidgin is by definition a second language: it has no native speakers. Pidgins are developed as a means of communication among speakers of various languages. The linguistic elements in a pidgin are simplified within a context of restricted use— usually for trade. Pidgins are neither broken languages nor distortions of the grammatical structure of the source languages. On the contrary, pidgins are quite regular in grammatical structure as the result of the simplification process, although their specific grammatical patterns may not be the same as those of any single source language. Whenever a pidgin is passed on to succeeding generations as a native tongue, it is said to be a creole language. Since creole languages must serve all the functions of a language, not just the limited linguistic interactions for which pidgins are devised, creole languages expand rapidly in complexity in succeeding generations. This intricate process in which a language based upon the convergence of other languages undergoes expansion in both use and form is called creolization.[17]

To gain some perspective on the creolization process in Gullah, it may be helpful to move back in time from All Saints Parish in the mid-nineteenth century to West Africa in the age of the slave trade, simply to note the varieties and structural similarities of West African languages. West Africa was a region of several hundred mutually unintelligible languages. With a constant need for communication with neighboring peoples who spoke diverse tongues, linguistic skills became highly developed among West Africans. Many in the Senegal-Gambia region, for instance, were bilingual, fluent in both Wolof and Mandingo, the two most widespread languages of the region. Bilingualism at some level was a necessity in polyglot West Africa. Despite their mutual unintelligibility, however, there were several similar linguistic patterns that African languages shared and that set them apart from other languages of the world. In particular, the two great West African language families, Bantu and Sudanese, shared strong structural similarities.[18]

Thus the process of pidginization began in Africa out of the need for speakers of disparate languages to communicate with one another, and the process was helped along by structural similarities among otherwise different tongues. Perhaps the most unusual catalyst for pidginization, and certainly the most ironic, was the slave trade. In the slave baracoons of the West African coast and in the wretched shipholds of the Middle Passage, enslaved Africans from various regions, speakers of distinct tongues with centuries of tradition behind them, were forced to seek similarities in their languages and to develop whatever means of communication they could. Wolof speakers from Senegambia may have served as interpreters among the enslaved Africans and between the slaves and their captors, lending a strong Wolof cast to the emerging pidgin.[19]

Pidginization became widespread among Africans in the New World. Those linguistic patterns among the mutually unintelligible languages most familiar to the largest number of Africans had the best chance of surviving in the new pidgin. Much of the vocabulary was supplied by the alien languages of the masters. Thus there developed an Afro-Dutch pidgin in the Virgin Islands; Afro-Portuguese pidgins in Brazil and Curaçao; Afro-Spanish pidgins in Cuba, Puerto Rico, and Colombia;

Afro-French pidgins in Louisiana, French Guiana (influenced by Portuguese), Haiti, Guadeloupe, Grenada, and other Antilles. There were both Afro-French and Afro-English pidgins in Trinidad and Tobago. Afro-English pidgins developed in Barbados, Antigua, Guyana, Jamaica, and South Carolina. The Dutch colony of Surinam was a special case. It developed an Afro-English pidgin as well as an Afro-Portuguese pidgin with strong English lexical influences, rather than an Afro-Dutch pidgin. Many of these pidgins were adopted by succeeding generations and became creoles.[20]

The first generation of slaves in South Carolina came mostly from the Caribbean, where they had already learned an Afro-English pidgin. Because they constituted only a small proportion of Carolina's small population, and because in their generation contacts between enslaved Africans and their English-speaking masters were of necessity close and personal, their speech may have been nearer to standard English than that of later generations who came directly from Africa. But the great expansion of rice culture in the early eighteenth century brought about an enormous increase in the young colony's slave trade. The expansion in both rice and slaves was caused in part by the opening up of the rich rice lands north of the Santee, including those along the Waccamaw. The importation of thousands of slaves annually from West Africa fostered intercultural contact on a scale unprecedented in South Carolina, not only between Africans and Europeans, but among diverse groups of Africans. With a higher ratio of Africans to Europeans than anywhere else on the North American mainland, Georgetown District became the mainland equivalent of a Caribbean colony in the eighteenth and nineteenth centuries. The rice planters, when they purchased slaves, preferred Africans from the Senegal-Gambia region, from the rice-growing regions of the Windward Coast, and from the Congo-Angola region. Nearly 40 percent of the Africans enslaved and brought to South Carolina between 1730 and the end of the legal slave trade came from Angola. Another 20 percent came from Senegambia, and the other 40 percent variously from the Windward and Gold coasts, Sierra Leone, and elsewhere. The growing Waccamaw plantations shared fully in these human imports.[21]

But the dominant linguistic features of the emerging pidgin were not necessarily the same as the dominant regional origins of the enslaved Africans. The linguistic features capable of being comprehended by the largest number of slaves, whatever their native tongues, were most likely to survive; those least comprehensible were least likely to survive. Some languages, such as Wolof, had been even more widespread as second languages in Africa than as native tongues. The chances that features of such languages would survive were far greater than those of a language that functioned only as a native tongue. Furthermore, if English and any given African language or languages shared some feature, it had a better chance of surviving than features that strongly differed. Certainly not all African features were retained, nor were all English features acquired.[22]

But most Africans coming into the Waccamaw region in the eighteenth century spoke little if any English. When confronted with the harsh dilemmas of their new environment—as slaves of alien, white-skinned people whose shouted commands they could not understand—their response must have been to lapse into silence, struggling to find meaning in the words yelled at them, straining to isolate some familiar sound in the stream of gibberish. Where once they had lived among family and friends whose languages and folkways they shared, now they found themselves among strangers who had also fallen victim to the slave trade, strangers who could understand neither one another nor their white masters. Two overwhelming needs—to comprehend the masters and to comprehend one another—had profound and complex, and sometimes contradictory, effects on the linguistic response of the Africans to their enslavement. If there were forces at work on the plantations to discourage retention of their native languages, there were also circumstances that had an opposite effect. While the social dominance of the masters served as a strong incentive to learn English, the numerical dominance of the blacks facilitated their retention of African patterns of speech. While they lacked a common linguistic heritage, through trial and error in their efforts to communicate with one another Africans increasingly became aware of common elements in their diverse tongues. More and more they found other speakers of their own or similar African languages. Out of these opposing tendencies—to learn English and to retain African speech patterns—they created a new language: Gullah.[23]

This new language took root to such an extent among enslaved Africans that it was passed on to succeeding generations on the Waccamaw and elsewhere in the lowcountry. To African-born slaves Gullah would have remained a pidgin, a second language, but to the American-born generations it was a creole, a native tongue. Once Gullah acquired native speakers and assumed all the functions of a language, it expanded rapidly in complexity. From then on, incoming Africans learned Gullah neither through trial-and-error nor from the plantation whites, but from American-born blacks.[24]

Gullah had not one but many African sources. Perhaps the most conspicuous was Wolof, but elements from Sierra Leone were especially important in the new language; and there were also influences from Fante, Ga, Kikongo, Kimbundu, Mandinka, Twi, Ewe, Ibo, and Yoruba. But African languages were not, of course, the only influences on the development of Gullah. As Gullah passed from the pidgin to the creole stage in the early eighteenth century, the Carolina lowcountry was one of the most linguistically diversified areas on the North American mainland. The sources of the All Saints population included not only slaves from various parts of West Africa but also the French Huguenot Belins, LaBruces, and Mazyks; the Allstons and Westons from England; the Frasers, Heriots, Nesbits, and Wards from Scotland; the Tuckers from the Bahamas; and the Middletons from Barbados. In Charleston were also heard Quakers with their distinctive use of English as well as other British settlers with regional accents from such places as Warwickshire, Lancashire, Ulster, and Jamaica. There were also speakers of German, Spanish, and Portuguese, and even of Creek and Cherokee. While the ultimate influence of these linguistic strains varied with their social and political valuation, a discernible lowcountry English—which was both influenced by, and influential upon, Gullah—emerged in this complex linguistic environment.[25]

If there was a European influence on the speech of the slaves, there was a corresponding African influence on the speech of the masters. In the lopsided demographic circumstances of the lowcountry nearly all whites necessarily had much contact with blacks, but many blacks had only limited contact with whites. The Waccamaw planters by and large learned to talk like their slaves rather than expecting their slaves to talk like them. Creolization on the Waccamaw was not limited to one race. It left its mark on the posterity of both transplanted Africans and transplanted Europeans and influenced their speech patterns in ways still apparent. It is not surprising, given the demographic dominance of Africans, that whites were affected by the linguistic patterns of the blacks. Northern and English visitors rarely failed to note the extent to which the planters, outnumbered nine to one by their slaves, absorbed elements of Gullah. An English traveler referred to the speech of the planters as "that peculiar accent derived from almost exclusive association with negroes." A northern correspondent wrote that "the children of the planters, brought up on the plantations, and allowed to run in the woods with the little negroes, acquired the same dialect; and to-day many a gentleman's son regrets that it is apparent in his speech." Many of the white plantation children perhaps learned their first language from a Gullah-speaking nurse, thus becoming native speakers of Gullah, and learned English as a second language. Some apparently never really mastered English. It was said of Benjamin Allston, Sr., of Turkey Hill, the father of Martha Allston Pyatt, that "his language was like a negro's, not only in pronunciation, but even in tone." Many of the Waccamaw rice planters remained fluently bilingual in Gullah and English from their childhood throughout their lives. Others would have been at least passively bilingual, able to comprehend the Gullah of their slaves but not to speak it.[26]

Those slaves who came into the greatest contact with whites also became actively or passively bilingual in Gullah and English. Creolization did not cause slave speech to develop in a completely uniform way; as early as the eighteenth century slaves were observed along a speech continuum ranging from the pidgin of the newly arrived Africans to fully standard and even elegant English, depending upon access to education. House servants played an important role in dual creolization. They helped to bring Gullah into the Big House and standard English—that is, the regional standard—to the cabins on the street.[27]

Thus Gullah developed in a situation of language contact on the Waccamaw, with reciprocal influences of African and English features upon both the creole language and the regional standard. The English of the whites and the Gullah of the blacks were similar enough in vocabulary to permit relatively easy communication, despite some occasional difficulties, but different enough for some whites to regard Gullah as a corrupted form of English and thus evidence of the mental indolence or incapacity of the slaves. Doubtless even the Waccamaw rice planters had occasional difficulties in understanding the slaves. Any number of factors might work to foster difficulties in master-slave communication. The masters' problems in comprehending the slaves' speech, however, did not always result from inherent difficulties in the interaction of languages that were similar but not identical. Thriving on ambiguity and paralinguistics, Gullah speakers proved their language to be as adept in impeding communication as in facilitating it. Gullah could reveal, but it could also conceal; and slaves had a stake in concealing information from the masters. By cloaking African words with their African meanings behind English words with similar sounds, slaves may have constructed a code through which they could communicate with one another while keeping the masters uninformed.[28]

4

The African penchant for using indirect and highly ambiguous speech, for speaking in parables, was adapted by slaves on the Waccamaw rice plantations to a new natural, social, and linguistic environment. This aspect of creolization was strikingly illustrated in their proverbs. African-born slaves undoubtedly brought with them numerous African proverbs, although none survived on the Waccamaw in its original African form. This loss is not surprising, for proverbs depend upon the skillful use of metaphor, and the translation of metaphor from one language to another is always difficult and sometimes impossible. Even today attempts to make literal translations of proverbs from one language to another are often meaningless to readers not conversant with the original tongue. Since the enslaved Africans came from many different linguistic stocks, and since their emerging pidgin language did not (in its pidgin stage) offer a sufficiently large metaphoric repertory from which to choose even roughly equivalent metaphors, poetic translations were even more difficult than literal ones. To say that African proverbs themselves did not survive on the Waccamaw is not to say, however, that the grammar of African proverb usage— both as a means of aesthetic variation upon drab everyday speech and as a means of avoiding the painful effects and insults of direct commentary—did not persist in the proverbs of the new language.[29]

By employing the grammar of African proverb performance and the largely English vocabulary of the new creole language, All Saints slaves were able to transform older African proverbs into metaphors of their collective experience on the Waccamaw rice plantations. Some African proverbs were retained virtually unchanged in Gullah. The Hausa proverb "Chattering doesn't cook the rice" continued in All Saints Parish as "Promisin' talk don' cook rice." Another Hausa proverb—"Does dog eat dog?"—retained even its rhetorical question format in the Gullah "Dat's dog eat dog, enty?" The Gullah proverb "Empty sack can't stand upright alone" was a Waccamaw version of the Mandingo "It is hard for an empty sack to stand upright." And the Dahomey distinction between rhetoric and reality, "The mouth talks plenty that the heart does not say," reappeared on the Waccamaw as "Heart don't mean ever thing mouth say."[30] Other African proverbs, however, underwent minor changes. The Fante proverb "One bird in the hand is worth ten in the sky" became the Gullah "Most kill bird don't make stew" (An almost killed bird does not make a stew). The Dahomey "Crooked wood makes crooked ashes" became "Onpossible [impossible] to get straight wood from crooked timber." And the Bantu proverb "Every beast roars in its own den" became the Gullah "Every frog praise its own pond if it dry."[31] The wording of proverbs was relatively fixed, but, like all forms of folklore, proverbs were subject to variation. Usually the variation was minor, but more radical changes in the imagery were not infrequent as African proverbs were adapted to a new environment. The difficulty of translating meaning and rhetoric at the same time made some African proverbs resistant to direct translation. In such cases, the slaves retained the meaning of the African proverbs but completely transmuted the rhetoric into metaphors more meaningful to their new environment. Thus the Gullah proverb "Most hook fish don't help dry hominy" (An almost hooked fish [one not quite caught] does not improve the taste of dry hominy) is related in meaning to the Yoruba proverb " 'Nearly' is an individual we invariably meet on the way"; but it is related in rhetoric to another Gullah proverb "Most kill bird don't make stew." Similarly, the Gullah proverb "Chip don't fall far from block" is related semantically, but not rhetorically, to the Fante proverb "No one needs to teach the leopard's child how to spring."[32]

The proverbs of the slaves were more fixed in their structural patterns than in their wording. Among the common structural patterns were the *If A then B* formula, as in "Ef you hol' you Mad e would kill eby Glad" (If you hold your anger, it will kill all your happiness), and the rhetorical question pattern—so common in Africa—as in "Don' hol' nuttin down deep een you heart. Ain' God gi' you mout fo talk 'em?" (Do not hold anything deep down in your heart. Did God not give you a mouth with which to talk about it?)[33] Perhaps the most common structural forms were simple positive or negative propositions ("Change gwine come" [is inevitable] or "One clean sheet can' soil another" [cannot soil another]); double propositions ("It takes a thief to catch a thief. Nightwalkers meet nightwalkers"); or even triple propositions ("So I totes mah powder en sulphur en I carries mah stick in mah han en I puts mah truss in Gawd" (So I carry my powder and sulfur and I carry my stick in my hand and I put my trust in God).[34] Multiple propositions in a proverb proved an apt structure for the slaves to use in making invidious distinctions, as in "Man p'int, but God disapp'int." Perhaps the most striking use of this structural form by the slaves was in their proverbs contrasting blacks and whites. "Black people rule sickness with magic," one such proverb contends, "but white people get sick and die." "People ain' got no business tryin' to be Gawd," another advises. "Not black people anyways. Let de white people go on. Dey is gwine to hell anyhow!"[35]

The slaves used their proverbs as metaphors of social relations, that is, to indicate relationships among the elements of the proverb, between the proverb and the real world, and, by extension, among the elements of the real world. Through their proverbs the slaves made distinctions by comparison and contrast and commented upon how things happened, affirming or denying equivalence ("Det wan ditch you ain fuh jump" [Death is one ditch you cannot jump] or "Hell ain' no hole. A hole 'ud git full")[36] and causation ("Likker'll make you not know you mama" [Liquor will make you not know your mother] or "The master didn't make all the world in a day"). A variation on negative equivalence was the proverb in which one element was greater than the other, such as "There are more ways to kill a dog than to choke him with butter."[37]

The slaves' use of proverbs in All Saints Parish cannot be completely understood without reference to the proverb's strategy, that is, to its plan for relating the situation described within the proverb to the real-life social relations to which the proverb was being applied. Perhaps the most frequent use of proverbs was to offer advice. A proverb might present either of two mutually exclusive strategies—it might recommend an action or it might suggest that the situation was normal and could not be changed, thereby promoting acceptance or resignation. These recommendations were, of course, given indirectly, metaphorically. "Work while it is day" and "Put yuh bess foot fo moss" (Put your best foot foremost [forward]) are examples of the *action* strategy. Hagar Brown's "Don't let 'em put dey hand in your eye! Some people gouge 'em" counseled defensive action. Gullah speakers on the Waccamaw had an interesting inversion of the widespread proverb "Still waters run deep," which reversed the strategy from a counsel of taciturnity and reticence to one of action, advice made more powerful by coupling the reversal of strategy with a metaphorical relationship between water and the ritual purification of baptism: "Still water gits stale an' scummy too quick. It can' wash away sin."[38] The practical experience of rice field and swamp found poetic expression in slave proverbs.

That trouble is a natural condition of the world was suggested by the Gullah proverb "Trouble goin' fall!" Here was an example of the *acceptance* strategy. "Trouble made for man," the proverb warned. "Ain't goin fall on the ground! Goin fall on somebody!" There was no way to anticipate trouble, another proverb cautioned, all one could do was "just take it like I takes it!" When asked, "How you take it?" the speaker replied, "As it come! As it come!" Still another proverb counseled patience, for troubles come and troubles go: "A march that comes in like a lion will go out as quiet as a new-born lamb."[39] Some proverbs suggested that the hearer was responsible for his or her own misfortunes and that nothing was to be done except to accept the consequences: "You's made a hard bed for you sef, now you got to lie in it." Other proverbs advised treating misfortune as a necessary learning experience, for example, "Sad we got to be burn 'fore we learn" and "Burn child dread fire, you know." Still others suggested that, however hard the misfortunes might be, they could be borne. According to one proverb, "Eby back is fitted to de bu'den" (Every back is fitted to the burden). According to Sabe Rutledge, "What God got lot out for a man he'll get it."[40]

Two important elements of Gullah proverbs were their sense of authority—a result of their detachment and generalization—and their ambiguous and allusive poetic nature, which made it possible for them to be used in a variety of ways. The proverbs of the slaves were set off from ordinary speech by such poetic devices as alliteration ("Sin is easier to stand dan shame"), rhyme ("Tit fuh tat, butter fuh fat, ef yuh kill my dawg, I kill yuh cat"), repetition ("Heavy hearts make heavy steps"), personification ("Every frog praise its own pond

if it dry!"), meter ("Rob Peter to pay Paul"), and parallelism
("Mo rain, mo ress, but fair wedder bin bess").[41] Because of
such poetic qualities and their allusiveness and ambiguity,
metaphoric proverbs were broadly applicable. They could be
cited with equal authority in a wide range of situations. Indeed, it was possible for a slave in All Saints Parish to advise
either action or inaction in any situation by means of an appropriate proverb. This flexibility has sometimes made proverbs seem contradictory to modern readers, but, just as a language gives its speakers words for saying either yes or no, the
Gullah proverb repertory enabled the slaves to offer whatever
advice seemed appropriate to the situation, and to do so in
heightened poetic language. The Gullah proverb repertory
contained proverbs touting boldness ("Cards an' dice is like all
in life; dey ever falls well for bold players") or caution ("Er
good run bettuh dan uh bad stan" [A good run is better than a
bad stand]) with equal art and with equal authority.[42]

The full meaning of any given proverb was only clear in
the context of its use. As a Fante proverb has it, "There is no
proverb without the situation." There were no specialized occasions for reciting proverbs on the rice plantations of the
Waccamaw. Some forms of folk expression, such as the telling
of folk tales, were set apart for the evening after the rice field
tasks were accomplished; but proverbs were recited on any occasion that language could be used. Proverbs could be used for
the artistic ornamentation of everyday discourse, or they could
be used in informal litigation—that is, in the settling of con-
flicts, tensions, and arguments among the slaves. Although the
Gullah proverbs were rather straightforward in their application of metaphor, they were one of the most complex folk-
lore genres in their extreme sensitivity to context.[43] Unfortunately, there are no known descriptions of the contexts of
proverb usage in All Saints Parish during slavery. In this regard, as in other linguistic matters, one must be more tentative
and less precise than one would wish.

5

Inevitably, personal accounts of language interaction among the slaves were rare. Like the languages of Africa, Gullah expressed a high degree of ambiguity and double entendre in face-to-face speech. Since Gullah was an oral rather than a written language, slaves on the Waccamaw rice plantations must have developed a heightened sensitivity to vocal intonation, gestures, and kinesics. The intonations of slave speech must be considered within the context of the tonal languages of some of the Africans who were brought to South Carolina as slaves—Bini, Ewe, Fante, Ga, Ibo, Mandingo, and others. Gullah speakers did not regularly use tone to distinguish meaning, as many African languages do. In slave parlance, however, words did sometimes carry different—or even opposite—meanings depending upon intonation. For example, the adjective *bad*, when intoned by a slave on a slow, falling tone (like *baaad*), could be an expression of admiration for another slave who successfully flouted Ole Maussa's rules. More common, however, was the retention of African intonation patterns in Gullah sentences without their African meanings. These included such practices as high or mid-level tones at the end of declarative sentences, rising tones at the end of declarative sentences, level tones throughout a statement, use of tones that fell from high to mid, use of tones that rose from low or mid to high, and the use of level tones at the end of questions. These intonation patterns did not occur under similar conditions in English. The typical expectations of English were that sentences would use generally level tones, with a falling tone at the end of statements and a rising tone at the end of questions. Not only did Gullah differ strongly from English in intonation but also in patterns of loudness or softness, of syllable and breath dynamics, and in the use of pitch and stress.[44]

The transition from an oral to a written language gave rise to increasing English influences upon Gullah—direct influences upon some slaves, indirect influences upon others. Despite legal prohibitions against teaching slaves to read and write in South Carolina, many masters and more mistresses, including Emily Weston of Hagley and Mary Vereen Magill of Richmond Hill, taught at least some of their slaves to read the Bible. Emily Weston gave Testaments to the graduates of her literacy classes. Surviving letters from such slaves as Mulatto Joe to Robert F. W. Allston, Samuel Taylor to Elizabeth Blyth, Mary Ann (surname unknown) to Emily Jordan, and George Simons to Francis Weston testify to the ability of some slaves to write as well as to read. Some slaves, such as Prince, the Westons' coachman, were even considered to be bookish. But while slave literacy seems to have been relatively widespread on the Waccamaw, it was not intensive. Only a small proportion of the slaves on any plantation ever learned to read or write.[45]

Literate slaves had a more intensive encounter with the language of highest prestige, English, than did other Gullah speakers. Their continuous contact with English was not only influential on their own speech but also on that of other slaves with whom they were in daily communication. Gullah gradually shed more and more of its creole characteristics and acquired a greater resemblance to English. This process was an example of decreolization, and during the nineteenth century it fostered an increasing degree of local variation in slave speech.[46] One of the most important changes in Gullah during decreolization was the tendency for it to lose more and more of its surviving African words and to replace them with words from English. Gullah also shifted grammatically in the direction of the regional standard, although it retained a number of structural differences that stemmed from differences in the histories of the two languages. Underlying these changes in vocabulary and grammar were such factors as the relative prestige of speakers, contact across social strata, and value orientations among each group.[47]

Decreolization is a more rapid form of linguistic change than the usual internal language change. What has all too often been considered an imperfect process of deletion from the regional standard can now be seen as an ongoing addition to a creole language. In decreolization, unlike other forms of linguistic change, grammar tends to change before sound. Decreolization tends to create a continuum among speakers from the creole toward the regional standard. The process of decreolization began in slavery, mainly affecting house servants, but the rapid linguistic change that is usually associated with decreolization had to wait until the breakdown of rigid social stratification, which was partially accomplished by emancipation.[48]

6

Another way in which the slaves preserved their African linguistic heritage was exemplified in their naming practices. For the slaves of All Saints Parish, as for their African ancestors, naming was socially significant, almost mystical, and illustrated personal and historical experiences, attitudes toward life, and human values. In many African societies the power to name was perceived as the power to control, to order reality. Thus the slaves and the masters vied with one another for the right to name the children. Probably most slave names on the vast Waccamaw rice plantations were chosen by the slaves themselves. Certainly with the high annual birth rate among the slaves many masters found it easier to leave such matters to the slaves. But other masters, perhaps in recognition of the power inherent in naming, insisted on their right to name the slave children. As a result, many slaves were given two names: one an outer or public name, given by the master, the other an inner or basket name, given by the parents and used only among kin and friends. Sabe Rutledge, for instance, although known by his African name *Sabe* among the other slaves, was called *Newman* by his master. His grandfather, the driver at The Ark plantation, was also known by different names in the Big House and on the slave street: "They called him Rodrick Rutledge for shortness," Sabe Rutledge later recalled. "My grandpa *real* name Jim."[49]

The use of basket names did not stem exclusively from master/slave competition over the right to name, but followed traditional African double-naming customs. Basket names, even as late as the mid-nineteenth century, were often words of African origins. In All Saints Parish, as in the Caribbean, one

general pattern was to name children one of the African day
names, after the day of the week on which they were born. All
seven African day names appear to have been still in use on the
Waccamaw as late as the Civil War.[50] See Table 10 for a comparison of the day names and African derivatives.

Day names were not the only African names common
among the slaves of All Saints Parish. The following list, although by no means exhaustive, does at least demonstrate an
extraordinary perpetuation of African names among Waccamaw slaves after several generations in the New World.[51]

English	*African*	*English*	*African*
Affa	Affy	Rinah	Rhina
Binah	Binah	Saby	Sabe
Binyky	Binky	Sambo	Sambo
Cotta	Cotta	Sango	Sancho
Congo	Kongy	Satirah	Satira
Fante	Fany	Sawny	Sawney, Sawne
Mingo	Mingo	Sena	Cinda
Minto	Minta, Minda	Sibbey	Sibby
Monda	Munder	Yono	Yanie

But African continuities were not manifested solely in the
static retention of easily recognized African names. On the contrary, behind many of the apparently English names in the
plantation records were African naming practices. The transition from the sound spoken by the slaves to the script written
by the masters was not always accomplished without a certain
cultural transformation. What the master thought a given spoken name to be and what a slave thought a given spoken name
to be were not always the same. In many cases the masters
wrote into their records whatever English name sounded most
like the name spoken by the slave. If a slave couple informed
their master that they had named their son *Keta*, a common
name among the Yoruba, Hausa, and Bambara, the master
might have understood the child's name to be *Cato*. Similarly,
if a slave couple told a planter that they had named their
daughter *Haga*, a Mandingo name, he might have written
Hagar into his records. The Mandingo name *Heke*, meaning a

Table 10.
Distribution of African Day Names in
Antebellum All Saints Parish

Day of Week	Ghana	Guyana	Jamaica	All Saints
		Masculine Names		
Sunday	Kouassi	Couachi	Quashee	Quashey, Quash
Monday	Kodio	Codio	Cudjo	Cudjo
Tuesday	Kouamina	Couamina	Cubbenah	Ben ?
Wednesday	Kouakau	Couacou	Quaco	Quacco
Thursday	Yao	Yao	Quao	Quauo
Friday	Kofi	Cofi	Cuffee	Cuffee
Saturday	Kouami	Couami	Quamin	Tommy ?
		Feminine Names		
Sunday	Akouassiba	Corrachiba	Quashiba	Quasheba
Monday	Adioula	Adioula	Juba	Juba
Tuesday	Aminaba	Amba	Beneba	Bina, Bhina, Venus, Venice
Wednesday	Akouba	Acouba	Cuba	Cupid
Thursday	Ayaba	Yaba	Abba	Abby
Friday	Afouba	Affiba	Phibba	Phoebe, Phebe, Pheby
Saturday	Amoriba	Abiniba	Mimba	Minda, Pemba

powerful animal, may have survived behind the English name
Hercules, often spelled Hackless in the slave lists (and still pronounced that way) in All Saints Parish. The following is a sam-
pling of English names from Waccamaw plantation records
that may have been homonyms of African names:[52]

English	African	English	African
Abby	Abanna	Jemmy	Jeminah
Abraham	Abra	Joe	Cudjo
Billy	Bilah	Lizzie	Liceta
Ben	Bungoh	Moses	Moosa
Dunkin	Dunke	Pat	Pattoe
Esther	Esher	Sam	Samba
Jack	Jaeceo	Quinny	Quenchy
		Trim	Tremba

In other cases the African meaning was retained behind a
direct translation of the name into English. Day names were
frequently translated from their African names into their English equivalents. Such day names as *Monday* and *Friday* were
quite common among All Saints slaves, as were such other sea-
sonal basket names as *March, April, August, Summer,* and
Winter. An ex-slave, Monday Holmes, described how he came
to be named: "My RIGHT name been Samson but I never been
call dat YET. Name Samson outer the Bible. Calls me MONDAY
'cause I born that day." [53]

The creolization process, by which African ways of using
language were applied to a new tongue, produced such new sea-
sonal basket names as *Christmas.* All Saints slaves continued
other African approaches to naming as well, although the specific names produced were not African. The African tradition
of naming children after conditions at the time of their birth—
the weather, the appearance or temperament of the child, or
the attitude of the parents toward the birth—was reflected on
the Waccamaw in such names as *Snow, Brass, Boney, Lazy,
Handful, Grace, Welcome, Fortune,* and *Hardtimes.* Similarly,
slave names on the Waccamaw revealed the adaptation to English of African patterns of naming after localities (*London,
Paris, Dublin,* and *Scotland*) and after titles (*King Agrippa,
Prince, Doctor,* and *Gentry*). On the other hand, the masters'
influence was clear in the abundance of classical (*Caesar, Bru-
tus, Nero, Cato, Juno,* and *Pompey*), literary (*Hamlet*), and
historical (*Washington* and *Napoleon*) names. Biblical names
seem to have been popular with both masters and slave parents
(*Abraham, Amos, Dan'l, Esau, Esther, Isaac, Israel, Lazrus,
Peter, Paul,* and *Mary*). Secondary names were often necessary
to distinguish among slaves who shared the same name. Occasionally occupational names (*Driver Sam, Cooper Sam, Driver
Primus,* or *Carpenter Tom*) were used to make such distinctions, but more commonly they were made on the basis of age
(*Big Joe, Little Joe, Old Nancy, New Rachel,* or *Grandma
Kit*), physical appearance (*Long Scipio*), or genealogy (*Cato's
Mary, Bob's Rachel,* or *Minder's Joe*).[54]

Sometimes genealogical relationships were reflected in

slave naming practices in other ways. At least some All Saints slaves continued to follow the African pattern of having children named by their grandparents. Hagar Brown's mother, for instance, insisted on naming her grandchild. As Hagar Brown recalled many years later, "Had me gang of chillun when ma die. I had Samuel, I had Elias, I had Arthur, I had Beck. Oh, my God! Man, go way! I had Sally! I had Sally again. I didn't want to give the name 'Sally' again. Say, 'First Sally come carry girl.' Ma say, 'Gin 'em name "Sally"' I faid (afraid) that other one come back for him. Had to do what Ma say. Had to please 'em. Ma name Sally."[55]

Plantation records fail to reveal the extent to which slaves on the Waccamaw, with or without their masters' permission, used surnames among themselves; but there are tantalizing glimpses in the memories of aged ex-slaves and the observations of perceptive visitors, such as Wyndham Malet. Malet noted, "The negroes have family names, but you never hear them used except among themselves, they call them 'titles,' e.g. Mrs. W's second footman is Gabriel, his family name Knox; Mary, the housemaid's title, is Green." Some slaves took their titles from their masters. According to ex-slave Mariah Heywood, "Grandma Harriet, (Harriet Mortor wuz her title but that time they always gone by they Master title). Joe Heywood was Joe Belin—he was Parson Belin man—he take the Heywood title after mancipation. Poinsette (Uncle Fred) ALWAYS carry that title. That day, all the right hand servant always take they Massa title." After emancipation some slaves—like Joe Heywood—refused to keep their master's surname and chose another. Others—like Fred Poinsette—retained the titles they had used in slavery, even if it had been the surname of their former masters. It should be remembered that the use of titles was not between master and slave, but among the slaves themselves. If some adopted their master's surname as a title, others chose their titles on the basis of personal characteristics. Margaret Bryant described how her husband had chosen his title on the basis of his preeminence as a carpenter. "Husband title, husband nichel (initial) been 'One.' Number one carpenter—give 'em that name Michael One—and he give 'em that name."

Few slaves appear to have adopted their owners' surnames as titles; fewer still adopted new titles at emancipation. Elizabeth Collins, a young English woman who served as housekeeper at Hagley plantation from 1859 to 1864, wrote, "It must be remembered the negroes have their *titles* as well as the white man. I have often noticed they used them among themselves, and have no doubt if slavery is abolished that they will claim the recognition of their *titles*." Apparently they did so. Certainly there was little correlation in the manuscript census records for All Saints Parish in 1870 between the surnames of the freedmen and the surnames of the largest slaveholders in 1860, such as Ward and Weston (although there were numerous black Allstons, Alstons, and Pyatts). It seems likely that some slaves adopted their owners' names as titles in bondage, but most did not. Many of those who did abandoned them upon emancipation.[56]

Through their insistence upon their right to name their own children, Waccamaw slaves successfully (for the most part) asserted control over a critical area of their lives. Through their adoption of titles, no less than through their perpetuation of African traditions of naming, the slaves of All Saints Parish proclaimed their sense of identity and community, and of continuities with their individual and communal pasts. In the creolization process they retained some African names outright, and they adopted some English names outright. More commonly, if less obviously, they adapted African grammars of naming to the needs of a new linguistic and social environment. Since one's name is his most basic label of identity, it was no trivial accomplishment.

7

Thus, by every device of sound and syntax, semantics and lexicon, gesture and intonation, the slaves combined elements of their various African heritages to create a new creole language. There were, of course, British contributions to Gullah, particularly in matters of vocabulary and to some extent in pronunciation. The sources of most, although not all, of the word forms in the creole were to be found in British regional dialects. There were no British parallels, however, for many of the grammatical patterns of Gullah, which shared many structural features with West African languages and with the creole languages of the Caribbean. The culture contact of transplanted Africans and transplanted Europeans in All Saints Parish fostered processes of creolization by which African pronunciations, meanings, and grammatical patterns converged with English vocabulary and some English pronunciations and meanings. Gullah, originating as a pidgin, became the native tongue of the black speech community. In the course of creolization Gullah passed from pidgin to creole to the beginnings of decreolization in the direction of the regional standard.[57]

Not the least of the ironies of Afro-American history is that aspects of black speech related to Gullah are now stigmatized by many blacks as well as whites as illiterate or associated with field hands, in contrast to the high prestige of "proper" English. In retrospect one should be more impressed with the success of the slaves, a people of diverse linguistic backgrounds and limited opportunities, in creating a creole language and culture than appalled at their "failure" to adopt *in toto* the language and culture of their masters. The continuing—and sometimes acrimonious—debate on the relationship among Gullah, other manifestations of black speech, and the speech of whites is beyond the scope of this study. Whatever its significance to present-day controversies, Gullah was critically important to the slaves, creating a special bond among them. The continuation of numerous features of Gullah into contemporary black English, indeed the continuation of Gullah itself, surely points to its importance as a potent symbol of cultural unity among the slaves who developed it and passed it on to posterity. The potent symbol stood for a potent reality. Speech communities, to an even greater extent than political communities, imply a shared culture and world view. Since Gullah was susceptible to individual manipulation, it was the shared property of everyone in the speech community, packed with the symbols of that community's culture and its values. Slaves could not communicate with one another, could not offer proverbial advice, and could not name their children without using the symbols held in common by the community and embodied in its language. Thus Gullah became perhaps the principal means by which the slave community molded the individual into its culture.[58] To create a living language would seem a greater accomplishment than to preserve one, and the slaves of All Saints Parish shared fully in that accomplishment. After the creolization of Gullah by the slaves, who could remain unaware of their linguistic achievement or doubt its central position in slave folklife?

CHAPTER EIGHT

"My Time Up with You"

For four years, off and on, there had been Civil War on the Waccamaw; in 1865 there was an uneasy peace. The slaves of All Saints Parish had endured four years of ambiguous service, marked by hope, fortitude, and short rations. Some had accompanied their masters to war; others had been evacuated inland with their masters' families; still others had remained behind to work the rice plantations, had seen Union gunboats on the Waccamaw, and had witnessed daring Marine raids on plantations and saltworks. Many slaves, field hands and house servants alike, abandoned the plantations at the first sound of Federal trumpets and eagerly set out in search of freedom. Their desire was for freedom from slavery itself, not merely from abusive masters or overseers; and slaves of kindly masters sought freedom as eagerly as those of cruel ones. From April 1862 on, a steady stream of runaways fled to Union ships. The risks they were willing to run evidenced the price they were willing to pay to be free. The dangers were great—apprehension typically meant death—but the desire for freedom was greater. Even those who remained behind were strongly on the side of the Union, for the Federal forces were regarded as liberators. As Welcome Beese put it, "Yankee fight fo' free we!" The Confederates, their government crumbling, their cities burning, and their armies routed in the West and in northern Virginia, had been forced to surrender at Appomattox. As the news of that transaction spread south, the slaves of All Saints could scarcely believe the Day of Jubilo was at hand: "Sunday we got our freedom. Bright day, too," Mariah Heywood recalled. "When the big gun shooting, old people in the yard. 'Tank God! Massa, HE COMING!' (referring to 'Freedom') 'HE COMING!' Chillun say, 'What coming? What coming? What

225

coming, Grandma?' 'You all will know! You all will know!'"
And so they did. "I know when Lincoln shoot the chain of
slavery off my neck," Mariah Heywood added. "And I hear the
gun. I hear SHOOT and the house shake and water shake out
the glass. The gun shoot to Georgetown." To Sabe Rutledge,
the coming of freedom was like having "been to the Devil and
come back now!" Ellen Godfrey was ecstatic: "I talk with
Abram Lincoln own son Johnny, and, bless your heart I glad
for Freedom till I fool!"

> Freedom forever! Freedom everymore!
> Want to see the Debbil run
> Let the Yankee fling a ball
> The Democrack will take the swamp!

An uneasy peace came to the Waccamaw in 1865, and
with it emancipation of the slaves. Notwithstanding the spe-
cious arguments and sanguine expectations that had activated
the eager secessionists of All Saints, once more the Stars and
Stripes flew over Georgetown, once more the divided sections
were united, and never again would men and women be bought
and sold at public auction in America.[1]

2

All Saints blacks could hardly believe that the vaunted Confederate armies had been so completely vanquished, although
they soon had the confirmation of returning troops who had
survived the failed campaigns. As the ragged Confederate columns trudged by, blacks were struck by the contrast with the
dashing, swaggering warriors who had marched off to war in
1861. The irony was not lost on Welcome Beese: "Mister
White carry forty or fifty tousan' (thousand) man from town,
say he goin to Washington to get Old Lincoln head. Come
back without old Lincoln head. Say he went out the notion.
Stid o' he gettin' Lincoln head fore he through Lincoln get
his'n." But the irony was not merely scornful. The complex
and intricate ties that had bound slave and master together in
the close and continuing relationships of slavery did not come

unraveled all at once. They conspired to produce equally complex reactions to emancipation, reactions born of the conflict between the slaves' innate longing for freedom and their inculcated (but, for some, no less genuine) loyalty to their "white folks." Young Elizabeth Allston noted the indignation of Aleck Parker, the family coachman, when her mother informed him that he would have to find another job, for she was unable to pay him: "Miss, I don' want no wagis! Aint I wuk fu yu sence I bin man grown, aint my fadder wuk fu Maussa fadder! En my grandfadder de same! . . . Ain't I drive yo!, de Guvna's lady all de time Maussa bin Guv'na, en now yu tink I gwine lef yu. . . . no ma'am, not Aleck Pa'ka, e aint mean enuf fu dat!" And Mariah Heywood, who had prayed for freedom for four years, seemed to take ironic pride that her former master, Charles Alston, had been the last of the All Saints rice planters to swear allegiance to the victorious Union and the last to acknowledge the emancipation of his slaves. "Major Charles the last man of Waccamaw gone under the flag!" she boasted. "Whole [Waccamaw] Neck free but us! Last people free on 'Neck.' MY MAJOR last one to went under flag to Georgetown!" Then, for emphasis, she reiterated, "LAST GENTLEMAN GONE UNDER THE FLAG!"[2]

Ambivalence was prompted, too, by the blacks' disillusioning encounters with their putative liberators, who were all too likely to possess the same prejudices, lack of sensitivity, and even cruelty previously thought to be peculiar to slaveholders. To some blacks, the blue-clad strangers seemed not liberators, but thieves. There is evidence that Federal troops seized the property of blacks as well as whites. A former slave named Margaret complained that Union soldiers had looted her personal possessions. "I always bin hear dat de Yankees was gwine help de Nigger!" she exclaimed. "W'a' kynd a help yu call dis! Tek ebery ting I got in de wurld, my t'ree gold broach."[3]

A more common response to emancipation was a personal assertion of freedom. The most obvious means by which slaves could assert their freedom was to cease working for their masters. Many of them took a holiday from their labors, depriving their former owners of servants to wait upon them as well as paralyzing rice production. A rice planter's daughter termed it the "intoxication of freedom." Charles Alston's house servants, for instance, refused to wait on the white family or to wash for them. Many freedmen continued to manifest the same cordiality and respect toward their former owners that had been required of them in slavery, but others asserted their freedom through what the whites regarded as an excessive propensity for insolence and insubordination. One striking example was described by the daughter of one of the planters, who told of a young freedman who "stood a little way off, balancing a sharp stone in his hand and aiming it at Mamma from time to time, now came nearer and leaned on the wheel of the carriage. Mamma thought he wanted to intimidate her."[4]

That the freedmen did not accept the paternalistic values of their former masters was evident in the rapidity with which they attacked the most visible symbols of their power—the Big House, the provision barn, and the overseer. Some of them called for vengeance upon the slaveholders, and many felt that robbery, vandalism, and violence were justifiable as retribution for years of enslavement. One plantation mistress wrote that an ex-slave named Charles "took down my Secretary and carried it into his house and the whole of my furniture, large presses too large to move were taken to pieces and every book carried off many torn and strewed over the place." Another complained to Federal officials: "My house," she wrote, "has been robbed of every article of furniture and much defaced and injured also all my provisions of meat, lard, coffee and tea taken. . . . we are left without a bed or blanket," adding that "all these necessary things are distributed among the negroes." There were said to be "hordes of blacks who like vultures hang around" the rice plantations, not all of them satisfied to pillage the plantations of their own former masters.[5]

Some of the blacks also plundered the store rooms and smokehouses, divided plantation livestock among themselves, and pulled down fences, barns, and other plantation outbuildings. An overseer reported that "the negroes still go on in puling building to Peicies [*sic*]." Another overseer "watched them take supplies from the barns, corn and rice, using the baskets which were always used in measuring grain." Of course, former slaves and former masters did not share a common definition of theft. What the whites saw as thievery, the freedmen may have considered overdue payments for their years of servitude, as Adele Allston tacitly conceded when she wrote to her son, "The conduct of the negroes in robbing our house, store room meat house etc. and refusing to restore anything shows you they *think it right* to steal from us."[6]

From the blacks' point of view, the overseers—because they had directed the slaves' labor, had enforced plantation discipline, and had dealt out punishments—were the most blatant symbol of bondage. Doubtless some of them fully deserved their reputations for cruelty. Doubtless, too, many slaves had personal scores to settle with particularly oppressive taskmasters. But often overseers, the only white men left on the rice plantations, had come to represent all that the freedmen hated in slavery, and often the overseers felt the full brunt of their long-seething bitterness. At least one hated overseer was murdered by ex-slaves on the "first day of 'mancipation." Another overseer admitted that he had lost control of the plantation. "I am not allowed to say any [thing] about Work and have not been to the barn in the last five days. Jacob is the worst man on the Place, then comes in Scipio Jackey Sawney & Paul," he complained. "Most all of them have arms." On another plantation the former bondsmen placed the overseer under house arrest, warning him that "if he left the house they would kill him, and they put a negro armed with a shotgun to guard the house and see that he did not leave alive."[7]

Other symbols of the masters' hegemony were attacked as well. The Reverend Alexander Glennie's black parishioners would no longer listen to his preaching, according to J. Motte Alston, "but would shout and sing after their own fashion, and surround themselves with their old African superstitions." The freedmen "flatly refused his ministrations," noted James R. Sparkman, "and declined the further services of the church as soon as their freedom was acknowledged and accepted by the whites." Glennie, he said, believed "the labors of his life time dissipated and lost in a single day." After the blacks at Hagley looted the All Saints parsonage, the astonished and disillusioned Glennie spoke despondently of giving up and returning to England.[8]

3

The slaves' deep longing for freedom, while unrecognized by most of their masters, was perceived by a few discerning travelers. One slave, Scipio, had told a northern visitor in 1860 that nearly all the blacks would fight for their freedom if they had the opportunity, although a few preferred slavery because they were certain of being cared for when they were old. In All Saints Parish blacks outnumbered whites nine to one. "Suppose," said Scipio, "dat one quarter ob dese niggas rise—de rest keep still—whar den would de white folks be?" The northern visitor observed that "most of you have kind masters and fare well." Scipio replied, "Dat's true, massa, but dat ain't freedom, and de black lub freedom as much as de white. De same blessed Lord made dem both, and He made dem all 'like, 'cep de skin. De blacks hab strong hands, and when de day come you'll see dey hab heads, too!" All Saints slaves recognized slavery as an evil institution quite independently of whether the master, overseer, or driver, was "good" or "bad," was brutal or permissive. A slave named Pompey told an English visitor:

> "'pears to me England must be a good country to lib in." "Why so?" "All free dar, sa!" "Why you'd have to work harder than you do here, and have nobody to take care of you. The climate wouldn't suit you, either, there's not enough sunshine. You couldn't have a kinder or better master than Colonel—I'm sure." "No, *sa!*" with a good deal of earnestness; "he fust-rate man, sa, dat a fac; and Mass Philip and de young ladies, dey berry good to us. But—" and the slave hesitated. "What is it, Pompey? Speak out!" "Well, den, some day de Cunnel he die, and den trouble come, *suah!* De ole plantation be sold, and de hands sold too, or we be divide 'tween Mass Phil, Miss Jule, and

Miss Emmy. Dey get married, ob course. Some go one way, some toder, we wid dem—neber lib together no more. Dat's what I keep t'inking ob, Sa!"

It might plausibly be argued that slavery in All Saints Parish was, in terms of physical and material treatment, among the more kindly and humane examples, standards for this dubious honor not being highly competitive. But, one might ask, how good could slavery be? That slaves on the rice plantations of All Saints Parish may have enjoyed better material treatment than their counterparts elsewhere does not imply the absence of other types of oppression. In fact, slaves there as elsewhere complained, stole, talked of tricking Ole Maussa, ran away, and rebelled. And even in the matter of material treatment one should be aware that contrary tendencies were always present. Instances of slaves who were relatively well housed, well clad, and well fed could be matched with instances of an opposite character. In this, as in other aspects of human history, the matter of relative proportion is both important and elusive. Granting that there were exceptions, and with no disposition to insist upon uniformity of practice on the Waccamaw, one might still note that the ex-slaves usually spoke well of their former masters. But even slavery at its best was still slavery, and the slaves of All Saints Parish longed for something more than just better treatment. They did not look forward to better masters: they wanted to be free.[9]

The world view of the slaves was sharply at variance with the slaveholders' paternalistic vision of them as "admirably suited to a state of subordination to superior intelligence." The slaves, as the rice planters saw them, were "docile, gentle under good treatment, capable of strong but superficial affection, incapable of deep thought, improvident and hating labor . . . but cheerful and happy in light work and sufficient food to meet their slightest wants." Since most of the rice planters considered themselves to be kindly and humane masters, they considered their slaves to be happy and contented with their status. Under such delusions a rice planter wrote to a Scottish cousin, "I am safe in saying that a large majority of them love me and would defend me, and my family." This was a dubious assumption, as some masters knew and others learned. But if the aristocratic, antibourgeois paternalism of the planters made them more or less blind to their slaves' aspirations for freedom, it also made them more or less vulnerable to their slaves' deceptions, as traditional African manners, indirection, and dissembling were put to new uses on the rice plantations. As one planter wrote to his son, "There is not one of your boys or girls either but will lie, and I would not take the pains or lose the time to train one who can not be depended on for the truth." [10]

To say that the slaves deliberately encouraged their masters to see them as docile and contented is not to say that they were willing to submit to any abuse without show of resistance. On the contrary, there were always men and women on the rice plantations who challenged the system, sometimes surreptitiously by lying or stealing, sometimes boldly by insolence, insubordination, desertion, or outright rebellion. The theft of rice, foodstuffs, and livestock was as persistent in reality as in the slave folktales. Occasionally slaves would respond to insults with insolence; a few slaves were forthright with their masters to the point of being sharp-tongued. When Scipio, an aged African at Woodbourne, was made the butt of a joke by his master, he responded, "Don't bodder me Mossa, enty you know I bin libbin in dese woods fo' erry udder [before any other] nigger mek track yer [make track here]—go way and don't bodder me, or I run way fo' tru—yerry wat I say." More often slaves resisted threatened beatings, sometimes successfully. Mary One, the mother of Margaret Bryant, refused to be beaten for allegedly having failed to complete her task. "Going drownded myself!" she threatened. "I done my work. Fore I take a lick, rather drownded meself." Her resistance succeeded. Her master decided she was too good a worker to drown and transferred her to the weave room. A more drastic form of resistance was running away. There had been runaways since the colonial period, but it was not until the presence of Union gunboats on the Waccamaw during the Civil War that the likelihood of successful escape outweighed the risks of capture. [11]

The most drastic form of slave resistance was outright insurrection. At least three insurrectionary plots disturbed the consciousness of All Saints planters in the nineteenth century. Since all three were aborted, their full dimensions remain unknown. Two of them, in 1802 and in 1810, may have been no more than rumors. In 1802, however, the rumors were sufficient to cause a hasty mobilization of the militia. Three slaves—Charles, Joe, and Wood—were executed for their part in an unsuccessful slave insurrection in July 1829. Their jury consisted of such prominent Waccamaw rice planters as Joseph Waties Allston, Edward Thomas Heriot, and Robert F. W. Allston. James L. Petigru wrote to his brother-in-law, Robert F. W. Allston, "I am afraid you will hang half the country."[12]

The slaves, through such examples of insubordination, desertion, and insurrection, kept the threat of a servile uprising alive in the planters' consciousness during the six decades preceding the Civil War. Still, for the most part, the planters continued to believe that their slaves were contented, loyal, and trustworthy. During the war itself, the slaves' bland, emotionless demeanor prompted speculation about their apparent indifference to the struggle over their future. As the war ground to a close, however, the black mask was dropped a bit; the slaves' countenances were less circumspect. Prayer meetings for freedom, once clandestine, became increasingly vociferous and often lasted all night. "Great many time the chicken crow for day," Mariah Heywood recalled. "Change clothes. Gone on in the house. Get that eight, seven o'clock breakfast." Some slaves dropped all pretense. The white housekeeper at Hagley, for instance, noted that Selina, a "good looking" slave, was "not very good tempered" and was given to casting "a very disagreeable look over her countenance." Despite such glimpses behind the mask of indifference, and notwithstanding the evidence of discontent, few masters were prepared either for the extent of their slaves' desertion during the war or for their behavior in its aftermath.[13]

4

Despite intense racial and social tension in the aftermath of slavery, there is no evidence that any former slave inflicted personal violence upon any former masters or mistresses, although some former slaveholders believed their lives to be endangered. Furthermore, while many overseers experienced "insubordination," only one was murdered. Another was placed under house arrest. Looting was relatively common, but there is little evidence that more than a fraction of the freedmen ever engaged in it. The freedmen exhibited neither the incendiarism of the French peasants of 1789 nor the violence of West Indian slave revolts. "No outrage has been committed against the whites except in the matter of property," acknowledged one plantation mistress.[14]

Such were the causes of ill feeling that at this time existed between the freedmen and their former masters: the freedmen complained that the planters were trying to keep them in slavery, the planters rejoining that the blacks were trying to take their land. There was some truth in both charges. After Appomattox the planters certainly wished to make the blacks return to their former labors, although they denied a desire to reinstate the blacks' former condition of servitude. Unable to compel black labor any longer by either promises or intimidation, they called on Federal authorities for assistance. Typical was Adele Allston, who wrote to Colonel P. P. Brown that "I acquiesce readily in the freeing of the negroes, but surely our property should not be taken from us and a portion of the crop should come to us as rent for the land planted." It was land—land the symbol of a new status to the blacks, land the symbol of their old status to the whites—that was the chief issue of contention. In the first year of freedom former slaves manifested an extraordinary determination to acquire land. Clearly land ownership was next to freedom itself as a priority. Some of the blacks settled in nearby pinelands, such as the Free Woods, where they could purchase land for a dollar an acre and could pay for it with rice. Others lay claim to the plantations on which they had spent their working lives. Many of the white planters had abandoned their Waccamaw plantations for inland safety during the war, leaving their slaves behind to work the land. In 1865 those slaves, now free, believed that the land and the crops should remain in their hands. The Freedmen's Bureau Act of March 3, 1865, authorized freedmen to preempt forty acres of abandoned or confiscated land at nominal rent for three years and to buy it for a fairly appraised price. Blacks thus had to occupy the land in order to gain it; whites had to occupy the land in order to retain it. Tension was inevitable; the closest former slaves and former masters came to armed conflict was over this question. In this contest the white planters ultimately prevailed, not because of any lack of will on the part of the freedmen, but because of the willingness of Federal authorities to sustain the planters' legal claim to the land.[15]

5

While former masters employed themselves in attempting to regain the plantations they had left in the hands of their slaves during the war, the day-to-day life of former slaves—with concerns of food, clothing, and shelter, work and off times, courtship and marriage, weddings and funerals, music and dance, storytelling and religion—went on as always, outside of either enmity or alliance with the whites, outside of the political struggles of Reconstruction.

The funeral remained a focal point of black culture on the Waccamaw, for death remained a central fact of black folklife, part of the everyday rhythm of life. Newborn babies perished, sometimes just before or just after their young mothers. The bereaved families consoled themselves as quickly as possible, widows and widowers remarried after a decent interval, and departed infants were supplanted within a few years. Of every one hundred children who survived infancy, twenty-six died before they were ten years old, twenty more never reached the age of twenty, and another forty-five died between twenty and fifty. Only four lived into their sixties. The one slave of one hundred who attained the age of seventy was accorded classical African deference, prestige, and authority. His children and half of his grandchildren were long dead. He alone had survived as the plantation's living repository of traditional wisdom, an ancient sage burdened by the tragic memory of long and terrible years of bondage, but proud of what he had seen three generations of his people accomplish.[16]

Such an ancient sage had been an unwilling participant in one of history's most massive cultural transformations. Ripped from his African family and friends in childhood, herded into the wretched and stinking hold of a slave ship, and sold at auction to a Waccamaw rice planter, he had found himself among various other enslaved Africans whose speech he could not understand and with whose customs he was unfamiliar. Their masters, in this strange new environment, shouted commands at them, commands they struggled to comprehend. Little by little in their efforts to communicate with one another, they discovered common grammatical patterns in their diverse African languages, as they were simultaneously learning more and more of their master's words. Out of the convergence of common structures in African grammars, applied to a growing English vocabulary, they devised a new language as a means of communicating with one another. What was a second language to enslaved Africans was the native tongue of their American-born children. The ancient sage had seen three generations of slaves on the Waccamaw develop this new language to a high degree of complexity. It retained only a few of the familiar African words he still recalled from his childhood, other than the day names still given to the children; but the English words were still put together in the appropriate African way. It bothered him that the children's day names were often in English, but he was pleased that the younger generations at least gave their children such names. And even if their proverbs were now in English, he was glad the younger generations had sufficient sense of manners to use proverbs for sensitive subjects rather than to give offense by direct speech.

The development of Gullah out of the convergence of common grammatical patterns in a multitude of African languages with a new English vocabulary was only one part of the transformation from African to Afro-American culture in which the ancient sage had participated. But changes in other aspects of culture were akin to the transformation in language. Implicit but pervasive grammatical principles of culture lay behind the transformation of slave folklife in all its various manifestations. It is axiomatic that any people must build their response to the challenges and demands of a new environment out of the materials at hand. But those materials are put together in the manner they perceive to be most appropriate to the situation. The response may be in itself innovative—the creation of a new language, a new house-type, or new folktales—but the perception of appropriateness is cultural. Traditional notions of appropriateness in work and worship, in feeling, thinking, and living—notions learned in childhood and passed down across the generations—influence the cultural choices forced by new conditions. Cultural continuity is rarely, if ever, completely shattered; and African traditions had a persistent way of asserting themselves time and again in the slave folklife of All Saints Parish.

In work patterns the sage had seen the slaves adapt African traditions to the masters' notions of labor organization in the cultivation of rice and its preparation for market. On one level there was relatively little adjustment. Many of his fellow Africans had come from rice-growing regions and knew more about its cultivation than their masters. Over the generations, however, he had seen the management techniques of the rice planters superimposed onto the work routine. The task system, in which each individual was assigned a specific task to be completed without regard to the work of others, was very different from African traditions of communal labor. The slaves had responded by developing their own informal version of the task system in which each accomplished his assigned task; but they worked side-by-side—hoeing in time to work songs—and helped slower slaves keep up, all of which reflected an African communal orientation toward work. In addition, the persistence of hoes as all-purpose implements and of the hand-coiled fanner baskets for winnowing rice exemplified continuity with African work patterns among the rice plantation slaves of the Waccamaw. Among non-field workers, African skills in woodworking and metalworking—brought over in the minds of enslaved Africans and taught to successive generations—continued on the rice plantations in the work of gifted carpenters and blacksmiths and were reflected in the esteem in which such skilled workers were held in the slave community.

In the time left to the slaves to use for their own purposes, the sage had supplemented his family's food allowances by hunting and fishing and by tending his own garden. Weekend visiting and partying—with music, dance, and storytelling—had been a welcome relief from work. In the early years he had learned many of the customs of other Africans, some of them much like his own, some of them quite strange to him. It was in such gatherings that the younger generation learned much of what they would come to know of the breadth and variety of African culture, although such things were also learned at home, by the fireside in the little cabins.

The ancient sage had observed successive generations of slaves on the Waccamaw make creative adaptations of African customs and beliefs to New World conditions. They adopted their masters' religion, but they worshiped their new God with the kind of exaltation considered appropriate to such a powerful deity in Africa. Life-cycle celebrations such as weddings and funerals continued to be marked by special patterns of behavior that reflected creative adaptations of African customs and beliefs to the rice plantations.

The animal trickster tales he had known and loved as a child in Africa had entertained and educated his children and grandchildren here in America. Many of the very same stories he remembered from childhood had been translated into Gullah. Rabbit continued to be the favorite character of the stories, although many local animals replaced their African originals. The slaves had created a new set of stories, too, about a slave trickster named John. The stories were much like the animal trickster stories, and John was much like Rabbit. But they applied more directly to plantation life than the Rabbit stories. The slaves told "John Tales" only within the slave community.

Here again both important lines of continuity with African tradition as well as the marked influence of the immediate environment were evident.

This description only suggests the various and complex cultural transformations that the ancient sage had witnessed and participated in over a long lifetime. These events made up an intricate process of cultural creolization analagous to linguistic creolization. Just as their original African languages had little utility on the rice plantations, so, too, was the case with many African work patterns, religions, food, and dress. And just as a new language was created out of English words put together in accordance with African grammars, so new cultural forms were put together out of Anglican Christianity, plantation foodstuffs, and white labor systems. But they were all organized according to appropriate African cultural grammars. If the content of slave religion was the Christianity preached by Alexander Glennie, the slaves' religious behavior was shaped by African cultural grammars. If the material ingredients of slave foodways were merely ordinary plantation foodstuffs, their preparation and spicing—and their symbolic meaning—were governed by African cultural grammars. If slave clothing consisted of the garments issued by the masters, how those garments were worn and what their wearing meant to the slaves reflected cultural continuity with Africa.

The old man had seen much change during his lifetime of bondage, but he also saw that much of the past persisted into the present. Slavery was ended, but emancipation did not automatically bring freedom. Appomattox ushered in an ambiguous time of transition in which the moribund folkways of slavery doddered on and the newborn folkways of freedom toddled about uncertainly. Emancipation meant losses as well as gains to some of the freedmen, who felt that their years of servitude entitled them to security and care in their old age. "Beat my Pa and Ma to death and turn me loose!" recalled Gabe Lance. "Ought to take care of me." Others, such as Ben Horry, recognized that emancipation only set in motion an unequal contest between former slave and former master: "You had the learning in you head! Give me that pencil to catch up dem thing. I couldn't to save my life." The end of slavery thus offered new possibilities, new challenges, and new burdens.[17]

This time of transition in the Waccamaw society following emancipation was analogous to the liminal period in an individual's rites of passage. All cultures are said to practice certain rituals to accompany the transition of individuals from one status to another, as, for example, those accompanying such life crises as marriage or death. These rituals are designed to cushion the social and individual disturbance of these transitions, which are considered uncertain. Three overlapping states characterize such rituals—the old status, the new status, and between them a liminal stage in which the standards of neither the old nor the new status are appropriate. This is considered a dangerous time, when one's status is ambiguous, suspended between two worlds. The transition from slavery to freedom was such a time, but it had to be faced without the aid of clearly established rituals.[18]

The new opportunities and the new burdens would fall most heavily on a new generation, at once the largest and most vital segment of the black population of All Saints Parish. This generation, its world view shaped in slavery, had as yet no knowledge of what lay ahead in the first generation of freedom. But they knew what lay behind. One of them, Matthew Grant, expressed it in a parable: "One time had a eagle been shut up in a cage for lo, many years! And he was in there long, comparable while. Maussa taut it was time for she to turn out. The door been open. He sit up there & commence to try his pinion. Commence to flewed off from cage. And after while he come back and flewed & look on the cage. Bid the cage 'farewell.' And she goned off again. And comed back. And after he comed back he went off after biddin' the cage farewell third time. He told the cage, 'My time up with YOU.'"[19] At the end of the Civil War the large numbers of slave children born in All Saints Parish in the 1830s and 1840s had reached maturity and were beginning to produce offspring of their own—"the freedom children." Those parents would face the task of carrying forward the creolized culture of slave folklife into the first generation of freedom—and beyond.

Epilogue

As we cross the gangplank of the *Island Queen* to the wooden dock of Wacca-Wache Marina and step ashore onto Wachesaw plantation, we are acutely conscious of the persistence of the past into the present. The sedans and station wagons of yachtsmen and tourists in the parking lot of the marina are shaded by giant live oaks that stood here while several generations of slaves grew rice for the Belins and the Flaggs. Scenes out of time, historical and contemporary at once, present themselves to our eyes. Sitting beneath one of the oaks, a young black man patiently mends his nets, as such men have done on the Waccamaw for more than two centuries. Across the river a small boat, performing a timeless ritual, returns Sandy Islanders to their homes after a day's work. It was here, on this river, that flatboats returned field hands to their homes on plantation streets after a day's work in the rice fields. Some of these same live oaks, their lower limbs brushing the dark waters of the Waccamaw with Spanish moss, stood as silent sentinels for their journeys then as for ours now.

Our river cruise has been for us a voyage into history, taking us past abandoned rice fields once made productive by the labor of thousands of human beings, past rice mills where slaves once prepared the crops for market, past forest clearings where once stood the legendary Big Houses in whose yards the slaves gathered on Sunday mornings. We are conscious that history really happened here, to real men and women whose names we know, over whose graves we have stood in silent homage, and of whose burdens and achievements considerable evidence remains. From the letters, diaries, and memoirs of the plantation whites and their visitors, from census and probate records, and especially from the testimonies of the slaves themselves and of their descendants, we have discovered a real world of slave folklife: of courage and passion, valor and pity, violation and redemption, faith and fear, love and resentment.

As we gaze beyond the broken trunks of the rice fields now reclaimed by river and swamp, we can almost see the workers keeping pace with one another as they move across the fields. We can almost hear their singing as their hoes rise and fall on the beat. Here, at the edge of the river, there is an eerie feeling that we can almost reach out and touch these people we have come to know over the years. We can almost see, glimmering through the river mists, All Saints Parish as it was in the era of slavery, where the talented carpenter Renty Tucker builds a chapel for his people, and Jemmy the preacher leads his flock in prayer, and little Sabe Rutledge listens in wide-eyed wonder to the fascinating tales of Buh Rabbit, and Prince, the bookish coachman, entertains the slave community with fiddle and banjo, and Ben Horry dodges the patrols to visit his first sweetheart, and Mary One threatens to drown herself rather than submit to a beating.

It was here, in All Saints Parish, and in hundreds of unremembered slave communities like All Saints Parish, that these men and women and thousands more played important, if unsung, roles in a momentous process of culture change. For out of pride and compassion as well as anguish and injustice, out of African traditions as well as American circumstances, they created a new language, a new religion—indeed, a new culture—that not only allowed them to endure the collective tragedy of slavery, but to bequeath a notable and enduring heritage to generations to come.

Notes

AA	*American Anthropologist*
AHR	*American Historical Review*
DUL	Duke University Library, Durham, N.C.
1850 Census	U.S. Census Bureau, Mss. Census Returns for 1850. Free and Slave Population Schedules, National Archives, Washington, D.C. Agriculture and Mortality Schedules, South Carolina Archives, Columbia.
1860 Census	U.S. Census Bureau, Mss. Census Returns for 1860. Free and Slave Population Schedules, National Archives, Washington, D.C. Agriculture and Mortality Schedules, South Carolina Archives, Columbia.
JAF	*Journal of American Folklore*
JAH	*Journal of American History*
JNH	*Journal of Negro History*
JSH	*Journal of Southern History*
LC	Library of Congress, Washington, D.C.
MHVR	*Mississippi Valley Historical Review*
OR Army	*Official Records of the Union and Confederate Armies, the War of the Rebellion.* Washington, D.C.: Government Printing Office, 1880–1901. 130 vols.
OR Navy	*Official Records of the Union and Confederate Navies, the War of the Rebellion.* Washington, D.C.: Government Printing Office, 1894–1914. 30 vols.
SCA	South Carolina Archives, Columbia.
SCHM	*South Carolina Historical Magazine*
SCHS	South Carolina Historical Society, Charleston.
SCL	South Caroliniana Library, University of South Carolina, Columbia.
SFQ	*Southern Folklore Quarterly*
SHC	Southern Historical Collection, University of North Carolina, Chapel Hill.

Quotations from the slave narratives are verbatim. All respellings to simulate the phonology of the slaves' Gullah speech patterns, as well as all parenthetical insertions, are those of the Work Projects Administration field worker, Genevieve Willcox Chandler.

Notes to "Introduction"

1. Ben Horry, Slave Narratives: A Folk History of Slavery in the United States from Interviews with Former Slaves. Typewritten records prepared by the Federal Writers' Project, 1936–38 (microfilm), 14, part ii, 298, 304, 308, 310, 311, 317; interviews with Genevieve Willcox Chandler, Murrells Inlet, S.C., Aug. 1969 and July 1975, Charlotte, N.C., Jan. 1972. A facsimile edition of the Slave Narratives, edited by George P. Rawick under the title *The American Slave: A Composite Autobiography* (Westport, Conn., 1972), includes parts i and ii of the South Carolina interviews in vol. 2 and parts iii and iv of the South Carolina interviews in vol. 4. Pagination is the same.

2. Cf. Paul D. Escott, *Slavery Remembered: A Record of Twentieth-Century Slave Narratives* (Chapel Hill, 1979), 3–17.

3. Cf. Robert E. Berkhofer, Jr., *A Behavioral Approach to Historical Analysis* (New York, 1969), 208; Clyde Kluckhohn, "Parts and Wholes in Cultural Analysis," in Daniel Lerner, ed., *Parts and Wholes* (New York, 1953), 121; Eric J. Hobsbawm, "From Social History to the History of Society," in *Essays in Social History* (London, 1974), 5; Conrad Arensberg, "The Community Study Method," *American Journal of Sociology*, 60 (1954), 120; G. B. Elton, *The Practice of History* (New York, 1967), 11; Clifford Geertz, *The Interpretation of Cultures* (New York, 1973), 22.

4. Henry Glassie, *Passing the Time in Ballymenone: Culture and History of an Ulster Community* (Philadelphia, 1982); Herman Baltl, "Folklore Research and Legal History in the German Language Area," *Journal of the Folklore Institute*, 5 (1968), 142–51; Ronald H. Buchanan, "A Decade of Folklife Study," *Ulster Folklife*, 2 (1965), 63–75, and "Geography and Folk Life," *Folk Life*, 1 (1963), 5–15; Sigurd Erixon, "European Ethnology in Our Time," *Ethnologia Europaea*, 1 (1967), 3–11, "Folklife Research in Our Time: From a Swedish Point of View," *Gwerin*, 3 (1962), 275–91, and "An Introduction to Folk Life Research or Nordic Ethnology," *Folkliv*, 14–15 (1950–51), 5–15; Alexander Fenton, "An Approach to Folk Life Studies," *Keystone Folklore Quarterly*, 12 (1967), 5–21, "Historical Ethnology in Scotland," *Ethnologia Europaea*, 1 (1967), 125–29, and "Material Culture as an Aid to Local History Studies in Scotland," *Journal of the Folklore Institute*, 2 (1965), 326–39; J. W. Y. Higgs, *Folk Life Collection and Classification* (London, 1963); Ake Hultkrantz, "The Conception of 'Folk' in Sigurd Erixon's Ethnological Theory," *Ethnologia Europaea*, 2–3 (1968–69), 18–20, and "Historical Approaches in American Ethnology: A Research Survey," *Ethnologia Europaea*, 1 (1967), 96–116; Hultkrantz, ed., *General Ethnological Concepts, International Dictionary of Regional Euro-*

pean Ethnology and Folklore, 1 (Copenhagen, 1960), 126–44; J. Geraint Jenkins, ed., *Studies in Folk Life: Essays in Honour of Iorwerth C. Peate* (New York, 1969); Iorwerth C. Peate, *Tradition and Folk Life: A Welsh View* (London, 1972); Francis L. Utley, "A Role for Folk Life Studies in the United States," *Ethnologia Europaea*, 4 (1970), 150–54. Perhaps the classic work of folklife scholarship is Richard Weiss, *Volkskunde der Schweiz: Grundriss* (Erlenbach-Zurich, 1946).

5. Don Yoder, "Folklife," in Tristram P. Coffin, ed., *Our Living Traditions* (New York, 1968), 47–48. See also Yoder, "The Folklife Studies Movement," *Pennsylvania Folklife*, 13 (July 1963), 43–56, and his "Folklife Studies in American Scholarship," in Yoder, ed., *American Folklife* (Austin, 1976).

6. Fernand Braudel, *The Mediterranean and the Mediterranean World in the Age of Philip II*, trans. Sian Reynolds, 2 vols. (New York, 1972–75), 20. Lucien Febvre used the phrase "a new kind of history" as the title of an article in *Revue de metaphysique et de morale*, 58 (1949), reprinted in Peter Burke, ed., *A New Kind of History: From the Writings of Lucien Febvre*, trans. K. Folka (New York, 1973), 27–43. The most important works of the *Annalistes* in English include a remarkable series of works by Emmanuel Le Roy Ladurie, *The Peasants of Languedoc*, trans. John Day (Urbana, 1974); *Montaillou: The Promised Land of Error*, trans. Barbara Bray (New York, 1978); and *Carnival in Romans*, trans. Mary Feeney (New York, 1979); Marc Bloch's pioneering works, *Land and Work in Medieval Europe*, trans. J. E. Anderson (New York, 1969), and *French Rural History: An Essay on Its Basic Characteristics*, trans. Janet Sondheimer (Berkeley, 1970); and Braudel's monumental *Capitalism and Material Life*, trans. Miriam Kochan, 2 vols. (New York, 1975–80). The *Annalistes'* achievement is impressive, but it has not been accomplished without loss. In some *Annaliste* scholarship change has become nonexistent ("l'histoire immobile"), and human beings have become imperceptible. People are buried under layers of "structures" that "incumber history," according to Braudel, "and thus control its flow" (*Capitalism and Material Life*, 422). The individual remains anonymous, "imprisoned within a destiny in which he himself has little hand," as Braudel sees it. "All efforts against the prevailing tide of history," he adds, "are doomed to failure" (*Mediterranean*, 1244). I do not share this deterministic view. Cf. the following by Le Roy Ladurie: *Times of Feast, Times of Famine: A History of Climate since the Year 1000*, trans. Barbara Bray (Garden City, N.Y., 1971), and *The Territory of the Historian*, trans. Ben and Sian Reynolds (Chicago, 1979), 285–319.

7. Julia Peterkin, "Seeing Things," *American Magazine*, 105 (Jan. 1928), 115–16; Braudel, *Mediterranean*, 16. On the "longue dureé," cf. Fernand Braudel, "Debats et combats," *Annales E.S.C.*, 4 (1958), 725–53.

8. There are numerous problems in the use of the ex-slave interviews: the length of time between emancipation and the interviews, the age of the informants at the time of the interview, the age of the informants in slavery,

the condition of the informants at the time of the interview during the Great Depression, the personal characteristics of the interviewer, the conduct of the interview, and the nature of the interviewer's transcription process, among others. See also John Blassingame, "Using the Testimonies of Ex-Slaves: Approaches and Problems," *JSH*, 41 (1975), 473–92; C. Vann Woodward, "History from Slave Sources," *AHR*, 79 (1974), 473–81; and Escott, *Slavery Remembered*. On special problems and special opportunities in oral history, see Charles W. Joyner, "Oral History as Communicative Event: A Folkloristic Perspective," *Oral History Review* (1979), 47–52.

9. The reader will recognize here the influence of anthropologist Clifford Geertz, who proposes a theory of culture change that attempts to steer a course between the essentially atheoretical empiricism, which characterized American anthropology in the first half of the twentieth century, and the neo-evolutionary determinism of the second half. Geertz denies the causal power of culture, instead viewing culture as "models for" and "models of" behavior in ecosystems. He refuses to assign primacy to either endogenic (cultural) or exogenic (environmental) factors in culture change. They are seen instead as contexts in which cultural processes may be "intelligibly— that is, thickly—described." See his *Agricultural Involution: The Process of Ecological Change in Indonesia* (Berkeley, 1963), 11, and *passim*, and *Interpretation of Cultures*, 14, 89, 93–94. Cf. Ward H. Goodenough, "Comment on Cultural Evolution," *Daedalus*, 90 (1961), 521–28, his *Change: An Anthropological Approach to Community Change* (New York, 1963), and his *Description and Comparison in Cultural Anthropology* (Chicago, 1970). Anthony B. Smith asserts the primacy of exogenic factors in *social* change (without carefully distinguishing between social change and culture change) in *The Concept of Social Change: A Critique of the Functionalist Theory of Social Change* (Boston, 1973).

10. On speech communities see Dell Hymes, *Foundations in Sociolinguistics: An Ethnographic Approach* (Philadelphia, 1974), 47–51; Pier Paolo Giglioli, ed., *Language and Social Context* (Harmondsworth, Middlesex, 1972), 219–31. Hymes defines linguistic creolization in his *Pidginization and Creolization of Languages* (Cambridge, 1971), 84. See also Robert A. Hall, *Pidgin and Creole Languages* (Ithaca, 1965), 15; William A. Stewart, "Sociolinguistic Factors in the History of American Negro Dialects," *Florida FL Reporter*, 5 (1967), 12–13.

11. E. P. Thompson, "Time, Work-Discipline, and Industrial Capitalism," *Past and Present*, 38 (1967), 80. Cf. Herbert G. Gutman, *Work, Culture, and Society in Industrializing America* (New York, 1977), 1–78.

12. Edward Brathwaite, *The Development of Creole Society in Jamaica, 1770–1820* (Oxford, 1971), 296; cf. 296–307. Somewhat similar interpretations of Afro-American culture change have been put forward by historians Peter H. Wood, Herbert G. Gutman, and Lawrence W. Levine and by anthropologists Sidney W. Mintz and Richard Price. Gutman alone applies the term "creolization" (always within quotation marks) in the broader

Brathwaitian sense, but for him it is merely a general term to describe the transformation of Africans into Afro-Americans (or "creoles"). He does not examine slave language, nor does he use a linguistic model of creolization. Levine does not use the term at all. Nevertheless, his understanding of culture as process and his analysis of continuities between African and Afro-American cultures in terms of transformations rather than of survivals runs parallel to recent linguists' understanding of the creolization process in language. Wood, in an important chapter on the development of Gullah as a creole language, uses an implicit creolization model, but he does not attempt to apply his linguistic insights to broader cultural processes. Mintz and Price also draw upon creolization theory to analyze Afro-American linguistic change, but stop short of proposing an explicitly creolist approach to other cultural formations. However, their approach, while admittedly hypothetical and tentative, is clearly influenced by their understanding of linguistic creolization. See Gutman, *The Black Family in Slavery and Freedom, 1750–1925* (New York, 1976), 34, 340–43; Levine, *Black Culture and Black Consciousness: Afro-American Folk Thought from Slavery to Freedom* (New York, 1977), 3–135; Wood, *Black Majority: Negroes in Colonial South Carolina from 1670 through the Stono Rebellion* (New York, 1974), 167–91; Mintz and Price, *An Anthropological Approach to the Afro-American Past: A Caribbean Perspective* (Philadelphia, 1976).

Notes to "Prologue"

1. Lower All Saints Parish was a subdivision of Georgetown District, while Upper All Saints Parish was a subdivision of Horry District. Georgetown and Horry districts became Georgetown and Horry counties in 1868. The standard account of Georgetown District is George C. Rogers, Jr., *The History of Georgetown County, South Carolina* (Columbia, 1970); for the prime years of rice culture, see 252–386. See also his "The Georgetown Rice Planters on the Eve of the Civil War," *South Carolina History Illustrated*, 1 (1970), 25–33. There is no standard history of Horry District. For the mid-nineteenth century, see Robert Mills, *Statistics of South Carolina* (Charleston, 1826), 579–84; Harry Hammond, ed., *South Carolina: Resources and Population, Institutions and Industries* (Charleston, 1883), 44–70, and *passim*; Julian J. Petty, *The Growth and Distribution of Population in South Carolina* (Columbia, 1943), 75–78.

2. Petty, *Growth and Distribution of Population*, 75–78; Philip D. Curtin, *The Atlantic Slave Trade: A Census* (Madison, 1969), 158; Peter H. Wood, *Black Majority: Negroes in Colonial South Carolina from 1670 through the Stono Rebellion* (New York, 1974), 131–66.

3. Interview with James H. Dusenbury, Garden City, S.C., May 13, 1979; *Along the Coast* (Myrtle Beach, S.C.), Apr. 15–21, 1979, 9. Interview with Ashby Ward, executive director of Greater Myrtle Beach Chamber of Commerce, May 28, 1979.

4. Elizabeth Bunting, *Out of Wacca Wache* (Columbia, 1978), reproduces Bunting's script as guide on the *Island Queen*. Her welcoming remarks are on p. 1. In our case the cruise was in the afternoon.

5. *Ibid.*, 7.

6. *Ibid.*, 12, 23. The Allston and Alston families are descended from two brothers, John and William Allston, who settled on the Waccamaw in 1734 and 1735. See Rogers, *History of Georgetown County*, 187–88, 520–23; Elizabeth Deas Allston, *The Allstons and Alstons of Waccamaw* (Charleston, 1936).

7. Bunting, *Out of Wacca Wache*, 29.

8. Julia Peterkin, *Scarlet Sister Mary* (Indianapolis, 1928), 102–3, 224. Her father, Dr. J. A. Mood, was a twentieth-century owner of Brookgreen plantation, where *Scarlet Sister Mary* was set. See Alberta Morel Lachicotte, *Georgetown Rice Plantations* (Columbia, 1955), 58.

9. Interview with Mrs. William A. Kimbel, Wachesaw Plantation, July 5, 1979; Lachicotte, *Georgetown Rice Plantations*, 67–68.

10. There are numerous popular publications that feature Waccamaw ghost legends. See, for example, Julian Stevenson Bolick, *Waccamaw Plantations* (Clinton, S.C., 1946); his *The Return of the Gray Man* (Clinton, S.C., 1956); his *Ghosts from the Coast* (Clinton, S.C., 1966); Nancy and Bruce Roberts, *Ghosts of the Carolinas* (Charlotte, N. C., 1971); and [Robbie L. Alford], *GhostsGhostsGhostsGhosts* (Georgetown, S.C., 1975).

11. Paul Quattlebaum, *The Land Called Chicora: The Carolinas under Spanish Rule with French Intrusions, 1520–1670* (Gainesville, 1956); J. G. Johnson, "A Spanish Settlement in Carolina, 1526," *Georgia Historical Quarterly*, 7 (1923), 339–45. Woodbury Lowery, *The Spanish Settlements within the Present Limits of the United States* (New York, 1901), 161–68, 447–52, details the slave revolt but estimates the location on the banks of the Pee Dee. Joseph C. Carroll, *Slave Insurrections in the United States, 1800–1860* (Boston, 1939), 13, believes the slave revolt was instigated by the Indians. Herbert Aptheker, *American Negro Slave Revolts* (New York, 1943), 163, believes that the Africans became permanent settlers. Paul E. Hoffman argues in an unpublished paper, "The Chicora Legend and Franco-Spanish Rivalry in *La Florida*," that San Miguel de Gualdape was in the Port Royal region, considerably south of the Waccamaw.

12. *South Carolina Gazette*, June 16, 1777; H. A. M. Smith, "The Baronies of South Carolina: Hobcaw," *SCHM*, 14 (1913), 70–83; Louis Gottschalk, *Lafayette Joins the American Army* (Chicago, 1937), 1–3.

13. Henry Lumpkin, *From Savannah to Yorktown: The American Revolution in the South* (Columbia, 1981), 68–79; Robert Duncan Bass, *The Swamp Fox: The Life and Campaigns of General Francis Marion* (New York, 1959), 88–210; Hugh F. Rankin, *Francis Marion: The Swamp Fox* (New York, 1973); Lucien Agniel, *Rebels Victorious, the American Revolution in the South, 1780–1781* (New York, 1972), 64–65; Rogers, *History of Georgetown County*, 127, 136–57.

14. Alexander S. Salley, *President Washington's Tour through South Carolina in 1791* (Columbia, 1932), 4–7; Archibald Henderson, *Washington's Southern Tour* (Boston, 1923), 125–26.

15. Rogers, *History of Georgetown County*, 362; Henry DeSaussure Bull, *All Saints Church, Waccamaw, 1739–1968* (Georgetown, 1968), 12–17.

16. Richard Lathers, *Reminiscences of Richard Lathers: Sixty Years of a Busy Life in South Carolina, Massachusetts, and New York* (New York, 1907), 7–8; Rogers, *History of Georgetown County*, 362.

17. Lachicotte, *Georgetown Rice Plantations*, 14–15; Rogers, *History of Georgetown County*, 487.

18. Bernard M. Baruch, *Baruch: The Public Years* (New York, 1957), 167, 177, 190, 299, 315–16; Lachicotte, *Georgetown Rice Plantations*, 14.

19. Jared B. Flagg, *The Life and Letters of Washington Allston* (New York, 1892), 1–21; Edgar P. Richardson, *Washington Allston: A Study of the Romantic Artist in America* (Chicago, 1948), 5–7.

20. Rogers, *History of Georgetown County*, 188–91, 196–97; Ronald Ray Swick, "Theodosia Burr Alston," *South Atlantic Quarterly*, 74 (Winter 1975), 495–506; [Robbie L. Alford], "Theodosia Burr Allston," *Historic Georgetown County Leaflet*, no. 1 (Georgetown, 1975). She was regarded by some writers as the best educated American woman of her time. See James Parton, *The Life and Times of Aaron Burr* (New York, 1864), 1:203; Samuel K. Knapp, *The Life of Aaron Burr* (New York, 1835), 195; John Davis, *Travels of Four Years and a Half in the United States of America during 1798, 1800, 1801, and 1802* (New York, 1909), 26. Julian Bolick (*Waccamaw Plantations*, 17) and Anya Seton (in her novel, *My Theodosia* [Boston, 1941], chs. 20–21) contend that Burr himself visited his daughter and son-in-law on their Waccamaw plantation. For the ghostly legends of Theodosia Burr Alston, see Bolick, *Return of the Gray Man*, 13–25, 115–40.

21. Genevieve Willcox Chandler, "Sandy Island across the Waccamaw: Before and After," in Clarke A. Willcox, *Musings of a Hermit, with Historical Sketches of the Waccamaw Neck*, 2d ed. (Charleston, 1967), 110.

22. Interview with Abraham Nelson, Jan. 21, 1972. Nelson was born and raised on Sandy Island.

23. Paul Herbert Wesley, *Bits of Driftwood* (Charleston, 1936), 101, 118.

24. *Ibid.*, 100–103.

25. *Ibid.*, 111.

26. Chandler's interviews with living ex-slaves in All Saints Parish are a part of volumes 14 and 15 of the Slave Narratives: A Folk History of Slavery in the United States from Interviews with Former Slaves. Typewritten records prepared by the Federal Writers' Project, 1936–38 (microfilm). Chandler's folklore collection for the Federal Writers' Project is housed in the Work Projects Administration Mss., SCL.

27. Chandler, "Sandy Island across the Waccamaw," 110.

28. *Ibid.*, 111.

29. Charles W. Joyner, "Folk Preaching on Sandy Island, South Carolina," paper read before the American Folklore Society annual meeting, New
Orleans, Nov. 1975.

Notes to *"Down by the Riverside"*

1. For many years the *Nina*, named for Christopher Columbus's flag-
ship, plied between Georgetown and Charleston, carrying passengers and
cargo between the two cities. See Dec. 27, 1859, diary of Emily Esdaile
Weston (Mrs. Plowden C. J. Weston) for 1859, in private possession, hereafter cited as Emily Weston diary; Elizabeth W. Allston Pringle, *Chronicles
of Chicora Wood* (New York, 1922), 173; Arney R. Childs, ed., *Rice Planter
and Sportsman: The Recollections of J. Motte Alston* (Columbia, 1953),
115; Edmund Kirke [James Roberts Gilmore], *Among the Pines: or, The
South in Secession-Time* (New York, 1862), 10–11. Capt. Arthur McGee,
master of the *Nina*, advertised that he embarked from Charleston on
Wednesdays and Saturdays at 7 A.M., and from Georgetown on Mondays
and Thursdays at 8 A.M. See, for example, advertisements in the Georgetown
newspapers *True Republican*, Mar. 27, 1852, and *Winyah Observer*, Apr. 3,
1853. William D. Morgan, Georgetown's last intendant and first mayor
(1891–1905), recalled the *Nina*'s last voyage. One day the vessel set out
from Georgetown for Nassau in the Bahamas and was never seen again. See
For Love of a Rebel (Georgetown, 1964), 63.

2. "Viator" [pseud.], "Notes of Travel in South Carolina," *Southern
Presbyterian*, rpt. *Winyah Observer*, June 2, 1852.

3. Kirke, *Among the Pines*, 11.

4. William Gilmore Simms, *Geography of South Carolina* (Charleston,
1843), 82; Almira Coffin to Mrs. J. G. Osgood, May 10, 1851, in J. Harold
Easterby, ed., "South Carolina through New England Eyes: Almira Coffin's
Visit to the Low Country in 1851," *SCHM*, 45 (1944), 127; *Winyah Observer*, June 2, 1852. See also James Stuart, *Three Years in America* (Edinburgh, 1833), and Charles Joseph Latrobe, *The Rambler in North America*
(London, 1835).

5. "Sketches of South Carolina, Number Four: 'Slaves and Slavery,'"
Knickerbocker Magazine, 21 (May 1843), 348; Kirke, *Among the Pines*,
11–17; *Winyah Observer*, June 2, 1852; Simms, *Geography of South Carolina*, 83; Laurence Oliphant, *Patriots and Filibusters; or Incidents of Political and Exploratory Travel* (Edinburgh, 1860), 144. See also Oliphant's
anonymously published "Rambles at Random through the Southern States,"
Blackwood's Magazine, Jan. 1860.

6. Childs, ed., *Rice Planter and Sportsman*, 5; *Winyah Observer*, June
2, 1852.

7. George C. Rogers, Jr., *The History of Georgetown County, South
Carolina* (Columbia, 1970), 335–36; Carl Bridenbaugh, *Myths and Reali-*

ties: Societies of the Colonial South (Baton Rouge, 1952; rpt. New York, 1973), 54.

8. This description is a composite of descriptions in Simms, *Geography of South Carolina*, 80–83; Robert Mills, *Statistics of South Carolina* (Charleston, 1826), 563–65; Coffin to Osgood, May 10, 1851, in Easterby, ed., "South Carolina through New England Eyes," 127–36; Pringle, *Chronicles of Chicora Wood*, 16, 68–69; Oliphant, *Patriots and Filibusters*, 141–45; William Wyndham Malet, *An Errand to the South in the Summer of 1862* (London, 1863), 79, 83, 118, 138; Thomas P. Lockwood, *A Geography of South Carolina* (Charleston, 1832), 32; Sam B. Hilliard, "The Tidewater Rice Plantation: An Ingenious Adaptation to Nature," *Geoscience and Man*, 12 (1975), 57–66.

9. Robert F. W. Allston, *Essay on Sea Coast Crops* (Charleston, 1854), 27–28; daily meteorological journal of Alexander Glennie, Waccamaw Island, S.C., 1830–80, in Meteorological Reports, and Meteorological Reports for Waccamaw, 1835–53, Plowden Weston Papers, both at College of Charleston Library, Charleston.

10. Pringle, *Chronicles of Chicora Wood*, 67. See also Zamba, *The Life and Adventures of Zamba, an African Negro King, and His Experience of Slavery in South Carolina, Written by Himself* (London, 1847), 220–21.

11. Easterby, ed., "South Carolina through New England Eyes," 127–36; Oliphant, *Patriots and Filibusters*, 137; Simms, *Geography of South Carolina*, 80; Rogers, *History of Georgetown County*, 324.

12. Peter H. Wood, *Black Majority: Negroes in Colonial South Carolina from 1670 through the Stono Rebellion* (New York, 1974), 13–34; Richard S. Dunn, "The English Sugar Islands and the Founding of South Carolina," *SCHM*, 72 (1971), 81–93, and his *Sugar and Slaves: The Rise of the Planter Class in the English West Indies, 1624–1713* (Chapel Hill, 1972), 115–16; John P. Thomas, Jr., "The Barbadians in Early South Carolina," *SCHM*, 31 (1930), 75–92; Adelaide B. Helwig, "The Early History of Barbados and Her Influence upon the Development of South Carolina" (Ph.D. diss., University of California, Berkeley, 1931); M. Eugene Sirmans, "The Legal Status of the Slave in South Carolina, 1670–1740," *JSH*, 28 (1962), 462–66, and his *Colonial South Carolina: A Political History, 1663–1763* (Chapel Hill, 1966), part one; Winthrop D. Jordan, *White over Black: American Attitudes toward the Negro, 1550–1812* (Chapel Hill, 1968), 142–47.

13. Alexander S. Salley, Jr., *The Introduction of Rice Culture into South Carolina*, Historical Commission of South Carolina Bulletin no. 6 (Columbia, 1919), 10–13; Duncan Clinch Heyward, *Seed from Madagascar* (Chapel Hill, 1937), 4; Allston, *Essay on Sea Coast Crops*, 29.

14. The African sources of South Carolina rice culture are best detailed in Daniel C. Littlefield, *Rice and Slaves: Ethnicity and the Slave Trade in Colonial South Carolina* (Baton Rouge, 1981), 74–114; but see also Wood, *Black Majority*, 35–63; Converse D. Clowse, *Economic Beginnings in Co-*

lonial South Carolina, 1670–1730 (Columbia, 1971), 124; William R. Bascom, "Acculturation among the Gullah Negroes," *AA*, 43 (1941), 44–45; Melville J. Herskovits, *The Myth of the Negro Past* (New York, 1941; rpt. Boston, 1958), 147; Philip D. Curtin, *The Atlantic Slave Trade: A Census* (Madison, 1969), 145; Douglas Grant, *The Fortunate Slave: An Illustration of African Slavery in the Early Eighteenth Century* (London, 1968), 24–25; Daniel F. McCall, *Africa in Time Perspective* (Boston, 1964), 29; Elliott P. Skinner, "West African Economic Systems," in Elliott P. Skinner, ed., *Peoples and Cultures of Africa* (Garden City, N.Y., 1973), 207.

15. Pringle, *Chronicles of Chicora Wood*, 15; Rogers, *History of Georgetown County*, 29; Verner W. Crane, *The Southern Frontier, 1670–1732* (Ann Arbor, 1929), 22; Wesley Frank Craven, *The Colonies in Transition, 1660–1713* (New York, 1968), 292; Aubrey C. Land, ed., *Bases of the Plantation Society* (New York, 1969). All of the above point out the correlation between rice exports and slave imports. Wood, *Black Majority*, 13–35, convincingly argues that the relationship was causal. See also Peter A. Coclanis, "Rice Prices in the 1720s and the Evolution of the South Carolina Economy," *JSH*, 48 (1982), 531–44.

16. W. Robert Higgins, "The Geographical Origins of Negro Slaves in Colonial South Carolina," *South Atlantic Quarterly*, 70 (1971), 40–45; Curtin, *Atlantic Slave Trade*, 145–57; Elizabeth Donnan, "The Slave Trade into South Carolina before the Revolution," *AHR*, 33 (1927–28), 816–17; Wood, *Black Majority*, 13–35, 340; Rogers, *History of Georgetown County*, 341; Simms, *Geography of South Carolina*, 81.

17. Pringle, *Chronicles of Chicora Wood*, 6, 53–54, 76; "Sketches of South Carolina, Number Four," 348.

18. Richard Lathers, *Reminiscences of Richard Lathers: Sixty Years of a Busy Life in South Carolina, Massachusetts, and New York* (New York, 1907); Malet, *Errand to the South*, 117–18; Pringle, *Chronicles of Chicora Wood*, 27–28, 69. Pringle named some of the following as rowing songs she often heard on the Waccamaw: "On Canaan's Happy Shore"; "Roll, Jordan, Roll"; "Run, Mary, Run"; "Drinkin' Wine, Drinkin' Wine"; and "Oh, Zion." Oliphant reported hearing "There's a Meeting Here Tonight"; "In That Morning"; "Daniel"; "Lord, I Must Go"; "The Heavenly Bell Is Ringing Loud"; and "Broders, Don't You Hear the Horn?" in his *Patriots and Filibusters*, 141–43.

19. Welcome Bees [*sic*], in WPA Mss., SCL. The name is consistently spelled "Bees" in the Slave Narratives and in the WPA Mss.; however, his son, daughter, and granddaughter spell the family name Beese. I have followed their practice in the text, but use the field worker's spelling in the citations.

20. Oliphant, *Patriots and Filibusters*, 141.

21. Mills, *Statistics of South Carolina*, 565; Simms, *Geography of South Carolina*, 81; Pringle, *Chronicles of Chicora Wood*, 68.

22. Chalmers Gaston Davidson, *The Last Foray: The South Carolina*

Planters of 1860: A Sociological Study (Columbia, 1971), 12, 80–81, 172–73; Alberta Morel Lachicotte, *Georgetown Rice Plantations* (Columbia, 1955), 11–13, 18–26; Rogers, *History of Georgetown County*, 267–68; Elizabeth Deas Allston, *The Allstons and Alstons of Waccamaw* (Charleston, 1936); Harriet Kershaw Leiding, *Historic Houses of South Carolina* (Philadelphia, 1921), 124; Julian Stevenson Bolick, *Waccamaw Plantations* (Clinton, S.C., 1946), 4–20; Childs, ed., *Rice Planter and Sportsman*, 7; 1860 Census, Agriculture and Slave Schedules.

23. Childs, ed., *Rice Planter and Sportsman*, 42–43; Rogers, *History of Georgetown County*, 267; Davidson, *Last Foray*, 172; Lachicotte, *Georgetown Rice Plantations*, 16–17, 25, 111; Bolick, *Waccamaw Plantations*, 39; Allston, *Allstons and Alstons*, 25–26; Barnwell Rhett Heyward, "The Descendants of Colonel William Rhett, of South Carolina," *SCHM*, 4 (1903), 114–57.

24. 1860 Census, Agriculture and Slave Schedules; Rogers, *History of Georgetown County*, 266–67; Davidson, *Last Foray*, 217–18; Lachicotte, *Georgetown Rice Plantations*, 21; Leiding, *Historic Houses of South Carolina*, 117; Bolick, *Waccamaw Plantations*, 40–41.

25. John Izard Middleton correspondence in Hering-Middleton Papers and in Middleton-Blake Papers, both at SCHS; 1860 Census, Agriculture and Slave Schedules; Rogers, *History of Georgetown County*, 266–372; Davidson, *Last Foray*, 7, 30–31, 57–58, 140, 217–18, 230; Lachicotte, *Georgetown Rice Plantations*, 13, 25; Bolick, *Waccamaw Plantations*, 42–43; John Amasa May and Joan Reynolds Faunt, *South Carolina Secedes* (Columbia, 1960), 101; Charles C. Cauthen, *South Carolina Goes to War, 1860–1865* (Chapel Hill, 1950), 89–91; *For Love of a Rebel*, 5.

26. Plantation accounts of Francis Weston, in Plowden Weston Papers, College of Charleston Library; Laurel Hill Mill Mss., in Francis Marion Weston Papers, SCHS; Rogers, *History of Georgetown County*, 267–69; Lachicotte, *Georgetown Rice Plantations*, 39–41, 65; Davidson, *Last Foray*, 260–61; Bolick, *Waccamaw Plantations*, 44, 48–52, 62–64; Malet, *Errand to the South*, 78–82; Henry A. M. Smith, "The Baronies of South Carolina," X. "Hobcaw Barony," *SCHM*, 14, (1913), 74, 78–79; Anthony Devereaux, *The Rice Princes: A Rice Epoch Revisited* (Columbia, 1973), 74–120; James Henry Rice, *The Aftermath of Glory* (Charleston, 1934), 105–10.

27. Elizabeth Collins, *Memories of the Southern States* (Taunton, England, 1865), 3–4. Cf. Oliphant's description of his welcome by the slaves on a Waccamaw rice plantation in *Patriots and Filibusters*, 137–38: "Broad-grinning visages greet you merrily as you pass through it; and if the occasion of your arrival is that also of the master, after his absence during the summer months, great is the commotion which is created; all the field hands come trooping in to welcome him; the old and decrepit hobble out of their cabins; and the juvenile portion of the population, under charge of a stalwart matron, are drawn up, a somewhat mutinous looking assemblage of curly

heads; and a shaking of hands commences, beginning with the master, and going through all his own family, and then on to the guest, so that by the time the latter has grasped 300 hands, whose owners are of both sexes, of every age, and are reeking at the moment with the effects of every description of manual labor, he is abundantly satisfied with the evidence of their goodwill."

28. Collins, *Memories of the Southern States*, 17, 50, 61–62, 76; Malet, *Errand to the South*, 49–50, 79; inventory of the estate of Francis Marion Weston, 1855, and inventory of the estate of Plowden C. J. Weston, 1864, both at Office of Probate Judge, Georgetown County Court House. Francis Weston was the father of Plowden C. J. Weston, who served as meticulous administrator of his father's estate. The careful inventory of what Plowden C. J. Weston inherited upon his father's death is a valuable document for the study of slave folklife in All Saints Parish.

29. All Saints Waccamaw Protestant Episcopal Church, vestry journal, Dec. 24, 1854, SCHS; Emily Weston diary, Jan. 4, 11–12, 25–26, Feb. 3–4, 17, 23, May 5, 1859; Francis Weston inventory; Plowden Weston inventory; 1870 Census, Population Schedule; Estate of Renty Tucker, June 27, 1913, Office of Probate Judge, Georgetown County Court House; Malet, *Errand to the South*, 134, 144–45; Rice, *Aftermath of Glory*, 195; Henry DeSaussure Bull, *All Saints Church, Waccamaw, 1739–1968* (Georgetown, 1968), 20–25.

30. Emily Weston diary, Jan. 30, Feb. 13, 26–27, Mar. 6, 13, Dec. 4, 1859; Collins, *Memories of the Southern States*, 71.

31. Diary of Benjamin F. Dunkin, Dec. 12, 1861–Jan. 24, 1862, SCHS; Rogers, *History of Georgetown County*, 264–65; Davidson, *Last Foray*, 8, 10, 24, 40, 56–57, 105, 195; Coffin to Osgood, May 10, 1851, in Easterby, ed., "South Carolina through New England Eyes"; Smith, "Baronies of South Carolina," 74; Daniel E. Huger Smith, *A Charlestonian's Recollections, 1846–1913* (Charleston, 1950), 46–55; May and Faunt, *South Carolina Secedes*, 137–38; Bolick, *Waccamaw Plantations*, 58–61; *For Love of a Rebel*, 2–3; Benjamin F. Perry, *Reminiscences of Public Men* (Philadelphia, 1883), 208–13. On the growing of oranges in the South Carolina lowcountry see Jonathan Daniels, *The Gentlemanly Serpent and Other Columns from a Newspaperman in Paradise* (Columbia, 1974), 32–33.

32. Mariah Heywood, in Slave Narratives: A Folk History of Slavery in the United States from Interviews with Former Slaves. Typewritten records prepared by the Federal Writers' Project, 1936–38 (microfilm). Vol. 14, part ii, 282; 1860 Census, Agriculture and Slave Schedules.

33. Rogers, *History of Georgetown County*, 263–64; Davidson, *Last Foray*, 6, 234; Lachicotte, *Georgetown Rice Plantations*, 25, 52; J. E. H. Galbraith, "All Saints Waccamaw: Mural Tablets and Tombstone Inscriptions," *SCHM*, 13 (1912), 168; Bolick, *Waccamaw Plantations*, 57; 1860 Census, Agriculture and Slave Schedules.

34. *Winyah Observer*, June 23, 1852.

35. J. Harold Easterby, ed., *The South Carolina Rice Plantation as Revealed in the Papers of Robert F. W. Allston* (Chicago, 1945), 36; Rogers, *History of Georgetown County*, 263; Davidson, *Last Foray*, 19, 81, 172; Lachicotte, *Georgetown Rice Plantations*, 30–37; Pringle, *Chronicles of Chicora Wood*, 33–71, esp. 33–37; Bolick, *Waccamaw Plantations*, 44–47, 53–56.

36. List of slaves sold by Hugh Fraser to Robert F. W. Allston, Mar. 4, 1851, Allston to Francis Weston and Alexander Robertson, Apr. 14, 1851, bill of sale, Ann Allston Tucker to R. Allston, Feb. 17, 1854, all in Robert F. W. Allston Papers, SCHS; 1860 Census, Agriculture and Slave Schedules. There is also information on individual Allston slaves in a bill to Waverly Plantation, 1853, Dr. Andrew Hasell Account Book, SCHS.

37. "Recollections of a Visit to the Waccamaw," *Living Age*, Aug. 1, 1857, 292–93; Rogers, *History of Georgetown County*, 262–63; Davidson, *Last Foray*, 126–27, 257; Lachicotte, *Georgetown Rice Plantations*, 46–54; Smith, "Baronies of South Carolina," 78; J. E. Galbraith, "Inscriptions from the Allston Burying Grounds at Turkey Hill Plantation near Waccamaw," *SCHM*, 10 (1909), 182; Leiding, *Historic Houses of South Carolina*, 120–21; Bolick, *Waccamaw Plantations*, 62–64, 94–95; Samuel Gaillard Stoney, ed., "Memoirs of Frederick Adolphus Porcher," *SCHM*, 47 (1946), 47–48; Childs, ed., *Rice Planter and Sportsman*, 34; Lathers, *Reminiscences*, 7–8; Bull, *All Saints Church, Waccamaw*, 32; Susan Markley Fickling, *Slave Conversion in South Carolina, 1830–1860* (Columbia, 1924), 37–49; 1860 Census, Agriculture and Slave Schedules.

38. Welcome Bees, Slave Narratives, 14, part i, 49; interview with John Beese, Pawleys Island, S.C., Jan. 18, 1972; Rogers, *History of Georgetown County*, 261–62; Davidson, *Last Foray*, 243; Galbraith, "Inscriptions from the Allston Burying Grounds," 172–73; Leiding, *Historic Houses of South Carolina*, 120; Bolick, *Waccamaw Plantations*, 92–93; 1860 Census, Agriculture and Slave Schedules.

39. Louisa Brown, Slave Narratives, 14, part i, 115; Rogers, *History of Georgetown County*, 261–62; Davidson, *Last Foray*, 85, 256–57; Bolick, *Waccamaw Plantations*, 96–97. Trapier apparently liked to see people eat and drink well. He has the distinction of having introduced mint juleps to New College, Oxford, in 1845. He presented New College with a family recipe for the beverage and an antique silver cup and endowed the college with funds for an annual mint julep festival to be held each June 1, a custom still observed at New College. See David Ogg, "New College, Oxford, and South Carolina: A Personal Link," *SCHM*, 59 (1958), 61–63.

40. When the estate was finally settled the plantations were divided among Joshua John Ward's three sons: Joshua, Maham, and Benjamin. See Rogers, *History of Georgetown County*, 260–61.

41. Ben Horry, Slave Narratives, 14, part ii, 308–9; Ellen Godfrey, Slave Narratives, 14, part ii, 159–61; Brookgreen-Springfield Plantation Book, Nov. 3, 1861, SCHS; Rogers, *History of Georgetown County*,

259–61; Davidson, *Last Foray*, 258; Lachicotte, *Georgetown Rice Plantations*, 18–26, 55–63; Galbraith, "All Saints Waccamaw," 172–73; Robin R. Salmon, "Historical Background of the Plantations Comprising Brookgreen Gardens," in Walton Rawls, ed., *A Century of American Sculpture: Treasures from Brookgreen Gardens* (New York, n.d. [1981]), 123–24; Susan Lowndes Allston, *Brookgreen Waccamaw in the Carolina Low Country* (Charleston, 1936), 23–27; Leiding, *Historic Houses of South Carolina*, 117–18; Bolick, *Waccamaw Plantations*, 103–8; 1860 Census, Agriculture and Slave Schedules; 1870 Census, Population Schedules; plat of Longwood Plantation, Plat Book 4, 94, Horry County Court House, Conway, S.C.

42. Ellen Godfrey, Slave Narratives, 14, part ii, 161; Ben Horry, Slave Narratives, 14, part ii, 305, 311, 317; Henry Small interview, Free Woods, S.C., Aug. 2, 1975.

43. Weston had offered to sell Laurel Hill to his cousin, Francis Weston, in 1856 and again in 1858, including the 200 slaves on the plantation. He wrote that he "would be obliged to ask a fair price, but the times of payment would be made very accommodating say 1/8 down, and the rest in ten or fifteen or twenty years." Plowden C. J. Weston to Francis Weston, Mar. 18, 1858, in Weston Family Papers, SCL. When the offer was declined, he sold the property, through his Charleston agents, to Daniel W. Jordan. Articles of Agreement for the Sale and Purchase of Laurel Hill Plantation, Mar. 12, 1859, Mazyck and Howard to Jordan, Nov. 1, 9, 10, 12, 30, Dec. 6, 15, 1859, Daniel W. Jordan Papers, DUL. Rice (*Aftermath of Glory*, 160–61) has a somewhat garbled account of this transaction. Jordan sold out his Little River holdings and took possession of Laurel Hill in January 1860. Deed Book, Jan. 5, 1860, Horry County Court House; Plowden Weston to Jordan, Jan. 26, 1860, Daniel W. Jordan Papers. I can find no record in the Jordan Papers or elsewhere of any military service on Jordan's part. He began using the title "Colonel" while attempting unsuccessfully to establish himself as a cotton planter in Mississippi in the 1830s. See also Rogers, *History of Georgetown County*, 258, 270; Davidson, *Last Foray*, 216; Lachicotte, *Georgetown Rice Plantations*, 39, 59; Connelly Burgin Berry, "Little River and Long Bay: An Historical Sketch of Coastal Horry County, South Carolina," in Clarke A. Willcox, *Musings of a Hermit, with Historical Sketches of the Waccamaw Neck*, 2d ed. (Charleston, 1967), 149; C. B. Berry, "Colonel Daniel W. Jordan," *Independent Republic Quarterly*, 13 (Oct. 1979), 12–15.

44. Mazyck and Robertson to Jordan, Nov. 12, 30, 1859, Daniel W. Jordan Papers.

45. Emily Weston diary, Dec. 24–27, 1859; Francis Weston inventory.

46. Frederick J. Shaffer to Jordan, Nov. 1, 1859, Daniel W. Jordan Papers.

47. 1860 Census, Agriculture and Slave Schedules; letters of Jan. 15, 1846, Apr. 29, 1859, Jan. 16, 1860, and list of Negroes, May 1862, Daniel W. Jordan Papers, DUL. There is ample evidence that the slaves used

surnames, or "titles," among themselves, with or without the knowledge of their masters. Jordan's is the *only* slave list I have seen that routinely uses surnames. The surnames listed thereon may, however, be names awarded by the master, and not necessarily what the slaves regarded their family name to be.

48. Samuel T. Atkinson to Jordan, Mar. 11, 1859, Daniel W. Jordan Papers.

49. *Ibid.*

50. *Ibid.* For a discussion of hernias among slaves, see Todd L. Savitt, *Medicine and Slavery: The Diseases and Health Care of Blacks in Antebellum Virginia* (Urbana, 1978), 134–35.

51. Atkinson to Jordan, Mar. 11, 1859, Daniel W. Jordan Papers.

52. Rogers, *History of Georgetown County*, 207; Davidson, *Last Foray*, 226; Lachicotte, *Georgetown Rice Plantations*, 67. Magill came from an old All Saints family. He married Mary Vereen in 1825, and at his death in 1864 he left Richmond Hill to his son, John D. Magill, Jr. See All Saints Vestry Records, SCHS; estate of John D. Magill, Apr. 8, 1864, Probate Office, Plat Book B, p. 100, and Deed Book A, all at the Georgetown County Court House.

53. Emily R. Reynolds and Joan Reynolds Faunt, *Biographical Directory of the Senate of the State of South Carolina, 1776–1964* (Columbia, 1964), 334; Lawrence C. Bryant, "Negro Legislators in South Carolina, 1868–1902," mimeograph copy, SCA.

54. John D. Magill inventory, Probate Office, Georgetown County Court House; 1870 Census, Population Schedules; 1880 Census, Population Schedules; Records Book 6, Sparkman Family Papers, SHC.

55. John D. Magill inventory; *1880 Census of Horry County, South Carolina* [State Census], Horry County Historical Society Publication No. 1 (Conway, S.C., 1970), 162. Toby Small was the father of Henry Small, whom I interviewed in Aug. 1975 for this study. He was also the father of Julia Small, whose interview with Helen Gardner Butler was published as Etrulia P. Dozier, ed., "Interview of Mrs. Julia Smalls [*sic*]," *Independent Republic Quarterly*, 4 (July 1970), 31–33.

56. Ellen Godfrey, Slave Narratives, 14, part ii, 161. Both Henry Small and Julia Small, whose father, Toby Small, and grandfather, Titus Small, were slaves of Magill, substantiated Ellen Godfrey's testimony. Henry Small interview, Aug. 2, 1975; Dozier, ed., "Interview of Mrs. Julia Smalls," 31–32.

57. See, for example, the *Pee Dee Times*, Jan. 21, Oct. 14, 1857, and July 21, 1858.

58. *Winyah Observer*, June 23–Dec. 29, 1852.

59. *OR Navy*, Ser. I, 13:213–15.

60. 1860 Census, Agriculture and Slave Schedules.

61. Rogers, *History of Georgetown County*, 256, 521; Lachicotte, *Georgetown Rice Plantations*, 64–68; Smith, "The Baronies of South Caro-

lina," 79; Mabel L. Webber, "Moore of St. Thomas Parish," *SCHM*, 27 (1926), 157–69; Bolick, *Waccamaw Plantations*, 109–11, 116–19. Allard Belin Flagg was the brother of Alice Flagg, whose untimely death at the age of fifteen inspired the ghostly legends of "Alice of the Hermitage." See Willcox, *Musings of a Hermit*, 40–41, 77–81, for the legend. See Charles W. Joyner, "Legend, Belief, and History: An Interdisciplinary Approach to Legend Formation and Communicative Strategy," *International Folklore Review*, 2 (1982): 53–60, for an analysis of the legend in historical perspective.

62. Margaret One grew up to be Margaret Bryant, an informant for the Federal Writers' Project Slave Narrative Collection. See Margaret Bryant, Slave Narratives, 14, part i, 145–47.

63. Childs, ed., *Rice Planter and Sportsman*, 6, 50–51, 66–69, 123–25, and *passim*; Rogers, *History of Georgetown County*, 265–66; Mabel C. Webber, "Inscriptions from the Alston Burying Grounds at 'The Oaks' Plantation, Waccamaw," *SCHM*, 12 (1911), 38–41; Heyward, "Descendants of Col. William Rhett," 56–114, 156–57.

64. Childs, ed., *Rice Planter and Sportsman*, 118–23.

65. *Ibid.*, 125–26.

66. Rogers, *History of Georgetown County*, 221; Davidson, *Last Foray*, 9, 13, 181; Kirke, *Among the Pines*, 31; "Henry Buck," *Independent Republic Quarterly*, 2 (Jan. 1969), 31–33. James Henry Rice, a not-always-reliable source, contends that Buck came to South Carolina as a peddler with a pack on his back and received a start in his career through the generosity of Robert F. W. Allston, who lent Buck two slaves but refused to sell or rent slaves to him (*Aftermath of Glory*, 161–62). This anecdote is not mentioned in either Easterby's scrupulous edition of Allston's papers, nor in the memoirs of Allston's daughter.

67. Kirke, *Among the Pines*, 31.

68. 1860 Census, Slave Schedules; Davidson, *Last Foray*, 181.

69. Kirke, *Among the Pines*, 13–32. A similar report was made by Mary Brookman of Bucksport, Me., who—despite her abolitionist sympathies—came to All Saints Parish to be governess to Buck's children in 1849. See Annette Reesor, "The Discordant Note," *Sandlapper*, 8 (Oct. 1973), 45.

70. Kirke, *Among the Pines*, 32.

71. *Ibid.*, 48.

72. *Ibid.*, 36. Gilmore describes in his memoirs an audience with President Abraham Lincoln, who "took from the drawer of his table a copy of 'Among the Pines,' every few leaves of which had a page turned down. Then looking at me searchingly, he asked, 'How much of this book is true?'" Gilmore assured him that "'every incident in it occurred as I related it, and under my own observation.'" James Roberts Gilmore, *Personal Recollections of Abraham Lincoln and the Civil War* (Boston, 1898), 78.

73. Henry L. Buck IV, "The Buck Family, 1861–1865," *Independent Republic Quarterly*, 3 (Oct. 1969), 11–14.

74. 1860 Census, Agriculture and Slave Schedules.

75. Sabe Rutledge, Slave Narratives, 14, part iv, 61–64; 1870 Census, Population Schedules; Sabe Rutledge, WPA Mss.

76. 1860 Census, Agriculture and Slave Schedules; William Oliver, Slave Narratives, 14, part iii, 218–20; 1870 Census, Population Schedules.

77. Bill of sale, Mary Ann LaBruce Petigru to R. Allston, Feb. 1, 1859, Robert F. W. Allston Papers; Rogers, *History of Georgetown County*, 254–55; Easterby, ed., *South Carolina Rice Plantation*, 22.

78. In addition to the holdings listed, Allston also managed Waverly and Woodville plantations on the Waccamaw until 1857. See Rogers, *History of Georgetown County*, 263–66; Davidson, *Last Foray*, 171–72; Lachicotte, *Georgetown Rice Plantations*, 119–25; Galbraith, "Inscriptions from the Allston Burying Grounds at Turkey Hill," 183; Joseph W. Barnwell, "Dr. Henry Woodward, the First English Settler of South Carolina and Some of His Descendants," *SCHM*, 8 (1907), 36; "Historical Notes," *ibid.*, 13 (1912), 179; "Georgetown Library Society," *ibid.*, 25 (1924), 99; Louise R. Johnson and Julia Rosa, "Inscriptions from the Churchyard of Prince George Winyah, Georgetown, South Carolina," *ibid.*, 31 (1930), 303. According to Yates Snowden, "The Administration of Gov. Allston was not marked by any noteworthy event in South Carolina." *History of South Carolina* (Chicago, 1920), 2:647.

79. James L. Petigru to R. Allston, Dec. 29, 1858, and bill of sale, M. Petigru to R. Allston, Feb. 1, 1859, both in Easterby, ed., *South Carolina Rice Plantation*, 148–49, 352–53; Pringle, *Chronicles of Chicora Wood*, 9–11.

80. See, for example, the petitions concerning the desire of William Jackson, a free black, to see his wife and children freed, in the Free Persons of Color During Slavery file, 1853, SCA. The petitions were rejected on grounds of "the principles and policy of the law which forbids the emancipation of slaves." On Allston's purchase and disposition of the Pipe Down slaves, see bill of sale, M. Petigru to R. Allston, 1859, and Robert F. W. Allston estate inventory, 1864, both in Robert F. W. Allston Papers. It should be noted that there were a great many elderly persons among the Pipe Down slaves purchased in 1859, and thus death may have been the principal reason for the disparity between the 1859 and 1864 lists. Allston's brother-in-law, the noted lawyer James L. Petigru, who served as broker for the sale, acknowledged that "with the number of mendicants in the population the acquisition is not as good a bargain as the purchase of Louisiana." James L. Petigru to R. Allston, Apr. 1, 1859, in Robert F. W. Allston Papers.

81. 1870 Census, Population Schedules; Pringle, *Chronicles of Chicora Wood*, 9–10; interview, Prince Washington (grandson of Philip Washington), Sandy Island, S.C., Jan. 17, 1972; interview, Rebecca Washington (widow of Prince Washington), Sandy Island, S.C., July 2, 1976.

82. Bills of sale, Jan. 13, 25, 1859, May 9, 1860, in Robert F. W. Allston Papers.

83. James R. Sparkman Books, vol. 3, SHC; family council, May 24,

1858, Sparkman Family Papers; Dirleton Plantation Memo Book, 1859, SCHS; Rogers, *History of Georgetown County*, 255–56; Davidson, *Last Foray*, 209; Lachicotte, *Georgetown Rice Plantations*, 105. See also Smith, "Baronies of South Carolina," 78-79; Galbraith, "All Saints Waccamaw," 176.

84. Gabe Lance, Slave Narratives, 14, part iii, 91–92.

85. Memorandum for the benefit of the parties interested, Jan. 17, 1859, Sparkman Family Papers; estate of Edward T. Heriot, Jan. 18, 1859, in Robert F. W. Allston Papers. Allston was one of the appraisers of the estate.

86. Francis W. Pickens to John C. Calhoun, Feb. 6, 1846, in John C. Calhoun Papers, Clemson University, Clemson, S.C.; R. Allston, *Essay on Sea Coast Crops*, 37; William W. Freehling, *Prelude to Civil War: The Nullification Controversy in South Carolina, 1816–1836* (New York, 1966), 28–29; Ulrich B. Phillips, "The Slave Labor Problem in the Charleston District," *Political Science Quarterly*, 22 (1907), 416–39; Lathers, *Reminiscences*, 5.

87. 1860 Census, Slave Schedules.

88. Winyah and All Saints Agricultural Society minutes, 1842–61, SCHS; Rogers, *History of Georgetown County*, 339–41; S. Allston, *Brookgreen Waccamaw*, 23–27.

89. Rogers, *History of Georgetown County*, chs. 13–17. A broader study of the antebellum rice industry finds the production of rice everywhere highly concentrated, with one-fifth of all producers accounting for 96 percent of the crop. Economies of scale enabled the large plantations to earn profitable rates of return denied to the vast majority of small producers. See Dale Evans Swan, "The Structure and Profitability of the Ante-bellum Rice Industry: 1859" (Ph.D. diss., University of North Carolina, 1972).

90. Simms, *Geography of South Carolina*, 81; R. Allston, *Essay on Sea Coast Crops*, 26–27; Pringle, *Chronicles of Chicora Wood*, 67; Zamba, *Life*, 220–21; Edward Thomas Heriot to Anna Bruce Cunningham, Apr. 1854, in Edward Thomas Heriot Papers, DUL; Benjamin Blossom to Jordan, July 23, 1859, in Daniel W. Jordan Papers; G.M., "South Carolina," *New England Magazine*, 1 (Oct. 1831), 337–41. Cf. Oliphant, *Patriots and Filibusters*, 144.

91. Sherman L. Ricards and George M. Blackburn, "A Demographic History of Slavery: Georgetown County, South Carolina, 1850," *SCHM*, 76 (1975), 215–24. Free blacks comprised 1.09 percent of the black population. The median age was 18.6, the sex ratio was 89.95 males per 100 females, and the dependency ratio was 116 slaves aged 0 to 20 per 100 slaves aged 21 to 64, and 1.6 aged 65 and over per 100 aged 21 to 64. My analysis of the 1860 census shows similar patterns: the proportion of free blacks, for instance, drops to 1.01 percent in 1860, the sex ratio rises to 102 males per 100 females, and the dependency ratio declines to 91.4 children and youth per 100 adults and rises to 5.9 aged per 100 adults. For additional discussion

of free blacks in Georgetown District, see Marina Wikramanayake, *A World in Shadow: The Free Black in Ante-Bellum South Carolina* (Columbia, 1973), 16–17, 22–23, 95.

92. Malet, *Errand to the South*, 50; Childs, ed., *Rice Planter and Sportsman*, 55–56; Pringle, *Chronicles of Chicora Wood*, 53–54; Albert Carolina, Slave Narratives, 14, part i, 199; Ben Horry, Slave Narratives, 14, part ii, 306, 311.

93. Pringle, *Chronicles of Chicora Wood*, 351.

Notes to "All Dem Rice Field"

1. Converse D. Clowse, *Economic Beginnings in Colonial South Carolina, 1670–1730* (Columbia, 1971), 122–32; Duncan Clinch Heyward, *Seed from Madagascar* (Chapel Hill, 1937), 41; M. Eugene Sirmans, *Colonial South Carolina: A Political History, 1663–1763* (Chapel Hill, 1966), 226; Carl Bridenbaugh, *Myths and Realities: Societies of the Colonial South* (Baton Rouge, 1952; rpt. New York, 1973), 67; George C. Rogers, Jr., *The History of Georgetown County, South Carolina* (Columbia, 1970), 324–39; Dale Evans Swan, "The Structure and Profitability of the Ante-bellum Rice Industry: 1859" (Ph.D. diss., University of North Carolina, 1972); Raymond C. Battalio and John Kagel, "The Structure of Southern Agriculture: South Carolina, a Case Study," *Agriculture History*, 44 (1970), 25–37.

2. Interview with A. H. Lachicotte, Jr., Pawleys Island, S.C., July 28, 1975; Etrulia P. Dozier, ed., "Interview of Mrs. Julia Smalls [*sic*]," *Independent Republic Quarterly*, 4 (July 1970), 32. I have observed these partly eroded dikes, sluice gates, and stobs at close range on boat trips down the Waccamaw. See also Zamba, *The Life and Adventures of Zamba, an African Negro King, and His Experience of Slavery in South Carolina, Written by Himself* (London, 1847), 220–21.

3. Gabe Lance, in Slave Narratives: A Folk History of Slavery in the United States from Interviews with Former Slaves. Typewritten records prepared by the Federal Writers' Project, 1936–38 (microfilm), 14, part iii, 52.

4. Ben Horry, Slave Narratives, 14, part ii, 312.

5. Bernard M. Baruch, *My Own Story* (New York, 1957), 292. Cf. Julia Peterkin, *Roll, Jordan, Roll* (New York, 1933), 11; James McBride Dabbs, "The Myth, the Movement, and the American Dream," *New South*, 18 (Dec. 1963), 6.

6. Arney R. Childs, ed., *Rice Planter and Sportsman: The Recollections of J. Motte Alston* (Columbia, 1953), 108. Bryan Edwards noted a similar sense of ownership among slaves in eighteenth-century Jamaica. See his *The History, Civil and Commercial, of the British Colonies in the West Indies* (London, 1793), 2:133.

7. Interview with John Beese, Pawleys Island, S.C., Jan. 18, 1972; interview with Henry Small, Free Woods, S.C., Aug. 2, 1975; Lachicotte interview; Gabe Lance, Slave Narratives, 14, part iii, 92; Rogers, *History of*

Georgetown County, 331; Childs, ed., *Rice Planter and Sportsman*, 46; J. Harold Easterby, ed., *The South Carolina Rice Plantation as Revealed in the Papers of Robert F. W. Allston* (Chicago, 1945), 31; Dennis T. Lawson, *No Heir to Take Its Place: The Story of Rice in Georgetown County, South Carolina* (Georgetown, 1972), 13. Cf. G.S.S., "Sketches of the South Santee," *Atlantic Monthly Magazine*, May 8, 1836, 431–32. According to the daughter of one rice planter, "That it was very moderate is proved by the fact that the smart, brisk workers can do two or three 'tasks' in a day, but the lazy ones can never be persuaded to do more than one task, though they may finish it by 11 o'clock." Patience Pennington [Elizabeth Allston Pringle], *A Woman Rice Planter* (New York, 1914), 41.

8. Childs, ed., *Rice Planter and Sportsman*, 46. Cf. Robert William Fogel and Stanley L. Engerman, *Time on the Cross: The Economics of American Negro Slavery* (Boston, 1974), 1:206.

9. H. Small interview; Lachicotte interview.

10. J. Beese interview; Lachicotte interview; William Oliver, Slave Narratives, 14, part iii, 220; William Wyndham Malet, *An Errand to the South in the Summer of 1862* (London, 1863), 57; Ben Horry, Slave Narratives, 14, part ii, 312; Gabe Lance, Slave Narratives, 14, part iii, 52; interview with Mary Small, Free Woods, S.C., Aug. 2, 1975. Like Malet, Laurence Oliphant, an earlier British visitor to All Saints Parish, considered task work "easy." See his *Patriots and Filibusters; or Incidents of Political and Exploratory Travel* (Edinburgh, 1860), 140.

11. Easterby, ed., *South Carolina Rice Plantation*, 31; Gabe Lance, Slave Narratives, 14, part iii, 92. Each slave was assigned his own hoe, with his name branded on it, and was held accountable for the tool. See account of tools, 1849, 1851, 1853, Hasell-Flagg Plantation Records, SCHS.

12. James R. Sparkman to Benjamin Allston, Mar. 10, 1858, in Robert F. W. Allston Papers, SCHS, printed in Easterby, ed., *South Carolina Rice Plantation*, 346; Elizabeth Collins, *Memories of the Southern States* (Taunton, England, 1865), 46; Lawson, *No Heir*, 13; Plowden C. J. Weston, "Rules and Management for the Plantation, 1859," quoted in Collins, *Memories of the Southern States*, 107. Collins (104–16) quotes the entire document. An earlier and somewhat shorter version of this overseer's contract was published as "Rules on the Rice Estate of P. C. Weston, S.C., 1856," *DeBow's Review*, 21 (1857), 38–44, and reprinted in Ulrich B. Phillips, ed., *Plantation and Frontier Documents* (Cleveland, 1910), 1:115–22.

13. Weston, "Rules and Management for the Plantation," 107.

14. M. Small interview; H. Small interview; Hagar Brown, Slave Narratives, 14, part i, 110–11; Gabe Lance, Slave Narratives, 14, part iii, 92; Albert Carolina, Slave Narratives, 14, part i, 147; Ben Horry, Slave Narratives, 14, part ii, 304, 310–11; Margaret Bryant, Slave Narratives, 14, part i, 147.

15. J. Beese interview; Sparkman to B. Allston, Mar. 10, 1858, in Easterby, ed., *South Carolina Rice Plantation*, 346; estate of Francis Marion Weston, 1855, Office of Probate Judge, Georgetown County Court House.

The slave list in Weston's inventory is extremely helpful because it lists each slave on his plantations by occupation. In Fante-Ashanti tradition women till the fields. See Roger Bastide, *African Civilisations in the New World*, trans. Peter Green (New York, 1971), 65.

16. Sparkman to B. Allston, Mar. 10, 1858, in Easterby, ed., *South Carolina Rice Plantation*, 346.

17. Almira Coffin to Mrs. J. G. Osgood, May 10, 1851, in J. Harold Easterby, ed., "South Carolina through New England Eyes: Almira Coffin's Visit to the Low Country in 1851," *SCHM*, 45 (1944), 127−36; Sparkman to B. Allston, Mar. 10, 1853, in Easterby, ed., *South Carolina Rice Plantation*, 346−50; Weston, "Rules and Management for the Plantation," 104−16; Lachicotte interview; Lawson, *No Heir*, 13.

18. The following description of the annual cycle of rice culture is taken from several sources. The most detailed information is found in the very thorough diary of rice tasks throughout the year in the Ben Sparkman Plantation Record, SHC. I have also drawn extensively from my interviews with Luther Allston (who still grew rice), Murrells Inlet, S.C., July 24, 1975, and with Lachicotte. Sociolinguist Patricia Causey Nichols furnished me with copies of her interviews on rice cultivation with William Collins and Prince Washington on Sandy Island, Dec. 1974. The following printed materials were also very useful: Robert F. W. Allston, *An Essay on Sea Coast Crops* (Charleston, 1854), esp. 31−36; Robert F. W. Allston, *Memoir on the Introduction and Planting of Rice* (Charleston, 1843), 4−17; Robert F. W. Allston, "Report by Robert F. W. Allston," *Southern Agriculturalist, Horticulturalist, and Register of Rural Affairs*, Jan. 1844, 6−29; T. Addison Richards, "The Rice Lands of the South," *Harper's New Monthly Magazine*, 19 (Nov. 1859), 727−28; A. R. Waud, "Sketches of a Rice Plantation," *Harper's Weekly*, Jan. 5, 1867, 8; David Doar, *Rice and Rice Planting in the South Carolina Low Country* (Charleston, 1936); Heyward, *Seed from Madagascar*, 27−44; Elizabeth Allston Pringle, *Chronicles of Chicora Wood* (New York, 1922), 14−17, 89−90; Rogers, *History of Georgetown County*, 330−34; Lawson, *No Heir*, 5−16; Clowse, *Economic Beginnings*, 126−30.

19. Ben Horry, Slave Narratives, 14, part ii, 302. Robert F. W. Allston noted that the task for sowing on the rice coast of South Carolina was a half acre. "This is the unit of land measurement among the negroes," he wrote, "and with practical planters" (*Essay on Sea Coast Crops*, 32). Allston's statement strongly suggests that the slaves had at least some influence on determining the dimensions of the task.

20. Mss. diary of Emily Weston, in private possession, Apr. 29, 1859, hereafter cited as Emily Weston diary.

21. R. Allston, *Essay on Sea Coast Crops*, 32−33. Allston emphasizes the importance of having expert sowers with his indication that "it is a good plan to make handsome presents to the best sowers after the planting." While Allston and many of the Waccamaw planters preferred the old method of coating the rice seeds with mud, others preferred the new method

of rolling the seed in clayed water, which was championed by Edmund Ruffin. See Ruffin's *Report on the Commencement and Progress of the Agricultural Survey of South Carolina for 1843* (Columbia, 1843), esp. 16, 99–120.

22. Ellen Godfrey, Slave Narratives, 14, part ii, 158–59; William Oliver, Slave Narratives, 14, part iii, 219.

23. Brookgreen and All Saints Agricultural Society Minutes, SCHS; Susan Lowndes Allston, *Brookgreen Waccamaw in the Carolina Low Country* (Charleston, 1936), 23–27.

24. R. Allston, *Essay on Sea Coast Crops*, 33–34.

25. Examples of fanner baskets from Georgetown District are on exhibit in the Rice Museum in Georgetown. They are quite similar to the fanner baskets on exhibit in the McKissick Museum at the University of South Carolina, Columbia, in the Old Slave Mart Museum in Charleston, and in the illustration opposite p. 128 of Nathan I. Huggins, Martin Kilson, and Daniel H. Fox, eds., *Key Issues in the Afro-American Experience* (New York, 1971), vol. 1. The mortar and pestle on exhibit at Brookgreen Gardens, Murrells Inlet, S.C., are from the same plantation as Ben Horry, who described the mortar and pestle pounding process in Slave Narratives, 14, ii, 309. See also the photographs of rice pounding in Heyward, *Seed from Madagascar*, facing p. 182, and Doar, *Rice and Rice Planting*, following p. 50.

26. Laurel Hill Mill Records, 1846–64, in Francis Marion Weston Papers, SCHS; Henry Middleton to Oliver Middleton, Jan. 12, [18??], Middleton-Blake Papers, SCHS; Rogers, *History of Georgetown County*, 335; Lawson, *No Heir*, 10–12.

27. Childs, ed., *Rice Planter and Sportsman*, 42.

28. R. Allston, *Essay on Sea Coast Crops*, 36–37.

29. Coffin to Osgood, May 10, 1851, in Easterby, ed., "South Carolina through New England Eyes," 127–36.

30. For example, the slave list for Laurel Hill Plantation in the inventory for the estate of Francis Marion Weston, 1855, shows one half-time and two full-time engineers among his rice mill workers. In addition, the mortality schedules of the 1850 federal census for Georgetown District shows that four slave millers died in the district between June 1849 and June 1850.

31. Weston, "Rules and Management for the Plantation," 111.

32. R. Allston, *Essay on Sea Coast Crops*, 35–36; J. Beese interview; Lachicotte interview.

33. On the controversy see Fogel and Engerman, *Time on the Cross*, 1:41, 147–52, and their numerous critics, especially Herbert Gutman and Richard Sutch, "Sambo Makes Good, or Were Slaves Imbued with the Protestant Work Ethic?" in Paul A. David *et al.*, *Reckoning with Slavery* (New York, 1976), 55–93.

34. Weston, "Rules and Management for the Plantation," 114.

35. *Ibid.*, 107; Childs, ed., *Rice Planter and Sportsman*, 46.

36. Diary of Robert F. W. Allston, Jan. 14, 1860, in Easterby, ed., *South Carolina Rice Plantation*, 454–55; Sparkman to B. Allston, Mar. 10, 1858, *ibid.*, 347–48; Pringle, *Chronicles of Chicora Wood*, 14–15; Pennington, *Woman Rice Planter*, 8. Cf. Raymond A. and Alice H. Bauer, "Day to Day Resistance to Slavery," *JNH*, 27 (1942), 388–410.

37. Emily Weston diary, Apr. 3, Dec. 13, 1859; Malet, *Errand to the South*, 57; James R. Sparkman Books, II, SHC; Ben Sparkman Plantation Record; "Agreement by Robert F. W. Allston to Purchase Hogs, 1859," in Easterby, ed., *South Carolina Rice Plantation*, 350. That such purchases from slaves were contrary to South Carolina law appeared not to bother the All Saints rice planters, who included among their numbers between 1850 and 1865 a governor, Robert F. W. Allston; two lieutenant-governors, Joshua John Ward and Plowden C. J. Weston; and a chancellor of the Court of Equity, Benjamin Faneuil Dunkin. See David J. McCord, ed., *Statutes at Large of South Carolina* (Columbia, 1840), 6:516–17.

38. R. Allston to Sarah Carr, Jan. 17, 1859, in Easterby, ed., *South Carolina Rice Plantation*, 34.

39. Malet, *Errand to the South*, 68–69.

40. Margaret Bryant, Slave Narratives, 14, part i, 147.

41. Albert Carolina, Slave Narratives, 14, part i, 197–98. Cf. Kenneth M. Stampp, *The Peculiar Institution: Slavery in the Ante-Bellum South* (New York, 1956), 174–81.

42. Hagar Brown, Slave Narratives, 14, part i, 113.

43. Gabe Lance, Slave Narratives, 14, part iii, 92.

44. Harman Pitman to R. Allston, May 6, 1860, in Easterby, ed. *South Carolina Rice Plantation*, 263.

45. Hagar Brown, Slave Narratives, 14, part i, 110; Ben Horry, Slave Narratives, 14, part ii, 304; Gabe Lance, Slave Narratives, 14, part iii, 92; Albert Carolina, Slave Narratives, 14, part i, 197–98.

46. Easterby, ed., *South Carolina Rice Plantation*, 34, concludes that "the lash does not appear to have been in general use."

47. Gabriel L. Ellis to R. Allston, Sept. 16, 1838, *ibid.*, 254–55.

48. Weston, "Rules and Management for the Plantation," 108, 115.

49. J. Beese interview.

50. "Robert F. W. Allston Diary, January 14, 1860," in Easterby, ed., *South Carolina Rice Plantation*, 454.

51. R. Allston to Adele Petigru Allston, Apr. 10, 1863, *ibid.*, 193–94. Brass was sold for $1,700. Robertson, Blacklock and Co. to R. Allston, May 9, 1863, *ibid.*, 426.

52. Collins, *Memories of the Southern States*, 71.

53. Hagar Brown, WPA Mss., SCL.

54. Ben Horry, Slave Narratives, 14, part ii, 303.

55. Henry A. Middleton to Mrs. Henry A. Middleton, Nov. 5, 1862, in Cheves Collection, Middleton Papers, SCHS; Mariah Heywood, Slave Narratives, 14, part ii, 286–87. The patrol was an organized police activity,

loosely related to the state militia, which played a major role in slave control. All adult white males in South Carolina were subject to patrol duty. See Howell M. Henry, *The Police Control of the Slave in South Carolina* (Emory, Va., 1914), 32–37.

56. Cf. Fogel and Engerman, *Time on the Cross*, 1:145; Herbert G. Gutman, *Slavery and the Numbers Game: A Critique of Time on the Cross* (Urbana, 1975), 18–41; David Brion Davis, *The Problem of Slavery in Western Culture* (Ithaca, 1966), 223–43.

57. Cf. Eugene D. Genovese, *Roll, Jordan, Roll: The World the Slaves Made* (New York, 1974), 3–7, and *passim*, and his *The Political Economy of Slavery: Studies in the Economy and Society of the Slave South* (New York, 1965), 28; Pierre L. van den Berghe, *Race and Racism: A Comparative Perspective* (New York, 1967), 31–33.

58. Heriot to Anna Bruce Cunningham, Apr. 20, 1853, in Edward Thomas Heriot Papers, DUL.

59. Cf. E. P. Thompson, "'Rough Music': Le Charavari Anglais," *Annales: E.S.C.*, 27 (1972), 285–313; Natalie Davis, "The Rites of Violence," in her *Society and Culture in Early Modern France* (Stanford, 1975); Clifford Geertz, "Deep Play: Notes on the Balinese Cockfight," *Daedalus*, 101 (1972), 1–37, and collected in his *The Interpretation of Cultures* (New York, 1973), 412–53.

60. African retentions in South Carolina rice seeding, hoeing, winnowing, and threshing practices are emphasized in William R. Bascom, "Acculturation among the Gullah Negroes," *AA*, 43 (1941), 44–45, and Peter H. Wood, *Black Majority: Negroes in Colonial South Carolina from 1670 through the Stono Rebellion* (New York, 1974), 61–62. Photographs taken on the Waccamaw in the 1930s by Bayard Wooten show the persistence of these patterns among All Saints blacks. On the African background, see Elliott P. Skinner, "West African Economic Systems," in Elliott P. Skinner, ed., *Peoples and Cultures of Africa* (Garden City, N.Y., 1973), 207; Daniel F. McCall, *Africa in Time Perspective* (Boston, 1964), 29; John J. McKelvey, Jr., "Agricultural Research," in Robert A. Lystad, ed., *The African World: A Survey of Social Research* (New York, 1965), 330; Douglas Grant, *The Fortunate Slave: An Illustration of African Slavery in the Early Eighteenth Century* (London, 1968), 24–25. African continuities in coil basketry will be discussed below.

61. On the question of retentions, see Melville J. Herskovits, *The Myth of the Negro Past* (New York, 1941; rpt. Boston, 1958), xxii, 167–86. On the Africans in All Saints Parish in the mid-nineteenth century, see Ben Horry, Slave Narratives, 14, part i, 306, 311; Albert Carolina, Slave Narratives, 14, part i, 199; Malet, *Errand to the South*, 50; Childs, ed., *Rice Planter and Sportsman*, 55–56; Pringle, *Chronicles of Chicora Wood*, 53–54, 351. On the introduction of the rice mills, see Doar, *Rice and Rice Planting*, 18–22.

62. R. Allston, *Essay on Sea Coast Crops*, 31–36; Hagar Brown, Slave

Narratives, 14, part i, 110; M. Small interview (Mary Small is the daughter of Hagar Brown); Sparkman to B. Allston, Mar. 10, 1858, in Easterby, ed., *South Carolina Rice Plantation*, 346; G.S.S., "Sketches of the South Santee," 318–19.

63. Estate of Francis Marion Weston, 1855.

64. U.S. Census, 1850 and 1860, Mortality Schedules, Georgetown District, S.C., SCA.

65. Estate of Francis Marion Weston, 1855; J. Beese interview; Sabe Rutledge, Slave Narratives, 14, part iv, 62. Of the twenty-seven elderly slaves on the Weston plantations, fifteen were between sixty and sixty-nine years of age, and twelve were over seventy years of age. Only one slave younger than seventy was retired; only one slave older than sixty-nine was still working.

66. Oliphant, *Patriots and Filibusters*, 140; Edmund Kirke [James Roberts Gilmore], *Among the Pines: or, The South in Secession-Time* (New York, 1862), 129.

67. M. Small interview; Dan Ben-Amos, "The Elusive Audience of Benin Storytellers," *Journal of the Folklore Institute*, 9 (1972), 177–84; James Boyd Christensen, "The Role of Proverbs in Fante Culture," in Skinner, ed., *Peoples and Cultures of Africa*, 516; "Grandma Kit and Aunt Mariah Heywood," in WPA Mss.; Peterkin, *Roll, Jordan, Roll*, 10. Cf. Leslie J. Pollard, "Aging and Slavery: A Gerontological Perspective," *JNH*, 66 (1981), 228–34; Genovese, *Roll, Jordan, Roll*, 522–23; Gilbert Osofsky, ed., *Puttin' On Ole Massa* (New York, 1969), 38; Orlando Patterson, *The Sociology of Slavery* (London, 1967), 150, 169–70; Sidney W. Mintz and Richard Price, *An Anthropological Approach to the Afro-American Past: A Caribbean Perspective* (Philadelphia, 1976), 35.

68. Malet, *Errand to the South*, 117–18; Collins, *Memories of the Southern States*, 14–15. Cf. John Hope Franklin, "Slaves Virtually Free in Ante-Bellum North Carolina," *JNH*, 28 (1943), 284–310.

69. Lawson, *No Heir*, 12. Cf. Randall M. Miller, "The Man in the Middle: The Black Slave Driver," *American Heritage*, 30 (Oct. 1979), 41–49; William L. Van Deburg, *The Slave Drivers: Black Agricultural Labor Supervisors in the Antebellum South* (Westport, Conn., 1979); Genovese, *Roll, Jordan, Roll*, 378–79; Stampp, *Peculiar Institution*, 151–52.

70. Gabe Lance, Slave Narratives, 14, part iii, 91.

71. Sabe Rutledge, Slave Narratives, 14, part iv, 61; Sabe Rutledge, WPA Mss.

72. William Oliver, Slave Narratives, 14, part iii, 218; Ben Horry, Slave Narratives, 14, part ii, 299–300.

73. Weston, "Rules and Management for the Plantation," 107–8, 112. Cf. Easterby, ed., *South Carolina Rice Plantation*, 31.

74. H. Small interview; Albert Carolina, Slave Narratives, 14, part i, 197–98; Hagar Brown, Slave Narratives, 14, part i, 113; Ben Horry, Slave Narratives, 14, part ii, 304.

75. Weston, "Rules and Management for the Plantation," 108.

76. Robert Nesbit to R. Allston, Dec. 26, 1837, in Easterby, ed., *South Carolina Rice Plantation*, 76; Childs, ed., *Rice Planter and Sportsman*, 108–9.

77. Lachicotte interview; Ben Horry, Slave Narratives, 14, part ii, 311; Albert Carolina, Slave Narratives, 14, part i, 197–98; Charlotte Ann Allston to R. Allston, Apr. 3, 1823, in Easterby, ed., *South Carolina Rice Plantation*, 58–59. Ben Horry succeeded his father as "head man" at Brookgreen. See Slave Narratives, 14, part ii, 311. Cf. Philip D. Morgan, "The Development of Slave Culture in Eighteenth Century Plantation America" (Ph.D. diss., University College, London, 1977), 116–26, 189–93.

78. B. Allston to R. Allston, Mar. 24, 1861, in Easterby, ed., *South Carolina Rice Plantation*, 73. On the importance of ritual in the symbolic enhancement of status, see Victor Turner, *The Forest of Symbols: Aspects of Ndembu Ritual* (Ithaca, 1967), 19; Raymond Firth, *Symbols: Public and Private* (Ithaca, 1975), 396; Edmund Leach, *Culture and Communication* (London, 1976), 6; and Eric Wolf, "Specific Aspects of Plantation Systems in the New World: Community, Sub-Cultures, and Social Classes," in Vera Rubin, ed., *Plantation Systems of the New World* (Washington, 1959), 136–46.

79. R. Allston to Joseph Blyth Allston, Jan. 13, 1859, in Easterby, ed., *South Carolina Rice Plantation*, 151; Ben Horry, Slave Narratives, 14, part ii, 299–300, 304; Gabe Lance, Slave Narratives, 14, part iii, 91; William Oliver, Slave Narratives, 14, part iii, 218; Sabe Rutledge, Slave Narratives, 14, part iv, 61; Pringle, *Chronicles of Chicora Wood*, 9–10; interview with Prince Washington, Sandy Island, S.C., Jan. 17, 1972. Cf. Leslie Howard Owens, *This Species of Property: Slave Life and Culture in the Old South* (New York, 1976), 121–35.

80. Doar, *Rice and Rice Planting*, 37; William K. Scarborough, *The Overseer: Plantation Management in the Old South* (Baton Rouge, 1966), 57; Easterby, ed., *South Carolina Rice Plantation*, 27. That overseers were constantly changing employers in All Saints Parish is indicated in the Laurel Hill Mill Records, 1846–64, Francis Marion Weston Papers. The importance attached to overseers may be seen in that Joshua John Ward, the largest and most powerful rice planter in the state, was charged in Horry District with "not having overseer on or in vicinity of a settled plantation." Horry General Sessions Court Journal, Spring Term, 1839, SCA.

81. Lachicotte interview; Easterby, ed., *South Carolina Rice Plantation*, 26–27; Malet, *Errand to the South*, 57; Ulrich B. Phillips, *Life and Labor in the Old South* (Boston, 1929), 307.

82. Lachicotte interview; Rogers, *History of Georgetown County*, 325–28.

83. William Jay, *Inquiry into the Character and Tendency of the American Anti-Slavery Societies* (New York, 1840), 22, in Marina Wikramanayake, *A World in Shadow: The Free Black in Antebellum South Carolina* (Columbia, 1973), 95. Fully one-third of colonial manumissions in South

Carolina were of mulatto children; two-thirds were women. See John D. Duncan, "Slave Emancipation in Colonial South Carolina," *American Chronicle*, 1 (1972), 66; John Donald Duncan, "Servitude and Slavery in Colonial South Carolina, 1670–1776" (Ph.D. diss., Emory University, 1971); John L. Bradley, "Slave Manumission in South Carolina, 1820–1860" (M.A. thesis, University of South Carolina, 1964).

84. Samuel T. Atkinson to Daniel W. Jordan, Mar. 11, 1859, Daniel W. Jordan Papers, DUL; Ben Horry, Slave Narratives, 14, part ii, 305. Cf. Genovese, *Roll, Jordan, Roll*, 366; Fogel and Engerman, *Time on the Cross*, 1:210–11; Jerome S. Handler and Frederick M. Lange, *Plantation Slavery in Barbados: An Archaeological and Historical Investigation* (Cambridge, Mass., 1978), 75.

85. Sabe Rutledge, WPA Mss.

86. Weston, "Rules and Management for the Plantation," 104.

87. Hagar Brown, Slave Narratives, 14, part i, 110–11; Easterby, ed., *South Carolina Rice Plantation*, 25; Ben Horry, Slave Narratives, 14, part ii, 305–6, 311, 317. James Henry Rice, Jr., in a popular account of the rice coast, considers the majority of overseers to be "a mere step above the brute." According to him, the overseers "hated the planters, along with everything decent and honorable"; they "robbed planters without stint or scruple"; and they "abused and oppressed the negroes." See his *Glories of the Carolina Coast* (Columbia, 1925), 11. Cf. William W. Freehling's negative evaluation of overseers' competence in his *Prelude to Civil War: The Nullification Controversy in South Carolina, 1816–1836* (New York, 1965), 34.

88. John Izard Middleton to Oliver Middleton, All Saints Beach, Aug. 20, 18??, Middleton-Blake Papers; Childs, ed., *Rice Planter and Sportsman*, 109–10; Pringle, *Chronicles of Chicora Wood*, 67; Ben Horry, Slave Narratives, 14, part ii, 306, 317, 323; Coffin to Osgood, Mar. 10, 1858, in Easterby, ed., "South Carolina through New England Eyes," 127–36; Oliphant, *Patriots and Filibusters*, 137–39; Lawrence Fay Brewster, *Summer Migrations and Resorts of South Carolina Planters* (Durham, N.C., 1947), 3–6; Rogers, *History of Georgetown County*, 312; Easterby, ed., *South Carolina Rice Plantation*, 9. Orlando Patterson, *Sociology of Slavery*, 33, emphasizes planter absenteeism as "the root of all the evils" of the Jamaican slave system. On absenteeism cross-culturally, see Patterson's *Slavery and Social Death: A Comparative Study* (Cambridge, Mass., 1982), 180–81.

89. Francis Marion Weston inventories, Georgetown County Court House; Sparkman Family Papers, SHC; Robert F. W. Allston Papers; Slave Narratives, vol. 14; Emily Weston diary; Malet, *Errand to the South*; Collins, *Memories of the Southern States*; Childs, ed., *Rice Planter and Sportsman*; Pringle, *Chronicles of Chicora Wood*; Easterby, ed., *The South Carolina Rice Plantation*.

90. George Fitzhugh, "The Freedman and His Future: A Rejoinder," *Lippincott's Magazine*, 5 (Feb. 1870), 191–97.

91. Roy Sieber, "The Visual Arts," in Lystad, ed., *African World*, 442–51; Robert Faris Thompson, *Black Gods and Kings: Yoruba Art at UCLA* (Los Angeles, 1971), ch. 3; Justine M. Cordwell, "African Art," in William R. Bascom and Melville J. Herskovits, eds., *Continuity and Change in African Cultures* (Chicago, 1959), 28–45; Paul Bohannon and Philip Curtin, *Africa and Africans*, rev. ed. (Garden City, N.Y., 1971), 84–100; Skinner, "West African Economic Systems," in Skinner, ed., *Peoples and Cultures of Africa*, 211–12; Robert Faris Thompson, "African Influences on the Art of the United States," in Armstead L. Robinson, *et al.*, eds., *Black Studies in the University* (New Haven, 1969), 156; Wood, *Black Majority*, 95–131; Winthrop D. Jordan, *White over Black: American Attitudes toward the Negro, 1550–1812* (Chapel Hill, 1968), 128–29.

92. Pringle, *Chronicles of Chicora Wood*, 13–14; Henry DeSaussure Bull, *All Saints Church, Waccamaw, 1739–1968* (Georgetown, S.C., 1968), 25; Easterby, ed., *South Carolina Rice Plantation*, 33; Lawson, *No Heir*, 13. On skilled black artisans more generally, see Daniel E. Huger Smith, *A Charlestonian's Recollections, 1846–1913* (Charleston, 1950), 17–25; Leonard Price Stavisky, "The Negro Artisan in the South Atlantic States, 1800–1860" (Ph.D. diss., Columbia University, 1958), and his "Negro Craftsmanship in Early America," *AHR*, 54 (1949), 315–25; Genovese, *Roll, Jordan, Roll*, 9, 365–98; Owens, *Species of Property*, 121–35. For a study of a traditional black craftsman in Charleston, see John Michael Vlach, *Charleston Blacksmith: The Work of Philip Simmons* (Athens, Ga., 1981). For the underlying African tradition see Rene S. Wassing, *African Art: Its Backgrounds and Traditions* (New York, 1968), 52, 117, 196–97; Michael Leiris and Jacquelyn DeLance, *African Art* (London, 1968), 99–210.

93. Sparkman Family Papers, Book 5; Ben Sparkman Plantation Record; Pringle, *Chronicles of Chicora Wood*, 14. For the African origins of the plantation dugout canoes, see Wood, *Black Majority*, 123–24.

94. Emily Weston diary, Jan. 4, 11–12, 25–26, Feb. 3–4, 17, 23, May 5, Dec. 2, 1859; Bull, *All Saints Church, Waccamaw*, 25; Collins, *Memories of the Southern States*, 7; Malet, *Errand to the South*, 80–81; Rogers, *History of Georgetown County*, 358; Susan Lowndes Allston, "Lives of the Westons Sparkled with Adventure," Charleston *News and Courier*, Nov. 6, 1938; Anthony Devereaux, *The Rice Princes: A Rice Epoch Revisited* (Columbia, 1973), 93.

95. Collins, *Memories of the Southern States*, 7–8; Doar, *Rice and Rice Planting*, 38; Devereaux, *Rice Princes*, 82. The structure, today known as the Pelican Inn, still stands on the southern end of the island. See Charlotte Kaminsky Prevost and Effie Leland Wilder, *Pawley's Island: A Living Legend* (Columbia, 1972), 20.

96. Childs, ed., *Rice Planter and Sportsman*, 118–19, 123–24. Since Motte Alston lived until 1909, Richmond's freedom came by way of the Civil War, not Alston's will.

97. Pringle, *Chronicles of Chicora Wood*, 14, 34–35.

98. Sparkman Family Papers, Book 5; Welcome Beese, Slave Narratives, 14, part i, 49; Brookgreen carpenters and tools, 1851, 1853, Hasell-Flagg Mss., SCHS.

99. James R. Sparkman Books, II. On Allston's hiring of carpenters, see, for example, R. Allston to H. W. Tilton, Feb. 6, 1854, in Allston Papers.

100. Sparkman Family Papers, Book 5; Brookgreen carpenters and tools, 1851, 1853, Hasell-Flagg Mss.

101. Pringle, *Chronicles of Chicora Wood*, 13; Easterby, ed., *South Carolina Rice Plantation*, 32, 277, 285, 425; Childs, ed., *Rice Planter and Sportsman*, 45; Ben Sparkman Plantation Record. Cf. Vlach, *Charleston Blacksmith*, 146. The inventory for Robert F. W. Allston's estate in 1864, SCHS, lists the following blacksmiths' tools: one anvil, two sledges, two small hammers, vice, screwplate, and five bars of iron. Cf. W. E. B. DuBois and Augustus Granville Dill, eds., *The Negro American Artisan* (Atlanta, 1912), 35.

102. Pringle, *Chronicles of Chicora Wood*, 14, 27; Thomas Hemingway to R. Allston, May 19, 1854, Allston Papers.

103. Sabe Rutledge, Slave Narratives, 14, part iii, 60; Margaret Bryant, Slave Narratives, 14, part i, 146–47.

104. William Oliver, Slave Narratives, 14, part iii, 218; Margaret Bryant, Slave Narratives, 14, part i, 147.

105. Emily Weston diary, Feb. 8, May 2, 7, Dec. 3, 1859.

106. Lesley M. Drucker, "A Cultural Resources Inventory of Selected Areas of the Oaks and Laurel Hill Plantations, Brookgreen Gardens, Georgetown County, South Carolina," unpublished report, 1980, in Brookgreen Gardens Archives, Murrells Inlet, S.C., 58, 75, 80. Drucker's preliminary survey is the only investigation of historic sites on the plantations of All Saints Parish. On Colono-ware, see Leland G. Ferguson, "Looking for the 'Afro' in Colono-Indian Pottery," in Robert L. Schuyler, ed., *Archaeological Perspectives on Ethnicity: Afro-American and Asian American Culture History* (Farmingdale, N.Y., 1980), 14–28. The term Colono-Indian was coined by Ivor Noel Hume to indicate his attribution of the pottery's source. See his "An Indian Ware of the Colonial Period," *Quarterly Bulletin of the Archaeological Society of Virginia*, 17 (Sept. 1962), 5. Ferguson suggests the more neutral term Colono-ware. For the Barbadian connection, see Handler and Lange, *Plantation Slavery in Barbados*, 136–37.

107. Pringle, *Chronicles of Chicora Wood*, 54. Photographs taken on the Waccamaw Neck in the 1930s by Bayard Wooten for the WPA show fanner baskets still in use. Alice R. Huger Smith's watercolors depict fanner baskets in use in the 1850s. See Alice R. Huger Smith and Herbert Ravenel Sass, eds., *A Carolina Rice Plantation of the Fifties* (New York, 1930). See also her sketches of fanner baskets in Pennington, *A Woman Rice Planter*, 272, 375. Similar scenes from the sea islands off Beaufort, S.C., in the early twentieth century are depicted in Edith Dabbs, *The Face of an Island: Leigh Rich-*

mond Miner's Photographs of Saint Helena Island (New York, 1971). I interviewed coil basketmakers Edna Rouse and Evelina Foreman, of Mt. Pleasant, S.C., on their methods of coil basketry in 1975. For additional studies of Afro-American coil basketry in the South Carolina lowcountry and its African roots, see Gerald L. Davis, "Afro-American Coil Basketry in Charleston County, South Carolina," in Don Yoder, ed., *American Folklife* (Austin, 1976), 151–84; Gregory Day, "Afro-Carolinian Art: Towards the History of a Southern Expressive Tradition," *Contemporary Art/Southeast*, 1 (Spring 1978), 17–19; Doris Adelaide Derby, "Black Women Basket Makers: A Study of Domestic Economy in Charleston, South Carolina" (Ph.D. diss., University of Illinois, 1980); Thompson, "African Influence on the Art of the United States," 127; Betty Myers, "Gullah Basketry," *Craft Horizons*, 36 (June 1976), 30–31; Robert E. Perdue, Jr., "African Baskets in South Carolina," *Economic Botany*, 22 (1968), 289–92; James A. Porter, "Four Problems in the History of Negro Art," *JNH*, 37 (1942), 9–36; Herbert L. Frazier, "Basket Weaving Traced to Ancient African Craft," Charleston *News and Courier*, Sept. 4, 1972, 5a; Wood, *Black Majority*, 61; Lawson, *No Heir*, 10–12; Doar, *Rice and Rice Planting*, 33; Bascom, "Acculturation among the Gullah Negroes," 45, 49; DuBois and Dill, *Negro American Craftsman*, 17–19; Herskovits, *Myth of the Negro Past*, 147; Cordwell, "African Art," 38; Elsie Clews Parsons, *Folk-Lore of the Sea Islands, South Carolina* (Cambridge, Mass., 1923), 208.

108. Thompson, "African Influence on the Art of the United States," *Black Studies in the University*, 127. Cf. Barry Higman, *Slave Population and Economy in Jamaica, 1807–1834* (Cambridge, 1976), 212–32. Both the craft itself and the act of craftsmanship elicited "that state of special grace" which makes one object art and another not, what Robert Plant Armstrong calls "*affecting things and events*" (*The Affecting Presence* [Urbana, 1971], 3–4).

109. Lachicotte interview; Welcome Beese, in WPA Mss.; James R. Sparkman Books, II; Ben Sparkman Plantation Record; Pringle, *Chronicles of Chicora Wood*, 16, 68–69; Malet, *Errand to the South*, 74, 117–18; Weston, "Rules and Management for the Plantation," 108; Gabriel L. Ellis to R. Allston, Aug. 4, 1838, in Easterby, ed., *South Carolina Rice Plantation*, 253.

110. Jane G. North to A. Allston, Dec. 29, 1860, in Easterby, ed., *South Carolina Rice Plantation*, 172; Collins, *Memories of the Southern States*, 55; Malet, *Errand to the South*, 79; Pringle, *Chronicles of Chicora Wood*, 168.

111. The numerous bills from physicians in the various mss. collections indicate that medical care of the slaves constituted an important portion of a rice planter's expenses: Dr. E. B. Flagg medical day book, no. 7, 1847–53, Dr. Andrew Hasell, Cedar Grove day book, 1841–50, Dr. Andrew Hasell, Cedar Grove account book, 1843–56, all at SCHS; Dr. Robert Nesbit account book, SCL; Daniel W. Jordan Papers; Robert F. W. Allston Papers. However, neither the slave narratives nor my interviews with the children

and grandchildren of All Saints slaves reflect medical treatment by physicians on the plantation. For general studies of medical aspects of slavery, see Todd L. Savitt, *Medicine and Slavery: The Diseases and Health Care of Blacks in Antebellum Virginia* (Urbana, 1978), esp. 49–82, 149–84; Kenneth F. and Virginia Kiple, "Black Tongue and Black Men: Pellagra and Slavery in the Ante-Bellum South," *JSH*, 43 (1977), 411–28, and their "Black Yellow Fever Immunities, Innate and Acquired, as Revealed in the American South," *Social Science History*, 4 (1977), 419–36; William D. Postell, *The Health of Slaves on Southern Plantations* (Baton Rouge, 1951), 11–28; John Duffy, "Medical Practice in the Ante-Bellum South," *JSH*, 25 (1959), 53–72; Bennett H. Wall, "Medical Care of Ebenezer Pettigrew's Slaves," *MVHR*, 38 (1950), 451–70; Richard H. Shryock, "Medical Practice in the Old South," *South Atlantic Quarterly*, 29 (1930), 172–82, and his "Medical Sources and the Social Historian," *AHR*, 41 (1936), 458–73; Charles S. Sydnor, "Life Span of Mississippi Slaves," *AHR*, 35 (1930), 566–74; Martha Carolyn Mitchell, "Health and the Medical Profession in the Lower South," *JSH*, 10 (1944), 424–46; Walter Fisher, "Physicians and Slavery in the Antebellum Southern Medical Journal," in August Meier and Elliott Rudwick, eds., *The Making of Black America* (New York, 1969), 153–64; Eugene D. Genovese, "The Medical and Insurance Costs of Slaveholding in the Cotton Belt," *JNH*, 45 (1960), 141–55, and his *Roll, Jordan, Roll*, 224–29, 454–519; Fogel and Engerman, *Time on the Cross*, 1:117–26; Richard Sutch, "The Care and Feeding of Slaves," in Paul A. David *et al.*, *Reckoning with Slavery: A Critical Study in the Quantitative History of American Negro Slavery* (New York, 1976), 282–92; Freehling, *Prelude to Civil War*, 33–36, 70–72; Stampp, *Peculiar Institution*, 307–18; Owens, *Species of Property*, 19–49; John W. Blassingame, *The Slave Community: Plantation Life in the Ante-Bellum South* (New York, 1972), 164–65. For a comparative perspective, see Patterson, *Sociology of Slavery*, 99–103, and Richard S. Dunn, *Sugar and Slaves: The Rise of the Planter Class in the English West Indies 1624–1713* (Chapel Hill, 1972), 303–5.

112. Weston, "Rules and Management for the Plantation," 108–10, 112–13; Sabe Rutledge, Slave Narratives, 14, part iv, 62; Pringle, *Chronicles of Chicora Wood*, 64; Cohen's Medical Depot to Daniel W. Jordan, Mar. 26, May 28, 1860, in Daniel W. Jordan Papers. In addition to the medicines listed, Jordan also purchased gum camphor, gum arabic, olive oil, alum, caustic, sulphur, blister plaster, sugar lead, iron by hydrogen, white mustard seed, Bermuda arrowroot, and Jamaica ginger. See also David Owen Whitten, "Medical Care of Slaves in South Carolina" (M.A. thesis, University of South Carolina, 1963).

113. Weston, "Rules and Management for the Plantation," 109; Emily Weston diary, esp. Jan. 12–20, Mar. 12, Dec. 1–5, 1859; medical bill, Dr. Andrew Hasell to estate of Joseph Waties Allston, 1853, in Robert F. W. Allston Papers; R. Allston to B. Allston, May 28, 1859, in Easterby, ed., *South Carolina Rice Plantation*, 158; Gabriel L. Ellis to R. Allston, Aug. 4, 1838,

ibid., 254; "Charleston Negro Hospital," *Charleston Medical Journal*, 12 (1857), 134.

114. Sabe Rutledge, Slave Narratives, 14, part iv, 62; Margaret Bryant, Slave Narratives, 14, part i, 146; Ben Horry, Slave Narratives, 14, part ii, 305. See also Jessie W. Parkhurst, "The Role of the Black Mammy in the Plantation Household," *JNH*, 23 (1938), 349–69; Genovese, *Roll, Jordan, Roll*, 540–50; James D. Anderson, "Aunt Jemima in Dialectics: Genovese on Slave Culture," *JNH*, 41 (1976), 99–114.

115. J. Beese interview; H. Small interview; M. Small interview; J. Sparkman to B. Allston, Mar. 10, 1858, in Easterby, ed., *South Carolina Rice Plantation*, 345–46; Weston, "Rules and Management for the Plantation," 105–7, 113; Charles W. Joyner, "Soul Food and the Sambo Stereotype: Foodlore from the Slave Narrative Collection," *Keystone Folklore Quarterly*, 16 (1971), 171–78.

116. Emily Weston diary, Feb. 22, 23, Apr. 7, 1859. See also her entries for Feb. 14, 18–24, Mar. 8, 26, 1859.

117. Weston, "Rules and Management for the Plantation," 110; Welcome Beese, Slave Narratives, 14, part i, 49.

118. Weston, "Rules and Management for the Plantation," 111–13; Emily Weston diary, Jan. 6, 1859.

119. Sparkman Family Papers; Emily Weston diary, Jan. 3, 8, May 9, Dec. 1, 1859; Sparkman to B. Allston, Mar. 10, 1858, in Easterby, ed., *South Carolina Rice Plantation*, 346; Coffin to Osgood, May 10, 1851, in Easterby, ed., "South Carolina through New England Eyes," 128–29; Collins, *Memories of the Southern States*, 54–55.

120. Warrant and appraisement, estate of Francis Marion Weston, Jan. 13, 1855, Probate Judge's Office, Georgetown County Court House. Cf. Frederick Douglass, *Life and Times of Frederick Douglass: Written by Himself* (New York, 1893), 44; E. Franklin Frazier, "The Negro Slave Family," *JNH*, 15 (1930), 213; Genovese, *Roll, Jordan, Roll*, 392–93.

121. Allston is quoted in Pringle, *Chronicles of Chicora Wood*, 61–62; see also Lachicotte interview; Rogers, *History of Georgetown County*, 347–48. Cf. Genovese, *Roll, Jordan, Roll*, 327–65; Fogel and Engerman, *Time on the Cross*, 1:206–7, 220–21; Stampp, *Peculiar Institution*, 41–42, 337–38; Owens, *Species of Property*, 106–20.

122. Emily Weston diary, Mar. 15–17, 19–22, 1859.

123. *Ibid.*, Jan. 1, 1859; Collins, *Memories of the Southern States*, 16.

124. Collins, *Memories of the Southern States*, 16–17, and *passim*; Pringle, *Chronicles of Chicora Wood*, 169–70, and *passim*; Robertson, Blacklock and Company to R. Allston, Aug. 31, 1863, in Easterby, ed., *South Carolina Rice Plantation*, 426. William Baron, one of R. Allston's most talented house servants, became a noted Charleston restauranteur and caterer after emancipation. See Pringle, *Chronicles of Chicora Wood*, 169–70; Jonathan Daniels, *The Gentlemanly Serpent and Other Columns from a Newspaperman in Paradise* (Columbia, 1974), 348–49.

125. Coffin to Osgood, May 10, 1851, in Easterby, ed., "South Carolina through New England Eyes," 129; Collins, *Memories of the Southern States*, 6, and *passim*.

126. Plowden C. J. Weston, *Rules and History of the Hot and Hot Fish Club of All Saints Parish, South Carolina* (Charleston, 1860); Richard B. Harwell, "The Hot and Hot Fish Club of All Saints Parish," *SCHM*, 48 (1947), 40–47; Rogers, *History of Georgetown County*, 347–48; Pringle, *Chronicles of Chicora Wood*, 170–73; Easterby, ed., *South Carolina Rice Plantation*, 33, 35, and *passim*; Peterkin, *Roll, Jordan, Roll*, 20; A. Allston to B. Allston, Oct. 3, 1854, in Easterby, ed., *South Carolina Rice Plantation*, 121.

127. H. Small interview; Pringle, *Chronicles of Chicora Wood*, 17, 253; Ben Horry, Slave Narratives, 14, part ii, 305; Mariah Heywood, Slave Narratives, 14, part ii, 282; Leon F. Litwack, *Been in the Storm so Long: The Aftermath of Slavery* (New York, 1979), 156. See also Archibald Rutledge's "Aristocrats of Africa," in his *Deep River* (Columbia, 1960). Cf. Rogers, *History of Georgetown County*, 347–48; Fogel and Engerman, *Time on the Cross*, 1:152–53; Phillips, *Life and Labor*, 206–17.

128. Childs, ed., *Rice Planter and Sportsman*, 12; will of James L. Belin, 1858, in *Our Benefactor: Commemorating 110 Years since His Death on May 19th, 1859* (Murrells Inlet, S.C., 1969), 12–13; R. Allston to A. Allston, Nov. 24, 1847, in Easterby, ed., *South Carolina Rice Plantation*, 97–98; R. Allston to B. Allston, Oct. 6, 1860, *ibid.*, 167–68; Pringle, *Chronicles of Chicora Wood*, 170–73; Emily Weston diary, Jan. 26, 1859; Ben Horry, Slave Narratives, 14, part ii, 311. See also Peterkin, *Roll, Jordan, Roll*, 9–10. Cf. Genovese, *Roll, Jordan, Roll*, 327–65; Stampp, *Peculiar Institution*, 333–40; Fogel and Engerman, *Time on the Cross*, 1:206–7, 220–21.

129. Sabe Rutledge, WPA Mss.; Richard Lathers, *Reminiscences of Richard Lathers: Sixty Years of a Busy Life in South Carolina, Massachusetts, and New York* (New York, 1907), 5; An Anonymous Englishman [Laurence Oliphant], "Rambles at Random through the Southern States," *Blackwood's Magazine*, Jan. 1860; Emily Weston diary, Dec. 22–28, 1859; Collins, *Memories of the Southern States*, 6; Weston, "Rules and Management for the Plantation," 107; Ben Horry, Slave Narratives, 14, part ii, 305; Peterkin, *Roll, Jordan, Roll*, 9–10. Cf. Bertram Wyatt-Brown's contention that slavery was actually least humane by twentieth-century standards when it was most humane by nineteenth-century standards, because of the enforced dependency involved. See his "The Ideal Typology and Ante-Bellum Southern History: A Testing of a New Approach," *Societas*, 5 (1975), 21n.

130. J. Beese interview; Collins, *Memories of the Southern States*, 71; A. Allston to Col. Francis W. Heriot, May 31, 1864, in Easterby, ed., *South Carolina Rice Plantation*, 199.

131. Peterkin, *Roll, Jordan, Roll*, 16–19; Erving Goffman, *Asylums: Essays on the Social Situation of Mental Patients and Other Inmates* (Gar-

den City, N.Y., 1961), xiii, 18–19. Cf. Roger D. Abrahams, "The Negro Stereotype: Negro Folklore and the Riots," *JAF*, 83 (1970), 231. Two works that have drawn explicitly upon Goffman's model are Roy Simon Bryce-Laporte, "The Conceptualization of the American Slave Plantation as a Total Institution" (Ph.D. diss., University of California, Los Angeles, 1968), and George M. Frederickson and Christopher Lasch, "Resistance to Slavery," *Civil War History*, 13 (1967), 315–29.

132. William Oliver, Slave Narratives, 14, part iii, 218; James R. Sparkman Books, II; Malet, *Errand to the South*, 114; Childs, ed. *Rice Planter and Sportsman*, 126; Easterby, ed., *South Carolina Rice Plantation*, 27–28, 32, 37; Rogers, *History of Georgetown County*, 339; Lawson, *No Heir*, 13. Cf. Phillips, *Life and Labor*, 181, 216; Stampp, *Peculiar Institution*, 72–73; Fogel and Engerman, *Time on the Cross*, 1:52–57; Genovese, *Roll, Jordan, Roll*, 390–92; Richard C. Wade, *Slavery in the Cities: The South, 1820–1860* (New York, 1964), 38–54; Frederick Bancroft, *Slave Trading in the Old South* (Baltimore, 1931), 145–64; Robert Starobin, *Industrial Slavery in the Old South* (New York, 1970), 128–37. For a comparative perspective see Carl Degler, *Neither Black Nor White: Slavery and Race Relations in Brazil and the United States* (New York, 1971), 245; Mary W. Williams, "The Treatment of Negro Slaves in the Brazilian Empire," *JNH*, 15 (1930), 334; Herbert Klein, *Slavery in the Americas: A Comparative Study of Cuba and Virginia* (Chicago, 1967), 56; Frank Tannenbaum, *Slave and Citizen: The Negro in the Americas* (New York, 1946), 58–59.

133. Kirke, *Among the Pines*, 18–19.

134. James R. Sparkman Books, II; All Saints Church Waccamaw Vestry Journal, SCHS; William Oliver, Slave Narratives, 14, part iii, 218; "List of Carpenters Hired to Rebuild Waverly Mill, 1837," in Easterby, ed., *South Carolina Rice Plantation*, 341.

135. South Carolina General Assembly, Bill to Amend Sixth Section of "An Act for the Better Regulation and Government of Free Negroes and Persons of Colour and for other Purposes" (ratified Dec. 23, 1822), Dec. 8, 1845, SCA; *Winyah Intelligencer*, Jan. 1, 1825.

136. War Department Collection of Confederate Records, RG 109, NA; Welcome Bees, WPA Mss.

Notes to "Sit at the Welcome Table"

1. Edmund Kirke [James Roberts Gilmore], *Among the Pines: or, The South in Secession Time* (New York, 1862), 120; Sabe Rutledge, WPA Mss., SCL; Sabe Rutledge, Slave Narratives: A Folk History of Slavery in the United States from Interviews with Former Slaves. Typewritten records prepared by the Federal Writers' Project, 1936–38 (microfilm), 14, part iii, 60; William Oliver, Slave Narratives, 14, part iii, 219; Margaret Bryant, Slave Narratives, 14, part i, 146; Ellen Godfrey, Slave Narratives, 14, part ii, 157–59; Etrulia P. Dozier, ed., "Interview of Mrs. Julia Smalls [*sic*]," *Inde-*

pendent Republic Quarterly, 4 (July 1970), 32; Arney R. Childs, ed., *Rice Planter and Sportsman: The Recollections of J. Motte Alston* (Columbia, 1953), 10, 46, 78; Mss. diary of Emily Esdaile Weston, in private possession, Apr. 2, 9, May 2, 7, Dec. 3, 12, 1859 (hereafter cited as Emily Weston diary); William Wyndham Malet, *An Errand to the South in the Summer of 1862* (London, 1863), 48–49, 82; Elizabeth Collins, *Memories of the Southern States* (Taunton, England, 1865), 5; Plowden C. J. Weston, "Rules and Management for the Plantation, 1859," in *ibid.*, 105–6; James R. Sparkman to Benjamin Allston, Mar. 10, 1858, in J. Harold Easterby, ed., *The South Carolina Rice Plantation as Revealed in the Papers of Robert F. W. Allston* (Chicago, 1945), 346–48. On the holistic folklife studies approach to the study of material culture, see Charles G. Zug III, "Introduction," *Material Culture in the South*, special issue of *SFQ*, 39 (1975), 303; Don Yoder, "Folklife Studies in American Scholarship," in Don Yoder, ed., *American Folklife*, (Austin, 1976), 3–18; Don Yoder, "The Folklife Studies Movement," *Pennsylvania Folklife*, 13 (1963), 43–56; Richard M. Dorson, "Concepts of Folklore and Folklife Studies," in Richard M. Dorson, ed., *Folklore and Folklife: An Introduction* (Chicago, 1972), 1–50. African historians have used archaeological artifacts to reveal, in some cases, more of certain aspects of life in preliterate Africa than written records have of more recent African history. See Daniel F. McCall, *Africa in Time-Perspective: A Discussion of Historical Reconstruction from Unwritten Sources* (New York, 1964), xv, 28–37. On material culture (as distinguished from material artifacts) in the pursuit of "a more human history," see Henry H. Glassie, *Pattern in the Material Culture of the Eastern United States* (Philadelphia, 1968), 2, and his *Folk Housing in Middle Virginia: A Structural Analysis of Historic Artifacts* (Knoxville, 1975), vii, 8–12.

2. "Foodways" is defined as "the whole interrelated system of food conceptualization and evaluation, procurement, distribution, preservation, preparation, consumption, and nutrition shared by all the members of a particular society." See Jay Allan Anderson, "The Study of Contemporary Foodways in American Folklife Research," *Keystone Folklore Quarterly*, 16 (1971), 156. On the reciprocal relations between food and culture, see Audrey I. Richards, *Hunger and Work in a Savage Tribe* (London, 1932), and her *Land, Labour, and Diet in Northern Rhodesia: An Economic Study of the Bemba Tribe* (London, 1939). On the significance of slave foodways, see Charles W. Joyner, "Soul Food and the Sambo Stereotype: Foodlore from the Slave Narrative Collection," *Keystone Folklore Quarterly*, 16 (1971), 171–78; and Roger Bastide, *African Civilizations in the New World*, trans. Peter Green (New York, 1971), 90. Cf. R. J. Bernard, "Peasant Diet in Eighteenth Century Gevaudan," in Elborg Forster and Robert Forster, eds., *European Diet from Pre-Industrial to Modern Times* (New York, 1976), 19–46; L. M. Cullen, "Irish History without the Potato," *Past and Present*, 40 (1968), 72–83; Margaret Cussler and Mary L. de Give, *'Twixt the Cup and the Lip: Cultural Factors Affecting Food Habits* (New York, 1952); Wil-

liam J. Darby, Paul Ghalioungui, and Louis Grivetti, *Food: The Gift of Osiris*, 2 vols. (New York, 1977); R. E. Dingle, "Drink and Working Class Living Standards in Britain, 1870–1914," *Economic History Review*, 25 (1972), 608–22; Brian Harrison, *Drink and the Victorians* (Pittsburgh, 1971); Bridget Ann Henisch, *Fast and Feast: Food in Medieval Society* (University Park, Pa., 1977); Emmanuel Le Roy Ladurie, *Times of Feast, Times of Famine: A History of Climate since the Year 1000*, trans. Barbara Bray (Garden City, N.Y., 1971); Claude Levi-Strauss, "The Culinary Triangle," *Partisan Review*, 33 (1966), 586–95, and his *The Raw and the Cooked: Introduction to a Science of Mythology*, trans. John and Doreen Weightman (New York, 1969); R. N. Salaman, *A Social History of the Potato* (London, 1949); Max Sorre, "The Geography of Diet," in Philip L. Wagner and Marvin W. Mikesell, eds., *Readings in Cultural Geography* (Chicago, 1962), 445–56; Robert Forster and Orest Ranum, eds., *Food and Drink in History: Selections from the Annales: Economies, Societies, Civilizations*, vol. 5, trans. Elborg Forster and Patricia M. Ranum (Baltimore, 1979); Don Yoder, "Historical Sources for American Foodways Research and Plans for an American Foodways Archive," *Ethnologica Scandinavica*, 2 (1971), 41–55.

3. Hagar Brown, Slave Narratives, 14, part i, 113; Ben Horry, Slave Narratives, 14, part ii, 309–10; interview with Henry Small, Free Woods, S.C., Aug. 2, 1975; Emily Weston diary, Jan. 22, Apr. 2, 9, Dec. 3, 1859; Malet, *Errand to the South*, 48–49. Richard Sutch distinguishes between *ration* and *diet*. The slaves' ration he regards as "monotonous, crude, and nutritionally suspect," but the diet, supplemented by the slaves' hunting, fishing, and gardening, may have been balanced nutritionally even when the ration was deficient. See his "The Care and Feeding of Slaves," in Paul A. David *et al.*, *Reckoning with Slavery: A Critical Study in the Quantitative History of American Negro Slavery* (New York, 1976), 281–82. The most thorough discussion of diet in the Old South is Sam Bowers Hilliard, *Hog Meat and Hoe Cake: Food Supply in the Old South, 1840–1860* (Carbondale, Ill., 1972), esp. chs. 3, 7, and 9. Cf. Kenneth M. Stampp, *The Peculiar Institution: Slavery in the Ante-Bellum South* (New York, 1956), 158–59; Eugene D. Genovese, *Roll, Jordan, Roll: The World the Slaves Made* (New York, 1974), 544.

4. Sparkman to Benjamin Allston, Mar. 10, 1858, in Easterby, ed., *South Carolina Rice Plantation*, 346. This would seem to represent a sizeable quantity of food, the equivalent of 40 cups of dry corn meal (or 240 cups of mush), 24 cups of dry rice or peas (or 72 cups cooked), and 128 cups of sweet potatoes per week, or 34 cups of mush, 10 cups of rice or beans, and 18 cups of sweet potatoes *daily*. Cf. Rosser Taylor, who maintains in his pioneer article, "Feeding Slaves," *JNH*, 9 (1924), 139–43, that the standard ration of an adult field hand was 3 ½ pounds of "salt pork" or "bacon" and 1 peck of corn per week.

5. Dozier, ed., "Interview of Mrs. Julia Smalls," 32.

6. Bill, Locke and Cheney to Daniel W. Jordan, Apr. 11, 1860, Daniel W.

Jordan Papers, DUL; Sparkman to B. Allston, Mar. 10, 1858, in Easterby, ed., *South Carolina Rice Plantation*, 346. Hilliard (*Hog Meat and Hoe Cake*, 104–5, 157, 272) believes that beef or molasses, or both, were commonly substituted for pork. Beef was substituted for pork in the diet of Moslem slaves. See Ball Plantation book, 1804–90, SCL.

7. Interview with John Beese, Pawleys Island, S.C., Jan. 18, 1972; H. Small interview; interview with Mary Small, Free Woods, S.C., Aug. 2, 1975; Almira Coffin to Mrs. J. G. Osgood, May 10, 1859, in J. Harold Easterby, ed., "South Carolina through New England Eyes: Almira Coffin's Visit to the Low Country in 1851," *SCHM*, 45 (1944), 127; interview with A. H. Lachicotte, Jr., Pawleys Island, S.C., July 28, 1975; Weston, "Rules and Management for the Plantation," 105–7, 113; Sparkman to B. Allston, Mar. 10, 1858, in Easterby, ed., *South Carolina Rice Plantation*, 346–47; Childs, ed., *Rice Planter and Sportsman*, 78; Malet, *Errand to the South*, 57. Cf. Julia Peterkin, *Roll, Jordan, Roll* (New York, 1933), 9; Stampp, *Peculiar Institution*, 287–88; Don Yoder, "Folk Cookery," in Dorson, ed., *Folklore and Folklife*, 338, 341–46. Note the folk belief among South Carolina lowcountry blacks that one who sings before breakfast will cry before supper, in Elsie Clews Parsons, *Folk-Lore of the Sea Islands, South Carolina* (Cambridge, Mass., 1923), 210. This was presumably an example of what Edward King termed the "peculiar superstitions and ceremonies" of the freedmen he observed in the lowcountry immediately after the Civil War. See his *The Great South: A Record of Journeys* (Hartford, Conn., 1875), 429.

8. Mariah Heywood, Slave Narratives, 14, part ii, 285; Lachicotte interview; Malet, *Errand to the South*, 138; Emily Weston diary. Cf. Sam Bowers Hilliard, "Hogmeat and Cornpone," *Proceedings of the American Philosophical Society*, 113 (1969), 12. For a general discussion of the time and size of meals, see Yoder, "Folk Cookery," 341–46. For a discussion of the eating patterns of house servants, see Stampp, *Peculiar Institution*, 288. During creolization the masters were as influenced by the culinary preferences of slave cooks as the other way around. For a Jamaican example, see Henry Preston Vaughan Nunn, *Lady Nugent's Journal of Her Residence in Jamaica from 1801 to 1805*, ed. P. Wright (Oxford, 1966), 92, 95, 121, 127.

9. 1860 Census, Slave Schedules; Weston, "Rules and Management for the Plantation," 105–7. The public pot is presumably not unlike the communal cooking pot on display in the remaining plantation kitchen at Brookgreen Gardens, on the site of Brookgreen plantation.

10. H. Small interview; Ellen Godfrey, Slave Narratives, 14, part ii, 158. For a general discussion of cooking utensils, see Yoder, "Folk Cookery," 341–46; John Solomon Otto, "A New Look at Slave Life," *Natural History*, 88 (1979), 8, 16, 20, 22, 24, 30, and his "Artifacts and Status Differences— A Comparison of Ceramic Differences from Planter, Overseer, and Slave Sites on an Antebellum Plantation," in Stanley South, ed., *Research Strategies in Historical Archaeology* (New York, 1977); Charles Fairbanks, "The Kingsley Slave Cabins in Duval County, Florida, 1968," *Conference on His-*

toric Site Archaeology Papers, 1972, No. 7 (Columbia, 1974), 62–93; Robert Asher and Charles Fairbanks, "Excavation of a Slave Cabin: Georgia, USA," *Historical Archaeology,* 5 (1971), 3–17.

11. Sparkman Family Papers, book 3, SHC.

12. Sabe Rutledge, Slave Narratives, 14, part iv, 59; Dozier, ed., "Interview of Mrs. Julia Smalls," 32; M. Small interview.

13. J. Beese interview; Weston, "Rules and Management for the Plantation," 105–7; Sparkman to B. Allston, Mar. 10, 1858, in Easterby, ed., *South Carolina Rice Plantation,* 346; Ellen Godfrey, Slave Narratives, 14, part ii, 159.

14. Lachicotte interview; Emily Weston diary, Apr. 3, 1859; Malet, *Errand to the South,* 57, 82; Sparkman to B. Allston, Mar. 10, 1858, in Easterby, ed., *South Carolina Rice Plantation,* 346–48; Ben Sparkman Plantation Record, SHC; Ellen Godfrey, Slave Narratives, 14, part ii, 157–58; William Oliver, Slave Narratives, 14, part iii, 219; Sabe Rutledge, WPA Mss., SCL; "Agricola," "Management of Negroes," *DeBow's Review,* 10 (Mar. 1851), 325. Cf. Peterkin, *Roll, Jordan, Roll,* 9. There is an abundance of vegetable planting lore in Afro-American folk belief in South Carolina. Peterkin included an Afro-American planting proverb in her novel of black folklife on Sandy Island, *Black April* (Indianapolis, 1927), 259: "Every pint of March dust brings a peck of September corn." Parsons reported (*Folk-Lore of the Sea Islands,* 350) a belief that potatoes should be planted at floodtide and peas at full moon, else the pods would not fill. Henry C. Davis noted the belief that corn should also be planted by moonlight. See his "Negro Folk-Lore in South Carolina," *JAF,* 27 (1914), 245.

15. Childs, ed., *Rice Planter and Sportsman,* 121; Elizabeth W. Allston Pringle, *Chronicles of Chicora Wood* (New York, 1922), 88–89; Collins, *Memories of the Southern States,* 4, 6, 12–13; Malet, *Errand to the South,* 82. On the growing of lemon and orange trees in the South Carolina lowcountry, see Lewis C. Gray, *History of Agriculture in the Southern United States in 1860* (Washington, D.C., 1933), 1:191; 2:1826; G.M., "South Carolina," *New England Magazine,* 1 (Sept.–Oct. 1831), 246–50, 337–41.

16. Ellen Godfrey, Slave Narratives, 14, part ii, 158–59; William Oliver, Slave Narratives, 14, part iii, 219; Lachicotte interview.

17. Quoted in Patience Pennington [Elizabeth Allston Pringle], *A Woman Rice Planter* (New York, 1914), 374. This recipe appears similar to what English visitor Wyndham Malet described as the "approved East Indian mode" of preparing rice (*Errand to the South,* 270–71): "Into a saucepan of two quarts of water, when boiling, throw a table-spoon of salt, then throw in one pint of rice after it has been well washed with cold water; let it boil twenty minutes; throw it out on to a colander, and strain off the water; when the water is well drained off put the rice back into the same saucepan dried by the fire, and let it stand near the fire some minutes, or till required to be dished up. Thus the grains will appear separate and not mashed into a pudding."

18. Childs, ed., *Rice Planter and Sportsman*, 78.
19. Lachicotte interview; Sparkman to B. Allston, Mar. 10, 1858, in Easterby, ed., *South Carolina Rice Plantation*, 345–46; cf. Otto, "New Look at Slave Life," 22.
20. Hasell-Flagg Plantation Papers, plantation account book, n.d., SCHS; Dozier, ed., "Interview of Mrs. Julia Smalls," 32; Ben Horry, Slave Narratives, 14, part ii, 317.
21. Sabe Rutledge, WPA Mss.; Lachicotte interview; cf. Sutch, "Care and Feeding of Slaves," 259; Otto, "New Look at Slave Life," 22; Genovese, *Roll, Jordan, Roll*, 549; Yoder, "Folk Cookery," 330. Note the Afro-American proverb from All Saints Parish, "Most hook fish don't help dry hominy" (Lillie Knox, WPA Mss.).
22. Sabe Rutledge, WPA Mss.
23. William Oliver, Slave Narratives, 14, part iii, 219; Ellen Godfrey, Slave Narratives, 14, part ii, 156; Sabe Rutledge, WPA Mss.; Sparkman to B. Allston, Mar. 10, 1858, in Easterby, *South Carolina Rice Plantation*, 346; Malet, *Errand to the South*, 48; E. B. Flagg Mss., SCHS; Louisa Brown, Slave Narratives, 14, part i, 115; Collins, *Memories of the Southern States*, 6, 12–13; Emily Weston diary, Dec. 22–28, 1859. A South Carolina planter who signed himself "Agricola" urged his fellow planters to sow "a small patch of wheat" for their slaves. See his "Management of Negroes," *De-Bow's Review*, 10 (Mar. 1851), 225. Cf. Hilliard, *Hog Meat and Hoe Cake*, 166–67. All of the All Saints rice planters grew sufficient corn for their plantations' needs, but none grew any wheat. Only Charles Alston, Sr. (ten bushels), Joseph Blyth Allston (three bushels), William Algernon Alston (ten bushels), and Benjamin F. Dunkin (thirty bushels) grew rye (1860 Census, Agriculture Schedules, SCA). Note the South Carolina black folk belief that breaking bread in another's hand will cause the two parties to quarrel, in M. H. Work, "Some Geechee Folklore," *Southern Workman*, 34 (1905), 697, and that cake must be stirred clockwise to turn out properly, in Newbell Niles Puckett, *Folk Beliefs of the Southern Negro* (Chapel Hill, 1926), 408. Breads seem to have held an important symbolic place in the memories of ex-slaves around the South who were informants for the WPA Slave Narrative project. See Joyner, "Soul Food and the Sambo Stereotype," 171–77.
24. Weston, "Rules and Management for the Plantation," 105–7; Sparkman to B. Allston, Mar. 10, 1858, in Easterby, ed., *South Carolina Rice Plantation*, 346; Emily Weston diary, Apr. 2, 9, 1859; Malet, *Errand to the South*, 48–49; Collins, *Memories of the Southern States*, 6. Molasses contains five times more iron than beef and six times more calcium than milk. The Agriculture Schedules of the 1860 census reveal that Joshua Ward had 102 cows for 1,121 slaves and Plowden Weston had 89 cows for 334 slaves. No other Waccamaw rice planter had more than 20 milk cows. Cf. Alfred W. Crosby, *The Columbian Exchange: Biological and Cultural Consequences of 1492* (Westport, Conn., 1972), ch. 5.

25. Ellen Godfrey, Slave Narratives, 14, part ii, 158 (who calls it "cow clabber"); Malet, *Errand to the South*, 48–49, 138; Collins, *Memories of the Southern States*, 138; Parsons, *Folk-Lore of the Sea Islands*, 209. The popularity of clabber is probably related to sour milk's being more easily digestible than fresh whole milk. Cf. William D. Postell, *The Health of Slaves on Southern Plantations* (Baton Rouge, 1951), 35; Hilliard, *Hog Meat and Hoe Cake*, 61, 120, 124–26. For an example of Afro-American folk belief regarding butter, see Davis, "Negro Folk-Lore in South Carolina," 247.

26. Sabe Rutledge, WPA Mss.; J. Beese interview; Lachicotte interview; Weston, "Rules and Management for the Plantation," 106; Sparkman to B. Allston, Mar. 10, 1858, in Easterby, ed., *South Carolina Rice Plantation*, 346; Coffin to Osgood, May 10, 1859, in Easterby, ed., "South Carolina through New England Eyes," 129; Gabe Lance, Slave Narratives, 14, part iii, 91; Pringle, *Chronicles of Chicora Wood*, 26; Childs, ed., *Rice Planter and Sportsman*, 124; Malet, *Errand to the South*, 48; Ben Horry, Slave Narratives, 14, part ii, 309. See also Peterkin, *Roll, Jordan, Roll*, 9. Cf. Gray, *History of Agriculture in the Southern United States*, 2:832, and Hilliard, *Hog Meat and Hoe Cake*, 45–46, on the alleged prejudice against mutton in the South. Portia Smiley describes the use of beef chunks in the making of love potions in her "Folk-Lore from Virginia, South Carolina, Alabama, Georgia, and Florida," *JAF*, 32 (1919), 380. On the importance of pork in the Old South, see Hilliard, *Hog Meat and Hoe Cake*, 42–44, 56–68, and his "Pork in the Antebellum South: The Geography of Self-Sufficiency," *Annals of the Association of American Geographers*, 57 (1969), 461–80.

27. William Gilmore Simms, *Geography of South Carolina* (Charleston, 1843), 81; G.M., "South Carolina," 337–41; Childs, ed., *Rice Planter and Sportsman*, 45–46, 124; Sparkman to B. Allston, Mar. 10, 1858, in Easterby, ed., *South Carolina Rice Plantation*, 346; Weston, "Rules and Management for the Plantation," 106; Lachicotte interview; Ben Horry, Slave Narratives, 14, part ii, 314–15, 321; Ellen Godfrey, Slave Narratives, 14, part ii, 159; Sabe Rutledge, WPA Mss.; William Oliver, Slave Narratives, 14, part iii, 219. Daniel W. Jordan ordered 200 fish hooks for his slaves from his Charleston supplier in the spring of 1860; B. C. Locke to Jordan, May 24, 1860, in Daniel W. Jordan Papers. Cf. Otto, "New Look at Slave Life," 20. Crabs were best caught at the dark of the moon because crabs were poor on a moonlight night (Parsons, *Folk-Lore of the Sea Islands*, 209). Crab claws were useful as amulets among Gullah slaves as well. See Childs, ed., *Rice Planter and Sportsman*, 45–46; Puckett, *Folk Beliefs of the Southern Negro*, 284.

28. Malet, *Errand to the South*, 118–19.

29. Hagar Brown and "Hackless," WPA Mss. Cf. Peter Wood, *Black Majority: Negroes in Colonial South Carolina from 1670 through the Stono Rebellion* (New York, 1974), 123–24.

30. Pringle, *Chronicles of Chicora Wood*, 89; Childs, ed., *Rice Planter and Sportsman*, 121; Simms, *Geography of South Carolina*, 81; William

Oliver, Slave Narratives, 14, part iii, 220; Laurence Oliphant, *Patriots and Filibusters; or Incidents of Political and Exploratory Travel* (Edinburgh, 1860), 145; Hagar Brown, WPA Mss.

31. Pringle, *Chronicles of Chicora Wood*, 89; Childs, ed., *Rice Planter and Sportsman*, 121; G.M., "South Carolina," 337–41. Archaeological investigations at Laurel Hill plantation have uncovered cartridges. See Lesley M. Drucker, "A Cultural Resources Inventory of Selected Areas of the Oaks and Laurel Hill Plantations, Brookgreen Gardens, Georgetown County, South Carolina," unpublished report, 1980, in Brookgreen Gardens Archives, Murrells Inlet, S.C., 275. Archaeologist John Solomon Otto found artifactual evidence of slaves' having owned firearms in slave cabin sites excavated along the Georgia and Florida coasts, as well as the remains of opossums, rabbits, racoons, and other game. See his "New Look at Slave Life," 20.

32. William Oliver, Slave Narratives, 14, part iii, 220.

33. Malet, *Errand to the South*, 68; Louisa Brown, Slave Narratives, 14, part i, 115; Peterkin, *Roll, Jordan, Roll*, 10.

34. Pringle, *Chronicles of Chicora Wood*, 151–53; Emily Weston diary, Dec. 22, 24, 1859; Weston, "Rules and Management for the Plantation," 106; Sparkman to B. Allston, Mar. 10, 1858, in Easterby, ed., *South Carolina Rice Plantation*, 347–48; Collins, *Memories of the Southern States*, 6, 12–13. Cf. Yoder, "Folk Cookery," 338–39.

35. Adele Petigru Allston to B. Allston, Jan. 1, 1857, in Easterby, ed., *South Carolina Rice Plantation*, 135–36; Louisa Brown, Slave Narratives, 14, part i, 115. Plowden Weston forbade his overseer to allow any slave to imbibe spirits without a physician's order. See "Rules and Management for the Plantation," 114. Otto found archaeological evidence for the use of alcoholic beverages by slaves on the Georgia and Florida coasts. See his "New Look at Slave Life," 30. Frederick Douglass believed such holidays "to be among the most effective means in the hands of the slaveholders in keeping down the spirit of insurrection." See his *Narrative of the Life of Frederick Douglass, an American Slave: Written by Himself* (Boston, 1845; rpt. Cambridge, Mass., 1960), 106–8.

36. Ben Horry, Slave Narratives, part ii, 309–10.

37. Dr. Andrew Hasell to Jordan, July 16, 1860, and Jordan to Hasell, July 19, 1860, in Daniel W. Jordan Papers. Historians have long noted the possibility of alcohol's turning social occasions into dangerous situations. See Richard W. Wade, *Slavery in the Cities: The South, 1820–1860* (New York, 1964), 150–58; Dingle, "Drink and Working Class Living Standards," 608–22. According to Douglass, slaveholders deliberately got slaves drunk in order "to disgust their slaves with freedom, by plunging them into the lowest depths of dissipation." See his *Narrative of the Life of Frederick Douglass*, 107. For two analyses of both positive and negative functions of alcohol in social interaction, see Louis J. Chiaramonte, "Mumming in 'Deep Harbour': Aspects of Social Organization in Mumming and Drinking" (esp.

84–88), and John F. Szwed, "The Mask of Friendship: Mumming as a Ritual of Social Relations" (esp. 109–16), both in Herbert Halpert and G. M. Story, eds., *Christmas Mumming in Newfoundland: Essays in Anthropology, Folklore, and History* (Toronto, 1969). On the question of role boundaries, see Mary Douglas, *Natural Symbols: Explorations in Cosmology* (New York, 1973), 147. Cf. Drew Gilpin Faust, *James Henry Hammond and the Old South: A Design for Mastery* (Baton Rouge, 1982), 93, for an example of slave theft of alcohol from the master's stock.

38. Hagar Brown, WPA Mss.

39. 1850 and 1860 Censuses, Mortality Schedules, SCA; medical bill of Dr. Hasell to the estate of Joseph Waties Allston, 1853, in Robert F. W. Allston Papers, Dr. E. B. Flagg medical day book, no. 7, 1847–53, Dr. Hasell, Cedar Grove day book, 1841–50, Dr. Hasell, Cedar Grove account book, 1843–56, all in SCHS; Dr. Robert Nesbit account book, SCL. Cf. Tyson Gibbs *et al.*, "An Anthropological Examination of Slave Nutritional Adequacy," *Medical Anthropology*, 4 (Spring 1980), 175–262; Kenneth F. and Virginia Kiple, "Black Tongue and Black Men: Pellagra and Slavery in the Ante-Bellum South," *JSH*, 43 (1977), 411–28; Richard H. Shryock, "Medical Sources and the Social Historian," *AHR*, 41 (1936), 460–67; Postell, *Health of Slaves*, 48–49, 85–86; Sutch, "Care and Feeding of Slaves," 234; Hilliard, *Hog Meat and Hoe Cake*, 64; Kenneth F. and Virginia Kiple, "Slave Child Mortality: Some Nutritional Answers to a Perennial Puzzle," *Journal of Social History*, 10 (1977), 284–309.

40. Childs, ed., *Rice Planter and Sportsman*, 46; Weston, "Rules and Management for the Plantation," 105; will of James L. Belin, 1858, in *Our Benefactor: Commemorating 110 Years since His Death on May 19th, 1859* (Murrells Inlet, S.C., 1969), 12–13.

41. Ellen Godfrey, Slave Narratives, 14, part ii, 159, 161; Gabe Lance, Slave Narratives, 14, part iii, 92; J. Beese interview; interviews with Mary Small and Henry Small, Free Woods, S.C., Aug. 2, 1975. Henry Small is the son of Toby Small and the grandson of Titus Small, both of whom were slaves of John D. Magill.

42. See Table 5 herein. Over half of the slaves on the Waccamaw lived on the plantations of the four wealthiest planters, and more than three-fourths of the slaves lived on plantations of 200 slaves or more. Cf. George C. Rogers, Jr., *The History of Georgetown County, South Carolina* (Columbia, 1970), 331; Dale Evans Swan, "The Structure and Profitability of the Antebellum Rice Industry: 1859" (Ph.D. diss., University of North Carolina, 1972). For a favorable account of the slave diet on southern plantations, see Robert William Fogel and Stanley L. Engerman, *Time on the Cross: The Economics of American Negro Slavery* (Boston, 1974), 44–46. For negative interpretations of slave diet, see Stampp, *Peculiar Institution*, 282–85; John W. Blassingame, *The Slave Community: Plantation Life in the Ante-Bellum South* (New York, 1972), 158. Cf. Richard Shryock, "Medical Practice in the Old South," *South Atlantic Quarterly*, 29 (1930), 160–61; Eu-

gene D. Genovese, "The Medical and Insurance Costs of Slaveholding in the Cotton Belt," *JNH*, 45 (1960), 141–55. The *Third Report of the Commissioners for Inquiring into the Condition of the Poorer Classes in Ireland* (1836) is quoted in E. P. Thompson, *The Making of the English Working Class* (New York, 1963), 432.

43. G.M., "South Carolina," 337–41; Ben Horry, Slave Narratives, 14, part ii, 309–10, 317; Ellen Godfrey, Slave Narratives, 14, part ii, 159; H. Small interview. Cf. Blassingame, *Slave Community*, 159; Gilbert Osofsky, *Puttin' On Ole Massa* (New York, 1969), 24–27. A slave caught stealing sugar in Jamaica expressed a similar interpretation of the meaning of theft: "As sugar belongs to Massa, and myself belongs to Massa, it all de same ting—dat make me tell Massa me don't tief; me only take it!" When the slave was asked what stealing meant, he replied, "When me broke into broder house and ground, and take away him ting, den me tief, massa." See James M. Phillippo, *Jamaica: Its Past and Present State* (London, 1843), 252.

44. The first proverb is quoted in Julia Peterkin's novel of Afro-American folklife on Sandy Island, *Black April*, 86. The second was collected from Lillie Knox, Murrells Inlet, S.C., 1937, by Genevieve Willcox Chandler, WPA Mss. See also Joyner, "Soul Food and the Sambo Stereotype," 171–77; Bastide, *African Civilisations in the New World*, 90.

45. David J. McCord, ed., *Statutes at Large of South Carolina* (Columbia, 1836–41), 7: 396. A 1690 statute that required slaveholders to furnish slaves with clothing once a year was repealed in 1696. See *ibid.*, 7: 343, 393. See also *South Carolina Gazette*, Nov. 5, 1744. For a discussion of slave clothing cross-culturally, see Orlando Patterson, *Slavery and Social Death: A Comparative Study* (Cambridge, Mass., 1982), 58, 381. On folk costume in general, see Don Yoder, "Folk Costume," in Dorson, ed., *Folklore and Folklife*, 296–302; Peter Michelsen and Holger Rasmussen, *Danish Peasant Culture* (Copenhagen, 1955), 47–54, and especially Petr Grigorijevic Bogatyrev, *The Functions of Folk Costume in Moravian Slovakia*, trans. R. G. Crum (The Hague, 1971).

46. Cf. Richard Weiss, *Volkskunde der Schweiz: Grundriss* (Erlenbach-Zurich, 1946), 140–41. The Jamaican scholar Edward Brathwaite notes a relationship between African and Afro-American clothing behavior in the Caribbean: "Even," he notes, "the way the dresses are worn—off the shoulder, rivered between the thighs when sitting—have clear resemblances on both sides of the Atlantic, though no comparative study of these and other essentials have yet been undertaken academically." See his "Cultural Diversity and Integration in the Caribbean," paper presented at Johns Hopkins University, April 1973, quoted in Sidney W. Mintz and Richard Price, *An Anthropological Approach to the Afro-American Past: A Caribbean Perspective*, (Philadelphia, 1976), 49–50.

47. Childs, ed., *Rice Planter and Sportsman*, 46; Kirke, *Among the Pines*, 129; Coffin to Osgood, May 10, 1859, in Easterby, ed., "South Caro-

lina through New England Eyes," 127; Collins, *Memories of the Southern States*, 4–5; Malet, *Errand to the South*, 49; Ellen Godfrey, Slave Narratives, 14, part ii, 159; Ben Horry, Slave Narratives, 14, part ii, 310; William Oliver, Slave Narratives, 14, part iii, 219.

48. Childs, ed., *Rice Planter and Sportsman*, 10; R. Allston to A. Allston, Dec. 1, 1844, in Easterby, ed., *South Carolina Rice Plantation*, 92; Collins, *Memories of the Southern States*, 70; Sabe Rutledge, Slave Narratives, 14, part iii, 60; Margaret Bryant, Slave Narratives, 14, part i, 146–47; William Oliver, Slave Narratives, 14, part iii, 218; Emily Weston diary, Feb. 8, May 2, 7, Dec. 3, 1859. Jordan purchased 250 needles and four dozen spools of thread for Laurel Hill plantation from Gilliland, Howell, and Co., Charleston, on Apr. 28, 1860. See Daniel W. Jordan Papers. Cf. Anne Firor Scott, *The Southern Lady: From Pedestal to Politics, 1830–1930* (Chicago, 1970), 30, 32–33.

49. Emily Weston diary, May 2, 7, Dec. 3, 1859; Collins, *Memories of the Southern States*, 6, 70.

50. William Oliver, Slave Narratives, 14, part iii, 219; Childs, ed., *Rice Planter and Sportsman*, 10, 12, 46; Collins, *Memories of the Southern States*, 5; R. Allston to A. Allston, Dec. 1, 1844, in Easterby, ed., *South Carolina Rice Plantation*, 92; Ben Horry, Slave Narratives, 14, part ii, 310; Emily Weston diary, May 7, Dec. 3, 1859. Sabe Rutledge, WPA Mss.; Daniel W. Jordan Papers. No cotton was grown on the Waccamaw. See 1850 and 1860 Censuses, Agriculture Schedules.

51. Dozier, ed., "Interview of Mrs. Julia Smalls," 143. This cloth may well be the same as the "Negro cloth" purchased by Elizabeth Blyth for her slaves in September 1823; Elizabeth Blyth Papers, DUL. See also R. Allston to A. Allston, Dec. 1, 1844, in Easterby, ed., *South Carolina Rice Plantation*, 92.

52. William Oliver, Slave Narratives, 14, part iii, 219; Ben Horry, Slave Narratives, 14, part ii, 310; Childs, ed., *Rice Planter and Sportsman*, 10, 12, 46; R. Allston to A. Allston, Dec. 1, 1844, in Easterby, ed., *South Carolina Rice Plantation*, 92; Collins, *Memories of the Southern States*, 4; Emily Weston diary, May 7, Dec. 3, 12, 1859; Sabe Rutledge, WPA Mss.; Kirke, *Among the Pines*, 129; Sabe Rutledge, Slave Narratives, 14, part iii, 60; Margaret Bryant, Slave Narratives, 14, i, 146. The slaves were said to prefer red. See Puckett, *Folk Beliefs of the Southern Negro*, 220–21; Genovese, *Roll, Jordan, Roll*, 557–58. See also Victor W. Turner, "Colour Classification in Ndembu Ritual: A Problem in Primitive Classification," in Michael Blanton, ed., *Anthropological Approaches to the Study of Religion* (London, 1966), 47–84; Claude Levi-Strauss, *The Savage Mind* (London, 1966), 64–65.

53. Cf. Victor W. Turner, *The Ritual Process: Structure and Anti-Structure* (Chicago, 1969), 42, and his *The Forest of Symbols: Aspects of Ndembu Ritual* (Ithaca, 1967), 19; Edmund Leach, *Culture and Communication* (London, 1976), 6; Eric R. Wolf, "Specific Aspects of Plantation Sys-

tems in the New World: Community, Sub-Cultures, and Social Classes," in Vera Rubin, ed., *Plantation Systems in the New World* (Washington, D.C., 1959), 136–46; Raymond Firth, *Symbols: Public and Private* (Ithaca, 1975), 396.

54. Pringle, *Chronicles of Chicora Wood*, 154.

55. Sparkman to B. Allston, Mar. 10, 1858, in Easterby, ed., *South Carolina Rice Plantation*, 347; Emily Weston diary, Apr. 2, 20, May 2, Dec. 3, 6, 8–10, 12, 16–17, 1859; Pringle, *Chronicles of Chicora Wood*, 152–53. Pringle's aunt and namesake ordered blue and white plains from Charleston for her slaves. See Elizabeth Blyth Papers, Oct. 1823.

56. Sparkman to B. Allston, Mar. 10, 1858, in Easterby, ed., *South Carolina Rice Plantation*, 347; Childs, ed., *Rice Planter and Sportsman*, 10; Pringle, *Chronicles of Chicora Wood*, 154.

57. Sparkman to B. Allston, Mar. 10, 1858, in Easterby, ed., *South Carolina Rice Plantation*, 347. Cf. Fogel and Engerman, *Time on the Cross*, 1:118; Sutch, "Care and Feeding of Slaves," 299.

58. Daniel W. Jordan Papers, Apr. 28, 1860; Sparkman to B. Allston, Mar. 10, 1858, in Easterby, ed., *South Carolina Rice Plantation*, 347; Pringle, *Chronicles of Chicora Wood*, 153; Childs, ed., *Rice Planter and Sportsman*, 10.

59. Collins, *Memories of the Southern States*, 4–6, 70, 76; Childs, ed., *Rice Planter and Sportsman*, 10; Coffin to Osgood, May 10, 1859, in Easterby, ed., "South Carolina through New England Eyes," 127; Ben Horry, Slave Narratives, 14, part ii, 310; Sparkman to B. Allston, Mar. 10, 1858, in Easterby, ed., *South Carolina Rice Plantation*, 347.

60. Sparkman to B. Allston, Mar. 10, 1858, in Easterby, ed., *South Carolina Rice Plantation*, 347; Childs, ed., *Rice Planter and Sportsman*, 12. Cf. Yoder, "Folk Costume," 304–5.

61. Childs, ed., *Rice Planter and Sportsman*, 46; Sparkman Family Papers, Book 6, SHC; Malet, *Errand to the South*, 56; Sabe Rutledge, in WPA Mss.; Emily Weston diary, Apr. 2, 1859.

62. Collins, *Memories of the Southern States*, 5. Cf. Genovese, *Roll, Jordan, Roll*, 558–59; Melville J. and Frances Herskovits, *Suriname Folk-Lore* (New York, 1936), 4–5. While the headkerchiefs were usually white in color, there were exceptions. A visiting Englishman reported lowcountry slave women wearing "gaily-colored handkerchiefs arranged turban fashion upon their heads." See "An Englishman in South Carolina," *Continental Monthly*, 3 (1863), 112. And Duncan Clinch Heyward, who grew up on a rice plantation on the Combahee, recalled that slave women there wore colored bandanas. See his *Seed from Madagascar* (Chapel Hill, 1937), 180.

63. Margaret Bryant, WPA Mss. Cf. Judith Wragg Chase, *Afro-American Art and Craft* (New York, 1971), 52–53; Paul Escott, *Slavery Remembered: A Record of Twentieth-Century Slave Narratives* (Chapel Hill, 1979), 101.

64. Ben Horry, Slave Narratives, 14, part ii, 310.

65. Emily Weston diary, Dec. 3, 16, 1859; Dozier, ed., "Interview of Mrs. Julia Smalls," 32; James R. Sparkman Books No. 2732, vol. 3, Sparkman Family Papers, SHC.

66. Emily Weston diary, May 7, Dec. 3, 6, 12, 1859; Sabe Rutledge, WPA Mss.; Ben Horry, Slave Narratives, 14, part ii, 310; R. Allston to A. Allston, Dec. 1, 1844, in Easterby, ed., *South Carolina Rice Plantation*, 92; Childs, ed., *Rice Planter and Sportsman*, 12; Collins, *Memories of the Southern States*, 76.

67. Emily Weston diary, May 7, 1859; Collins, *Memories of the Southern States*, 4.

68. Ellen Godfrey, Slave Narratives, 14, part ii, 159; William Oliver, Slave Narratives, 14, part iii, 219; shoe distribution list, 1861, in Hasell-Flagg Mss., SCHS. Sabe Rutledge, WPA Mss.; M. Small interview. Jordan, at Laurel Hill, purchased brogans and boots for his slaves from Murray and Blaney in Wilmington, N.C. (Jan. 1, 1859), and Edward Daly in Charleston (Nov. 8, 1860), Daniel W. Jordan Papers.

69. Pringle, *Chronicles of Chicora Wood*, 155–56.

70. Sparkman to B. Allston, Mar. 10, 1858, in Easterby, ed., *South Carolina Rice Plantation*, 347; Emily Weston diary, Apr. 2, 1859; Pringle, *Chronicles of Chicora Wood*, 155.

71. Interviews with Genevieve Willcox Chandler, Murrells Inlet, S.C., Aug. 1969, Aug. 1975, Charlotte, N.C., Jan. 1972; Heyward, *Seed from Madagascar*, 182.

72. Childs, ed., *Rice Planter and Sportsman*, 10, 46; Sparkman to B. Allston, Mar. 10, 1858, in Easterby, ed., *South Carolina Rice Plantation*, 347; Adele Petigru Allston memorandum, Nov. 15, 1851, in Robert F. W. Allston Papers.

73. Coffin to Osgood, May 10, 1859, in Easterby, ed., "South Carolina through New England Eyes," 127; Weston, "Rules and Management for the Plantation," 104; "Recollections of a Visit to the Waccamaw," *Living Age*, Aug. 1, 1857, 292–93; Collins, *Memories of the Southern States*, 5. Cf. Stampp, *Peculiar Institution*, 290; Genovese, *Roll, Jordan, Roll*, 552–57.

74. Cf. Erving Goffman, *The Presentation of Self in Everyday Life* (Garden City, N.Y., 1959), 106–40; Genovese, *Roll, Jordan, Roll*, 560–61; Stampp, *Peculiar Institution*, 290.

75. J. Beese interview; Lachicotte interview; interview with Sarah Ann Goback, Murrells Inlet, S.C., Aug. 7, 1975; Malet, *Errand to the South*, 49, 79; David Doar, *Rice and Rice Planting in the South Carolina Low Country* (Charleston, 1936), 38; An Anonymous Englishman, "Rambles at Random through the Southern States," *Blackwood's Magazine*, Jan. 1860; Pringle, *Chronicles of Chicora Wood*, 53, 63–64; Peterkin, *Roll, Jordan, Roll*, 9–10. Photographs of surviving slave houses at the turn of the century are housed in the William D. Morgan Photograph Collection, Georgetown County Library. Ulrich B. Phillips describes a typical plantation layout in his *American Negro Slavery: A Survey of the Supply, Employment, and Control of Negro*

Labor as Determined by the Plantation Regime (New York, 1918; rpt. Baton Rouge, 1966), 309–10. Carl Anthony contends that plantation outbuildings were related to African building practices. See his "The Big House and the Slave Quarters," Part I, *Landscape*, 20 (1976), 8–19.

76. James Deetz, *In Small Things Forgotten: The Archeology of Early American Life* (New York, 1977), 92; Warren Roberts, "Folk Architecture," in Dorson, ed., *Folklore and Folklife*, 288; Edward T. Hall, "The Language of Space," *Landscape*, 10 (1960), 45, and his *The Hidden Dimension* (New York, 1966), 105. Glassie, *Folk Housing in Middle Virginia*, 17–65, 171; Amos Rapaport, *House Form and Culture* (Englewood Cliffs, N.J., 1969), 47. Cf. Fred Kniffen, "American Cultural Geography and Folklife," in Yoder, ed., *American Folklife*, 51–70; Fred Kniffen, "Louisiana House Types," *Annals of the Association of American Geographers*, 26 (1936), 179–93; and Henry Glassie, "The Types of the Southern Mountain Cabin," in Jan Harold Brunvand, *The Study of American Folklore* (New York, 1968), 338–70. For an examination of the houses of slaves and their descendants in southern Maryland, see George W. McDaniel, *Hearth and Home: Preserving a People's Culture* (Philadelphia, 1982).

77. The only investigations in historical archaeology in All Saints Parish thus far are tentative and preliminary. One brief survey was reported by Lesley M. Drucker, "Archeological Investigations at Brookgreen Gardens: The Oaks and Laurel Hill Plantations," paper presented to the Sixth Annual Conference on South Carolina Archeology, University of South Carolina, Columbia, Apr. 19, 1980, and in her unpublished report, "A Cultural Resources Inventory of Selected Areas of the Oaks and Laurel Hill Plantations, Brookgreen Gardens." Stanley South reported on his contracted "'one day' examination" (which actually took nine days) of an eighteenth-century dwelling on Pawleys Island in his "The Pawley House," Research Manuscript Series No. 16, Institute of Archeology and Anthropology, University of South Carolina (Columbia, 1971). I examined in late March 1980 the extant slave cabins in three villages, or "streets," at Hobcaw Barony, a composite plantation formed by Bernard M. Baruch 1905–7 from the combined purchases of what had been in 1860 Marietta, Strawberry Hill, Friendfield, Michaux's Point, Calais, Bellefield, Youngville, Annandale, Alderly, and Oryzantia plantations. Slave cabin archaeology is an exciting new subfield in historical archaeology. Perhaps the most impressive work thus far is Jerome S. Handler and Frederick W. Lange, *Plantation Slavery in Barbados: An Archaeological and Historical Investigation* (Cambridge, Mass., 1978), but important work is being done in the United States as well. See especially Otto, "Artifacts and Status Differences," 91–118; John Solomon Otto, "Race and Class on Antebellum Plantations," in Robert L. Schuyler, ed., *Archaeological Perspectives on Ethnicity in America* (Farmingdale, N.Y., 1979), ch. 1; Fairbanks, "Kingsley Slave Cabins," 62–93; Asher and Fairbanks, "Excavation of a Slave Cabin," 3–17. For archeological studies of plantations elsewhere in the South Carolina lowcountry, see Kenneth E.

Lewis and Donald L. Hardesty, "Middleton Place: Initial Archeological Investigations at an Ashley River Rice Plantation," Research Manuscript Series No. 148, Institute of Archeology and Anthropology, University of South Carolina (Columbia, 1979), and Lynne G. Lewis, *Drayton Hall: Preliminary Archaeological Investigations at a Low Country Plantation* (Charlottesville, 1977). For discussions of the theoretical and methodological underpinnings of historical archaeology, see Ivor Noel Hume, *Historical Archaeology* (New York, 1968); Stanley South, *Method and Theory in Historical Archeology* (New York, 1977); and the essays in Robert L. Schuyler, ed., *Historical Archaeology: A Guide to Substantive and Theoretical Contributions* (Farmingdale, N.Y., 1979). Kenneth E. Lewis demonstrates that archaeology can be simultaneously historical and anthropological in his *Camden: A Frontier Town*, Anthropological Studies, No. 2, Institute of Archeology and Anthropology, University of South Carolina (Columbia, 1976).

78. Malet, *Errand to the South*, 49; Doar, *Rice and Rice Planting*, 38. Cf. Glassie, *Pattern in Material Folk Culture*, 64–69, 75.

79. Sparkman to B. Allston, Mar. 10, 1858, in Easterby, ed., *South Carolina Rice Plantation*, 348; E. Estyn Evans, *Irish Heritage: The Landscape, the People, and Their Work* (Dundalk, Ireland, 1963); M. W. Barley, *The English Farmhouse and Cottage* (London, 1961); Glassie, *Folk Housing in Middle Virginia*, 74–77, and his *Pattern in Material Folk Culture*, 65–66, 80–81; John Michael Vlach, *The Afro-American Tradition in Decorative Arts* (Cleveland, 1978), 125.

80. Solon Robinson, in *American Agriculturalist*, 9 (1850), 187–88, rpt. *DeBow's Review*, 9 (1850), 201–3; Glassie, *Pattern in Material Culture*, 78–79, 82–83; Vlach, *Afro-American Tradition*, 133–35.

81. Here is the nexus between the hall-and-parlor house and the Afro-American shotgun house. The shotgun, as it originated in Haiti, merged the striking gable entrance favored by Arawak Indians with the Yoruba floor plan and European construction techniques. In All Saints Parish a similar creolization process took place, but without the Arawak gable entrance: the convergence of the British hall-and-parlor house and the Yoruba two-room house. See Vlach, *Afro-American Tradition*, 125, 133, and his "Sources of the Shotgun House: African and Caribbean Antecedents for Afro-American Architecture" (Ph.D. diss., Indiana University, 1975); Julius F. P. Gluck, "African Architecture," in Douglas Fraser, ed., *The Many Faces of Primitive Art: A Critical Anthology* (Englewood Cliffs, N.J., 1968), 224–43.

82. Sparkman to B. Allston, Mar. 10, 1858, in Easterby, ed., *South Carolina Rice Plantation*, 348. For smaller estimates of the size of southern slave cabins, see Fogel and Engerman, *Time on the Cross*, 1 : 116; Genovese, *Roll, Jordan, Roll*, 524; Sutch, "Care and Feeding of Slaves," 293; Otto, "New Look at Slave Life," 30. On Plymouth houses see John Demos, *A Little Commonwealth: Family Life in Plymouth Colony* (New York, 1970), 30. It should be noted, however, that West African houses were for sleeping and for shelter when needed; they did not constitute "living space." See Gluck,

"African Architecture," 230–31; John Michael Vlach, "Affecting Architecture of the Yoruba," *African Arts*, 10 (1976), 48–57; Jean Cuvelier, *Relations sur le Congo du pere Laurent de Lucques*, quoted in Vlach, *Afro-American Tradition*, 135.

83. Kirke, *Among the Pines*, 120. Cf. Benjamin A. Brawley, *The Negro Genius* (New York, 1937), 1; Frederick Law Olmstead, *A Journey in the Seaboard Slave States with Remarks on Their Economy* (New York, 1856), 418–48.

84. Sparkman to B. Allston, Mar. 10, 1858, in Easterby, ed., *South Carolina Rice Plantation*, 348; Kirke, *Among the Pines*, 128. Cf. Vlach, *Afro-American Tradition*, 135; Genovese, *Roll, Jordan, Roll*, 524–25.

85. Cf. Vlach, *Afro-American Tradition*, 136–38; Carl Anthony, "The Big House and the Slave Quarters," Part II, 13; Glassie, *Folk Housing in Middle Virginia*, 137–38.

86. Malet, *Errand to the South*, 49; Doar, *Rice and Rice Planting*, 38; Sparkman to B. Allston, Mar. 10, 1858, in Easterby, ed., *South Carolina Rice Plantation*, 348; Kirke, *Among the Pines*, 122, 128. Cf. Otto, "New Look at Slave Life," 30; Genovese, *Roll, Jordan, Roll*, 524–25; Lucien Febvre, "History and Psychology," in Peter Burke, ed., *A New Kind of History: From the Writings of Lucien Febvre*, trans. K. Folca (New York, 1973), 7–8.

87. Kirke, *Among the Pines*, 122, 128; Dozier, ed., "Interview of Mrs. Julia Smalls," 32; Peterkin, *Black April*, 112; William Oliver, Slave Narratives, 14, part iii, 217; Childs, ed., *Rice Planter and Sportsman*, 46; Sparkman to B. Allston, Mar. 10, 1858, in Easterby, ed., *South Carolina Rice Plantation*, 348; cf. Genovese, *Roll, Jordan, Roll*, 525.

88. Cf. Febvre, "History and Psychology," 8.

89. Dozier, ed., "Interview of Julia Smalls," 32; Memorandum of A. Allston, Nov. 15, 1851, in Robert F. W. Allston Papers; Childs, ed., *Rice Planter and Sportsman*, 10, 46; Sparkman to B. Allston, Mar. 10, 1858, in Easterby, ed., *South Carolina Rice Plantation*, 347; J. Beese interview; Kirke, *Among the Pines*, 128. See also Susan Burrows Swan, *Plain and Fancy: American Women and Their Needlework, 1700–1850* (New York, 1977), 208–16, and her *A Winterthur Guide to American Needlework* (New York, 1976); Rose Wilder Lane, *Women's Day Book of American Needlework* (New York, 1963), 76–123; Jonathan Holstein, *The Pieced Quilt: An American Design Tradition* (New York, 1973), 10; Vlach, *Afro-American Tradition*, 44–75; Roy Sieber, *African Textiles and Decorative Arts* (New York, 1972), 155; Geoffrey Williams, *African Designs from Traditional Sources* (New York, 1971), 63–65. African continuities in the work of Afro-American quilters are discussed in Gladys-Marie Fry, "Harriet Powers: Portrait of a Black Quilter," in *Missing Pieces: Georgia Folk Art, 1770–1976* (Atlanta, 1976), 16–23, and Maude Southwell Walman and John Scully, *Black Quilters* (New Haven, 1979). Wahlman's "The Art of Afro-American Quiltmaking: Origins, Development, and Significance" (Ph.D.

diss., Yale University, 1980) is being published in revised form by Indiana University Press.

90. Emily Weston diary, Dec. 13, 1859; Coffin to Osgood, May 10, 1859, in Easterby, ed., "South Carolina through New England Eyes," 133; Kirke, *Among the Pines*, 122, 128–29. On the slave carpenters, see Collins, *Memories of the Southern States*, 7–8; Malet, *Errand to the South*, 80–81, and Emily Weston diary, for Renty Tucker; Sparkman Family Papers, Book 5, for Hardtimes Sparkman; Pringle, *Chronicles of Chicora Wood*, 14, 34–35, for Thomas Bonneau; Childs, ed., *Rice Planter and Sportsman*, 118–19, 123–24, for Richmond; and Welcome Beese, Slave Narratives, 14, part i, 49.

91. Dozier, ed., "Interview of Mrs. Julia Smalls," 32; Kirke, *Among the Pines*, 122, 128–29; Coffin to Osgood, May 10, 1859, in Easterby, ed., "South Carolina through New England Eyes," 133.

92. Cf. Genovese, *Roll, Jordan, Roll*, 528–29.

93. Sparkman to B. Allston, Mar. 10, 1858, in Easterby, ed., *South Carolina Rice Plantation*, 347; Coffin to Osgood, May 10, 1859, in Easterby, ed., "South Carolina through New England Eyes," 133. James Henry Hammond prescribed an elaborate cleaning of the slave quarters on his Edgefield District plantation twice annually. See James Hammond Plantation Manual, SCL.

94. Edward Thomas Heriot to Anna Bruce Cunningham, Apr. 20, 1853, in Edward Thomas Heriot Papers, DUL.

95. Michael Craton, *Sinews of Empire: A Short History of British Slavery* (London, 1974), 188–89; Richard S. Dunn, *Sugar and Slaves: The Rise of the Planter Class in the English West Indies, 1624–1713* (Chapel Hill, 1972), 248; Alexander Humboldt, *The Island of Cuba* (New York, 1856); Gwendolyn Midlo Hall, *Social Control in Slave Plantation Societies: A Comparison of St. Domingue and Cuba* (Baltimore, 1978), 90–92, 124; Cyril Outerbridge Packwood, *Chained on the Rock: Slavery in Bermuda* (New York, 1975), 87–88; Avery O. Craven, "Poor Whites and Negroes in the Ante-Bellum South," *JNH*, 15 (1930), 16; Fogel and Engerman, *Time on the Cross*, 1:115–16; *Third Report of the Commissioners for Inquiring into the Condition of the Poorer Classes in Ireland* (1836), quoted in Thompson, *Making of the English Working Class*, 432; Conrad Arensberg, *The Irish Countryman* (New York, 1961), 64; Friedrich Engels, *The Condition of the Working Class in England in 1844* (London, 1968), 27–37.

96. Emily Weston diary, Jan. 1, 3, Feb. 7, 1859; Coffin to Osgood, May 10, 1859, in Easterby, ed., "South Carolina through New England Eyes," 133; J. Beese interview; Lachicotte interview; Sparkman to B. Allston, Mar. 10, 1858, in Easterby, ed., *South Carolina Rice Plantation*, 348. Herbert G. Gutman has some insightful comments on the relationship between household and family in his "Le phenomene invisible: la composition de la famille et des foyer noir apres la Guerre de Secession," *Annales, E.S.C.*, 27 (1972), 1197–1218. See also his *The Black Family in Slavery and Freedom, 1750–1925* (New York, 1976), 96–97. W. E. B. DuBois stressed the relationships

between household and family life in his "The Problem of Housing the Negro—the Home of the Slave," *Southern Workman*, 30 (1901), 486–93. For other studies of relationships between household and family, see Peter Laslett, *The World We Have Lost* (New York, 1965); Conrad Arensberg and Solon T. Kimball, *Family and Community in Ireland* (Cambridge, Mass., 1968); Peter Laslett, ed., *Household and Family in Past Time: Comparative Studies in the Size and Structure of the Domestic Group over the Last Three Centuries in England, France, Serbia, Japan, and Colonial North America, with Further Materials from Western Europe* (Cambridge, Mass., 1972).

97. Cf. Vlach, *Afro-American Tradition*, 123.

98. Hagar Brown, WPA Mss.

Notes to *"Off Times"*

1. Plowden C. J. Weston, "Rules and Management for the Plantation, 1859," in Elizabeth Collins, *Memories of the Southern States* (Taunton, England, 1865), 107. An earlier and somewhat shorter version of this overseer's contract was published as "Rules on the Rice Estate of P. C. Weston, S.C., 1856," *DeBow's Review*, 21 (1857), 38–44, and reprinted in Ulrich B. Phillips, ed., *Plantation and Frontier Documents* (Cleveland, 1910), 1:115–22. My interpretation of the evidence on off times in this passage and elsewhere in this chapter is based upon an assumption that the social relations of All Saints rice plantations were dynamic, rather than static, and that the slaves' role in these social relations was active, rather than passive. Such customary rights were insisted upon by slaves as early as the ancient world. See W. L. Westermann, "Slave Maintenance and Slave Revolts," *Classical Philology*, 40 (1945), 8. Cf. Eugene D. Genovese, *Roll, Jordan, Roll: The World the Slaves Made* (New York, 1974), 566–84.

2. Cf. Mary Douglas, *Purity and Danger: An Analysis of Concepts of Pollution* (London, 1966), 62–63.

3. Weston, "Rules and Management for the Plantation," 107. Victor W. Turner contends that the contrast of work and leisure developed only after the industrial revolution. In pre-industrial societies the salient contrast was between sacred and profane work. See his "From Liminal to Liminoid in Play, Flow, and Ritual: An Essay in Comparative Symbology," in Edward Norbeck, ed., *The Anthropological Study of Human Play* (Houston, 1974), 53–90. Cf. Gregory Bateson, "A Theory of Play and Fantasy," in his *Steps to an Ecology of Mind* (New York, 1972), 177–93; Johan Huizinga, *Homo Ludens: A Study of the Play-Element in Culture* (Boston, 1955), 13; D. L. Miller, *Gods and Games: Toward a Theology of Play* (New York, 1973), 97; Barbara Kirshenblatt-Gimblett, ed., *Speech Play: Research and Resources for the Study of Linguistic Creativity* (Philadelphia, 1976), 184. On the questions of continuity and creativity, cf. Julia Peterkin, *Roll, Jordan, Roll* (New York, 1933), 12—which is concerned with All Saints Parish—and, for a comparative perspective, Sidney Mintz, "Toward an Afro-American His-

tory," *Cahiers d'histoire mondiale*, 13 (1971), 317–31, and Roger Bastide, *African Civilisations in the New World*, trans. Peter Green (New York, 1971), 23–43.

4. Laurence Oliphant, *Patriots and Filibusters; or Incidents of Political and Exploratory Travel* (Edinburgh, 1860), 140; William Wyndham Malet, *An Errand to the South in the Summer of 1862* (London, 1863), 117–18; Elizabeth W. Allston Pringle, *Chronicles of Chicora Wood* (New York, 1922), 68–69; Richard Lathers, *Reminiscences of Richard Lathers: Sixty Years of a Busy Life in South Carolina, Massachusetts, and New York* (New York, 1907), 5; Sabe Rutledge, in WPA Mss., SCL.

5. Interview with John Beese (son of Welcome Beese, a slave at Oatland plantation on the Waccamaw), Pawleys Island, S.C., Jan. 18, 1972; J. Harold Easterby, ed., *The South Carolina Rice Plantation as Revealed in the Papers of Robert F. W. Allston* (Chicago, 1945), 31; Arney R. Childs, ed., *Rice Planter and Sportsman: The Recollections of J. Motte Alston* (Columbia, 1953), 45; Dennis T. Lawson, *No Heir to Take Its Place: The Story of Rice in Georgetown County, South Carolina* (Georgetown, 1972), 13; George C. Rogers, Jr., *The History of Georgetown County, South Carolina* (Columbia, 1970), 331; Weston, "Rules and Management for the Plantation," 107; Malet, *Errand to the South*, 57; Almira Coffin to Mrs. J. G. Osgood, May 10, 1851, in J. Harold Easterby, ed., "South Carolina through New England Eyes: Almira Coffin's Visit to the Low Country in 1851," *SCHM*, 45 (1944), 127–36. These descriptions are supported by oral tradition among both blacks and whites: interview with Henry Small (son of Titus Small, a slave of John D. Magill), Free Woods, S.C., Aug. 2, 1975; A. H. Lachicotte (great-grandson of Phillip Rossignol Lachicotte, who supervised the rice mill at Brookgreen plantation in the 1850s), Pawleys Island, S.C., July 28, 1975. Elsewhere in the Georgetown District the task system operated in much the same way. See G.S.S., "Sketches of the South Santee," *Atlantic Monthly Magazine*, May 8, 1836, 431–32.

6. Lachicotte interview; Rogers, *History of Georgetown County*, 348; Mss. Diary of Emily Weston for 1859, in private possession (hereafter cited as Emily Weston diary), Apr. 3, Dec. 13, 1859; Malet, *Errand to the South*, 57; James R. Sparkman to Benjamin Allston, Mar. 10, 1858, in Easterby, ed., *South Carolina Rice Plantation*, 347–48; Ben Sparkman Plantation Record, SHC; David J. McCord, ed., *Statutes at Large of South Carolina* (Columbia, 1840), 6:516–17. See also Philip D. Morgan, "The Development of Slave Culture in Eighteenth Century Plantation America" (Ph.D. diss., University College, London, 1977), 189–93. H. J. Nieboer, in his pioneering *Slavery as an Industrial System* (Rotterdam, 1910), 35, called attention to the universality of the *peculium*, or provision ground, in slave societies. For a description of the peculium cross-culturally, see Orlando Patterson, *Slavery and Social Death: A Comparative Study* (Cambridge, Mass., 1982), 182–86. For a comparative perspective, see Patterson's *The Sociology of Slavery* (London, 1967), 69; Sidney W. Mintz and Richard

Price, *An Anthropological Approach to the Afro-American Past: A Caribbean Perspective* (Philadelphia, 1976), 47. On protopeasant economy see A. V. Chayanov, *The Theory of Peasant Economy*, trans. and ed. Daniel Thoner (Homewood, Ill., 1966), 171. On the moral economy, see E. P. Thompson, "The Moral Economy of the English Crowd in the Eighteenth Century," *Past and Present*, 50 (1971), 76–136.

7. Ben Horry, Slave Narratives: A Folk History of Slavery in the United States from Interviews with Former Slaves. Typewritten records prepared by the Federal Writers' Project, 1936–38 (microfilm), 14, part ii, 399–400; Julia Small, daughter of a slave on John D. Magill's plantation, described the house meetings in an interview in Etrulia P. Dozier, ed., "Interview of Mrs. Julia Smalls [*sic*]," *Independent Republic Quarterly*, 4 (July 1970), 32. See also Malet, *Errand to the South*, 74; Oliphant, *Patriots and Filibusters*, 140–41; Albert Carolina, Slave Narratives, 14, part i, 198; and John Hunter to Benjamin Allston, Mar. 6, 1858, in Benjamin Allston Papers, DUL.

8. Childs, ed., *Rice Planter and Sportsman*, 46; Weston, "Rules and Management for the Plantation," 107; Lachicotte interview. The abundance of seafood of all kinds in the Waccamaw River and the salt water creeks of All Saints Parish are attested by Robert Mills, *Statistics of South Carolina* (Charleston, 1826), 564–65; William Gilmore Simms, *Geography of South Carolina* (Charleston, 1843), 81.

9. Weston, "Rules and Management for the Plantation," 107; Malet, *Errand to the South*, 57; Collins, *Memories of the Southern States*, 56; Childs, ed., *Rice Planter and Sportsman*, 46; Easterby, ed., *South Carolina Rice Plantation*, 31; Patience Pennington [Elizabeth Allston Pringle], *A Woman Rice Planter* (New York, 1914), 14.

10. Malet, *Errand to the South*, 49, 111; Collins, *Memories of the Southern States*, 17, 61; Ben Horry, Slave Narratives, 14, part ii, 309. Cf. Paul A. Cimbala, "Fortunate Bondsmen: Black 'Musicianers' and Their Role as an Antebellum Slave Elite," *Southern Studies*, 18 (1979), 291–303, and his "Fortunate Bondsmen: Black 'Musicianers' and Their Place in Antebellum Southern Plantation Life" (M.A. thesis, Emory University, 1977); Eileen Southern, *The Music of Black Americans: A History* (New York, 1971), 45–47, 66–67, 157; Harold Courlander, *Negro Folk Music, U.S.A.* (New York, 1971), 219–20; Dena J. Epstein, *Sinful Tunes and Spirituals: Black Folk Music to the Civil War* (Urbana, 1977), 112–15, 144–56, 343–45. Epstein discusses in detail the African origins of the banjo (30–38). A classic depiction of a slave fiddler is Solomon Northup's autobiography, *Twelve Years a Slave: The Narrative of Solomon Northup, a Citizen of New-York, Kidnapped in Washington City in 1841 and Rescued in 1853, from a Cotton Plantation near the Red River in Louisiana* (Auburn, N.Y., 1853), esp. 216–17.

11. Edmund Kirke [James Roberts Gilmore], *Among the Pines: Or, The South in Secession Time* (New York, 1862), 145–48. Early in the eighteenth century, it had "been customary among them to have their feasts, dances,

and merry Meetings upon the Lord's day," as the Reverend Francis Le Jau had lamented (Frank Klingberg, ed., *The Carolina Chronicle of Dr. Francis Le Jau, 1706–1717* [Berkeley, 1956], 61), but by the nineteenth century Saturday had become the day for such festivities. A most interesting description of one such "frolic" was discovered in the *South Carolina Gazette* by Hennig Cohen: "It consisted of about 60 people . . . provided with Music, Cards, Dice, &c. The entertainment was opened, by the men copying (or *taking off*) the manners of their masters, and the women those of their mistresses, and relating some highly curious anecdotes, to the inexpressible diversion of that company. They then *danced*." See his "A Negro 'Folk Game' in Colonial South Carolina," *SFQ*, 16 (1952), 183–84.

12. Kirke, *Among the Pines*, 22. Cantometric analysis of Afro-American spirituals and work songs recorded in All Saints Parish by John A. Lomax for the Library of Congress indicates a striking persistence of continuities with West African singing style as late as the 1930s. These disc recordings, made in Genevieve Chandler's yard in the summers of 1936, 1937, and 1939, are housed in the Library of Congress: AFS 830 A1–B2, 832 A1–834 B3, 868 A–B2, 877 A1–B2, 903 A1–904 B4, 909 A1–910B2, 946 A1–B3, 950 A1–B2, 1031 A2–1046 B2, 1300 A1–1300 B3, 1301 A–1303B, 2692 A–B, 2702 B3, 2711 B1–B3, 2719 A1–B4, 2720 A2-2721 A3, 2722 A1–B2. On the principles of cantometric analysis see Alan Lomax *et al.*, *Folksong Style and Culture* (Washington, D.C., 1968). For other studies of relationships of slave singing style to West African singing style, see Richard Alan Waterman, "African Influence on the Music of the Americas," in Sol Tax, ed., *Acculturation in the Americas* (Chicago, 1952), 207–18; John F. Szwed, "Musical Adaptation among Afro-Americans," *JAF*, 82 (1969), 115; Alan Lomax, "The Homogeneity of African–Afro-American Musical Style," in Norman E. Whitten and John F. Szwed, eds., *Afro-American Anthropology* (New York, 1970), 181–201.

13. Ben Horry, Slave Narratives, 14, part ii, 304. Similar punishments by the patrol were described by Mary Small (daughter of Hagar Brown) and by H. Small in interviews in August 1975 in Free Woods, S.C. On the patrol, see Robert F. W. Allston to Benjamin Allston, Sept. 6, 1860, in Easterby, ed., *South Carolina Rice Plantation*, 165; Rogers, *History of Georgetown County*, 343–44; Howell M. Henry, *Police Control of the Slave in South Carolina* (Emory, Va., 1914), 32–37; Kenneth M. Stampp, *The Peculiar Institution: Slavery in the Ante-Bellum South* (New York, 1956), 214–15; George M. Frederickson and Christopher Lasch, "Resistance to Slavery," *Civil War History*, 13 (1967), 315–29; Gilbert Osofsky, *Puttin' On Ole Massa* (New York, 1969), 18; and Genovese, *Roll, Jordan, Roll*, 617–19. Something of the seriousness with which patrol duty was taken by the planters is indicated in the fact that Daniel W. Jordan, master of Laurel Hill, was fined $12 plus $1 court costs in September 1860 for defaulting on patrol duty. Daniel W. Jordan Papers, DUL.

14. Kirke, *Among the Pines*, 48. Cf. Bastide, *African Civilisations in the New World*, 91–92.

15. Childs, ed., *Rice Planter and Sportsman*, 47, 75–87; Emily Weston diary; "Recollections of a Visit to the Waccamaw," *Living Age*, Aug. 1, 1857, 292–93; Coffin to Osgood, May 10, 1851, in Easterby, ed., "South Carolina through New England Eyes," 131; William Oliver, Slave Narratives, 14, part iii, 220; Pringle, *Chronicles of Chicora Wood*, 89. Cf. Oliphant, *Patriots and Filibusters*, 145, who describes how, on the Waccamaw, "dense flocks of wild ducks, of numerous varieties, come winding past in long single-file, or, closing their ranks, settle in dense masses with noisy quack and flutter, all around you." See also Peterkin, *Roll, Jordan, Roll*, 10; Rogers, *History of Georgetown County*, 349–58. Slaves were allowed to hunt on their masters' property, but they were forbidden by law to carry firearms beyond the boundaries of the plantation unless they carried written permission from their master or were accompanied by a white. See Cooper and McCord, eds., *Statutes at Large of South Carolina*, 7:348, 353–54.

16. Ben Horry, Slave Narratives, 14, part ii, 310; Pringle, *Chronicles of Chicora Wood*, 93; Easterby, ed., *South Carolina Rice Plantation*, 31.

17. Weston, "Rules and Management for the Plantation," 107; Easterby, ed., *South Carolina Rice Plantation*, 33; John Pierpont, journal, 10–13, Mss. Pierpont Morgan Library, N.Y., quoted in Epstein, *Sinful Tunes and Spirituals*, 84; Abe Ravitz, "John Pierpont and the Slaves' Christmas," *Phylon*, 21 (1960), 383–86; John K. Winkler, *Morgan the Magnificent* (New York, 1930), 27.

18. "Sketches of South Carolina, Number Three: 'Merry Christmas,'" *Knickerbocker Magazine*, 21 (Mar. 1843), 228–29.

19. Emily Weston diary, Dec. 22–28, 1859; Collins, *Memories of the Southern States*, 6.

20. Pringle, *Chronicles of Chicora Wood*, 150–52. On the preference of James Henry Hammond's slaves for celebrating Christmas without their master's presence, see Drew Gilpin Faust, *James Henry Hammond and the Old South: A Design for Mastery* (Baton Rouge, 1982), 381.

21. Adele Petigru Allston to B. Allston, Jan. 1, 1857, in Easterby, ed., *South Carolina Rice Plantation*, 135–36.

22. Collins, *Memories of the Southern States*, 12–13.

23. Sparkman to B. Allston, Mar. 10, 1858, in Easterby, ed., *South Carolina Rice Plantation*, 347.

24. Emily Weston diary, Dec. 27, 1859; Malet, *Errand to the South*, 57–58, 68; Mary Petigru to A. Allston, Dec. 27, 1860, in Easterby, ed., *South Carolina Rice Plantation*, 171; Robert F. W. Allston diary, Dec. 25, 1860, in Easterby, ed., *South Carolina Rice Plantation*, 453–54. Cf. Arnold van Gennep, *The Rites of Passage*, trans. Monika B. Vizedom and Gabrielle L. Caffee (Chicago, 1960), esp. 116–65, and his "On the Rites of Passage," in Talcott Parsons, ed., *Theories of Society* (Glencoe, Ill., 1961),

2:950; Victor W. Turner, *The Forest of Symbols: Aspects of Ndembu Ritual* (Ithaca, 1967), esp. 151–279, and his *The Drums of Affliction* (Oxford, 1968), 15–16.

25. Louisa Brown, Slave Narratives, 14, part i, 115; Emily Weston diary, Dec. 27, 1859; Malet, *Errand to the South*, 57–58, 68; Peterkin, *Roll, Jordan, Roll*, 10; Genovese, *Roll, Jordan, Roll*, 451–54, 463–82; John Blassingame, *The Slave Community: Plantation Life in the Ante-Bellum South* (New York, 1972), 77–103; Donald G. Matthews, *Religion in the Old South* (Chicago, 1977), 44. For an analysis of slave marriage cross-culturally, see Patterson, *Slavery and Social Death*, 186–90.

26. The importance of the family in All Saints slave folklife is indicated by Sabe Rutledge, Slave Narratives, 14, part iv, 59; Welcome Bees, Slave Narratives, 14, part i, 49–50; Ben Horry, Slave Narratives, 14, part ii, 311; Hagar Brown, Slave Narratives, 14, part i, 110–14; Margaret Bryant, Slave Narratives, 14, part i, 146–47; Ella Small, WPA Mss. Such studies as E. Franklin Frazier, *The Negro Family in the United States* (Chicago, 1939), 40–41, 89–107, and his "The Negro Slave Family," *JNH*, 15 (1930), 198–259; and Stanley M. Elkins, *Slavery: A Problem in American Institutional and Intellectual Life* (Chicago, 1959), 53–54, contend that slavery destroyed the black family. Herbert G. Gutman, in *The Black Family in Slavery and Freedom, 1750–1925* (New York, 1976), esp. 45–100, emphasizes the strength of the slave family, attributing that strength to continuities with African cultural patterns of which the masters were unaware. That the slave family in All Saints Parish drew from both remembered African sources and encountered Euro-American sources is suggested by comparison of the following works: A. R. Radcliffe-Brown and Daryll Forde, eds., *African Systems of Kinship and Marriage* (London, 1950); Lawrence Stone, *The Family, Sex and Marriage in England, 1500–1800* (New York, 1977); Daniel Scott Smith, "Population, Family and Society in Hingham, Massachusetts, 1635–1880" (Ph.D. diss., University of California, Berkeley, 1973); Charles Rosenberg, ed., *The Family in History* (Philadelphia, 1975).

27. Malet, *Errand to the South*, 68; Louisa Brown, Slave Narratives, 14, part i, 115; Peterkin, *Roll, Jordan, Roll*, 10. Cf. Gutman, *Black Family*, 269–77, 281–84. On the analysis of focused gatherings, see Erving Goffman, *Encounters: Two Studies in the Sociology of Interaction* (Indianapolis, 1961), 9–10.

28. M. Small interview; J. Beese interview; Lachicotte interview; "Debbil Brew," collected by Genevieve Chandler, July 22, 1936, and ex-slave interviewed by Genevieve Chandler, Aug. 25, 1936, both in WPA Mss.; Emily Weston diary, Jan. 22, 1859. Cf. Genovese, *Roll, Jordan, Roll*, 194–202; Stampp, *Peculiar Institution*, 318–21; Richard C. Wade, *Slavery in the Cities: The South, 1820–1860* (New York, 1964), 169–70; Frazier, "Negro Slave Family," 215–16; Newbell Niles Puckett, *Folk Beliefs of the Southern Negro* (Chapel Hill, 1926), 79–113; Mary A. Waring, "Mortuary Customs and Beliefs of South Carolina Negroes," *JAF*, 7 (1894), 318–19, and her

"Negro Superstitions in South Carolina," *JAF*, 8 (1895); Portia Smiley, "Folk-Lore from Virginia, South Carolina, Alabama, Georgia, and Florida," *JAF*, 32 (1919), 357–83; H. C. Bolton, "Decoration of Graves of Negroes in South Carolina," *JAF*, 7 (1894), 305. On the African tradition, see Geoffrey Parrinder, *African Traditional Religion* (London, 1962), 99; Melville J. Herskovits, *The Myth of the Negro Past* (New York, 1941; rpt. Boston, 1958), 63, 201; Robert Faris Thompson, "African Influences on the Art of the United States," in Armstead L. Robinson *et al.*, eds., *Black Studies in the University* (New Haven, 1969), 122–70, esp. 149. For a description of Afro-American funeral practices in a comparative context, see Frank Tannenbaum, *Slave and Citizen: The Negro in the Americas* (New York, 1946), 85–86; Bastide, *African Civilisations in the New World*, 57–58, 79–82, 103–4, 161–62; Richard S. Dunn, *Sugar and Slaves: The Rise of the Planter Class in the English West Indies, 1624–1713* (Chapel Hill, 1972), 250–51.

29. J. Beese interview; Hagar Brown, Slave Narratives, 14, part i, 113–14; M. Small interview (according to Small, both her mother [Hagar Brown] and her grandmother are buried in the plantation cemetery at the Oaks); James R. Sparkman, "The Negro," Sparkman Family Papers, SHC. For a description of a black funeral on the Waccamaw in the 1930s see John A. Lomax, *Adventures of a Ballad Hunter* (New York, 1947), 209–14. Cf. Puckett, *Folk Beliefs of the Southern Negro*, 87–89; Susan Showers, "A Weddin' and a Buryin' in the Black Belt," *New England Magazine*, 18 (1898), 478–83, rpt. Bruce Jackson, ed., *The Negro and His Folklore in Nineteenth Century Periodicals* (Austin, 1967), 293–301; "Beliefs and Customs Connected with Death and Burial," *Southern Workman*, 4 (1912), 246–48; Martha Emmons, "Dyin' Easy," *Publications of the Texas Folklore Society*, 10 (1932), 55–61; E. Horace Fitchett, "Superstitions in South Carolina," *The Crisis*, 43 (1936), 360–61, 370; Glenn Sisk, "Funeral Customs in the Alabama Black Belt, 1870–1910," *SFQ*, 23 (1959), 169–71; Waring, "Mortuary Beliefs," 318.

30. This rudimentary classification of genres is based upon the system of Roger D. Abrahams, "The Complex Relations of Simple Forms," *Genre*, 2 (1969), 104–28.

Notes to "Come by Here, Lord"

1. William Wyndham Malet, *An Errand to the South in the Summer of 1862* (London 1863), 74, 114–15, 194; Edmund Kirke [James Roberts Gilmore], *Among the Pines: Or, The South in Secession-Time* (New York, 1862), 43–44; Laurence Oliphant, *Patriots and Filibusters; or Incidents of Political and Exploratory Travel* (Edinburgh, 1860); "Recollections of a Visit to the Waccamaw," *Living Age*, Aug. 1, 1857, 292–96. Cf. Dominique Zahan, *The Religion, Spirituality, and Thought of Traditional Africa*, trans. Kate Ezra Martin and Lawrence M. Martin (Chicago, 1979); Robin Hor-

ton, "African Traditional Thought and Western Science," parts 1 and 2, *Africa*, 37 (June and Sept. 1967); Albert J. Raboteau, *Slave Religion: The "Invisible Institution" in the Antebellum South* (New York, 1978), 16; Donald G. Matthews, *Religion in the Old South* (Chicago, 1977), 185; Paul Radin, "Status, Fantasy, and the Christian Dogma," in A. P. Watson, Paul Radin, and Charles S. Johnson, eds., *God Struck Me Dead: Religious Conversion Experiences and Autobiographies of Negro Ex-Slaves* (Nashville, 1945), reprinted as vol. 19 of George P. Rawick, ed., *The American Slave: A Composite Autobiography* (Westport, Conn., 1972); Joseph R. Washington, Jr., *Black Religion: The Negro and Christianity in the United States* (Boston, 1964), 31–33; Mary Douglas, *Purity and Danger: An Analysis of Concepts of Pollution* (London, 1966), 68; Mercea Eliade, *The Sacred and the Profane* (New York, 1961), 5. For an examination of slave religion cross-culturally, see Orlando Patterson, *Slavery and Social Death: A Comparative Study* (Cambridge, Mass., 1982), 66–76, esp. 73–75.

2. For a similar fragmentation of African religion in Jamaica, see Roger Bastide, *African Civilisations in the New World*, trans. Peter Green (New York, 1971), 103. That all three streams should be considered aspects of slave religion is suggested by Anthony F. C. Wallace's definition of religion as "that kind of behavior which can be classified as belief and ritual concerned with supernatural beings, powers, and forces" in his *Religion: An Anthropological View* (New York, 1966), 5.

3. For continuities of African function in Afro-American religions, see George Eaton Simpson and Peter B. Hammond, "Discussion," in Vera Rubin, ed., *Caribbean Studies: A Symposium* (Seattle, 1957), 48. On the influence of the spirits in human affairs, see John Mbiti, *African Religions and Philosophy* (Garden City, N.Y., 1969), 83. On European belief in witchcraft, astrology, and other occult phenomena, see Keith Thomas, *Religion and the Decline of Magic* (London, 1971).

4. Alexander Hewat, *An Historical Account of the Rise and Progress of the Colonies of South Carolina and Georgia* (London, 1779), rpt. in Bartholomew R. Carroll, ed., *Historical Collections of South Carolina; Embracing Many Rare and Valuable Pamphlets, and Other Documents, Relating to the History of That State, from Its First Discovery to Its Independence in the Year 1776* (New York, 1836), 1:347–48; Elizabeth W. Allston Pringle, *Chronicles of Chicora Wood* (New York, 1922), 351–52; Mariah Heywood, Slave Narratives: A Folk History of Slavery in the United States from Interviews with Former Slaves. Typewritten records prepared by the Federal Writers' Project, 1936–38 (microfilm), 14, part ii, 284–85; Philip D. Curtin, *The Atlantic Slave Trade: A Census* (Madison, 1969), 145–58; Elizabeth Donnan, "The Slave Trade into South Carolina before the Revolution," *AHR*, 33 (1927–28), 816–17; Peter H. Wood, *Black Majority: Negroes in Colonial South Carolina from 1670 through the Stono Rebellion* (New York, 1974), 13–35; Daniel C. Littlefield, *Rice and Slaves: Ethnicity and the Slave Trade in Colonial South Carolina* (Baton Rouge, 1981), 115–77; Zahan,

Religion, Spirituality, and Thought of Traditional Africa; Bastide, *African Civilisations in the New World*, 102, 112; Janheinz Jahn, *Muntu: An Outline of the New African Culture* (New York, 1961); Sidney W. Mintz and Richard Price, *An Anthropological Approach to the Afro-American Past: A Caribbean Perspective* (Philadelphia, 1976), 26; Raboteau, *Slave Religion*, 4; Olli Alho, *The Religion of the Slaves: A Study of the Religious Tradition and Behavior of Plantation Slaves in the United States, 1830–1865* (Helsinki, 1976), 43; Vincent Harding, "The Uses of the Afro-American Past," in Donald R. Cutter, ed., *The Religious Situation* (Boston, 1969), 829–40; Erskine Clarke, *Wrestlin' Jacob: A Portrait of Religion in the Old South* (Atlanta, 1979).

5. James R. Sparkman, "The Negro," in Sparkman Family Papers, SHC. Cf. Drew Gilpin Faust, *James Henry Hammond and the Old South: A Design for Mastery* (Baton Rouge, 1982), 93.

6. Cf. George Eaton Simpson, "The Shango Cult in Nigeria and Trinidad," *AA*, 54 (1962), 1204–29, and his *The Shango Cult in Trinidad* (San Juan, 1965); Harold Courlander, *The Dream and the Hoe: The Life and Lore of the Haitian People* (Berkeley, 1960); Alfred Metraux, *Voodoo in Haiti*, trans. Hugo Charteris (New York, 1959); Melville J. Herskovits, *Life in a Haitian Valley* (New York, 1937); Mbiti, *African Religions*, 83; Bastide, *African Civilisations in the New World*, 59–60, 101–3; Martha Beckwith, "Some Religious Cults in Jamaica," *American Journal of Psychology*, 34 (1923), 32–45; Donald Hogg, "The Convince Cult in Jamaica," in Sidney Mintz, ed., *Papers in Caribbean Anthropology* (New Haven, 1960); George Eaton Simpson, "Jamaican Revivalist Cults," *Social and Economic Studies*, 5 (1956), 321–42; Newbell Niles Puckett, *Folk Beliefs of the Southern Negro* (Chapel Hill, 1926), 167–310; E. Horace Fitchett, "Superstitions in South Carolina," *The Crisis*, 43 (1936), 360–71; Monica Shuler, "Afro-American Slave Culture," in Michael Craton, ed., *Roots and Branches: Current Directions in Slave Studies* (Willowdale, Ontario, 1979), 129–37.

7. "Hackless," Pawleys Island, S.C., WPA Mss., SCL. Julia Peterkin's novels of Afro-American folklife in All Saints Parish are virtually catalogs of such folk beliefs. See, for instance, *Black April* (Indianapolis, 1927), 147–48, 245, and *Bright Skin* (Indianapolis, 1932), 59. Cf. Henry C. Davis, "Negro Folk-Lore in South Carolina," *JAF*, 27 (1914), 245; B. A. Botkin, "'Folk-Say' and Folk-Lore," in W. T. Couch, ed., *Culture in the South* (Chapel Hill, 1934), 590; Bastide, *African Civilisations in the New World*, 134–47; Paul D. Escott, *Slavery Remembered: A Record of Twentieth-Century Slave Narratives* (Chapel Hill, 1979), 105; Eugene D. Genovese, *Roll, Jordan, Roll: The World the Slaves Made* (New York, 1974), 220; John W. Blassingame, *The Slave Community: Plantation Life in the Ante-Bellum South*, 2d ed. (New York, 1979), 41; Zora Neale Hurston, *Mules and Men* (Philadelphia, 1935), 247; Zora Neale Hurston, "Hoodoo in America," *JAF*, 44 (1931), 317–417; Leonora Herron and Alice M. Bacon, "Conjuring and Conjure-Doctors," *Southern Workman*, 24 (1895), 118.

8. [Lillie Knox], "Lizard in the Head," collected by Genevieve Willcox Chandler, in *South Carolina Folk Tales*, compiled by Workers of the Writers' Program of the Work Projects Administration in the State of South Carolina (Columbia, 1941), 82; Julia Peterkin, *Green Thursday* (New York, 1924), 158–63; Peterkin, *Black April*, 123; Peterkin, *Bright Skin*, 114; Davis, "Negro Folk-Lore," 245–48; Fitchett, "Superstitions," 360–71; Puckett, *Folk Beliefs*, 200; Herron and Bacon, "Conjuring and Conjure-Doctors," 193–94; Blassingame, *Slave Community*, 109; Eugene D. Genovese, *In Red and Black: Marxian Explorations in Southern and Afro-American History* (New York, 1968), 108–9; Gilbert Osofsky, ed., *Puttin' On Ole Massa* (New York, 1969), 37; W. E. B. DuBois, "Religion of the American Negro," *New World*, 9 (1900), 618, and his *The Souls of Black Folk* (Chicago, 1903), 144. Cf. Norman E. Whitten, Jr., "Contemporary Patterns of Malign Occultism among Negroes in North Carolina," *JAF*, 75 (1962), 311–25; Bastide, *African Civilisations in the New World*, 46. For a Brazilian parallel, see Gilberto Freyre, *The Masters and the Slaves* (New York, 1967), 289.

9. "Hant House," *South Carolina Folk Tales*, 77–79; Hagar Brown and Lillie Knox, WPA Mss.; Margaret Bryant, Slave Narratives, 14, part i, 146–47; Peterkin, *Black April*, 26. Cf. William R. Bascom, "Acculturation among the Gullah Negroes," *AA*, 43 (1941), 48; J. E. McTeer, *High Sheriff of the Low Country* (Beaufort, S.C., 1970), 22; Elsie Clews Parsons, *Folk-Lore of the Sea Islands, South Carolina* (Cambridge, Mass., 1923), 197; Roland Steiner, "Braziel Robinson Possessed of Two Spirits," *JAF*, 13 (1900), 226–28; Puckett, *Folk Beliefs*, 137; Herron and Bacon, "Conjuring and Conjure-Doctors," 117. On the African derivation of these beliefs, see Melville J. Herskovits, *The Myth of the Negro Past* (New York, 1941; rpt. Boston, 1958), 190.

10. Minnie Knox and Ellen Carolina, WPA Mss. Cf. Davis, "Negro Folk-Lore," 247; Herron and Bacon, "Conjure and Conjure-Doctors," 117; Elsie Clews Parsons, "Tales from Guilford County, North Carolina," *JAF*, 30 (1917), 168–200; Louis Pendleton, "Notes on Negro Folk-Lore and Witchcraft in the South," *JAF*, 3 (1890), 201–7. For comparative perspectives, see Suzanne Comhaire-Sylvain, "Creole Tales from Haiti," *JAF*, 51 (1938), 219–346; Bastide, *African Civilisations in the New World*, 147.

11. Unidentified, collected by Chandler, and Hagar Brown, both in WPA Mss.; "Uncle Gabe's Conjuh Ball," *South Carolina Folk Tales*, 103. Cf. Davis, "Negro Folk-Lore," 247; Herron and Bacon, "Conjure and Conjure-Doctors," 193–94. On the African provenience of using graveyard dirt, see Bascom, "Acculturation among the Gullah Negroes," 49.

12. On pharmaceutical treatment of slave illnesses, see Margaret Bryant, Slave Narratives, 14, part i, 146; Hagar Brown, WPA. Mss.; Peterkin, *Black April*, 7. Cf. Julia F. Morton, *Folk Remedies of the Low Country* (Miami, 1974), 16, 109–10, 125–26; Davis, "Negro Folk-Lore," 246; Wood, *Black Majority*, 120; Wayland D. Hand, *Popular Beliefs and Superstitions from North Carolina*, vol. 6 of the *Frank C. Brown Collection of*

North Carolina Folklore (Durham, N.C., 1961), 858–62. On healing by conjuration, see "Lizard in the Head," *South Carolina Folk Tales*, 82–83; Lillie Knox, Zackie Knox, and Ella Small, all in WPA Mss. Cf. Steiner, "Braziel Robinson," 226–28; Charles W. Chesnutt, "Superstitions and Folklore of the South," *Modern Culture*, 13 (1901), 231–35; Herron and Bacon, "Conjure and Conjure-Doctors," 210–11. The distrust of white doctors in All Saints Parish was indicated in interviews with John Beese, son of Welcome Beese, Pawleys Island, S.C., Jan. 18, 1972, and with Henry Small, son of Titus Small, Free Woods, S.C., Aug. 2, 1975. The distrust by All Saints blacks of white medicine is portrayed in Peterkin's novel of Sandy Island folklife, *Black April*, 71, 275, 281–83.

13. Sabe Rutledge, Slave Narratives, 14, part iii, 62; Lillie Knox, in "Lizard in the Head," *South Carolina Folk Tales*, 83; "Uncle Gabe's Conjuh Ball," collected by Chandler, WPA Mss. One must be wary of such protestations of disbelief by ex-slaves to middle-class white interviewers in the 1930s. Since, however, other ex-slaves had no hesitation in expressing their belief in conjuration to Chandler, there is no more reason to assume that one group dissembled than the other, unless we wish to impute our own attitudes on the subject, one way or the other, to the ex-slaves.

14. "Hant House," "Hag," and "Hag's Trade," *South Carolina Folk Tales*, 77–78, 90, 97. Cf. Davis, "Negro Folk-Lore," 247; Puckett, *Folk Beliefs*, 147; Bascom, "Acculturation among the Gullah Negroes," 49; Bastide, *African Civilisations in the New World*, 108–10.

15. "Hag," *South Carolina Folk Tales*, 90–91. Cf. Bastide, *African Civilisations in the New World*, 103.

16. Liza Small, interviewed by Chandler, WPA Mss.

17. "Hant House," *South Carolina Folk Tales*, 77. Cf. David J. Hufford, "A New Approach to the 'Old Hag': The Nightmare Tradition Reexamined," in Wayland D. Hand, ed., *American Folk Medicine: A Symposium* (Berkeley, 1976), 73–85.

18. "Hant House," *South Carolina Folk Tales*, 77–78.

19. "Hag," *ibid.*, 90. Cf. Davis, "Negro Folk-Lore," 247; Bascom, "Acculturation among the Gullah Negroes," 49. Peterkin describes the same folk belief in her novel *Black April*, 100.

20. "Hag's Trade," *South Carolina Folk Tales*, 97; Lillie Knox, WPA Mss.; Bascom, "Acculturation among the Gullah Negroes," 49.

21. "Hant House" and "Bring Back Us Teef!" *South Carolina Folk Tales*, 78, 75–76; [Zackie Knox], interviewed by Chandler, Aug. 25, 1936, WPA Mss. Cf. Bastide, *African Civilisations in the New World*, 108–10.

22. "Trus' Gawd," collected by Chandler, WPA Mss.; "Trus' Gawd or Ad's Plat-Eye," *South Carolina Folk Tales*, 86–89; Hagar Brown and Matthew Grant, WPA Mss. Cf. Peterkin, *Green Thursday*, 77–78; Davis, "Negro Folk-Lore," 248; Puckett, *Folk-Beliefs*, 130; Ambrose E. Gonzales, *The Black Border: Gullah Stories of the Carolina Coast* (Columbia, 1922), 33.

23. Hackless, interviewed by Chandler, Aug. 3, 1936, and Liza Small, interviewed by Chandler, n.d., WPA Mss. Cf. Peterkin, *Bright Skin*, 51.

24. Sabe Rutledge, WPA Mss.; Arney R. Childs, ed., *Rice Planter and Sportsman: The Recollections of J. Motte Alston* (Columbia, 1953), 121–22; journal of Bishop T. F. Davis, Apr. 2, 1855, quoted in Henry DeSassure Bull, *All Saints Church, Waccamaw, 1739–1968* (Georgetown, 1968), 27. Mariah Heywood, Slave Narratives, 14, part i, 285. On Belin and the Methodist mission to the slaves, see *Our Benefactor: Commemorating 110 Years since His Death on May 19th, 1859* (Murrells Inlet, S.C., 1969); Richard Cameron, *Methodism and Society in Historical Perspective* (Nashville, 1961), 182; William P. Harrison, *The Gospel among the Slaves: A Short Account of Missionary Operations among the African Slaves of the Southern States* (Nashville, 1893), 131, 181, 267–68; Albert Shipp, *History of Methodism in South Carolina* (Nashville, 1884), 452–60. On Glennie and the Episcopal mission to the slaves, see Anthony Toomer Porter, *Led On! Step by Step: Scenes from Clerical, Military, Educational, and Plantation Life in the South, 1828–1898* (New York, 1898), 82–83 (Porter began his career as an assistant to Glennie); "Recollections of a Visit to the Waccamaw," 292–93; *Southern Christian Advocate*, May 23, 1861; *Southern Episcopalian*, 2 (1855), 92–94; Bull, *All Saints Church, Waccamaw*, 24–33; Mason Crum, *Gullah: Negro Life in the Carolina Sea Islands* (Durham, N.C., 1940), 173–231; Susan Markey Fickling, *Slave Conversion in South Carolina, 1830–1860* (Columbia, 1924), 37–39; W. D. Weatherford, *American Churches and the Negro: An Historical Study from Early Slave Days to the Present* (Boston, 1957), 91. Cf. Randall M. Miller's study of Catholic missionaries' largely unsuccessful efforts at slave conversion, "The Failed Mission: The Catholic Church and Black Catholicism in the Old South," in Edward Magdol and Jon Wakelyn, eds., *The Southern Common People: Studies in Nineteenth Century Social History* (Westport, Conn., 1980), 37–54. On the planters' half-hearted support for slave conversion in early South Carolina, see Wood, *Black Majority*, 133–36.

25. Kirke, *Among the Pines*, 43–44.

26. *Ibid.*; "Recollections of a Visit to the Waccamaw," 292–96; Childs, ed., *Rice Planter and Sportsman*, 121; Manuscript diary of Emily Esdaile Weston, 1859, in private possession, *passim* (hereafter cited as Emily Weston diary).

27. Alexander Glennie, *Sermons Preached on Plantations to Congregations of Slaves* (Charleston, 1844), 22–26. But cf. Howard Thurman, *Jesus and the Disinherited* (New York, 1949), 30–31, for examples of slaves' resentment of such texts.

28. James R. Sparkman to Benjamin Allston, March 10, 1858, in J. Harold Easterby, ed., *The South Carolina Rice Plantation as Revealed in the Papers of Robert F. W. Allston* (Chicago, 1945), 349; George C. Rogers, Jr., *The History of Georgetown County, South Carolina* (Columbia, 1970), 357.

29. Whitemarsh Seabrook, quoted in William W. Freehling, *Prelude to*

Civil War: The Nullification Controversy in South Carolina, 1816–1836 (New York, 1966), 335; Whitemarsh Seabrook, *Essay on the Management of Slaves* (Charleston, 1834), 15, 28–30.

30. Glennie, *Sermons.*

31. *Ibid.*, 1–5, 21–27.

32. Malet, *Errand to the South*, 120; Robert F. W. Allston, *Essay on Sea Coast Crops* (Charleston, 1854), 41. On the problem of role boundaries in culture, see Douglas, *Purity and Danger*, 143.

33. Cf. Daryll Forde, ed., *African Worlds: Studies in the Cosmological Ideas and Social Values of African Peoples* (London, 1954); Meyer Fortes, *Oedipus and Job in West African Religion* (Cambridge, 1959); Geoffrey Parrinder, *African Traditional Religion* (London, 1962); William R. Bascom, *Ifa Divination: Communication between Gods and Men in West Africa* (Bloomington, Ind., 1969); E. E. Evans-Pritchard, *Nuer Religion* (Oxford, 1956), and his *Witchcraft, Oracles, and Magic among the Azande* (Oxford, 1937); W. E. Abraham, *The Mind of Africa* (London, 1962), ch. 2; R. S. Rattray, *Religion and Art in Ashanti* (Oxford, 1927); Mbiti, *African Religions*, ch. 3; Melville J. and Frances S. Herskovits, *An Outline of Dahomean Religious Belief* (New York, 1933); Martha Warren Beckwith, *Black Roadways: A Study of Jamaican Folk Life* (Chapel Hill, 1929), chs. 2, 6; Zahan, *Religion, Spirituality, and Thought of Traditional Africa*; Mechal Sobel, *Trabelin' On: The Slave Journey to an Afro-Baptist Faith* (Westport, Conn., 1979). The importance of a continuing Yoruba and Ashanti influence in Afro-American religion and of the declining Bantu religious influence despite Bantu demographic dominance in the New World is discussed in Bastide, *African Civilisations in the New World*, 104–15.

34. Sparkman, "The Negro," in Sparkman Family Papers; Etrulia P. Dozier, ed., "Interview of Mrs. Julia Smalls [*sic*]," *Independent Republic Quarterly*, 4 (July 1970), 32; Rev. John Hunter to Benjamin Allston, Mar. 6, 1858, Benjamin Allston Papers, DUL; Hagar Brown, WPA Mss. On the "shouts" see William Francis Allen, Charles P. Ware, and Lucy McKim Garrison, eds., *Slave Songs of the United States* (New York, 1867), xiv; Charlotte Forten, "Life on the Sea Islands," *Atlantic Monthly*, 13 (May 1864), 593–94, and her *The Journal of Charlotte L. Forten*, ed. Ray L. Billington (New York, 1953), 153, 184, 190, 205; Thomas Wentworth Higginson, "Negro Spirituals," *Atlantic Monthly*, 19 (June 1867), 685–94, and his *Army Life in a Black Regiment* (Boston, 1870), 197–98; Rupert S. Holland, ed., *Letters and Diary of Laura M. Towne: Written from the Sea Islands of South Carolina, 1862–1884* (Cambridge, Mass., 1912), 20–23; Elizabeth Ware Pearson, ed., *Letters from Port Royal* (Boston, 1906), 22–28; Daniel E. Huger Smith, "A Plantation Boyhood," in Alice R. Huger Smith and Herbert Ravenel Sass, eds., *A Carolina Rice Plantation of the Fifties* (New York, 1930), 75–76; [Henry George Spaulding], "Under the Palmetto," *Continental Monthly*, 4 (Aug. 1863), 196–200; Guy Carawan, "Spiritual Singing in the South Carolina Sea Islands," 1959 report in High-

lander Folk School Mss. Records Collection, Tennessee State Library and Archives, Nashville; Dena J. Epstein, *Sinful Tunes and Spirituals: Black Folk Music to the Civil War* (Urbana, 1977), 232–34, 278–87; Robert Winslow Gordon, "Negro 'Shouts' from Georgia," *New York Times Magazine*, Apr. 24, 1927; Zora Neale Hurston, "Shouting," in Nancy Cunard, ed., *Negro: An Anthology* (London, 1934), 49–50; Charles W. Joyner, *Folk Song in South Carolina* (Columbia, 1971), 71–73; Willie Lee Rose, *Rehearsal for Reconstruction: The Port Royal Experiment* (Indianapolis, 1964), 91; Society for the Preservation of Spirituals, *The Carolina Low Country* (New York, 1931), 198–201; Marshall W. Stearns, *The Story of Jazz* (New York, 1958), 68; G. R. Wilson, "The Religion of the American Negro Slave: His Attitude toward Life and Death," *JNH*, 8 (1923), 56. On the relation of hand-clapping and foot-stamping in the "shout" to African drumming, see John Miller Chernoff, *African Rhythm and African Sensibility: Aesthetics and Social Action in African Musical Idioms* (Chicago, 1979); Jahn, *Muntu*, 218–20; Alan Lomax, ed., *Folk Song U.S.A.* (New York, 1947), 421–22. On the African dance tradition see Geoffrey Gorer, *Africa Dances* (London, 1935), and Robert Faris Thompson, "An Aesthetic of the Cool: West African Dance," *Freedomways*, 2 (1966), 97. For examples of the fusion of African dance and spirit possession with Christianity in Afro-Caribbean cultures, see Elsa Goveia, *Slave Society in the British Leeward Islands at the End of the Eighteenth Century* (New Haven, 1965), 247–48; Edward Brathwaite, *The Development of Creole Society in Jamaica, 1770–1820* (Oxford, 1971), 219; Simpson, *Shango Cult in Trinidad*, 155; Erika Bourguignon, "Spirit Possession and Altered States of Consciousness: The Evolution of an Inquiry," in George D. Spindler, ed., *The Making of Psychological Anthropology* (Berkeley, 1978), 479–515.

35. Lillie Knox and Hagar Brown, WPA Mss.; Peterkin, "Finding Peace," in *Green Thursday*, 94–101. Cf. Roland Steiner, "Seeking Jesus," *JAF*, 14 (1901), 672; Watson *et al.*, eds., *God Struck Me Dead*; Beckwith, *Black Roadways*, 163–67; Melville J. Herskovits and Frances S. Herskovits, *Trinidad Village* (New York, 1964), 199–202; George Eaton Simpson, "'Baptismal,' 'Mourning,' and 'Building' Ceremonies of the Shouters of Trinidad," *JAF*, 79 (1965), 537–50; Erika Bourguignon, "Ritual Dissociation and Possession Belief in Caribbean Negro Religion," in Norman E. Whitten, Jr., and John F. Szwed, eds., *Afro-American Anthropology: Contemporary Perspectives* (New York, 1970), 87–101.

36. Malet, *Errand to the South*, 74; Oliphant, *Patriots and Filibusters*, 140–41; Albert Carolina, Slave Narratives, 14, part i, 98; "The Religious Life of the Negro Slave," *Harper's New Monthly Magazine*, 27 (1863), 677; Almira Coffin to Mrs. J. G. Osgood, May 10, 1851, in J. Harold Easterby, ed., "South Carolina through New England Eyes: Almira Coffin's Visit to the Low Country in 1851," *SCHM*, 45 (1944), 131. For a description of the call-and-response pattern in slave music on the Waccamaw, see Malet, *Errand to the South*, 114–15. I presented a paper on the continuing call-and-response

pattern in black preaching based on fieldwork on the Waccamaw in "The Unusual Task of the Gospel Preacher: Afro-American Folk Preaching on Sandy Island, South Carolina" at the American Folklore Society annual meeting in New Orleans in Nov. 1975. Cf. John F. Szwed, "Musical Adaptation among Afro-Americans," *JAF*, 82 (1969), 115, and Alan Lomax, "The Homogeneity of African–Afro-American Musical Style," in Whitten and Szwed, eds., *Afro-American Anthropology*, 181–201. On the emotional quality differentiating black and white versions of Christianity, the master of Mt. Arena on Sandy Island noted, "Constitutionally the negro is emotional, in no case more pronounced than in his religion" (Sparkman, "The Negro," in Sparkman Family Papers). A similar view is expressed by Carter G. Woodson, in his *The History of the Negro Church* (Washington, D.C., 1921), 142–43. A somewhat different interpretation of the differences between black and white Christianity is offered by E. Franklin Frazier, *The Negro Church in America* (New York, 1956), 1–20, and Blassingame, *Slave Community*, 64.

37. Glennie, *Sermons*, 4–5; Coffin to Osgood, May 10, 1851, in Easterby, ed., "South Carolina through New England Eyes," 131; "Recollections of a Visit to the Waccamaw," 292–96.

38. "Read Nineteenth Chapter Matthew," WPA Mss. This and the spirituals cited below were collected in All Saints Parish in the 1930s by Genevieve Willcox Chandler. Her transcriptions of the texts are housed in the WPA Mss. Chandler was instrumental in having John A. Lomax record many of these songs for the Library of Congress in the summers of 1936, 1937, and 1939. His original discs, never pressed for public release, are deposited in the Archive of Folk Culture, LC: AFS 830 A1–B2, 832 A1–B3, 868 A–B2, 877 A1–B2, 903 A1–904 B4, 909 A1–910 B2, 946 A1–B3, 950 A1–B2, 1031 A2–1046 B2, 1300 A1–B3, 1301 A–1303 B, 2692 A–B, 2702 B3, 2711 B1–B3, 2719 A1–B4, 2720 A2–2721 A3, 2722 A1–B2. In his field notes Lomax observes that "the people live in a very primitive style and sing tunes that go back to slavery and earlier times." See John A. Lomax Field Notes, June 6–8, 1939, LC. I have also recorded numerous spirituals still alive in oral tradition in the 1960s and 1970s on the Waccamaw. There are similar references to the Old Testament heroes of the Jews and to Revelation and the Judgment Day in each kind of source.

39. "Don't You Do That," WPA Mss.

40. Pringle, *Chronicles of Chicora Wood*, 27–28; Oliphant, *Patriots and Filibusters*, 141–43; Malet, *Errand to the South*, 117–18; Richard Lathers, *Reminiscences of Richard Lathers: Sixty Years of a Busy Life in South Carolina, Massachusetts, and New York* (New York, 1907), 5. Cf. LeRoy Moore, Jr., "The Spiritual: Soul of Black Religion," *American Quarterly*, 23 (1971), 658–76; Wayman B. McLaughlin, "Symbolism and Mysticism in the Spirituals," *Phylon*, 24 (1963), 69–77.

41. "Sign in the Judgment," WPA Mss. Cf. Frederick Douglass, *Narrative of the Life of Frederick Douglass, an American Slave: Written by Him-*

self (Boston, 1845; rpt. Cambridge, Mass., 1960), 38. On the relation of the spirituals to their African sources, see Marion Alexander Haskell, "Negro 'Spirituals,'" *Century Magazine*, 36 (Aug. 1899), 577–81; Henry Edward Krehbiel, *Afro-American Folk Songs* (New York, 1914), 43, 83ff.; Nicholas G. J. Ballanta-Taylor, *St. Helena Island Spirituals* (New York, 1925), xiv, 61; Erich M. von Hornbostel, "African Negro Music," *International Institute of African Languages and Cultures*, Memorandum 4 (New York, 1928), 33, and his "American Negro Music," *International Review of Missions*, 15 (1926), 748–53; Newman Ivey White, *American Negro Folk Songs* (Cambridge, Mass., 1928), 19–25; Guy B. Johnson, *Folk Culture on St. Helena Island, South Carolina* (Chapel Hill, 1930), 97–126; Guy B. Johnson, "The Negro Spiritual: A Problem in Anthropology," *AA*, 33 (1931), 162–63; George Pullen Jackson, *White and Negro Spirituals* (New York, 1943), 267; Gilbert Chase, *America's Music from the Pilgrims to the Present*, 2d ed. (New York, 1966), 254; Jahn, *Muntu*, 218–20; Janheinz Jahn, *Neo-African Literature: A History of Black Writing* (New York, 1968), 155–66; Bruno Nettl, *An Introduction to Folk Music in the United States* (Detroit, 1960), 54, and his *Folk and Traditional Music of the Western Continents* (Englewood Cliffs, N.J., 1965), 53–75, 118–46; Alan P. Merriam, "Characteristics of African Music," *Journal of the International Folk Music Council*, 11 (1959), 13–19; Alan P. Merriam, "The African Idiom in Music," *JAF*, 75 (1962), 120–30; Le Roi Jones [Amiri Amamu Baraka], *Blues People: Negro Music in White America* (New York, 1963), 44; Irving L. Sablosky, *American Music* (Chicago, 1969), 43; Eileen Southern, *The Music of Black Americans: A History* (New York, 1971), 215–24; Charles W. Joyner, "Music: Origins of Spirituals," in W. Augustus Low and Virgil A. Clift, eds., *Encyclopedia of Black America* (New York, 1981), 581–96.

42. "I'm Hunting for the Stone," WPA Mss.
43. II Kings 5: 1–19; "March Down to Jordan, Halleloo!" WPA Mss.
44. "Little David," WPA Mss.
45. "I Done Started for the Kingdom," WPA Mss.
46. "Come by Here, Lord," WPA Mss.
47. "Listen to the Roll," WPA Mss.
48. "I Will Overcome Some Day," WPA Mss.
49. "How Many Angels in the Band," as sung by Mr. and Mrs. James Moody, Murrells Inlet, S.C., Aug. 20, 1969, recorded by Charles Joyner. Cf. Raboteau, *Slave Religion*, 86; Bastide, *African Civilisations in the New World*, 165; Melville J. Herskovits, "African Gods and Catholic Saints in New World Negro Belief," *AA*, 39 (1937), 635–43.
50. "Don't Get Weary, We're Almost Done," 910 A2, Archive of Folk Culture; "Got to Move My Campin' Ground" and "Way By-and-Bye," WPA Mss. Jacob Stroyer recalled that when slaves were sold from the South Carolina plantation on which he grew up, those left behind would sing "little hymns that they had been accustomed to for the consolation of those who

were going away, such as 'When we all meet in Heaven, There is no parting there.'" *My Life in the South* (Salem, Mass., 1890), 41.

51. Oliphant, *Patriots and Filibusters*, 144.

52. Pringle, *Chronicles of Chicora Wood*, 27–28; "Let's Go to Cane-yun" (Canaan), 903 B2, "Just a Goin' Over Jordan," 1038 A3, "See John the Writer," 1037 B1, Archive of Folk Culture; "I Done Started for the Kingdom" and "If You See John the Writer," WPA Mss.

53. Joyner, *Folk Song*, 93; John Greenway, *American Folksongs of Protest* (Philadelphia, 1953), 78; Higginson, "Negro Spirituals," 691; Welcome Bees, WPA Mss.

54. Malet, *Errand to the South*, 74; Oliphant, *Patriots and Filibusters*, 140–41; Albert Carolina, Slave Narratives, 14, part i, 198. Cf. Woodson, *History of the Negro Church*, 41; Weatherford, *American Churches and the Negro*, 114–15.

55. Jemmy, quoted in Malet, *Errand to the South*, 49–50. On the social position of the man-of-words in African societies, see Dan Ben-Amos, *Sweet Words: Storytelling Events in Benin* (Philadelphia, 1975); Judith Irvine, "Caste and Communication in a Woloj Village" (Ph.D. diss., University of Pennsylvania, 1973); Ruth Finnegan, *Limba Stories and Storytelling* (Oxford, 1966), 64–85; Dan Ben-Amos, "Two Benin Storytellers," in Richard M. Dorson, ed., *American Folklore* (Garden City, N.Y., 1972), 103–14; S. A. Babalola, *The Content and Form of Yoruba Ijala* (Oxford, 1966), 40–55. On the importance of the man-of-words in the African diaspora, see Roger D. Abrahams, *The Man of Words in the West Indies: Performance and the Emergence of Creole Culture* (Baltimore, 1983). For a discussion of such "phenomena of mid-transition" who straddle sacred and secular worlds, see Victor W. Turner, *The Forest of Symbols: Aspects of Ndembu Ritual* (Ithaca, 1967), 110.

56. Malet, *Errand to the South*, 49; Sparkman, "The Negro," Sparkman Family Papers; "Uncle Gabe's Conjur Ball," *South Carolina Folk Tales*, 103; Zackie Knox and Lillie Knox, interviewed by Chandler, WPA Mss. Julia Peterkin, in her novel of Afro-American folklife on the Waccamaw, *Scarlet Sister Mary* (Indianapolis, 1928), 218, describes the continuing power of the black church after emancipation: "They all belonged to Heaven's Gate Church, whose strict rules tried to curb their conduct. They allowed no ground between sinners and Christians. Church members were all Christians, saved from sin. They, only, were the children of God and brothers and sisters of little King Jesus. Everybody else would be damned in Hell." Cf. Raboteau, *Slave Religion*, 136–37; Patricia Guthrie, "Rights of Plantation Members: An Analysis of Praise House Worship and Litigation among 'Gullah' Blacks of St. Helena Island, South Carolina," paper presented at the annual meeting of American Anthropological Association, Dec. 3, 1977. For a comparative perspective on similar phenomena in Brazil, see Bastide, *African Civilisations in the New World*, 92. On the slave preacher's role as a

role model in the slave community, see John W. Blassingame, "Status and Social Structure in the Slave Community," in Randall M. Miller, ed., *The Afro-American Slaves: Community or Chaos* (Malabar, Fla., 1981), 114, 120–21.

57. Sparkman, "The Negro," Sparkman Family Papers; Mariah Heywood, Slave Narratives, 14, part ii, 284; interviews with Mary Small and Henry Small, Aug. 2, 1975, Free Woods, S.C. Such gatherings, without the supervision of whites, were illegal in South Carolina. See David J. McCord, ed., *Statutes at Large of South Carolina* (Columbia, 1840), 8:354. On the Gabriel Prosser and Nat Turner revolts, see Gerald W. Mullin, "Gabriel's Insurrection," in Peter I. Rose, ed., *Americans from Africa*, vol. 2, *Old Memories, New Moods* (New York, 1970), and John B. Duff and Peter M. Mitchell, eds., *The Nat Turner Rebellion: The Historical Event and the Modern Controversy* (New York, 1971). The standard source for the Denmark Vesey plot is Lionel H. Kennedy and Thomas Parker, eds., *An Official Report of the Trials of Sundry Negroes Charged with an Attempt to Raise an Insurrection* (Charleston, 1822), rpt. as John Oliver Killens, ed., *The Trial Record of Denmark Vesey* (Boston, 1970). Other contemporary sources include Edwin C. Holland, *A Refutation of the Calumnies against Southern and Western States: An Account of the Late Intended Insurrection among Blacks* (Charleston, 1822), and [James Hamilton, Jr.], *Narrative of the Conspiracy and Intended Insurrection among a Portion of the Blacks in the State of South Carolina in the Year 1822* (Boston, 1822). There is a ms. trial transcript in [Thomas Bennett], Governor's Message No. 2 to the State Legislature, Nov. 2, 1822, Governors' Papers, SCA. Secondary accounts of the Vesey affair include John Lofton, *Insurrection in South Carolina: The Turbulent World of Denmark Vesey* (Yellow Springs, Ohio, 1964); Richard Wade, "The Vesey Plot: A Reconsideration," *JSH*, 30 (1964), 143–61; Sterling Stuckey, "Remembering Denmark Vesey," *Negro Digest*, 15 (Feb. 1966); Freehling, *Prelude to Civil War*, 52–61; Robert S. Starobin, ed., *Insurrection in South Carolina: The Slave Controversy of 1822* (Englewood Cliffs, N.J., 1970). According to Howard A. Ohline, "Georgetown, South Carolina: Racial Anxieties and Militant Behavior," *SCHM*, 73 (1972), 130–40, the putative slave revolt of 1802 existed only in the anxiety-ridden minds of hysterical whites. The extent of the 1829 insurrection remains unknown, but a few documents in the SCA testify that it did take place and that at least three slaves were executed for their part in it. See the following petitions to the South Carolina State Legislature praying for compensation for executed slaves: Hannah Tait, Nov. 16, 1829, Francis Kinlock, Nov. 19, 1829, and John Coachman, Dec. 15, 1829. See also William Vaught to Senate and House of Representatives praying for compensation for a horse injured while suppressing a supposed insurrection, Nov. 18, 1829; petition of Town Council of Georgetown to State Legislature praying for a refund of money spent in an effort to suppress an insurrection; and [Stephen D. Miller], Governor's Message No. 2 to State Legislature, Dec. 3, 1830, all in SCA.

On the role of slave preachers in stirring up discontent, see Washington, *Black Religion*, 202–4; Raboteau, *Slave Religion*, 318; Vincent Harding, "Religion and Resistance among Ante-Bellum Negroes, 1800–1860," in August Meier and Elliot Rudwick, eds., *The Making of Black America* (New York, 1969), 1:179–97; William C. Suttles, "African Religious Survivals as Factors in American Slave Revolts," *JNH*, 56 (1971), 97–104; Bastide, *African Civilisations in the New World*, 46–47, 104; John Hammond Moore, "A Hymn of Freedom—South Carolina, 1813," *JNH*, 50 (1965), 50–53.

    58. Ball Family Papers, SCL; William Meade, *Sermons Addressed to Masters and Servants, and Published in the Year 1743, by the Rev. Thomas Bacon. . . .* (Winchester, Va., 1813), 197–206.

Notes to "All De Bes' Story"

    1. Cf. W. E. B. DuBois, *The Souls of Black Folk* (Chicago, 1903), 378. For a discussion of important relationships between personal experience narratives (or memorates) and culture, see Lauri Honko, "Memorates and Folk Beliefs," *Journal of the Folklore Institute*, 1 (1963), 5–19. On language as symbolic action, see Kenneth Burke, *Language as Symbolic Action: Essays in Life, Literature, and Method* (Berkeley, 1971), 391; Peter Berger and Thomas Luckmann, *The Social Construction of Reality: A Treatise in the Sociology of Knowledge* (New York, 1966), 47–49; Joseph Church, *Language and the Discovery of Reality* (New York, 1961), 95.

    2. William Wyndham Malet, *An Errand to the South in the Summer of 1862* (London, 1863), 50; Arney R. Childs, ed., *Rice Planter and Sportsman: The Recollections of J. Motte Allston* (Columbia, S.C., 1953), 55–56; Elizabeth W. Allston Pringle, *Chronicles of Chicora Wood* (New York, 1922), 53–54; Albert Carolina, Slave Narratives: A Folk History of Slavery in the United States from Interviews with Former Slaves. Typewritten records prepared by the Federal Writers' Project, 1936–38 (microfilm), 14, part i, 199; Ben Horry, Slave Narratives, 14, part ii, 306, 311.

    3. Pringle, *Chronicles of Chicora Wood*, 351. According to Richard M. Dorson, *American Negro Folk Tales* (New York, 1967), 15, these tales did not come from Africa. Dorson reached this conclusion on the basis of comparison of tale types. The standard indices are Antti Aarne and Stith Thompson, *The Types of the Folk-Tale* (Helsinki, 1961); Erastus Ojo Arewa, "A Classification of the Folktales of Northern East African Cattle Area by Types" (Ph.D. diss., University of California, Berkeley, 1966); Winifred Lambrecht, "A Tale Type Index for Central Africa" (Ph.D. diss., University of California, 1967); Kenneth W. Clarke, "Motif-Index of Folk-Tales from Culture-Area V West Africa" (Ph.D. diss., Indiana University, 1958). For an opposing view, see Daniel J. Crowley, "African Folktales in Afro-America," in John F. Szwed, ed., *Black America* (New York, 1970), 181–83; Daniel J. Crowley, *I Could Talk Old-Story Good: Creativity in Bahamian Folklore* (New York, 1966), and Crowley, ed., *African Folklore in the New World*

(Austin, 1977), all of which emphasize a strongly Africanist position regarding the origin of Afro-American folktales.

4. For folktales from All Saints Parish, see *South Carolina Folk Tales*, compiled by Workers of the Writers' Program of the Work Projects Administration in the State of South Carolina (Columbia, 1941). Those folktales initialed G.W.C. were collected in All Saints Parish by Genevieve Willcox Chandler. Her animal tales are found on pages 2–42. In addition, numerous variants of the animal trickster tales and her extensive collection of human trickster tales are housed in the WPA Mss., SCL. For a discussion of Afro-American folktales in general, see Lawrence W. Levine, *Black Culture and Black Consciousness: Afro-American Folk Thought from Slavery to Freedom* (New York, 1977), 81–135. For a discussion of African folktales, see Ruth Finnegan, *Oral Literature in Africa* (Oxford, 1970), 315–88. On symbolic functions, cf. Victor W. Turner, *The Forest of Symbols: Aspects of Ndembu Ritual* (Ithaca, 1967), 30; Roger D. Abrahams, "Trickster, the Outrageous Hero," in Tristram Potter Coffin, ed., *Our Living Traditions* (New York, 1968), 170.

5. Cf. Arna Bontemps, ed., *The Book of Negro Folklore* (New York, 1958), viii; Roger Bastide, *African Civilisations in the New World*, trans. Peter Green (New York, 1971), 61, 65; Paul Radin, *African Folktales* (Princeton, 1960), 5, and his *The Trickster: A Study in American Indian Mythology* (London, 1956); Melville J. and Frances S. Herskovits, *Dahomean Narrative* (Evanston, Ill., 1958), 99–101; Alan Dundes, "African Tales among the North American Indians," *SFQ*, 29 (1965), 207–19.

6. Cf. Finnegan, *Oral Literature in Africa*, 341–51; Levine, *Black Culture and Black Consciousness*, 102–21; Janheinz Jahn, *Muntu: An Outline of the New African Culture* (New York, 1961), 221.

7. A. M. H. Christensen, *Afro-American Folk Lore Told Round Cabin Fires on the Sea Islands of South Carolina* (Boston, 1892), ix; Mary Douglas, *Natural Symbols: Explorations in Cosmology* (New York, 1973); E. E. Evans-Pritchard, *The Zande Trickster* (Oxford, 1967), 28–30.

8. The trickster-figure in the All Saints tales is a partridge in "Buh Rabbit and Buh Partridge" and "Buh Partridge Pay Buh Rabbit Back" (27–29), a turtle in "Buh Cootah and Buh Deer" (23), and a squirrel in "Buddah Frog, Buddah Squel, and Buddah Rabbit" (25–27), in *South Carolina Folk Tales*. In the savannah areas of West Africa, as among the Bantu peoples generally, the trickster is a little hare. Among the Yoruba he is a tortoise, among the Limba and Luba an antelope, among the Zulu a jackal. In the forested regions of the Ivory Coast, Ghana, and Sierra Leone, as among the Hausa, the Luo, and the Zande, the trickster is a spider. Among the Fante-Ashanti the spider trickster is the famous Anansi. See Denise Paulme, "Literature orde et comportements sociaux en Afrique noire," *L'homme*, 1 (1961), 37–49; Finnegan, *Oral Literature in Africa*, 344–45; Bastide, *African Civilisations in the New World*, 252.

9. WPA Mss.; *South Carolina Folk Tales,* 7–11. Tale Type 122D. Motif K 553.1. This tale is found in Africa and among Afro-Americans but is extremely rare in Europe. See Alan Dundes, "African and Afro-American Tales," in Crowley, ed., *African Folklore,* 48–49. Cf. Dorson, *American Negro Folk Tales,* 83–86. See also Guy B. Johnson, *Folk Culture on St. Helena Island, South Carolina* (Chapel Hill, 1930), 137; Charles C. Jones, Jr., *Negro Myths from the Georgia Coast* (New York, 1888), 123; Joel Chandler Harris, *Nights with Uncle Remus* (Boston, 1881), 12; Franz Boas, "Notes on Mexican Folk-Lore," *JAF,* 25 (1912), 204–60; Emily N. Harvey, "A Br'er Rabbit Story," *ibid.,* 32 (1919), 443–44; John H. Johnson, "Folklore from Antigua, British West Indies," *ibid.,* 34 (1921), 40–88; W. T. Cleare, "Four Folk-Tales from Fortune Island, Bahamas," *ibid.,* 30 (1917), 228–29; "Folk Tales from Students in Tuskegee Institute, Alabama," *ibid.,* 32 (1919), 397; A. M. Bacon and Elsie Clews Parsons, "Folk-Lore from Elizabeth City County, Virginia," *ibid.,* 35 (1922), 250–327; and the following by Elsie Clews Parsons: *Folk-Lore of the Sea Islands, South Carolina* (Cambridge, Mass., 1923), 14, 19, 35, 40–42; *Folk-Lore of the Antilles, French and English* (Cambridge, Mass., 1923), 41–47; "Folk-Lore from Aiken, S.C.," *JAF,* 34 (1921), 1–39; "Tales from Guilford County, North Carolina," *ibid.,* 30 (1917), 168–200; Finnegan, *Oral Literature in Africa,* 352. Mary Douglas notes that "food sharing symbolizes social relationships and can therefore express both intimacy and distance," in "Deciphering a Meal," *Daedalus,* 101 (1972), 61–81. Morton H. Fried emphasizes that "who eats with whom?" has always been a political question, in "The Study of Politics in Anthropology," in Sol Tax and Leslie G. Freeman, eds., *Horizons of Anthropology,* 2d ed. (Chicago, 1977), 270.

10. WPA Mss.; *South Carolina Folk Tales,* 20–21. Tale Type 1525. Motif K 1860. Cf. Dorson, *American Negro Folk Tales,* 91–92. See also Dorson's articles, "Negro Tales," *Western Folklore,* 13 (1954), 83–84, and "Negro Tales from Bolivar County, Mississippi," *SFQ,* 19 (1955), 105–6; G. Johnson, *Folk Culture,* 146; Christensen, *Afro-American Folk Lore,* 26; Joel Chandler Harris, *Uncle Remus, His Songs and His Sayings: The Folklore of the Old Plantation* (New York, 1881), 72; and the following by Elsie Clews Parsons: "The Provenience of Certain Negro Folk-Tales," *Folk-Lore,* 38 (1917), 408–14; "Folk-Lore from Aiken," 1–39; "Tales from Guilford County," 168–200; *Folk-Lore of the Antilles,* 29–31; and *Folk-Lore of the Sea Islands,* 44.

11. *South Carolina Folk Tales,* 38–39. Tale Type 15. Motifs K 72 and K401.1. There is a similar Waccamaw Neck version in the WPA Mss. This tale is quite widely reported in Africa and in Afro-American tradition, but not in Anglo-American tradition. Arewa ("Classification of the Folktales") cites five African versions, Lambrecht ("Tale Type Index") four, and Clarke ("Motif-Index") two. Cf. Dorson, *American Negro Folk Tales,* 68–71. See also G. Johnson, *Folk Culture,* 139–40; Sadie E. Stewart, "Seven Folk Tales

from the Sea Islands, South Carolina," *JAF*, 32 (1919), 394–96; Christensen, *Afro-American Folk Lore*, 13; Elsie Clews Parsons, *Folk-Tales of Andros Island, Bahamas* (Cambridge, Mass., 1918), 1–2, and her *Folk-Lore of the Sea Islands*, 5–11.

12. *South Carolina Folk Tales*, 35; interview with Henry Small, Free Woods, S.C., Aug. 2, 1975; Ellen Godfrey, Slave Narratives, 14, part ii, 161; Ben Horry, Slave Narratives, 14, part ii, 309–10, 317.

13. *South Carolina Folk Tales*, 25–27. Tale Type 73. Motif K 611. Aarne and Thompson (*Types of the Folk-Tale*) list no fewer than ten African versions of this tale type. Arewa ("Classification of the Folktales") gives African versions of this as his type 2057; Clarke ("Motif-Index") lists African versions under motif K 621. Cf. Parsons, *Folk-Lore of the Sea Islands*, 26–78. See also Parsons, "Tales from Guilford County," 168–200; Bacon and Parsons, "Folklore from Elizabeth City County," 250–327; Dundes, "African and Afro-American Tales," 42. The same motif (K 611 "Escape by Putting the Captor off Guard"), although by different means, is found in Dorson, *American Negro Folk Tales*, 105.

14. *South Carolina Folk Tales*, 32–33. Cf. the following by Parsons: *Folk-Lore of the Sea Islands*, 30–32; "Folk-Lore from Aiken," 1–39; and "Ten Folk Tales from the Cape Verde Islands," *JAF*, 30 (1917), 230–38; see also A. Gerber, "Uncle Remus Traced to the Old World," *ibid.*, 6 (1893), 245–57; Cleare, "Four Folk Tales from Fortune Island," 228–29; Harris's *Uncle Remus Songs and Sayings*, 98, *Nights with Uncle Remus*, 230–41, and *Uncle Remus and His Friends* (Boston, 1892), 77; Christensen, *Afro-American Folk Lore*, 73–80.

15. WPA Mss.; *South Carolina Folk Tales*, 3–4. Motifs K 1055, H 1376.5. Dundes ("African and Afro-American Tales," 44) points out that this tale has clear-cut African parallels but not European ones. See also Edwin W. Smith and Andrew M. Dale, *The Ila-Speaking People of Northern Rhodesia* (London, 1920), 2:378–90. Cf. Dorson, *American Negro Folk Tales*, 79–80; Parsons, *Folk-Lore of the Sea Islands*, 19, 59. See also Harris, *Nights with Uncle Remus*, 141; Christensen, *Afro-American Folk Lore*, 54–57; Jones, *Negro Myths from the Georgia Coast*, 1; Zora Neale Hurston, *Mules and Men* (Philadelphia, 1935), 141–42. There is a recorded version of this tale on Folkways Record P417B, *Negro Folk Music of Alabama*, vol. 1. For an interesting exchange over a version of this tale collected by Richard Dorson, see William D. Piersen, "An African Background for Afro-American Folktales?" *JAF*, 84 (1971), 212–13, and Dorson's response in "African and Afro-American Folklore," *ibid.*, 88 (1975), 160.

16. *South Carolina Folk Tales*, 28–29. Motifs K 585, J 2413.42. Cf. G. Johnson, *Folk Culture*, 146; Joel Chandler Harris, *Told By Uncle Remus* (New York, 1905), 126–41; Arthur Huff Fauset, "Negro Folk-Tales from the South (Alabama, Mississippi, Louisiana)," *JAF*, 40 (1927), 213–303; and the following by Elsie Clews Parsons: "Folk Tales Collected at Miami, Florida," *ibid.*, 30 (1917), 226; "Folk Tales from Students in Tuskegee Insti-

tute," 397; *Folk-Lore of the Sea Islands*, 33; "Folk-Lore from Aiken," 1–39. This tale is not reported in Europe but is well known in Africa. See Franz Boas and Kamba Simango, "Tales and Proverbs of the Vandau of Portuguese South Africa," *JAF*, 35 (1922), 180. Lambrecht ("Tale Type Index") reports this tale in Central Africa, and Arewa ("Classification of the Folktales") lists four versions from East Africa.

17. WPA Mss.; *South Carolina Folk Tales*, 21–23. Tale Type 1074. Motifs K 11.1, K 1840. Dundes concludes the tale is African, not European ("African and Afro-American Tales," 43). Cf. Dorson, *American Negro Folk Tales*, 86–87. See also Stewart, "Seven Folk Tales from the Sea Islands," 394–96; Christensen, *Afro-American Folk Lore*, 5; Jones, *Negro Myths*, 5; Harris, *Uncle Remus Songs and Sayings*, xiii–xiv, 86; G. Johnson, *Folk Culture*, 148; Parsons, *Folk-Lore of the Antilles*, 78–80; Dorson, "Negro Tales from Bolivar County," 106.

18. WPA Mss. Tale Types 4, 72. Arewa ("A Classification of the Folktales") reports this tale from East Africa as his type 1631. Clarke ("Motif-Index of Folk-Tales") cites five West African versions. Cf. Parsons, *Folk-Lore of the Sea Islands*, 53–55; Bacon and Parsons, "Folklore from Elizabeth City County," 265–66; Jones, *Negro Myths*, 27–31. For an interesting dispute over the appropriate classification of this tale, see William R. Bascom, "Africa and the Folklorist," *JAF*, 86 (1973), 258, and Dorson, "African and Afro-American Folklore," 160n. Dorson himself collected an African version of this tale, but continued to regard it as European. See Richard M. Dorson, ed., *African Folklore* (Bloomington, Ind., 1972), 15. Victor W. Turner discusses various forms of symbolic inversions in ritual in the second chapter of his *The Ritual Process: Structure and Anti-Structure* (Chicago, 1969).

19. *South Carolina Folk Tales*, 25–27, 28–29, 32–33.

20. WPA Mss.; *South Carolina Folk Tales*, 31–32. Motif A 2494.4.4. Cf. Dorson, *American Negro Folk Tales*, 94–96. See also Hurston, *Mules and Men*, 146–47, and Dorson, "Negro Tales from Bolivar County," 107. There is a recorded Gullah version of the tale on Library of Congress recording L464A4, recited by a white man in an imitation of the Gullah creole.

21. WPA Mss.; *South Carolina Folk Tales*, 19–20. Tale Type 66B. Motif K6707.3. The tale is widely reported in Africa, but not in Europe. Lambrecht ("A Tale-Type Index") lists it under her Type 1233. See also the Caribbean listings in Helen L. Flowers, "A Classification of the Folktales of the West Indies by Types and Motifs" (Ph.D. diss., Indiana University, 1952). For a description of an Egyptian version of the same story see D. J. M. Muffett, "Uncle Remus Was a Hausaman?" *SFQ*, 39 (1975), 153. Cf. Parsons, *Folk-Lore of the Sea Islands*, 143, and her "Tales from Guilford County," 168–200; Christensen, *Afro-American Folk Lore*, 62; Emma M. Backus, "Folk Tales from Georgia," *JAF*, 13 (1900), 19–32; William Owens, "Folklore of the Southern Negroes" (1877), in Jackson, ed., *The Negro and His Folklore in Nineteenth Century Periodicals* (Austin, 1967), 151. Attempts by

larger animals to trick smaller creatures into thinking them dead are discussed in Levine, *Black Culture and Black Consciousness*, 119.

22. *South Carolina Folk Tales*, 29–31. Tale Type 175. Motif K 741.
Alan Dundes makes a strong case for an African source in Afro-American
versions of this tale in "African and Afro-American Tales," 43. For other
South Carolina versions of the "Tar Baby" tale, see Parsons, *Folk-Lore of the
Sea Islands*, 12, 25; Ambrose E. Gonzales, *The Black Border: Gullah Stories
of the Carolina Coast* (Columbia, 1922), 343–46; Henry C. Davis, "Negro
Folk-Lore in South Carolina," *JAF*, 27 (1914), 241–54; Christensen, *Afro-
American Folk Lore*, 62. See also Parsons, *Folk-Lore of the Antilles*, 48–52,
and Harris, *Uncle Remus Songs and Sayings*, 7. The Tar Baby is well known
in creole languages other than Gullah: it is told in the Krio creole of Sierra
Leone as well as in Seychellois creole, according to Loreto Todd, *Pidgins and
Creoles* (London, 1974), 70. The same story is told among the Akan of
Ghana as "Anansi and the Gum Ball," in which the trickster hero is a spider.
An Ewe version is found in A. B. Ellis, *The Ewe Speaking Peoples of the Slave
Coast of West Africa* (1890; rpt. Netherlands, 1966), 276–77. James Fer-
nandez calls the rhetorical device "compensatory compensation." See his
"Persuasions and Performances: Of the Beast in Every Body . . . and the
Metaphors of Everyman," in Clifford Geertz, ed., *Myth, Symbol, and Cul-
ture* (New York, 1971), 39–60.

23. *South Carolina Folk Tales*, 27–28. Motif J 2413.42. Cf. Dorson,
American Negro Folk Tales, 349–50. See also Parsons, *Folk-Lore of the Sea
Islands*, 33–35; G. Johnson, *Folk Culture*, 146–47; Fauset, "Negro Folk-
Tales," 213–303; Harris, *Told by Uncle Remus*, 126–41.

24. Sabe Rutledge, WPA Mss. Cf. Finnegan, *Oral Literature in Africa*,
351; Ethel M. Albert, " 'Rhetoric,' 'Logic,' and 'Poetics' in Burundi," *AA*, 66
(1964), 35–54; John C. Messenger's analysis of how indirection serves the
same function in a different context: "The Role of Proverbs in a Nigerian
Judicial System," *Southwestern Journal of Anthropology*, 15 (1959), 64–73.

25. "John" tales were first brought to national attention by two black
folklorists, Zora Neale Hurston and J. Mason Brewer. See Hurston's "High
John de Conquer," *American Mercury*, 57 (1943), 450–58, and Brewer's
"John Tales," *Publications of the Texas Folklore Society*, 21 (1946), 81–104.
For additional discussions of the John cycle, see Richard M. Dorson, *Ameri-
can Folklore* (Chicago, 1959), 186; Abrahams, "Trickster," 175; Harry C.
Oster, "Negro Humor: John and Old Marster," *Journal of the Folklore Insti-
tute*, 5 (1968), 42–57; John Q. Anderson, "Old John and the Master," *SFQ*,
25 (1961), 195–97; Fred O. Weldon, "Negro Folktale Heroes," *Publications of the Texas Folklore Society*, 24 (1959), 170–89; Sterling Stuckey,
"Through the Prism of Folklore: The Black Ethos in Slavery," *Massachusetts
Review*, 9 (1968), 426–27. For a comparative perspective, see Roger Bastide's discussion of Père Jean tales from elsewhere in the New World, in his
African Civilisation in the New World, 179–80. The rhetorical strategy that
identifies unpleasant necessities with accepted values is discussed by James

Fernandez, in "Poetry in Motion: Being Moved by Amusement, by Mockery, and by Mortality in the Asturian Countryside," *New Literary History*, 8 (1977), 459–80, as moving things through "quality space."

26. WPA Mss. Motif K 842. For examples of the same tale with animal trickster figures, rather than the human trickster, see G. Johnson, *Folk Culture*, 137–38; Parsons, *Folk-Lore of the Sea Islands*, 40–42; Dorson, *American Negro Folk Tales*, 84–86; Harris, *Uncle Remus Songs and Sayings*, nos. 23, 29, and *Nights with Uncle Remus*, nos. 31–32. For a discussion of the social interaction involved in such fabrication, see Erving Goffman, *Frame Analysis* (New York, 1974), ch. 4. See also Gilbert Osofsky's introduction to his *Puttin' On Ole Massa* (New York, 1969).

27. "The One 'Bout Jack," WPA Mss. For comparative versions see n. 26 above.

28. "Story 'Bout John," WPA Mss. There are at least two other All Saints versions of this tale—"John's Richness," WPA Mss., and "Caught the Old Coon," which I collected from Henry Small, Free Woods, S.C., Aug. 2, 1975. Motif K 1956. Cf. Dorson, *American Negro Folk Tales*, 126–29; Hurston, *Mules and Men*, 111–12; Parsons, *Folk-Lore of the Antilles*, 282–84; Roger D. Abrahams, *Deep Down in the Jungle: Negro Narrative Folklore from the Streets of Philadelphia* (Hatboro, Pa., 1964), 222–24. On the complexities of plantation paternalism, cf. Eugene D. Genovese, *Roll, Jordan, Roll: The World the Slaves Made* (New York, 1974), 3–7, 656–58.

29. "Strong Man Jack," in WPA Mss. Type 1612. Motif K 1961. Cf. J. Mason Brewer, *Humorous Folk Tales of the South Carolina Negro* (Orangeburg, S.C., 1945), 3–4; Dorson, *American Negro Folk Tales*, 131–32; Oster, "Negro Humor," 43–44; Parsons, *Folk-Lore of the Antilles*, 284–85.

30. "Go-lias and the Devil," WPA Mss. I collected a version of this tale in July 1964 in DeLand, Fla., from a black informant who called the hero "John Henry." Cf. Hurston, *Mules and Men*, 197–98; Dorson, *American Negro Folk Tales*, 132–35, 262–63.

31. "Another One Mom Phillipa Tales," WPA Mss. This story is similar to Dorson's "Efan and the Panter," in his *American Negro Folk Tales*, 130–31. A related motif is K 1951.

32. Cf. Evans-Pritchard, *Zande Trickster*, 28–30; Levine, *Black Culture and Black Consciousness*, 131; Abrahams, "Trickster," 170.

33. Cf. Hurston, "High John de Conquer," 451–52; Kenneth Burke, *Permanence and Change* (Indianapolis, 1965), 69–70.

34. Sabe Rutledge, WPA Mss. On the use of paralinguistics in storytelling, see Parsons, *Folk-Lore of the Sea Islands*, xx–xxi; Gregory Bateson, "A Theory of Play and Fantasy," in his *Steps toward an Ecology of Mind* (New York, 1972), 177–93, and his "The Position of Humor in Human Communication," in Heinz von Foerster, ed., *Cybernetics* (New York, 1953), 1–47. On the relations between storytellers and their communities, see Barbara Kirshenblatt-Gimblett, "A Parable in Context: A Social Interactional Analysis of Storytelling Performance," in Dan Ben-Amos and Kenneth S. Gold-

stein, eds., *Folklore: Performance and Communication* (The Hague, 1975), 105–30; Linda Degh, *Folktales and Society: Storytelling in a Hungarian Peasant Community* (Bloomington, Ind., 1969), 61, and *passim*; and Douglas, *Natural Symbols*, 44. On such social situations as storytelling, see Erving Goffman, "The Neglected Situation," *AA*, 66 (1964), 133–36. For a discussion of the social features of folk narrative performance, see Dan Ben-Amos, "Folklore in African Society," in Bernth Lindfors, ed., *The Forms of Folklore in Africa: Narrative, Poetic, Gnomic, Dramatic* (Austin, 1977), 22–29. Both the verbal action of the story and the behavioral response of the audience were part of a continuum of social action. In many respects, judging from my own observation of modern Afro-American storytelling contexts in All Saints Parish, storytelling is nearly as communal an experience as singing or religious services.

35. Cf. Levine, *Black Culture and Black Consciousness*, 90; James Peacock, *Rites of Modernization: Symbolic and Social Aspects of Indonesian Proletarian Drama* (Chicago, 1968), 236; Mary Douglas, *Purity and Danger: An Analysis of Concepts of Pollution* (London, 1966), 62–63; Richard Bauman, "Verbal Art as Performance," *AA*, 77 (1975), 293.

36. Sabe Rutledge, WPA Mss. For a description of similar paralinguistic aspects of African narration, see Dan Ben-Amos, "The Elusive Audience of Benin Storytellers," *Journal of the Folklore Institute*, 9 (1972), 39–43, and his "Two Benin Storytellers," in Dorson, ed., *African Folklore*, 177–84; S. A. Babalola, *The Content and Form of Yoruba Ijala* (Oxford, 1966), 40–86; Gordon Innes, "Some Features of Theme and Style in Mende Folktales," *Sierra Leone Language Review*, 3 (1964), 6–19; Finnegan, *Oral Literature in Africa*, 346–50. On the distinction between functions and uses, see Alan P. Merriam, *The Anthropology of Music* (Evanston, Ill., 1964), 209–27. Cf. A. R. Radcliffe-Browne, "On the Concept of Function in Social Science," *AA*, 37 (1935), 394–402, and his *Structure and Function in Primitive Society* (London, 1952). Radcliffe-Browne was a leader of the structural-functional school of British social anthropologists, whose interest in folktales was limited to such narratives as could be shown to have a social function.

37. *South Carolina Folk Tales*, 7. Cf. Dorson, *American Negro Folk Tales*, 114–15; Hurston, *Mules and Men*, 153; Fauset, "Negro Folk-Tales," 241–42; Parsons, *Folk-Lore of the Sea Islands*, 118–19; Jones, *Negro Myths*, 25–26; Harris, *Nights with Uncle Remus*, 362; Melville J. and Francis S. Herskovits, *Suriname Folk-Lore* (New York, 1936), 141.

38. WPA Mss.; *South Carolina Folk Tales*, 40–41. Tale Type 2. Motifs K 1021, A 2325.1, A 2332.4.1. Cf. Dorson, *American Negro Folk Tales*, 89–91; Parsons, *Folk-Lore of the Sea Islands*, 14ff.; Portia Smiley, "Folk-Lore from Virginia, South Carolina, Alabama, Georgia, and Florida," *JAF*, 32 (1919), 361; Harris, *Uncle Remus Songs and Sayings*, 122, and *Nights with Uncle Remus*, 185; Emma Backus, "Tales of the Rabbit from Georgia Negroes," *JAF*, 12 (1899), 108–15; Gerber, "Uncle Remus Traced to the Old World," 245–57; Christensen, *Afro-American Folk Lore*, 26. For more

general discussion of this widely diffused tale type, see Stith Thompson, *The Folktale* (New York, 1946), 119–20, and Alexander H. Krappe, *The Science of Folklore* (New York, 1930), 61.

39. On the application of psychological analysis to folktales, see J. L. Fischer, "The Sociopsychological Analysis of Folktales," *Current Anthropology*, 4 (1963), 235–95; Erich Fromm, *The Forgotten Language: An Introduction to the Understanding of Dreams, Fairy Tales, and Myths* (New York, 1951); Eric Berne, "The Mythology of Dark and Fair: Psychiatric Use of Folklore," *JAF*, 72 (1959), 1–13; Bruno Bettelheim, *The Uses of Enchantment: The Meaning and Importance of Fairy Tales* (New York, 1976). On psychological approaches to trickster tales specifically, see Carl G. Jung, "On the Psychology of the Trickster Figure," in Radin, *The Trickster*, 195–211. Essentially psychological approaches to Afro-American folktales are taken by Marshall Fishwick in "Uncle Remus vs. John Henry: Folk Tension," *Western Folklore*, 20 (1961), 77–82, and Bernard Wolfe in "Uncle Remus and the Malevolent Rabbit," *Commentary*, 8 (1949), 31–41. For a discussion of the importance of status in antebellum and modern southern society, see James McBride Dabbs, *The Southern Heritage* (New York, 1958), 30–34, 110–11, 196–97.

40. Hagar Brown, Slave Narratives, 14, part i, 110; Gullah proverb, collected by Genevieve Willcox Chandler, Murrells Inlet, S.C., WPA Mss. Cf. a Gullah version of a widely diffused proverb that Julia Peterkin used in her story-cycle of black folklife in All Saints Parish, *Green Thursday* (New York, 1924), 130: "Eby back is fitted to de bu'den." The rhetorical phenomenon by which the definition of a situation embraces a strategy for handling the situation is termed "entitlement" by Kenneth Burke (*Language as Symbolic Action*, 359–79).

41. Cf. Stuckey, "Through the Prism of Folklore," 417–37; Osofsky, ed., *Puttin' On Ole Massa*, 21; Donald C. Simmons, "Protest Humor: Folkloristic Reaction to Prejudice," *American Journal of Psychiatry*, 120 (1963), 567–70; Abrahams, "Trickster," 172; Raymond A. and Alice H. Bauer, "Day to Day Resistance to Slavery," *JNH*, 27 (1942), 388–419; Eugene D. Genovese, "Rebelliousness and Docility in the Negro Slave: A Critique of the Elkins Thesis," *Civil War History*, 13 (1967), 293–314; George M. Frederickson and Christopher Lasch, "Resistance to Slavery," *Civil War History*, 13 (1967), 315–29; Levine, *Black Culture and Black Consciousness*, 116–24. The proverb is quoted in Genovese, *Roll, Jordan, Roll*, 605.

42. Cf. Genovese, *Roll, Jordan, Roll*, 656–68; Eric J. Hobsbawm, *Primitive Rebels: Studies in Archaic Forms of Social Movement in the Nineteenth and Twentieth Centuries* (Manchester, England, 1959), 24–25.

43. A straightforward expression of the masters' stereotype of their slaves in All Saints Parish was written by Edward Thomas Heriot to his Scottish cousin, Anna Bruce Cunningham, Apr. 20, 1853: "I manage them as my children." See Edward Thomas Heriot Papers, DUL. See also Malet, *Errand to the South*, 116. On closed systems, see Erving Goffman, *Asylums: Essays*

on the Social Situation of Mental Patients and Other Inmates (Garden City, N.Y., 1961), xiii. On the response to stereotypes, see Roger D. Abrahams, "The Negro Stereotype: Negro Folklore and the Riots," *JAF*, 83 (1970), 231. On storytelling as a form of cultural action, see Clifford Geertz, *The Interpretation of Cultures* (New York, 1973), 448–53; Paul Ricoeur, "The Model of the Text: Meaningful Action Considered as Text," *Social Research*, 38 (1971), 529–62.

Notes to *"Gullah: A Creole Language"*

1. Elizabeth W. Allston Pringle, *Chronicles of Chicora Wood* (New York, 1922), 53–4, 351; Edmund Kirke [James Roberts Gilmore], *Among the Pines: or, The South in Secession-Time* (New York, 1862), 18–19; Arney R. Childs, ed., *Rice Planter and Sportsman: The Recollections of J. Motte Alston* (Columbia, 1953), 55–56; William Wyndham Malet, *An Errand to the South in the Summer of 1862* (London, 1863), 49–50; Joseph LeConte, *The Autobiography of Joseph LeConte* (New York, 1903), 28–30; Henry W. Ravenel, "Recollections of Southern Plantation Life," *Yale Review*, 25 (1936), 775–77; William P. Harrison, *The Gospel among the Slaves: A Short Account of Missionary Operations among the African Slaves of the Southern States* (Nashville, 1893), 306; Laurence Oliphant, *Patriots and Filibusters; or Incidents of Political and Exploratory Travel* (Edinburgh, 1860), 140, 144; "An Englishman in South Carolina," *Continental Monthly*, 2 (1862), 692–93; Edward King, *The Great South: A Record of Journeys* (Hartford, Conn., 1875), 429.

2. A speech community is defined linguistically as "a community sharing knowledge of rules for the conduct and interpretation of speech. Such sharing comprises knowledge of at least one form of speech, and knowledge also of its patterns of use. Both conditions are necessary." See Dell Hymes, *Foundations in Sociolinguistics: An Ethnographic Approach* (Philadelphia, 1974), 51; John Gumperz, "The Speech Community," in Pier Paolo Giglioli, ed., *Language and Social Context* (Harmondsworth, England, 1972), 219–31. For a discussion of the relationships between language and community, see Roger D. Abrahams, "Talking My Talk: Black English and Social Segmentation in Black Communities," *Florida FL Reporter*, 10 (1972), 29–58. On relationships between culture and identity, see A. Irving Hallowell, *Culture and Experience* (Philadelphia, 1955), 75–100. On the role of language in the pressure of groups upon individuals, see Lucien Febvre, "History and Psychology," in Peter Burke, ed., *A New Kind of History: From the Writings of Lucien Febvre*, trans. K. Folka (New York, 1973), 4.

3. Ben Horry, in Slave Narratives: A Folk History of Slavery in the United States from Interviews with Former Slaves. Typewritten records prepared by the Federal Writers' Project, 1936–38 (microfilm), 14, part ii, 323, 325; Welcome Bees, Slave Narratives, 14, part i, 49; Patricia Causey Nichols, "Linguistic Change in Gullah: Sex, Age, and Mobility" (Ph.D. diss.,

Stanford University, 1976), 86–111, esp. 104–7. Nichols's dissertation was based on fieldwork in All Saints Parish in the 1970s. See also Irma Cunningham, "A Syntactic Analysis of Sea Island Creole ('Gullah')" (Ph.D. diss., University of Michigan, 1970), 21–22, 200–201; William A. Stewart, "Continuity and Change in American Negro Dialects," *Florida FL Reporter*, 6 (1968), 3; Loreto Todd, *Pidgins and Creoles* (London, 1974), 17. Cf. Dennis R. Craig, "Education and Creole English in the West Indies: Some Sociolinguistic Factors," in Dell Hymes, ed., *Pidginization and Creolization of Languages* (Cambridge, 1971), 382.

4. Welcome Bees, Slave Narratives, 14, part i, 50; Gabe Lance, Slave Narratives, 14, part iii, 91; Ben Horry, Slave Narratives, 14, part ii, 320; Ellen Godfrey, Slave Narratives, 14, part ii, 154.

5. Louisa Brown, Slave Narratives, 14, part i, 115; Pringle, *Chronicles of Chicora Wood*, 168.

6. Mariah Heywood, Slave Narratives, 14, part ii, 284; Ben Horry, Slave Narratives, 14, part ii, 322, 309.

7. Mariah Heywood, Slave Narratives, 14, part ii, 285; Ben Horry, Slave Narratives, 14, part ii, 310; Patricia C. Nichols, "*To* and *From* in Gullah: An Evolutionary View," paper presented at annual meeting of Linguistic Society of America, San Diego, Calif., Dec. 1973; Nichols, "Linguistic Change in Gullah," 65–82.

8. Welcome Bees, Slave Narratives, 14, part i, 49; Elizabeth Collins, *Memories of the Southern States* (Taunton, England, 1865), 17; Charles A. Ferguson, "Aspects of Copula and the Notion of Simplicity: A Study of Normal Speech, Baby Talk, and Pidgins," in Hymes, ed., *Pidginization and Creolization of Languages*, 141–50; Ralph W. Fasold, "One Hundred Years from Syntax to Phonology," in Sanford Steever *et al.*, eds., *Diachronic Syntax* (Chicago, 1976), 79–87; J. L. Dillard, *Black English: Its History and Usage in the United States* (New York, 1972), 49; Stewart, "Continuity and Change in American Negro Dialects," 3.

9. Hagar Brown, Slave Narratives, 14, part i, 110; Ellen Godfrey, Slave Narratives, 14, part ii, 156; Lorenzo Dow Turner, *Africanisms in the Gullah Dialect* (Chicago, 1949), 216.

10. Collins, *Memories of the Southern States*, 19; Hagar Brown, Slave Narratives, 14, part i, 109; Turner, *Africanisms in the Gullah Dialect*, 209–13.

11. Turner, *Africanisms in the Gullah Dialect*, 225–27; Todd, *Pidgins and Creoles*, 67; Joseph H. Greenberg, "Africa as a Linguistic Area," in William R. Bascom and Melville J. Herskovits, eds., *Continuity and Change in African Cultures* (Chicago, 1959), 23; William A. Stewart, "Foreign Language Teaching Methods in Quasi-Foreign Language Situations," in William A. Stewart, ed., *Non-Standard Speech and the Teaching of English* (Washington, D.C., 1964), 18; B. Comrie, *Aspect* (Cambridge, 1976); Ralph W. Fasold, *Tense Marking in Black English: A Linguistic and Social Analysis* (Arlington, Va., 1972).

12. Ellen Godfrey, Slave Narratives, 14, part ii, 154, 159, 162; *South Carolina Folk Tales*, compiled by Workers of the Writers' Program of the Work Projects Administration in the State of South Carolina (Columbia, 1941), 93 (collected by Genevieve Willcox Chandler in All Saints Parish); Ben Horry, Slave Narratives, 14, part ii, 312, 300. Cf. John Rickford, "The Insights of the Mesolect," in David DeCamp and Ian F. Hancock, eds., *Pidgins and Creoles: Current Trends and Prospects* (Washington, D.C., 1974).

13. Ellen Godfrey, Slave Narratives, 14, part ii, 165; Welcome Bees, Slave Narratives, 14, part i, 50; Ben Horry, Slave Narratives, 14, part ii, 299; Cunningham, "Syntactic Analysis of Sea Island Creole," 84; "Grandma Kit and Aunt Mariah Heywood," WPA Mss., SCL.

14. Hagar Brown, Slave Narratives, 14, part i, 283; Collins, *Memories of the Southern States*, 80. This continuity was also manifested in Afro-American speech communities elsewhere in the slave South and in the Caribbean as well. See Melville J. Herskovits, *The Myth of the Negro Past* (New York, 1941; rpt. Boston, 1958), 283; Todd, *Pidgins and Creoles*, 283.

15. Margaret Bryant, Slave Narratives, 14, part i, 145; Hagar Brown, Slave Narratives, 14, part i, 110; Hagar Brown, WPA Mss.; David DeCamp, "Toward a Generative Analysis of a Post-Creole Speech Continuum," in Hymes, ed., *Pidginization and Creolization of Languages*, 363; Ben Horry, Slave Narratives, 14, part ii, 316; William A. Stewart, "Patterns of Grammatical Change in Gullah," paper read in symposium Society and Culture in South Carolina, Charleston, Mar. 27, 1976; Turner, *Africanisms in the Gullah Dialect*, 247. Patricia C. Nichols analyzes *enty* as *ain't ee*, personal communication, Oct. 19, 1981.

16. John Bennett, "Gullah: A Negro Patois," *South Atlantic Quarterly*, 7 (1908), 340. For similar sentiments see Reed Smith, *Gullah* (Columbia, 1926), 22–23; Ambrose Gonzales, *The Black Border: Gullah Stories of the Carolina Coast* (Columbia, 1922), 10–17.

17. Systematic study of pidgin and creole languages is a relatively recent phenomenon. Hugo Schuchardt, who published an article on Lingua Franca early in this century ("Die Lingua Franca," *Zietschrift fur Romanische Philologie*, 33 [1909], 441–61), is generally considered the father of pidgin scholarship. Creole scholarship did not commence until the 1930s with the work of John Reinecke on Hawaiian Creole (*Language and Dialect in Hawaii: A Sociolinguistic History to 1835* [Honolulu, 1969]) and that of Turner on Gullah (*Africanisms in the Gullah Dialect*). Since the 1960s creole scholarship has expanded rapidly. On Gullah as a creole language, see Robert A. Hall, *Pidgin and Creole Languages* (Ithaca, 1965), 15; William A. Stewart, "Sociolinguistic Factors in the History of American Negro Dialects," *Florida FL Reporter*, 5 (1967), 12–13; Todd, *Pidgins and Creoles*, 5–6, 54, 67; Dillard, *Black English*, 76. On the definition of creolization, see Hymes, introduction to part iii of Hymes, ed., *Pidginization and Creolization of Languages*, 84. On the complexity of interrelationships in the cre-

olization process, see the following essays in Hymes, ed., *Pidginization and Creolization of Languages*: Sidney Mintz, "The Socio-historical Background of Pidginization and Creolization" (153–68); Mervyn C. Alleyne, "Acculturation and the Cultural Matrix of Creolization" (169–86); David De-Camp, "Introduction: The Study of Pidgin and Creole Languages" (13–39).

18. Basil Davidson, *Black Mother: The Years of the African Slave Trade* (Boston, 1961), 218; Greenberg, "Africa as a Linguistic Area," 15–27; Herskovits, *Myth of the Negro Past*, 50; Ivan Vansertima, "African Linguistic and Mythological Structures in the World," in Rhoda Goldstein, ed., *Black Life and Culture in the United States* (New York, 1971), 12–35. On the one hand, African languages tended to feature simple vowel and consonant systems with implosive consonant sounds and few consonant blends. On the other hand, African languages tended to have rather complex morphologies with complicated nominal taxonomies and intricate verbal derivatives that expressed causative, reflexive, passive, and motional action or being.

19. Todd, *Pidgins and Creoles*, 67; Hall, *Pidgin and Creole Languages*, 9, 25; Peter H. Wood, *Black Majority: Negroes in Colonial South Carolina from 1670 through the Stono Rebellion* (New York, 1974), 173–74; David Dalby, "Americanisms That May Once Have Been Africanisms," *The Times* (London), June 19, 1969, 9. There are still numerous pidgin and creole languages in West Africa, including a pidginized Kikongo in the Congo-Angolan area and a pidginized Hausa in Nigeria, Arabic-based pidgins in Nigeria, French-based pidgins on the Ivory Coast, Portuguese-based pidgins and creoles in Guinea and Senegal, and English-based pidgins and creoles in the Cameroons, Liberia, Sierra Leone, and Gambia. See Ian F. Hancock, "A Survey of the Pidgins and Creoles of the World," in Hymes, ed., *Pidginization and Creolization of Languages*, 516–19.

20. William A. Stewart, "Nonstandard Speech Patterns," *Baltimore Bulletin of Education*, 43 (1967), 52–65; J. L. Dillard, "Non-standard Negro Dialects: Convergence or Divergence?" *Florida FL Reporter*, 6 (1968), 9–12, rpt. in Norman E. Whitten, Jr., and John F. Szwed, eds., *Afro-American Anthropology: Contemporary Perspectives* (New York, 1970), 119–26; Ralph W. Fasold, "Decreolization and Autonomous Language Change," *Florida FL Reporter*, 10 (1972), 9; Hancock, "Survey of the Pidgins and Creoles of the World," 512–15. On the development of an Afro-English creole in Dutch Surinam, see Charles R. Boxer, *The Dutch Seaborne Empire, 1600–1800* (New York, 1965), 241.

21. Wood, *Black Majority*, 174–75, 179, 340; George C. Rogers, Jr., *The History of Georgetown County, South Carolina* (Columbia, 1970), 29, 53–54, 342–43; Converse D. Clowse, *Economic Beginnings in Colonial South Carolina, 1670–1730* (Columbia, 1971), 122–32, 230–34; Philip D. Curtin, *The Atlantic Slave Trade: A Census* (Madison, 1969), 145, 156–58; Elizabeth Donnan, "The Slave Trade into South Carolina before the Revolu-

tion," *AHR*, 33 (1927–28), 816–17; Daniel C. Littlefield, *Rice and Slaves: Ethnicity and the Slave Trade in Colonial South Carolina* (Baton Rouge, 1981), 33–55.

22. Wood, *Black Majority*, 185; Dalby, "Americanisms That May Once Have Been Africanisms," 9; Stewart, "Nonstandard Speech Patterns," 52–65; Dillard, "Non-standard Negro Dialects," 119–26; Fasold, "Decreolization," 9. Cf. Frederic G. Cassidy, *Jamaica Talk: Three Hundred Years of the English Language in Jamaica* (London, 1961), 49–50.

23. Nichols, "Linguistic Change in Gullah," 1–2; Todd, *Pidgins and Creoles*, 7, 9–10, 15, 25–27, 50–51; Stewart, "Sociolinguistic Factors in the History of American Negro Dialects," 11–29; Vansertima, "African Linguistic and Mythological Structures," 12–35; Wood, *Black Majority*, 175–80. Cf. Cassidy, *Jamaica Talk*, 15–19; Littlefield, *Rice and Slaves*, 156–60.

24. Stewart, "Sociolinguistic Factors in the History of American Negro Dialects," 12; Wood, *Black Majority*, 186–87; Todd, *Pidgins and Creoles*, 5–6, 54, 67; Dillard, *Black English*, 76.

25. Dalby, "Americanisms That May Once Have Been Africanisms," 9; Greenberg, "Africa as a Linguistic Area," 23; P. E. H. Hair, "Sierra Leone Items in the Gullah Dialect of American English," *Sierra Leone Language Review*, 4 (1965), 79–84; Turner, *Africanisms in the Gullah Dialect*, 209–16, 225–27, 278–91; Nichols, "Linguistic Change in Gullah," 104–7; Todd, *Pidgins and Creoles*, 17, 67; Stewart, "Continuity and Change in American Negro Dialects," 3, and his "Foreign Language Teaching Methods in Quasi-Foreign Language Situations," 18; Dillard, *Black English*, 56–57; Wood, *Black Majority*, 169–70; George C. Rogers, Jr., *Charleston in the Age of the Pinckneys* (Norman, 1969), 76–77.

26. "An Englishman in South Carolina," 693; King, *Great South*, 429; G.M., "South Carolina," *New England Magazine*, 1 (Sept.–Oct. 1831), 249–50; William A. Stewart, "More on Black-White Speech Relationships," *Florida FL Reporter*, 11 (1973), 35–40; Bennett, "Gullah," 339; Samuel Gaillard Stoney, ed., "The Memoirs of Frederick Adolphus Porcher," *SCHM*, 47 (1946), 92–93; Rogers, *Charleston*, 79; Raven I. McDavid, Jr., and Virginia Glenn McDavid, "The Relationship of the Speech of American Negroes to the Speech of the Whites," *American Speech*, 26 (1951), 3–17. A similar linguistic situation prevailed in the Caribbean. In Jamaica, for example, Lady Nugent complained that "the Creole language is not confined to the negroes. Many of the ladies who have not been educated in England, speak a sort of Broken English, with an indolent drawling out of their words, that is tiresome if not disgusting." See Henry Preston Vaughan Nunn, *Lady Nugent's Journal of Her Residence in Jamaica from 1801 to 1805*, ed. P. Wright (Oxford, 1966), 98. Cf. Cassidy, *Jamaica Talk*, 21–23.

27. Allen W. Read, "The Speech of Negroes in Colonial America," *JNH*, 24 (1939), 247–58; Stewart, "Sociolinguistic Factors in the History of American Negro Dialects," 29; Duncan Clinch Heyward, *Seed from Mada-*

gascar (Chapel Hill, 1937), 188–89. Cf. Allen W. Read, "Bilingualism in the Middle Colonies," *American Speech*, 12 (1937), 93–99. What I am describing as bilingualism would be considered *diglossia* by those who consider Gullah to be a dialect of English rather than a creole language. Diglossia is the use of two or more varieties of the same language under different conditions. See Charles A. Ferguson, "Diglossia," in Giglioli, ed., *Language and Social Context*, 232–51.

28. Elizabeth C. Traugott, "Principles in the History of American English—A Reply," *Florida FL Reporter*, 10 (1972), 5–6, 56; Stewart, "Sociolinguistic Factors in the History of American Negro Dialects," 11, 13, 29; Dalby, "Americanisms That May Once Have Been Africanisms," 9; Gilbert Osofsky, ed., *Puttin' On Ole Massa* (New York, 1969), 26. Apparently some planters regarded Gullah and other creoles to be a kind of baby-talk. See Edgar T. Thompson, *Plantation Societies, Race Relations, and the South: The Regimentation of Populations* (Durham, N.C., 1975), 133–34. Linguists who have espoused the baby-talk thesis included Leonard Bloomfield, *Language* (New York, 1933), 472–75, and Hall, *Pidgin and Creole Languages*, 5, 86. DeCamp convincingly challenges the baby-talk thesis in his "Introduction: The Study of Pidgin and Creole Languages," 18–23. A sophisticated restatement, emphasizing that all languages tend to simplify in similar ways for those who are regarded as unable to comprehend the community's "normal" speech, is Ferguson, "Aspects of Copula," 141–50. On the dynamics of linguistic contact, see Uriel Weinreich, *Languages in Contact* (New York, 1953). A recent overview of the literature is Ralph W. Fasold, "The Relation between Black and White Speech in the South," *American Speech*, 56 (1981), 168–89. On Afro-American uses of language to conceal, cf. M. G. Smith, "Some Aspects of Social Structure in the British Caribbean about 1820," *Social and Economic Studies*, 1 (1953), 70; Grace Sims Holt, "'Inversion' in Black Communication," in Thomas Kochman, ed., *Rappin' and Stylin' Out: Communication in Urban Black America* (Urbana, 1972), 152–59. Such interpretations may be taken to injudicious and unreliable extremes, and have been by Miles Mark Fisher in his *Negro Slave Songs of the United States* (New York, 1953). It should be noted in fairness that planters often perceived that they were being "put on," but played the game out of a sense of *noblesse oblige*.

29. Cf. Lawrence W. Levine, *Black Culture and Black Consciousness: Afro-American Folk Thought from Slavery to Freedom* (New York, 1977), 6, 444; Alan Dundes, *Mother Wit from the Laughing Barrel: Readings in the Interpretation of Afro-American Folklore* (Englewood Cliffs, N.J., 1973), 246–47. On the functions of proverbs and indirect speech in Africa, see Ethel M. Albert, "'Rhetoric,' 'Logic,' and 'Poetics' in Burundi," *AA*, 66 (1964), 35–54; John C. Messenger, "The Role of Proverbs in a Nigerian Judicial System," *Southwestern Journal of Anthropology*, 15 (1959), 64–73;

Ruth Finnegan, *Oral Literature in Africa* (Oxford, 1970), 393–408; Peter Seitel, "Proverbs: A Social Use of Metaphor," *Genre*, 2 (1969), 146–60; David Dwyer, *An Introduction to West African Pidgin English* (East Lansing, 1967), 98.

30. Selwyn Gurney Champion, *Racial Proverbs: A Selection of the World's Proverbs, Arranged Linguistically.* . . . (London, 1938), 515, 524, 533, 599; Julia Peterkin, *Scarlet Sister Mary* (Indianapolis, 1928), 215, and her *Black April* (Indianapolis, 1927), 43; Lillie Knox, in WPA Mss. On the importance of the oral rhetorical question format in Africa see Finnegan, *Oral Literature*, 401. While ethnographic writings (even reports in travel accounts by undiscerning amateurs) are readily accepted by scholars as primary sources, an explanation is required for attempting to use fiction as a source of factual information. This is all the more necessary if one wishes to use fiction written by a southern white woman in the age of Jim Crow as a source for facts on Afro-American culture. Peterkin spent part of her early life on the Waccamaw Neck and remained a part-time resident for most of her adult life. Her novels are recognizably set in the area—*Scarlet Sister Mary* on "Blue Brook" (Brookgreen) plantation, *Black April* on Sandy Island. Many environmental and cultural features of her novels are still verifiable on the Waccamaw Neck. Other cultural features have been reported by folklorists and linguists in other Gullah-speaking communities (see Richard M. Dorson, *American Folklore* [Chicago, 1959], 7; Ann Sullivan Haskell, "The Representation of Gullah-Influenced Dialects in Twentieth Century South Carolina Prose" [Ph.D. diss., University of Pennsylvania, 1968]; and Stewart, "More on Black-White Speech Relationships," 38). Thus by the tests of exposure to the culture and verification of specific cultural details within the community and of general cultural details in other Gullah-speaking communities, one is ready to credit Peterkin's primary knowledge of Gullah proverbs on the Waccamaw. See also Francis W. Bradley, "South Carolina Proverbs," *SFQ*, 1 (1937), 57–101.

31. Lillie Knox, in WPA Mss.; James Boyd Christensen, "The Role of Proverbs in Fante Culture," in Elliott P. Skinner, ed., *Peoples and Cultures of Africa* (Garden City, N.Y., 1973), 523 (cf. Bradley, "South Carolina Proverbs," 78); Champion, *Racial Proverbs*, 509, 525.

32. Lillie Knox, in WPA Mss.; Champion, *Racial Proverbs*, 606 (cf. Finnegan, *Oral Literature*, 401–2); Christensen, "The Role of Proverbs in Fante Culture," 523.

33. Julia Peterkin, in *Poetry: A Magazine of Verse*, 27 (1923), 60.

34. Ella Small, in WPA Mss.; Peterkin, *Black April*, 56, 131; cf. Bradley, "South Carolina Proverbs," 69, 77.

35. Patience Pennington [Elizabeth Allston Pringle], *A Woman Rice Planter* (New York, 1914), 37; Peterkin, *Black April*, 125, 247.

36. Informant unknown, WPA Mss.; Julia Peterkin, in *Poetry: A Magazine of Verse*, 25 (1925), 240–43 (cf. her *Scarlet Sister Mary*, 173).

37. Hagar Brown and Lillie Knox, both in WPA Mss. (cf. Bradley,

"South Carolina Proverbs," 70, and the African novelist Chinua Achebe, *Arrow of God* [Garden City, N.Y., 1965], 213).

38. On strategy, see Kenneth Burke, *The Philosophy of Literary Form* (New York, 1957), 3–4; Seitel, "Proverbs," 150–51; Lillie Knox and Hagar Brown, both in WPA Mss.; Peterkin, *Black April*, 68 (cf. Bradley, "South Carolina Proverbs," 96).

39. Informant unknown, WPA Mss.; Peterkin, *Black April*, 68 (cf. Bradley, "South Carolina Proverbs," 84, 99).

40. Peterkin, *Scarlet Sister Mary*, 132; Lillie Knox, in WPA Mss.; Julia Peterkin, "Teaching Jim," in Frank Durham, ed., *The Collected Short Stories of Julia Peterkin* (Columbia, 1970), 218–23 (cf. Bradley, "South Carolina Proverbs," 65); Julia Peterkin, *Green Thursday* (New York, 1924), 130; Sabe Rutledge, Slave Narratives, 14, part iv, 63.

41. Peterkin, *Black April*, 146 (cf. the Hausa proverb "Doing mischief is pleasanter than repairing it" in Champion, *Racial Proverbs*, 534); WPA Mss. (cf. Bradley, "South Carolina Proverbs," 95); Peterkin, *Green Thursday*, 129; Lillie Knox, in WPA Mss.; WPA Mss.; WPA Mss. (cf. Bradley, "South Carolina Proverbs," 90).

42. Peterkin, *Bright Skin* (Indianapolis, 1932), 39; WPA Mss. Cf. Elsie Clews Parsons, "Folk-Lore from St. Helena Island, South Carolina," *JAF*, 38 (1925), 228.

43. Christensen, "The Roll of Proverbs in Fante Culture," 510. Cf. Finnegan, *Oral Literature*, 394–418; E. Ojo Arewa and Alan Dundes, "Proverbs and the Ethnography of Speaking Folklore," *AA*, 66, pt. 2 (1964), 70–85; Charles Bird, "Heroic Songs of the Mande Hunters," in Richard M. Dorson, ed., *African Folklore* (Garden City, N.Y., 1972), 275–93; Roger D. Abrahams, "A Rhetoric of Everyday Life: Conversational Genres," *SFQ*, 32 (1968), 44–59, and his "Introductory Remarks to a Rhetorical Theory of Folklore," *JAF*, 81 (1968), 143–57; Dan Ben-Amos, "Folklore in African Society," in Bernth Lindfors, ed., *Forms of Folklore in Africa: Narrative, Poetic, Gnomic, Dramatic* (Austin, 1977), 22.

44. On the importance of speech interaction in culture, see Bertram Wyatt-Brown, "The Ideal Typology and Ante-Bellum Southern History: A Testing of a New Approach," *Societas*, 5 (1975), 4; Richard Bauman, "Verbal Art as Performance," *AA*, 77 (1975), 293; Erving Goffman's: "The Neglected Situation," *ibid.*, 66 (1964), 133–36, *Encounters: Two Studies in the Sociology of Interaction* (Indianapolis, 1961), and *Behavior in Public Places* (New York, 1963); Kenneth R. Johnson, "Black Kinesics—Some Non-Verbal Communication Patterns in the Black Culture," *Florida FL Reporter*, 9 (1971), 17–20, 57; Dell Hymes, "Competence and Performance in Linguistic Theory," in R. Huxley and E. Ingram, eds., *Language Acquisition: Models and Methods* (New York, 1971), 3–23; Beryl L. Bailey, "Towards a New Perspective in Negro English Dialectology," *American Speech*, 40 (1965), 171–77. On the distinction between *bad* and *baaad* in Afro-American culture, see H. C. Brearley, "Ba-ad Nigger," *South Atlantic Quar-*

terly, 38 (1939), 75–81; William H. Wiggins, Jr., "Jack Johnson as Bad Nigger: The Folklore of His Life," *Black Scholar*, 2 (1971), 39. On ambiguity and intonation in African languages, see Dwyer, *Introduction to West African Pidgin English*, 98; Greenberg, "Africa as a Linguistic Area," 23; Lorenzo Dow Turner, "Problems Confronting the Investigator of Gullah," *Publications of the American Dialect Society*, 9 (1947), 74–84. On Gullah's distinctive uses of syllable and breath dynamics, pitch, volume, and stress, see William A. Stewart, "Observations on the Problems of Defining Negro Dialect," *Florida FL Reporter*, 9 (1971), 48–49.

45. David J. McCord, ed., *Statutes at Large of South Carolina* (Columbia, 1840), 7:468; Mss. Diary of Emily Esdaile Weston for 1859, in private possession, Jan. 30, Feb. 13, 26–27, Mar. 6, 13, Dec. 4, 1859 (hereafter cited as Emily Weston diary); Malet, *Errand to the South*, 50, 57, 68, 204–5; Emily R. Reynolds and Joan Reynolds Faunt, *Biographical Directory of the Senate of the State of South Carolina, 1776–1964* (Columbia, 1964), 334; Lawrence C. Bryant, "Negro Legislators in South Carolina, 1868–1902" (mimeograph), SCA (Bruce Williams, one of the Richmond Hill slaves taught to read and write by Mary Vereen Magill, served as state senator from 1876 to 1902); Mulatto Joe to Robert F. W. Allston, Sept. 23, 1823, and Samuel Taylor to Elizabeth Blyth, Sept. 2, 1838, both in Robert F. W. Allston Papers, SCHS; Mary Ann (surname unknown) to Emily Jordan, Feb. 23, 1861, in Daniel W. Jordan Papers, DUL; George Simons to Francis Weston, June 5, 1864, in Weston Family Papers, SCL. The low proportion of black literacy is strikingly evident in the mss. federal census population schedules for 1870, SCA. Even allowing for the possibility that the most literate slaves left the parish after emancipation, the estimate of W. E. B. DuBois that about 5 percent of the slaves were literate by 1860 seems about right for All Saints Parish. See his *Black Reconstruction: An Essay toward a History for the Part which Black Folk Played in the Attempt to Reconstruct Democracy in America* (New York, 1935), 638.

46. Fasold, "Decreolization and Autonomous Language Change," 9; Stewart, "Sociolinguistic Factors in the History of American Negro Dialects," 12–13, and his "Patterns of Grammatical Change in Gullah"; Hall, *Pidgin and Creole Languages*, 15; Bennett, "Gullah," 336*n*.

47. Stewart, "Continuity and Change in American Negro Dialects," 3. Linguists call the replacement of words while maintaining the structure relexification. One theory claims that creoles originated as Portuguese trade pidgins and were relexified with English words on the West African coast. See Todd, *Pidgins and Creoles*, 33–42.

48. Nichols, "Linguistic Change in Gullah," 3–4; J. L. Dillard, "The Historian's History and the Reconstructionist's History in the Tracing of Linguistic Variants," *Florida FL Reporter*, 11 (1973), 41, and his *Black English*, 102; William A. Stewart, "Historical and Structural Bases for the Recognition of Negro Dialect," *Monograph Series on Languages and Linguistics*, 22 (Washington, D.C., 1969), 239–47, and his "Sociolinguistic Factors

in the History of American Negro Dialects," 13, 29; John J. Gumperz, "Linguistic Anthropology in Society," *AA*, 76 (1974), 791; DeCamp, "Toward a Generative Analysis of a Post-Creole Speech Continuum," 349–70.

49. Sabe Rutledge, Slave Narratives, 14, part iv, 59, and in WPA Mss. On the importance given to naming in African societies, see H. A. Wieschoff, "The Social Significance of Names among the Ibo of Nigeria," *AA*, 43 (1941), 212–22. Orlando Patterson offers an incisive discussion of the importance of naming cross-culturally in his *Slavery and Social Death: A Comparative Study* (Cambridge, Mass., 1982), 54–55. See also William F. Murphy, "A Note on the Significance of Names," *Psychoanalytic Quarterly*, 26 (1957), 91–106. On the planters' contribution to slave naming, see Newbell Niles Puckett, "Names of American Negro Slaves," in George Peter Murdock, ed., *Studies in the Science of Society Presented to Albert Galloway Keller* (New Haven, 1937), 471–94. Cf. Hennig Cohen, "Slave Names in Colonial South Carolina," *American Speech*, 28 (1952), 102–7; Naomi C. Chappell, "Negro Names," *American Speech*, 4 (1929), 272–75; Urban T. Holmes, "A Study in Negro Onomastics," *American Speech*, 5 (1930), 462–67; Arthur Palmer Hudson, "Some Curious Negro Names," *Southern Folklore Quarterly*, 2 (1938), 179–93; Ruby Terrill Lomax, "Negro Nicknames," *Publications of the Texas Folklore Society*, 18 (1943), 163–71.

50. Slave lists, estate of Francis Marion Weston, 1855, slave lists, estate of Plowden C. J. Weston, 1864, and slave lists, estate of John D. Magill, 1864, all in Office of Probate Judge, Georgetown County Court House; Emily Weston to William St. J. Mazyck, conveyance of real and personal estate, Aug. 14, 1864, Temporary Deeds, Book A, Register of Deeds, Georgetown County Court House; "Book of Things Given Out March 27, 1809," Charlotte Ann Allston Mss., 1804–20, in private possession. On African day names, see John Mbiti, *African Religions and Philosophy* (Garden City, N.Y., 1969), ch. 3; Roger Bastide, *African Civilisations in the New World*, trans. Peter Green (New York, 1971), 100; Edward Long, *The History of Jamaica* (London, 1774), 3:417; David DeCamp, "African Day Names in Jamaica," *Language*, 43 (1967), 139–49; Orlando Patterson, *The Sociology of Slavery* (London, 1967), 174; M. Delafosse, "De quelques persistances d'ordre ethnographique chez les descendants des Nègres transplantés aux Antilles et a la Guyane," *Revue d'Ethnologie et de Sociologie*, 3 (1912), 234–37; Turner, *Africanisms in the Gullah Dialect*, 31–43; Dillard, *Black English*, 123–35; Wood, *Black Majority*, 181.

51. The slave names in the list above and in the discussions that follow are from a master sample of more than 700 separate names, many of them occurring ten times or more, which I compiled from the above inventories; the Slave Narratives of All Saints Parish; the Emily Weston diary; the Daniel W. Jordan Papers; and the Robert F. W. Allston Papers. For the African names see Puckett, "Names of American Negro Slaves," 471–94; H. L. Mencken, *The American Language*, 4th ed. (New York, 1936), 524; Wood, *Black Majority*, 181–82. On New World continuities with African naming

practices, see Herskovits, *Myth of the Negro Past*, 190–94; Turner, *African-isms in the Gullah Dialect*, 31–43, and his "Problems Confronting the In-vestigator of Gullah," 74–84; Daniel E. Huger Smith, "A Plantation Boy-hood," in Alice R. Huger Smith and Herbert Ravenel Sass, eds., *A Carolina Rice Plantation of the Fifties* (New York, 1930), 71; Duncan Clinch Hey-ward, *Seed from Madagascar* (Chapel Hill, 1937), 97; Willie Lee Rose, *Re-hearsal for Reconstruction: The Port Royal Experiment* (Indianapolis, 1964), 97; Richard and Sally Price, "Sarameka Onomastics: An Afro-American Naming System," *Ethnology*, 11 (1972), 341–67.

52. These names are found *passim* in the Slave Narratives from All Saints Parish and the Emily Weston diary, as well as in slave lists in Francis Marion Weston estate; Plowden C. J. Weston estate; John D. Magill estate; Charlotte Ann Allston Mss.; Robert F. W. Allston Papers; Daniel W. Jordan Papers. For the African names, see Puckett, "Names of American Negro Slaves," 471–94; Mencken, *American Language*, 524; Wood, *Black Major-ity*, 181–85. Cf. Turner, *Africanisms in the Gullah Dialect*, 92–109; Dil-lard, *Black English*, 129–32.

53. Robert F. W. Allston Papers; Francis Marion Weston inventory; Plowden Weston inventory; Emily Weston diary; Monday Samson Holmes, Free Woods, S.C., WPA Mss. Cf. Cohen, "Slave Names in Colonial South Carolina," 104.

54. These names are found *passim* in the Slave Narratives and WPA Mss. from All Saints Parish; Robert F. W. Allston Papers; Emily Weston diary.

55. Hagar Brown, Slave Narratives, 14, part i, 112. On the African tra-dition of children's being named by grandparents, see Meyer Fortes, "Kin-ship and Marriage among the Ashanti," in A. R. Radcliffe-Brown and Daryll Forde, eds., *African Systems of Kinship and Marriage* (London, 1950), 276.

56. Malet, *Errand to the South*, 6; Mariah Heywood, Slave Narratives, 14, part ii, 284; Margaret Bryant, Slave Narratives, 14, part i, 146; Collins, *Memories of the Southern States*, 5. Cf. Heyward, *Seed from Madagascar*, 98. For a discussion of surnames cross-culturally, see Patterson, *Slavery and Social Death*, 56–58.

57. Stewart, "Sociolinguistic Factors in the History of American Negro Dialects," 29, and his "Continuity and Change," 3–14; Cassidy, *Jamaica Talk*, 17–20; Melville J. and Frances S. Herskovits, *Suriname Folk-Lore* (New York, 1936), 78–81, 116–18; David Dalby, *Black through White: Patterns of Communication* (Bloomington, Ind., 1970), 6; Hymes, "Intro-duction," 84; Elizabeth C. Traugott, "Pidgins, Creoles, and the Origins of Vernacular Black English," in D. S. Harrison and T. Trabasso, *Black English: A Seminar* (Hillsdale, N.J., 1976), 84–85.

58. On the stigma of non-standard English, see Claudia Mitchell-Kernan, *Language Behavior in a Black Urban Community* (Berkeley, 1969), 42–48, 60–66; William Labov, *The Social Stratification of English in New York City* (Washington, D.C., 1966), 495–96. On language as a symbol of

shared culture, see David G. Mandelbaum, ed., *Selected Writings of Edward Sapir in Culture, Language, and Personality* (Berkeley, 1949), 15; William C. Spengemann and L. R. Lundquist, "Autobiography and the American Myth," in Hennig Cohen, ed., *The American Culture: Approaches to the Study of the United States* (Boston, 1968), 495–96; C. Wright Mills, "Language, Logic, and Culture," *American Sociological Review*, 4 (1939), 677. On the impact of language on culture (rather than language as a reflector of culture), see Michael Silverstein, "Language as a Part of Culture," in Sol Tax and Leslie G. Freeman, eds., *Horizons of Anthropology*, 2d ed. (Chicago, 1977), 130. This interpretation has been taken to deterministic extremes by Benjamin Lee Whorf ("Science and Linguistics," in Eleanor Maccoby, ed., *Readings in Social Psychology* [New York, 1958], 5) and Basil L. Bernstein ("Social Class and Linguistic Development: A Theory of Social Learning," in A. H. Halsey *et al.*, eds., *Education, Economy, and Society* [New York, 1961]). See also the critique by Gary J. Miller, "Linguistic Constructions of Reality," in Howard Shapiro, ed., *Human Perspectives* (New York, 1972), 84–93.

Notes to *"My Time Up with You"*

1. Mariah Heywood, Slave Narratives: A Folk History of Slavery in the United States from Interviews with Former Slaves. Typewritten records prepared by the Federal Writers' Project, 1936–38 (microfilm), 14, part ii, 284; William Wyndham Malet, *An Errand to the South in the Summer of 1862* (London, 1863), 73; Elizabeth Collins, *Memories of the Southern States* (Taunton, England, 1865), 12–13. On slaves' accompanying their masters to war, see Elizabeth W. Allston Pringle, *Chronicles of Chicora Wood* (New York, 1922), 194, 276–77; Arthur Manigault Chapter of the United Daughters of the Confederacy, *For Love of a Rebel* (Georgetown, S.C., 1964), 16. On slaves evacuated inland with their masters' families, see Ellen Godfrey, Slave Narratives, 14, part ii, 159, 162; Pringle, *Chronicles of Chicora Wood*, 194ff. Marine raids and Union gunboats on the Waccamaw are detailed in Margaret Bryant, Slave Narratives, 14, part i, 145; Sabe Rutledge, Slave Narratives, 14, part iv, 61; George C. Rogers, Jr., *The History of Georgetown County, South Carolina* (Columbia, 1970), 401–15 *passim*; OR Army, Series I, 14:577–78; OR Navy, Series I, 12:123; 13:202–4, 212–15. On slave runaways during the war and the execution of captured fugitives, see Hagar Brown, Slave Narratives, 14, part i, 110; Mariah Heywood, Slave Narratives, 14, part ii, 287–88; Sabe Rutledge, Slave Narratives, 14, part iii, 61, 63; Henry A. Middleton to Mrs. Henry A. Middleton, Nov. 5, 1862, Middleton Papers, SCHS; Petition to military commander at Georgetown, Mar. 6, 1865, Sparkman Family Papers, SHC; Rogers, *History of Georgetown County*, 399–402. On runaway slaves' joining the Union army, see Jesse Belflowers to Adele Petigru Allston, Mar. 20, 1865, in J. Harold Easterby, ed., *The South Carolina Rice Plantation as Revealed in the Papers*

of Robert F. W. Allston (Chicago, 1945), 328–29; *New South* (Port Royal), Dec. 6, 1862, Jan. 13, 31, 1863, in Joel Williamson, *After Slavery: The Negro in South Carolina during Reconstruction, 1861–1877* (Chapel Hill, 1965), 17; *OR Army*, Series I, 14:290–91, 301–8, 463. On the slaves' immediate reaction to emancipation, see Welcome Bees, WPA Mss., SCL; Mariah Heywood, Slave Narratives, 14, part ii, 284; Sabe Rutledge, Slave Narratives, 14, part iv, 61; Ellen Godfrey, Slave Narratives, 14, part ii, 156–57.

2. Welcome Bees, WPA Mss.; Mariah Heywood, Slave Narratives, 14, part ii, 287; Pringle, *Chronicles of Chicora Wood*, 283–84.

3. Pringle, *Chronicles of Chicora Wood*, 233. Cf. Leon F. Litwack, *Been in the Storm so Long: The Aftermath of Slavery* (New York, 1979), 108, 128, 212.

4. Pringle, *Chronicles of Chicora Wood*, 264–66; Elizabeth Weston to A. Allston, Mar. 17, 1865, in Easterby, ed., *South Carolina Rice Plantation*, 207.

5. E. Weston to A. Allston, Mar. 17, 1865, Belflowers to A. Allston, Apr. 2, 1865, A. Allston to Capt. Morris, Mar. 1865, A. Allston to Col. Brown, Mar. 1865, Jane Pringle to A. Allston, Apr. 1, 1865, all in Easterby, ed., *South Carolina Rice Plantation*, 207–8, 209, 210, 329.

6. Belflowers to A. Allston, Apr. 2, 1865, A. Allston to Benjamin Allston, Sept. 10, 1865, *ibid.*, 329, 213. See also A. Allston to Col. Brown, Mar. 1865, Pringle to A. Allston, Apr. 1, 1865, E. Weston to A. Allston, Mar. 17, 1865, *ibid.*, 208, 211; Pringle, *Chronicles of Chicora Wood*, 264–65.

7. Ben Horry, Slave Narratives, 14, part ii, 305, 307; Mariah Heywood, WPA Mss.; Belflowers to A. Allston, Mar. 20, 1865, A. Allston to B. Allston, Sept. 10, 1865, in Easterby, ed., *South Carolina Rice Plantation*, 328–29, 213; Pringle, *Chronicles of Chicora Wood*, 264–65.

8. Arney R. Childs, ed., *Rice Planter and Sportsman: The Recollections of J. Motte Alston* (Columbia, 1953), 48; James R. Sparkman, "The Negro," Sparkman Family Papers; E. Weston to A. Allston, Mar. 17, 1865, Belflowers to A. Allston, Apr. 2, 1865, in Easterby, ed., *South Carolina Rice Plantation*, 207, 329.

9. Edmund Kirke [James Roberts Gilmore], *Among the Pines: or, The South in Secession-Time* (New York, 1862), 20; "An Englishman in South Carolina," *Continental Monthly*, 2 (1862), 110–11. Cf. Philip S. Foner, ed., *Life and Writings of Frederick Douglass* (New York, 1950), 1:157.

10. Charleston *Daily Courier*, June 27, 1855; Edward T. Heriot to Anna Bruce Cunningham, Apr. 20, 1853, in Edward Thomas Heriot Papers, DUL; Robert F. W. Allston to B. Allston, May 25, 1855, in Easterby, ed., *South Carolina Rice Plantation*, 123. Cf. Margaret Bryant, in Slave Narratives, 14, part i, 147. On the "guiltlessness" of southern slaveholders, see Bertram Wyatt-Brown, *Southern Honor: Ethics and Behavior in the Old South* (New York, 1982), 28–29. On the general question of paternalism, see Eugene D. Genovese, *Roll, Jordan, Roll: The World the Slaves Made* (New York, 1974), 3–7, and *passim*, and his *The World the Slaveholders*

Made (New York, 1969), 96, 101, 131, 199; Pierre L. van den Berghe, *Race and Racism: A Comparative Perspective* (New York, 1967), 25–37; Roger Bastide, "The Development of Race Relations in Brazil," in Guy Hunter, ed., *Industrialization and Race Relations: A Symposium* (London, 1965), 14–15. Insofar as All Saints Parish is concerned, paternalism is descriptive of the planters' world view but not that of the slaves. Tensions between the two faces of master-slave relationships—the paternalistic manorial one and the exploitative commercial one—caused inner contradictions and instabilities in slave societies. Such contradictions and instabilities are examined in William W. Freehling, *Prelude to Civil War: The Nullification Crisis in South Carolina, 1816–1836* (New York, 1966), 64–72; Moses I. Finley, *Slavery in Classical Antiquity* (Cambridge, 1960), 162; Roy Simon Bryce-LaPorte, "The Slave Plantation: Background to Present Conditions of Urban Blacks," in P. Orleans and W. R. Ellis, eds., *Race, Change, and Urban Society* (Beverly Hills, 1971), 265–66. For a comparative perspective on the racial ideology of slavery, see George M. Frederickson, *White Supremacy: A Comparative Study in American and South African History* (New York, 1981), xii–xiii, 70–75.

11. Ellen Godfrey, Slave Narratives, 14, part ii, 161; Ben Horry, Slave Narratives, 14, part ii, 299–300, 309–10; Margaret Bryant, Slave Narratives, 14, part i, 147; Childs, ed., *Rice Planter and Sportsman*, 46, 56, 61; R. Allston to A. Allston, Nov. 27, 1853, James R. Sparkman to B. Allston, Mar. 10, 1858, in Easterby, ed., *South Carolina Rice Plantation*, 117, 349; Rogers, *History of Georgetown County*, 44, 66, 399–402, 405–7.

12. On the putative revolt of 1802 see Howard A. Ohline, "Georgetown, South Carolina: Racial Anxieties and Militant Behavior," *SCHM*, 73 (1972), 130–40. On the alleged plot of 1810, see the letter, with signature missing, dated Apr. 22, 1810, in William Johnston Papers, SCL. On the 1829 insurrection, see the following petitions to the South Carolina State Legislature praying for compensation for executed slaves: John Coachman for Charles, Dec. 15, 1829; Hannah Tait for Joe, Nov. 16, 1829; and Francis Kinloch for Wood, Nov. 19, 1829, all in Legislative System, Slavery, Insurrection, SCA. The 1829 insurrection is also briefly treated in Freehling, *Prelude to Civil War*, 62, and Rogers, *History of Georgetown County*, 236. See also James L. Petigru to R. Allston, 1829, in J. P. Carson, ed., *Life, Letters, and Speeches of James Louis Petigru* (Washington, D.C., 1920), 66. On the response of slaveholders generally to slave insurrectionary scares, see Wyatt-Brown, *Southern Honor*, 402–34.

13. Childs, ed., *Rice Planter and Sportsman*, 61–62; Mss. Diary of Emily Esdaile Weston, in private possession, Dec. 6, 1859; Mariah Heywood, Slave Narratives, 14, part ii, 285; Collins, *Memories of the Southern States*, 4. Cf. C. Vann Woodward, ed., *Mary Chesnut's Civil War* (New Haven, 1981), 464.

14. Belflowers to A. Allston, Apr. 2, 1865, Pringle to A. Allston, Apr. 1, 1865, in Easterby, ed. *South Carolina Rice Plantation*, 329, 209–10. Prin-

gle, *Chronicles of Chicora Wood*, 264–65, 296–75; Ben Horry, Slave Narratives, 14, part ii, 305, 307; Mariah Heywood, WPA Mss. Cf. Litwack, *Been in the Storm so Long*, 148–49; Willie Lee Rose, *Slavery and Freedom*, ed. William W. Freehling (New York, 1981), 93–98.

15. A. Allston to Col. Brown, Mar. 1865, in Easterby, ed., *South Carolina Rice Plantation*, 207–8; Sparkman, "The Negro," in Sparkman Family Papers; Etrulia P. Dozier, ed., "Interview of Mrs. Julia Smalls [*sic*]," *Independent Republic Quarterly*, 4 (July 1970), 32; interview with Henry Small, Free Woods, S.C., Aug. 2, 1975. Such abandoned plantations as Hagley, True Blue, Turkey Hill, Friendfield, Strawberry Hill, Marietta, Forlorn Hope, and Clifton were managed by the Freedmen's Bureau, with half the proceeds from the sale of rice going to the freedmen and half to the government, until they were restored to their prewar owners or heirs in December 1865. See Rogers, *History of Georgetown County*, 423–28. On the desire of slaves elsewhere in South Carolina to own land, see Elizabeth Rauh Bethel, *Promiseland: A Century of Life in a Negro Community* (Philadelphia, 1981), part 1. Cf. Litwack, *Been in the Storm so Long*, 205–12, 403; Williamson, *After Slavery*, 63; Rose, *Slavery and Freedom*, 93–94. For a detailed account of Adele Allston's successful efforts to reclaim her plantations (and the role of Union authorities in those efforts), see Pringle, *Chronicles of Chicora Wood*, 269–75. For a cross-cultural discussion of post-emancipation relations between former slaves and former masters, see Orlando Patterson, *Slavery and Social Death: A Comparative Study* (Cambridge, Mass., 1982), 240–47.

16. 1860 Census, Georgetown County, S.C., Slave Schedules. For a comparative perspective on slave demography, see Michael Craton, *Searching for the Invisible Man: Slaves and Plantation Life in Jamaica* (Cambridge, Mass., 1978), 85–134, 385–87, and Drew Gilpin Faust, *James Henry Hammond and the Old South: A Design for Mastery* (Baton Rouge, 1982), 75–82.

17. Gabe Lance, Slave Narratives, 14, part iii, 92; Ben Horry, WPA Mss.

18. See Arnold van Gennep, *The Rites of Passage*, trans. Monika B. Vizedom and Gabrielle L. Caffee (Chicago, 1960), 116–65; Victor W. Turner, *The Forest of Symbols: Aspects of Ndembu Ritual* (Ithaca, 1967), 151–279.

19. Matthew Grant, Parkersville, S.C., WPA Mss.

Index

Aaron, 73
Abby, 32
Abraham, 116
Adam, 25–26
Addie ("Maum Addie"), 152–53
Affie, 25–26
Africa: basketry, 76; continuities in Afro-American culture, xxii, 15, 37; craftsmen, 71; culture, xxi; funereal traditions, 138; languages, 198, 199–200, 204, 215; metalwork, 71; naming patterns, 217–18; occultism, 144–50; pharmacopoeia, 148; pottery, 71; proverbs, 210–11; religion, 141–45, 159–60; singing styles, 131–32; storytelling, 172–75; textiles, 71; woodworking, 71; work patterns, 58
African-born slaves, 39, 173, 196
Agrippa, 18, 79
Albert, 116
Alcoholic beverages: consumed by slaves, 32, 102–3, 136, 212
Alice, 116
Allen, William Francis, 169
All Saints Church, Waccamaw, 20, 23, 87, 154, 161
Allston, Adele Petigru, 80–81, 83, 85, 102, 116, 227, 228–29, 234
Allston, Benjamin (son of R.F.W. and Adele Allston), 67, 88, 132
Allston, Benjamin, Sr. (proprietor of Turkey Hill), 208
Allston, Joseph Blythe, 19, 22, 125
Allston, Joseph Waties, 233
Allston, Robert F. W., 12, 22, 31, 33, 46, 49, 52–54, 65, 67, 69, 70, 73, 74, 77, 81, 87, 88, 96,

99, 101, 102, 109, 110, 115, 117, 129, 135–36, 137, 159, 233
Allston, Washington, 6, 28
Allston, William Allan, 19, 22, 125
Allston family, 3, 5, 6, 207
Alston, Charles, 16, 21, 29, 88, 227–28
Alston, Charles Cotesworth Pinckney, 18
Alston, Charles, Sr., 19
Alston, Charles, Jr., 125
Alston, Jacob Motte, 11, 28–29, 43, 48, 70, 72–73, 92, 96, 99, 101, 104, 107, 109, 111, 112–13, 114, 130, 154, 156, 229
Alston, Joseph, 6, 68
Alston, Theodosia Burr, 6
Alston, Thomas Pinckney, 72–73, 157
Alston, Washington Dunkin, 21
Alston, William Algernon, Jr., 16, 19, 125
American Revolution, 5, 30
Among the Pines, 86–87
Amy, 25–26
Ancrum, 40
Andrew, 25–26
Angola, 14, 119, 205
Animal raisers, 70
Animal trickster tales, 173–83
Annales school, xix–xxi
"Anniversary" preaching, 8
Anthony, 73
Antigua, 13, 205
Antilles, 205
Appomattox, 225, 239
Apprentices, 65, 71, 74

335

A NOTE ON THE AUTHOR

CHARLES W. JOYNER earned his Ph.D. in history
from the University of South Carolina and his Ph.D. in
folklore and folklife from the University of Pennsylvania. He is the author of *Folk Song in South Carolina*
and has published and lectured widely here and abroad
on many aspects of southern culture. He is also involved in the production of historical documentaries
for television.

BOOKS IN THE SERIES BLACKS IN THE NEW WORLD

Before the Ghetto: Black Detroit in the Nineteenth Century
David M. Katzman

Black Business in the New South: A Social History of the North Carolina
Mutual Life Insurance Company *Walter B. Weare*

The Search for a Black Nationality: Black Colonization and Emigration,
1787-1863 *Floyd J. Miller*

Black Americans and the White Man's Burden, 1898-1903
Willard B. Gatewood, Jr.

Slavery and the Numbers Game: A Critique of *Time on the Cross*
Herbert G. Gutman

A Ghetto Takes Shape: Black Cleveland, 1870-1930 *Kenneth L. Kusmer*

Freedmen, Philanthropy, and Fraud: A History of the Freedman's Savings
Bank *Carl R. Osthaus*

The Democratic Party and the Negro: Northern and National Politics,
1868-92 *Lawrence Grossman*

Black Ohio and the Color Line, 1860-1915 *David A. Gerber*

Along the Color Line: Explorations in the Black Experience
August Meier and Elliott Rudwick

Black over White: Negro Political Leadership in South Carolina during
Reconstruction *Thomas Holt*

Keeping the Faith: A. Philip Randolph, Milton P. Webster, and the
Brotherhood of Sleeping Car Porters, 1925-37 *William H. Harris*

Abolitionism: The Brazilian Antislavery Struggle *Joaquim Nabuco,
translated and edited by Robert Conrad*

Black Georgia in the Progressive Era, 1900-1920 *John Dittmer*

Medicine and Slavery: Health Care of Blacks in Antebellum
Virginia *Todd L. Savitt*

Alley Life in Washington: Family, Community, Religion, and Folklife in
the City, 1850-1970 *James Borchert*

Human Cargoes: The British Slave Trade to Spanish America, 1700-
1739 *Colin A. Palmer*

Southern Black Leaders of the Reconstruction Era *Edited by Howard N.
Rabinowitz*

Black Leaders of the Twentieth Century *Edited by John Hope Franklin
and August Meier*

Slaves and Missionaries: The Disintegration of Jamaican Slave Society,
1787-1834 *Mary Turner*

Father Divine and the Struggle for Racial Equality *Robert Weisbrot*

Communists in Harlem during the Depression *Mark Naison*

Down from Equality: Black Chicagoans and the Public Schools, 1920-41
Michael W. Homel

For a complete list of black-studies publications, write to the University of Iu Press (54 East Gregory Drive, Champaign, Illinois 61820).